COMMUNITY, PRAXIS, AND VALUES
IN A POSTMETAPHYSICAL AGE

COMMUNITY, PRAXIS, AND VALUES IN A POSTMETAPHYSICAL AGE

Studies on Exclusion and Social Integration
in Feminist Theory and Contemporary Philosophy

Edited by
YVANKA B. RAYNOVA

Axia Academic Publishers
♦ Vienna ♦

Bibliographic Information of the German National Library
The German National Library lists this Publication in the German National Bibliography; detailed bibliographic data is available in the internet:
http://dnb.dnb.de
Bibliographische Information der Deutschen Nationalbibliothek
Die Deutsche Nationalbibliothek verzeichnet diese Publikation in der Deutschen Nationalbibliographie, detaillierte bibliographische Daten sind im Internet unter http://dnb.dnb.de aufrufbar.

Published with the Support of the City of Vienna,
Cultural Department – Science and Research Promotion

Cover © Institute for Axiological Research
Cover image: Painting from the Berlin Wall - East Side Gallery

© Axia Academic Publishers
Vienna 2015
All Rights Reserved.
Printed in Germany

All parts of this publication are protected by copyright.

Any utilization outside the strict limits of the copyright law, without the permission of the publisher, is forbidden and liable to prosecution. This applies in particular to reproductions, translations, microfilming, storage and processing in electronic retrieval systems.

ISBN 978-3-903068-15-5

www.axia-verlag.at
www.axia.pub

TABLE OF CONTENTS

Introduction   7

PART I

WOMEN'S SITUATION BETWEEN THEORY AND PRAXIS

1. *Alison M. Jaggar*
   The Problem of Moral Justification in Contemporary
   Feminist Debates   15

2. *Yvanka B. Raynova*
   Human Rights, Women's Rights, Gender Mainstreaming,
   and Diversity: The Language Question   38

3. *Susanne Moser*
   The Concept of Recognition in Simone de Beauvoir's
   The Second Sex   90

4. *Sonia Kruks*
   Beauvoir, Foucault and "Postmodern Feminism"   108

5. *María Luisa Femínias*
   Judith Butler and the "Gender" Question   128

6. *Tatyana Batuleva*
   Rethinking Identity and Otherness:
   Luce Irigaray's shared world   140

7. *Mary-Kate G. Smith*
   Western Liberal Feminism, Liberal Values,
   and the Diversity of Women's Situations   158

8. *Yvanka B. Raynova*
   Civil Society and "Women's Movements" in Post-Communist
   Europe. An Apparaisal 25 Years after the Fall of the Berlin Wall   184

PART II

COMMUNITY VALUES AND THE PRAXIS OF SOCIAL INTEGRATION AND EXCLUSION

9. *Enrique Dussel*
   Globalization and the Victims of Exclusion
   from a Liberation Ethics Perspective ... 207

10. *Lester Embree*
    Schutz's Theory of the Historical Sciences in the light
    of the Women's Liberation Movement ... 241

11. *Dimitrios E. Akrivoulis*
    The Efficacity of History and the Limits of Emancipation:
    Reinhart Koselleck and Paul Ricoeur ... 274

12. *Tatyana Batuleva*
    Responsibility between Ontology and Ethics:
    Hans Jonas and Emmanuel Levinas ... 289

13. *Mark Zlomislic*
    Derrida and the Ethics of Community ... 306

14. *Susanne Moser*
    The Importance of Values for the Social and Political
    Integration in Europe ... 321

15. *Yvanka B. Raynova*
    The European Values: A "Dictatorship" or a Chance for Union? ... 333

Contributors ... 351

Introduction

The following volume is published on the occasion of the 15th anniversary of the establishment of the Institute for Axiological Research (Institut für Axiologische Forschungen) in Vienna – the first European Institute for the advanced philosophical and interdisciplinary study of values. Its main objective is to give an idea about the work of the Institute and to present the research results on some important topics and issues in the field of contemporary value theory and practical philosophy. Most of the articles included in this collection have been part of extensive research projects. They have been presented and discussed at conferences and workshops. Some of them were also published in *Labyrinth: An International Journal for Philosophy, Value Theory and Sociocultural Hermeneutics* or in other serial publications of the Institute, but there are also several new, unpublished studies. The choice of the essays here is also driven by the intention to cover more or less the focal points of the Institute's research program which are:
- classical and contemporary value theories
- value shifts in gender relations
- social, religious and cultural hermeneutics
- current sociopolitical transformations: identity, democracy, globalization and justice
- values and praxis

The volume is divided in two parts. The first one treats specific problems of women's struggle for rights, freedoms, and recognition, and moves successively to thematically broader methodological and hermeneutical approaches of the phenomena of exclusion and the possibilities of social integration, which are discussed in the second part. It is not my purpose here to present a summary of all the articles included in this collection. Rather, I would like to focus on a keyword of the title, namely on the Habermasian notion of "postmetaphysical age," and hence to sketch some interpretative lines and approaches to the core axiological questions of the book: How do we think today of community, praxis and values in front of the old and new problems of injustice, oppression and exclusion? How should we consider personal and group identity in the contexts of social and cultural diversity, of world view pluralism and incommensurable lifeworlds, lifestyles and values? Moreover, what is the meaning of the key concept of "European values," can it offer a real basis for integration, i.e. for "unity in diversity," or does it serve rather as a new form of "dictatorship" and exclusion of otherness?

Before I expand on Habermas' concepts of "postmetaphysical age" and "postmetaphysical thinking," let me recall that he was not the first to use the notion of the "postmetaphysical,"[1] but he is explaining more in detail its meaning and also since 1988 still maintains that we do not have any alternative to "postmetaphysical thinking."[2] Some scholars like Dieter Heinrich, Karen Gloy, and Erwin Sonderegger[3] reject this position and even the notion of the "postmetaphysical" itself. Others like Herta Nagl-Docekal accept the notion, but show the limits of the proposed postmetaphysical alternatives, in particular those of Habermas, Rawls and Honneth.[4] The articles, included in the present volume, tend rather in the second direction and some of them include even an explicit critique on Habermas or/and Rawls.

It should be made clear that the notion of "postmetaphysical age" is not identical to "postmetaphysical thinking"; even though they are interrelated, they have different characteristics. Habermas uses the expression "postmetaphysical age" to designate, on the one hand, the philosophical epoch after Hegel, which is characterized by criticism and rejection of metaphysics or by an "unclear"[5] position towards it and which is, in this sense, a "post"-metaphysical thinking. But, on the

---

[1] Richard Taft f.ex. is stating that the "post-metaphysical thinking" is best addressed as a problem of style ("Style and the Post-Metaphysical Project," Research in Phenomenology, Vol. 15, 1985/1, pp. 113-132.). Also conceptions of postmetaphysical ethics have been proposed by different authors like John D. Caputo (in idem, Radical Hermeneutics: Repetition, Deconstruction, and the Hermeneutic Project, Bloomington: Indiana University Press, pp. 236-240) and Wolfgang Schirmacher ("The Faces of Compassion: Toward a Post-Metaphysical Ethics," Analecta Husserliana, Volume 22, 1987, pp. 313-325).
[2] Jürgen Habermas, *Nachmetaphysisches Denken II*, Frankfurt: Suhrkamp, 2012, p. 8.
[3] Dieter Heinrich, "Was ist Metaphysik – was Moderne? Thesen gegen Jürgen Habermas", in: Merkur 6 (1986), pp. 495-508; Karen Gloy (ed.), *Unser Zeitalter – ein postmetaphysisches?* Würzburg: Königshausen & Neumann, 2004.
[4] Herta Nagl-Docekal, *Innere Freiheit. Grenzen der nachmetaphysischen Moralkonzeptionen*. Berlin/Boston: De Gruyter, 2014.
[5] Jürgen Habermas, *Nachmetaphysisches Denken*, Frankfurt: Suhrkamp, 1988, p. 35.

other hand, "postmetaphysical age" means not just a change in the way of philosophizing, but also the "spiritual situation of our time" (*die geistige Situation der Zeit*), which according Habermas is divided by two contrary tendencies – the spread of naturalistic (scientist) worldviews and the political influence of religious orthodoxies.[6] To this pluralism of secular views and religious beliefs Habermas adds the plurality of values and understandings about the "good life" (morals). Hence the question about "what we should do" (ethics) to achieve a harmonious and successful life, which was answered in the past in the metaphysical doctrines of the good life and of a just society based on a unifying identity thinking of the whole (cosmos, society, human being), is actually avoided by philosophers as it is too formal and abstract to allow an existential self-understanding:

> At first glance, moral theory and ethics appear to be oriented to the same question: What ought I, or what ought we, to do? But the "ought" has a different sense once we are no longer asking about rights and duties that everyone ascribes to one another from an inclusive we-perspective, but: instead are concerned with our own life from the first person perspective and ask what is best "for me" or "for us" in the long run and all things considered. Such ethical questions regarding our own weal and woe arise in the context of a particular life history or a unique form of life. They are wedded to questions of identity: how we should understand ourselves, who we are and want to be. Obviously there is no answer to such questions that would be independent of the given context and thus would bind all persons in the same way.[7]

In other words, philosophers in the "post-metaphysical age" have lost their privileged status and have no more "authority over the supposedly established [metaphysical] frameworks in to which the human life of individuals and communities had to fit."[8] That is why they should abdicate of the principles of metaphysics, which are: (a) the identity-thinking of being and reason, hence of the true, the good and the beautiful, (b) the ideal order of an all-embracing, harmonious whole as the absolute good, (c) the idea of eternal truths, and (d) the primacy of theory to praxis.[9] Consequently, philosophy has to be a

---

[6] See Jürgen Habermas, *Zwischen Naturalismus und Religion*, pp. 7-13.
[7] Jürgen Habermas, *The Future of Human Nature*, Polity. 3.
[8] Ibid., p. 2.
[9] Jürgen Habermas, *Nachmetaphysisches Denken*, op. cit., pp. 36-42.

thinking of difference, it should reevaluate norms and values in their different social contexts and renounce a universal "we"-perspective based on eternal truths and norms in favor of discourse and communicative praxis.

Although the defended positions of the essays in the present volume are different from those of Habermas, they should be conceived in relation to the issues he discusses in the context of the postmetaphysical turn. In an age in which philosophy has lost its privileged position of an all-embracing knowledge, of grand narrative vindicating the prerogative of ethical normativity, the problems of identity and diversity, of moral justification, and of rights and values are becoming especially challenging for philosophy and its own place in the human and social sciences. The question about how substantive moral assertions could be confirmed or disconfirmed is discussed by Alison Jaggar in her study "Feminist Ethics and Moral Justification." Jaggar asks, in particular, how feminists can justify their critiques of those actions, practices and institutions that rationalize or maintain male dominance. By presenting different feminist points of view on this subject she also evokes the feminist critiques of two leading moral theories of the 20th century – John Rawls' theory of justice and Jürgen Habermas' discourse ethics. According Jaggar both theories reflect a certain human type – the white middle class rationally acting man – as family head. This concept carries authoritarian traits as it denies women of the capacities to make rational decisions and puts them on a morally lower level compared to the sober justice-oriented attitude of men. Even though Habermas speaks of a "power-free discourse," in which everyone has an equal opportunity to speak and to be heard, there are many underprivileged groups that do not arrive to express their situation. Jaggar accuses these theories of ignoring the conditions necessary for such opportunities to be real rather than merely formal. The challenge lies not in the postulate of equality, but rather in the question about how an open and egalitarian discourse can be made possible for moral agents who are in different, unequal positions: "Speaking requires a language" – outlines Jaggar – "but dominant vocabularies may lack the resources necessary to express the perspectives of subordinated groups."

The question about language that Jaggar poses is examined specifically in Yvanka B. Raynova's study "Human Rights, Women's Rights, Gender Mainstreaming, and Diversity: The Language Question." Raynova shows how by changing the grammatical gender and the feminization of language women were able to articulate themselves as a subject of rights and not just of duties. Similar to Mary-Kate Smith, who evokes "the problem of speaking for others" (Linda Alcoff), and to Tatyana Batuleva, who stresses the importance of having "an own identity" in order to be independent, Raynova shows the interrelation between identity, language and women's human rights claims: "Feminists and philosophers may dispute the meanings and ambiguities of the notions of 'subject,' 'sex,' 'gender' etc., but in law, where every word counts, the univocal denomination of the subject is a *sine qua non* for any rights claims."

The thesis of the connection between recognition and identity, which has been brought up by Charles Taylor, is further examined by Susanne Moser in the context of the *Second Sex* of Simone de Beauvoir. While Moser indicates that Beauvoir's concept of recognition is based on Hegel's master-slave dialectics, which makes it difficult to find a solution to the problem, Sonia Kruks and María Luisa Femínias show how Beauvoir's notion of the subject as transcendence and freedom can serve as corrective to the post-Enlightenment theories of Michel Foucault and Judith Butler about the constructedness and instability of the subject and gender categories. If in *The Second Sex* Beauvoir thematizes women's exclusion through subjection and mythical construction as absolute otherness, Enrique Dussel, for his part, points out that the concepts of the other and the subject should be revisited in the light of the poor and the new victims of exclusion produced by the actual process of globalization. Thus he opens the doors for a new contextualization, as well as for a new rereading of history through globalization and the four stages of the "World System." The problems of history are also investigated by Lester Embree and Dimitrios Akrivoulis. Similar to Dussel, Embree emphasizes the tension between historical theory and the praxis of historical subjects as agents of social movements. Analyzing Alfred Schutz's contribution to the theory of the historical sciences, he shows the problem with his position that the social sciences in the strict signification are about the world of contemporaries while the historical sciences are about the world of predecessors, a position clearly incompatible with that of some contemporary history understandings dealing with the Women's liberation movement. Dimitrios Akrivoulis discusses a related topic, posing questions about the meaning of emancipation, the justification of emancipation claims and its limits. By comparing Reinhart Koselleck's and Paul Ricoeur's analyses of the receptivity and efficacity of the past, as well as their accounts of two core *meta*-historical categories conditioning history, namely the "space of experience" and "the horizon of expectation", he reveals the initial disproportionality marking the concept of emancipation.

Last but not least, the volume ends with a discussion about values and community in contemporary Western/European societies. While Mark Zlomislic develops Derrida's thesis that deconstruction, which has been wrongly labelled to be a destruction of ethical values, leads to a more powerful ethics of community than metaphysics, Susanne Moser complements Habermas' and Honneth's axiological conceptions in order to show the importance of values for the self-understanding and identity of Europeans as well as for the social and political integration in Europe. Yet, if Moser deplores the fact that the European Union has failed to open a sustained discussion about values, Yvanka Raynova pushes the critique further by asserting that most citizens of Europe do not understand what the expression "European values" means and that there are a lot paradoxes, contradictions and confusion in the current value controversy.

The themes and the questions discussed in this volume are of course not closed; they are open for further research and debates. But for now I want to thank on behalf the Institute for Axiological Research all participants of this collective work for their valuable contributions and support.

Yvanka B. Raynova

PART I

WOMEN'S SITUATION BETWEEN THEORY AND PRAXIS

1

Alison M. Jaggar

THE PROBLEM OF MORAL JUSTIFICATION IN CONTEMPORARY FEMINIST DEBATES

The philosophical question of moral justification enquires how substantive moral assertions – claims that particular actions or practices are right or wrong, permissible or impermissible – may be confirmed or disconfirmed. This question has always been central in Western moral philosophy and it holds special significance for feminism, which is defined by its moral opposition to male dominance. Feminists need some means of establishing that their critiques of those actions, practices and institutions that rationalize or maintain male dominance are not merely personal opinions but instead are objectively justified.

This paper discusses some recent feminist contributions to the philosophical debate about moral justification. Part I traces feminist engagements with four major moral theorists of the twentieth century, and Part II makes explicit several common themes running through those feminist critiques. Part III outlines some elements of an alternative feminist approach to moral justification, informed by the earlier critiques. Part IV offers some feminist reflections on the project of providing a philosophical account of moral justification, suggesting that philosophers' claims to authority in defining moral justification may themselves constitute practice of dominance.

I. Feminist challenges to the analytic canon

1. Intuitionism: Elizabeth Anderson on G. E. Moore

Analytic ethics is often said to begin in 1903 with the publication of G. E. Moore's *Principia Ethica.* Moore is credited with being the father of the linguistic turn in moral philosophy, directing philosophical attention away from explicit consideration of normative issues and refocusing it on the analysis of moral language. Moore's best-known contribution to ethics is his analysis of what he took to be its central concept, namely, the concept "good." Moore wanted to determine the intrinsic, as opposed to instrumental, meaning of "good," and, in his attempt to ascertain this, he sought to discover what was good in isolation from everything else. In order to avoid what he termed the naturalistic fallacy of identifying the meaning of "good" with some empirical property, he assumed that the word referred instead to some non-natural property which, he thought, must be simple and indefinable. Being non-natural, this property could not be identified through empirical observation, and so Moore concluded that it must be discovered by internal contemplation or moral intuition.

Moore's intuitionist method has received much criticism. Here I shall focus on the critique offered by Elizabeth Anderson, whose larger project is to refute Moore's account of value. Anderson begins by observing that Moore's conclusion, that only personal relations, beauty, and knowledge are intrinsically good, is incompatible with the intuitions of many people, who value such things as meaningful work, athletic achievement, justice and freedom. Anderson initially attributes Moore's surprising conclusion to the extremely narrow range of intuitions he consulted. She remarks:

> Moore and his followers removed themselves from active engagements in the larger world, withdrew to private spaces in the company of intimate friends, and introspectively contemplated the isolated objects of their imaginations. It is not surprising that many goods were not salient to people in such a privileged, exclusive aristocratic setting, insulated from the experiences of work and practical activity with strangers.[1]

Anderson observes that Moore, in addition to consulting an unrepresentative sample of intuitions, gave little credence to any that conflicted with his own. She quotes John Maynard Keynes's description of the manipulation and bullying through which Moore produced consensus among his friends in the Bloomsbury group.

---

[1] Elizabeth Anderson, *Value in Ethics and Economics,* Cambridge and London: Harvard University Press, 1993, p. 120.

> Victory was with those who could speak with the greatest appearance of clear, undoubting conviction and could best use the accents of infallibility. Moore... was a great master of this method – greeting one's remarks with a gasp of incredulity – Do you really think that, an expression of face as if to hear such a thing said reduced him to a state of wonder verging on imbecility, with his mouth wide open and wagging his head in the negative so violently that his hair shook. 'Oh!' he would say, goggling at you as if either you or he must be mad; and no reply was possible... In practice it was a kind of combat in which strength of character was really much more valuable than subtlety of mind.[2]

Anderson shows that Moore's conclusions concerning 'our' moral intuitions in fact reflected the beliefs of those with the most social power even within his own narrow and elite circle; she suggests that such a biased outcome was not accidental but reflected a tendency endemic in individualist intuitionism. If individuals' value judgements are construed as unmediated and ineffable perceptions, insusceptible to rational argument, then intuitionism is incapable of grounding a publicly accessible distinction between objective judgements and subjective preferences. In these circumstances, either moral claims are undecidable or, if treated as decidable, then the intuitions of those with the greatest social authority are the most likely to be accepted. Thus, individualist intuitionism not only has a tendency to rationalize conventional moral beliefs but, in a hierarchical social context, lends itself to justifying the moral beliefs of the powerful. In Moore's case, and notwithstanding Virginia Woolf's presence in the Bloomsbury group, these were the beliefs of people privileged by class, race, gender and empire.

2. *Universal prescriptivism: Lynne S. Arnault on Richard M. Hare*

Like Moore, Richard Hare aims to derive substantive moral claims from supposedly neutral investigations of the logical properties of moral concepts; his first book is aptly entitled, *The Language of Morals*. Hare also analyses concepts of moral evaluation, including "good," but he reaches different conclusions from Moore's. He contends that moral terms do not refer to anything, natural or non-natural, but instead are

---

[2] John Maynard Keynes, "My Early Beliefs," in *Two Memoirs*, New York: Augustus M. Kelley, 1949, pp. 85-88, quoted in Anderson, op. cit., p. 121.

characterized by their action-guiding function. To fulfil this function, moral claims require reasons and these, Hare argues, must take the form of arguments that a particular course of action could be prescribed universally. Hare considers universalizability to be the criterion of moral rationality; if a course of action can be prescribed universally, then it is objectively justified.

In order to determine whether a proposed course of action is universalizable, Hare recommends that a moral deliberator should identify sympathetically with each of the parties who will be affected if the proposal is implemented, imaginatively representing to herself each party's desires and aversions in turn.

When I have been the round of all the affected parties, and come back, in my own person, to make an impartial moral judgment giving equal weight to the interests of all parties, what can I possibly do except advocate that course which will, taken all in all, least frustrate the desires which I have imagined myself having? But this (it is plausible to go on) is to maximize satisfactions.[3]

Hare concludes that asking the classic Kantian question will produce the classic utilitarian answer.

Hare observes that reasoning with universalizability requires humans to think like 'ideal observers' or 'archangels,' beings that are fully rational and impartial and possess perfect knowledge. Hare acknowledges that no one can really think like an archangel, since human reason is imperfect and human knowledge, including self-knowledge, is finite, but he finds here an empirical rather than a logical impossibility, a difficulty of practice rather than principle. Hare acknowledges that there are 'practical difficulties in getting to know the states of mind of other sentient beings, which increase with the remoteness of their experiences from ours,' but he believes that these difficulties can 'be overcome by getting as closely acquainted as we can with their circumstances, verbal and other behaviour, anatomies, etc., and comparing them with our

---

[3] Richard M. Hare, *Freedom and Reason*, Oxford: Clarendon Press, 1963, p. 123. Quoted by Lynne S. Arnault, "The Radical Future of a Classic Moral Theory," in *Gender/Body/Knowledge: Feminist Reconstructions of Being and Knowing,* edited by Alison M. Jaggar and Susan Bordo, New Brunswick and London: Rutgers University Press, 1989, p. 191.

own.'[4] When a moral deliberator follows Hare's methodological recommendations, *inter*personal conflicts of preferences or prescriptions move 'inside' that individual to become *intra*personal ones.[5]

Hare is explicit about the assumptions underlying his method of moral justification. One is that people are fundamentally alike: 'people's inclinations about most of the important matters in life tend to be the same (very few people, for example, like being starved or run over by motor cars)'.[6] In addition to assuming that people are basically similar, Hare also supposes a particular conception of what they are like: in his view, individuals' primary inclination or desire is to have their own interests satisfied and he explains away apparent counter-examples. For example, as Lynne Arnault notes, Hare interprets people's 'particular loyalties and affections' in sociobiological terms that reduce them to strategies for preserving an individual's genes; this move enables him to deny that they are genuine manifestations of noninstrumental care about others.[7] Arnault concludes that Hare's universal prescriptivist method relies on the classically liberal conception of the person as an instrumentally rational, self-interested, fundamentally isolated individual who cooperates with others only in order to promote his own interests.

Arnault contends that both of Hare's assumptions about human motivation are empirically unwarranted: not only are people's conceptions of their own interests quite diverse, but many people also care about others for noninstrumental reasons. In Arnault's view, differences among individuals tend to be linked systematically with their differing social identities; she sees these identities as having profound epistemic significance, shaping not only people's needs and values but also their perceptions and interpretations of situations.

Individuals define what the situation is, and their constructions depend on their life-history, social experience and social situatedness. Thus, for example, a male manager may define the situation as simple flirtation, but a female secretary may construct it as sexual harassment.[8]

---

[4] Richard M. Hare, *Moral Thinking: Its Levels, Method and Point*, Oxford: Clarendon Press, 1981, pp. 126-127.
[5] Hare, *Moral Thinking,* op. cit., p. 110.
[6] Richard M. Hare, *Freedom and Reason*, Oxford: Clarendon Press, 1963, p. 97.
[7] Hare, *Moral Thinking,* op. cit., p. 137.
[8] Arnault, op. cit., p. 197.

If the epistemological consequences of differences among individuals were taken seriously, Arnault contends, Hare's method of moral justification would be revealed as evidently unworkable: his recommendation to adopt the standpoint of the other would be exposed as incoherent, impossible not only in practice but in principle.[9] Arnault's point may be elaborated by considering how the issue of sexual harassment might be addressed by Hare's method. The male manager might attempt to stand imaginatively in the shoes of his secretary but the individual wearing those shoes would be the manager, with his distinctive perceptions and values, rather than the secretary, with her different perceptions and values. That many men have expressed the wish that someone would sexually harass them illustrates the unreliability of the method of sympathetic identification; one cannot imaginatively identify with a different person and still remain oneself. If Hare is mistaken in believing that people's social identities are irrelevant to their moral thinking, his theory of moral justification encounters fatal difficulties.

Arnault adds that Hare's model of the moral agent is ill-suited to represent experiences involving ongoing dependence, such as occur within families, or 'to give voice to the forms of connectedness and solidarity those members of a subordinated group experience.[10] If the 'possessive individualist' is taken as the paradigm of individual rationality, then anyone who attempts to express experiences of connectedness and interdependence risks having her words dismissed as confused or irrational. Because Hare's theory of moral justification does not provide for women or members of disadvantaged or marginalized groups representing their experiences in undistorted, nonrepressed ways, Arnault concludes that it is biased against them.

3. Hypothetical contractarianism: Susan Okin on John Rawls; Alison Jaggar on Susan Okin

In the latter half of the twentieth century, John Rawls revived normative ethics from the near-death state induced in it by the neo-positivist assumption that philosophical ethics must be restricted to the analysis of

---

[9] Arnault, op. cit., p. 196.
[10] Arnault, op. cit., p. 192.

concepts. Rawls not only propounds a substantive normative theory of justice as fairness but also defends his theory with an original account of moral justification. To overcome the problems he perceives in, intuitionism and ideal utilitarianism, Rawls's account draws on the contractarian tradition in political philosophy.[11]

Rawls's account of moral justification postulates an imaginary original position, corresponding to the state of nature in political contract theories, in which parties meet to conclude a permanently binding agreement on the principles for regulating the 'basic structure' or 'major social institutions' of the society they are to inhabit.[12] The parties in the original position are conceived as free, equal and rational 'in the narrow sense, standard in economic theory, of taking the most effective means to given ends.'[13] They are located behind a 'veil of ignorance' which ensures that 'no one knows his place in society, his class position or social status, nor does anyone know his fortune in the distribution of natural assets and abilities, his intelligence, strength and the like.' The parties do not even know 'their conceptions of the good or their special psychological propensities'.[14] Despite their purportedly generic nature, the parties do retain two markers of social identity: they are heads of households, a stipulation that Rawls makes in order to ensure justice for the next generation, and each may be viewed as 'the least advantaged representative man,' a condition intended to guarantee that the interests of the worst off receive due weight in the deliberations that occur behind the veil of ignorance.

The various features of the original position are designed to ensure that the principles of justice generated in it are fair, impartial and reached autonomously; this design encourages Rawls to assert that the point of view embedded in the principles provides 'an Archimedean

---

[11] Some version of Rawls''s method of moral justification was adopted by many major philosophers in the 1970s and 1980s, including: Bruce Ackerman, Charles Beitz, Gerald Dworkin, David Gauthier, Alan Gweirth, Robert Nozick, Jeffrey Reiman and Thomas Scanlon.
[12] John Rawls, *A Theory of Justice,* Cambridge, MA: Harvard University Press, 1971, p. 7.
[13] Ibid., p. 14.
[14] Ibid., p. 12.

point from which the basic structure (of society) itself can be judged'.[15] However, the original position is not a moral foundation from which the principles of justice are deduced; on the contrary, Rawls's account of moral justification is ultimately coherentist, 'a matter of the mutual support of many considerations, of everything fitting together into one coherent view'.[16] Our accounts of the original position are to be revised in conjunction with making modifications to various formulations of the principles of justice and to what Rawls calls 'our considered (moral) judgments,' with a view to making all three mutually consistent. The goal is to produce the state of affairs that Rawls calls 'reflective equilibrium'.[17] Reflective equilibrium is a state of mind that responsible moral individuals should aspire to achieve.

Several feminists have argued that Rawls's method, as he describes it, is biased against women.[18] One obvious problem is that Rawls's supposedly generic party in the original position, 'the representative man,' is described as the head of a household; assigning "him" this social identity has the effect of excluding from the domain of justice issues concerning relations among family members. Susan Okin argues forcefully that marriage and family life must be subjected to the scrutiny of justice in order to address the unjust burdens that traditional family roles assign to women. These burdens include: a disproportionate share of housework and child-care; less decision-making power, leisure and nurture; and vulnerability to domestic violence. In addition, when women bear the main responsibility for domestic work, they are deprived of equal opportunities for economic or political power and prestige in the public world outside the home.[19]

---

[15] Ibid., p. 260.
[16] Ibid., p. 21.
[17] Ibid., p. 20.
[18] Objectors include Jane English, "Justice Between Generations," *Philosophical Studies* 31:2 (1977) and Sybil Schwartzenbach, "Rawls and Ownership: The Forgotten Category of Reproductive Labour," in *Science, Morality and Feminist Theory*, edited by Marsha Hanen and Kai Nielsen, Calgary, Canada: University of Calgary Press 1987.
[19] Susan Moller Okin, *Justice, Gender and the Family*, New York: Basic Books, 1989.

Okin proposes to remedy the male bias inherent in Rawls's method of moral justification by modifying his characterization of the original position in two ways. First, sex should be identified explicitly as a characteristic which is hidden behind the veil of ignorance; second, the social organization of gender, especially the family, should be recognized explicitly and consistently as falling within the domain of justice.[20] Okin believes that these modifications would ensure that the interests of 'the least advantaged representative woman' would be considered equally with those of the least advantaged representative man[21] and would enable the revised original position to serve as a theoretical device facilitating thinking from the standpoint of women.[22] Like Hare, Okin recognizes that thinking from the standpoint of less advantaged others involves some practical difficulties; she also acknowledges that it assumes considerable knowledge of the social world, knowledge requiring empathy and concern for others. Again like Hare, however, Okin does not view the problem of limited knowledge as an insuperable obstacle to moral justification via reflective equilibrium.

In opposition to both Rawls and Okin, I have argued elsewhere that hypothetical contractarianism is inadequate in principle as a method of moral justification.[23] Using this method requires formulating conceptions of human needs and interests and principles of rational choice that are at once sufficiently abstract to be universal and sufficiently determinate that they will not invite endless disputes over their interpretation. Because the natures of human needs and interests, as well as of the principles of reason, are essentially contested, I contend that it is impossible

---

[20] Okin notes that Rawls occasionally includes both these conditions in various descriptions of the original position. At the very outset of his theory, he includes the family among the major social institutions determining the basic structure of a society, though he goes on to assume rather than establish its justice, and he fails to mention it in a later article. In another paper subsequent to *A Theory of Justice*, Rawls includes sex among the contingencies hided by the veil of ignorance. These occasional concessions appear to have no impact on Rawls"s overall theory.
[21] Susan Moller Okin, "Reason and Feeling in Thinking about Justice," *Ethics: An International Journal of Social, Political, and Legal Philosophy*, 99:2 (1989).
[22] Okin, *Justice, Gender and the Family*, op. cit., pp. 106-9.
[23] Alison M. Jaggar, "Taking Consent Seriously: Feminist Practical Ethics and Actual Moral Dialogue," in *Applied Ethics: A Reader*, edited by Earl R. Winkler and Jerrold R. Coombs, Oxford: Blackwell, 1993.

to substitute private reflection for public discussion about principles of morality and justice. I go on to argue that the method of justifying moral claims by appeal to a postulated but hypothetical agreement is covertly elitist because it requires the construction of elaborate philosophical arguments for which most people have no inclination, time or training. (The early Rawls even says it requires complex mathematics.) A method of justification that ordinary people cannot use necessarily assigns final moral authority to those few philosophical experts who are able to use it. In Western societies, such people are generally white, male and middle-class.

Because the deliberation attributed to parties in the original position is hypothetical, Rawls's method remains essentially monological, reflecting only the views of the individual theorist–as illustrated by the male bias we have observed in Rawls's account of justice as fairness. The hypothetical contractarian method is unreliable, no matter how well-meaning the individual who uses it. However, its elaborate theoretical machinery obscures its monological character and gives the impression of generating a theory of justice that is objective in the sense of transcending the subjective views of any given individual. These unjustified pretensions to objectivity give the method an authoritarian potential, encouraging those who use it to dismiss the expressed views of real people (of sex workers, perhaps, or of welfare recipients) by alleging that their opinions are incompatible with the conclusions that would be reached by parties in the original position.

4. Domination-free discourse: Seyla Benhabib on Jürgen Habermas; Iris Young and others on Seyla Benhabib

The communicative or discourse ethics of Karl-Otto Apel and Juergen Habermas offers a contrast with the Anglo-American theories of moral justification considered above. Habermas accepts the Kantian intuition that the moral validity of any norm is to be defined in terms of what could be agreed in free and equal discussion among all those affected; however, he insists that the substantive content of moral agreements cannot be inferred through philosophical thought experiments but instead requires real-world discourse.

Its insistence on the need for actual public discussion reveals discourse ethics's recognition that moral subjects are diverse; at the same time, its requirement that such discussion should be domination-free moves discourse ethics beyond the conventionalism often thought to threaten both, communitarianism and postmodernism, the main contemporary challengers of neo-Enlightenment moral philosophy. Seyla Benhabib regards discourse ethics as offering the most promising model of moral justification available to feminism but suggests some modifications to Habermas's account, in order that this promise may be fulfilled.[24] Of the several revisions she recommends, I mention here only two.

First, Benhabib challenges Habermas's acceptance of the standard liberal distinction between a public 'moral' domain, regulated by objective principles of justice or right, and a private 'ethical' domain, in which people may pursue their various subjective conceptions of value or goodness. She notes that this distinction has served to exclude from moral scrutiny many questions of special concern to women, such as questions about abortion, pornography and domestic violence. Benhabib disputes the assumption that the distinction between moral issues of justice and ethical issues of goodness is unproblematic; she asserts that the distinction itself must be questioned in moral discourse. Second, Benhabib revises Habermas's account of moral judgement, denying the pre-eminence he assigns to the culturally masculine ability to formulate general norms through abstraction from concrete situations; she asserts that it is equally important to be able to perceive sensitively the specificities of particular contexts, an ability requiring the culturally feminine capacities for moral imagination, interpretation and sympathy. Benhabib argues that moral judgment involves enlarged thinking or reciprocal recognition, the ability to reverse perspectives with others in order to see the world as they see it.

Some feminist philosophers welcome Benhabib's revisions to discourse ethics but contend that they do not go far enough. Nancy Fraser notes that language is not a neutral means of communication, but reflects culturally specific ways of interpreting the world. She criticizes

---

[24] Seyla Benhabib, *Situating the Self: Gender, Community and Postmodernism in Contemporary Ethics,* New York: Routledge, 1992.

Benhabib for neglecting to address the problem that dominant discourses may well be incapable of expressing the interests and concerns of subordinated groups.[25] Iris Young argues that Benhabib's conception of enlarged thinking is ultimately incoherent, because the idea of reversing perspectives with someone else is unintelligible.

The reciprocal recognition by which I know that I am other for you just as you are other for me cannot entail a reversibility of perspectives, precisely because our positions are partly constituted by the perspectives each of us has on the others.[26]

Young further contends that the belief that we can adopt other peoples' standpoints is disrespectful and presumptuous: in assuming that other people are similar to us, it obscures their differences from us. This belief is problematic politically as well as morally, because privileged people who try to put themselves in the position of those who are less privileged are likely to rely on projections and fantasies and so to misrepresent the situations of the disadvantaged. Moreover, 'asking the oppressed to reverse perspectives with the privileged in adjudicating a conflict may itself be an injustice and an insult.'[27] Benhabib's proposals, like Habermas's, surely remain overly idealized in failing to address the inevitable problems of systematic inequality among participants in practical discourses.

II. 'The master's tools will never dismantle the master's house' – Audre Lorde

The parallels among these various critiques of the most eminent theorists of analytic ethics suggest that feminists have identified several male-biased assumptions that are not held idiosyncratically by a few isolated philosophers but that instead infect a whole tradition of thinking about moral justification. This is the liberal tradition descending from the European Enlightenment.

---

[25] Nancy Fraser, "Toward a Discourse Ethic of Solidarity," *Praxis International*, 5:4 (1986).
[26] Iris Marion Young, *Intersecting Voices: Dilemmas of Gender, Political Philosophy and Policy*, Princeton, NJ: Princeton University Press, 1997.
[27] Young, *Intersecting Voices*, op. cit., p. 48.

1. First, 'the' moral subject of this tradition appears to be generic but in fact reflects a specific social type: he is a Western male head of household, upper or middle class and therefore probably white. The motivations and style of reasoning characteristic of this social type are ascribed to all rational moral subjects, despite the overwhelming empirical evidence that many people have different motivations and employ alternative styles of reasoning.[28]
2. When this social type is taken as the moral norm, people whose thinking deviates from his are presented as deficient in moral rationality. Idealizing his mode of thinking is thus covertly authoritarian because it invalidates the moral thinking of many women as well as of male members of subordinated groups.
3. The sphere of moral reason is arbitrarily limited so as to exclude matters of intimate and family relations.
4. In consequence, numerous issues that have special importance for women's lives become morally undecidable; there is no conceptual space for criticizing many practices oppressive to women.
5. The foregoing points together entail that mainstream conceptions of moral justification deny the conceptual resources that would permit women and male members of subordinated groups to express their own moral perspectives in their own terms.
6. Despite the impartiality and universality claimed by these conceptions of moral justification, they are in fact self-serving and circular because they rationalize the views of the philosopher who invokes them while silencing dissenting voices.

For these reasons, the very conceptual tools that purport to guarantee moral objectivity are biased in favour of the privileged.

Implicit in feminists' criticisms of mainstream ethics is an expectation that any adequate account of moral justification must not only be able to distinguish justified moral claims from both subjective desires and established conventions; it must also fulfil the following conditions:

---

[28] For instance, empirical research shows that many women value care over justice, as do many African American, Native American and working class men, not to mention persons from Nonwestern cultures.

1. Its conception of the moral subject must be carefully scrutinized to eliminate covert bias on the basis of race, class, gender or any other axis of domination.
2. Therefore, it must take care not to discredit nor disregard the moral narratives, vocabularies and styles of thinking characteristic of women, lower-class and marginalized persons.
3. It must be practically available for use by all moral subjects, including those with little formal education; thus, it should not be highly technical nor rely on overly-idealized, counter-factual assumptions.
4. It must not exclude from moral scrutiny aspects of life that are of special concern to women or to male members of disadvantaged and marginalized groups.

In short, a feminist account of moral justification must be non-elitist and truly unbiased; it must not privilege the perspectives of the powerful nor assign disproportionate moral authority to their voices. The next section of this essay sketches some feminist work that moves in the direction of meeting these conditions.

III. Towards a feminist conception of moral justification

1. Positioning the moral subject

Liberal moral theory has typically discussed moral subjects at a high level of abstraction, presenting them as generic rational agents who are essentially – though not empirically – solitary. The classic liberal theorists were certainly aware that empirical subjects are embodied members of specific communities, but they dismissed people's bodies and community memberships as 'accidental' properties, inessential to their moral subjectivity. Some may have supposed that treating moral subjects as indistinguishable was required by the Enlightenment commitment to the equal moral value of every human individual. By focusing on people's commonalities and ignoring their differences, liberalism implies that moral subjects are indiscernible in all theoretical respects. In Seyla Benhabib's words, it treats them as 'generalized' rather than 'concrete.'

Over the past twenty-five years, the liberal conception of the moral subject has been challenged from many directions. Communitarian critics have been particularly vocal in insisting that moral subjects are essentially embodied, thereby entailing that they are 'embedded' in communities and 'encumbered' by particular loyalties and obligations that constitute essential aspects of their identities. Many feminist accounts of moral subjects resemble communitarianism in emphasizing bodies, communities and relationships, but feminist work is distinguished by its attention to inequality. Feminist discussions of embodiment, for instance, typically treat the body neither merely as an individuator of persons nor merely as a universal condition of human life but as a bearer of contingent and varying social meanings which locate bodies and their persons not only in particular communities but also in specific structures of privilege and power.[29] Similarly, feminists not only present moral subjects as constituted by particular relations but also assert that that these relations invariably involve dimensions of systematic dominance and inequality. Finally, feminists typically focus on those aspects of moral subjects' identities that are constituted by their membership in distinct – though overlapping – social collectivities defined not only by history and geography but also by categories such as gender, class and race, in which power inequalities are inherent.

Feminists do not deny that moral subjects are alike on some level of abstraction but their consciousness of the much false humanisms that have purveyed generalizations about specific populations as universal truths of human nature motivates them to highlight human differences over human commonalities. Nor do feminists dispute the equal moral worth of each individual but, when individuals are so differently situated, they insist that a genuine commitment to moral equality requires sensitivity to actual inequalities. Feminists further contend that the differences and inequalities that are most important for moral theory are systematic rather than idiosyncratic, and that they separate groups or collectivities rather than particular individuals.

Those features of moral subjectivity emphasized by feminists have implications for moral justification. For relationally constituted subjects,

---

[29] Excellent discussions of some of the gendered power dimensions of embodiment are offered by Susan Bordo, *Unbearable Weight: Feminism, Western Culture, and the Body,* Berkeley, Los Angeles and London: University of California Press, 1993, and Susan Wendell, *The Rejected Body: Feminist Philosophical Reflections on Disability,* New York: Routledge, 1996.

possessive individualism is not a natural – let alone rational – human motivation. For embodied subjects, the only knowledge they can hope to attain is finite and situated. Subjects who are socially constituted by their membership in different collectivities, especially collectivities that stand to each other in relations of dominance and subordination, are likely to have disparate moral viewpoints and styles of reasoning. Such disparities and inequalities create obstacles to projects of imaginative identification and even to productive discussion. To recognize these obstacles is challenge mainstream assumptions that there exists a single correct model of moral reason, and that moral subjects are interchangeable. Abandoning these assumptions requires rejecting monological conceptions of moral justification.

2. *Socializing moral rationality*

Most contemporary feminist philosophers repudiate the possibility of moral justification through solitary reflection, whether this take the form of consulting one's intuition, staging a hypothetical discourse or pretending to be someone else. Monological thought experiments may sometimes have heuristic value but they are equally likely to mislead. Many feminists argue that recommendations that moral agents think from the standpoint of others, reverse perspectives with them, and so on, are not only disrespectful of others but epistemically incoherent. There exists no substitute for listening to real people or to explain their moral perspectives in their own terms.

Engaging in actual discussion not only permits the collective assessment of what Hare calls proposed courses of action, alternative resolutions of a given moral problem; it also permits 'the' problem itself to be problematized. Empirical discourse allows people to raise questions such as: For whom is this situation problematic and what criteria are used to identify 'those affected'? In whose terms is the situation described, and what is highlighted and what obscured by those terms? What are the interests and values at stake and how do these change if the problem is redescribed? Who is responsible for addressing the situation and according to what account of responsibility? A monological method might be plausible if moral reasoning involved no more than consulting a moral calculus, but in fact every identification of a moral problem presupposes an interpretive point of view that should be made explicit and examined. It is because moral reasoning is inevitably hermeneutic that it must be pluralist and interactive.[30]

A full theory of moral rationality must include an account of individual rationality but, because of their scepticism about monological approaches, feminists' positive work on moral rationality has focused more on social processes than on individual capacities. Some feminist work has been done on the topic of individual rationality but there is no space to consider it here. One theme running throughout this work is that dominant philosophical accounts of individual moral rationality are biased by gender, class, race and ethnicity insofar as they reflect and rationalize the culturally specific values held by modern, Western, bourgeois, men. However, few feminists believe that the remedy for existing bias is to replace one singular model that covertly represents moral rationality as bourgeois and masculine with another singular model that has more features considered characteristically feminine; there no more exists a representative or generic woman than a generic human or a representative man. Instead, many feminists argue that the remedy is to reconstruct moral rationality as a charactric primarily of social processes and only secondarily as a property of individuals. On this view, individual rationality is no longer defined by the possession of specific motivations or values or by the utilization of a particular style of moral thinking; instead, it consists in proficiency in those interactive skills and virtues necessary to participate as an equal in productive moral discourse.

A considerable number of feminists, including myself, concurs with the long Western philosophical tradition, stretching from Plato through Locke and Kant, to Rawls and Habermas, that holds moral conclusions to be rationally justified when they are reached by rational people through discursive processes that are open, inclusive and egalitarian. But even though philosophers in this tradition are aware that real people are not all alike, they have ignored the practical and theoretical problems posed for egalitarian discourse by systematic difference and inequality.

---

[30] Maria C. Lugones, "On the Logic of Pluralist Feminism," in *Feminist Ethics,* edited by Claudia Card, Lawrence, KS: University of Kansas Press, 1991.

Feminists, by contrast, have been deeply troubled by those problems; in response, they have developed an extensive literature on discursive communication, including its ethical and political aspects. In what follows, I indicate a few of the avenues feminists have explored in considering how open and egalitarian discourse might be possible among moral subjects who are inevitably diverse and unequal.

Mainstream accounts of domination-free discourse require that each participant equally has an opportunity to speak and be heard; however, they neglect to examine the conditions necessary for such opportunities to be real rather than merely formal. Speaking requires a language but dominant vocabularies may lack the resources necessary to express the perspectives of subordinated groups; as a young woman, for instance, I was unable to articulate many vague and confused feelings and perceptions because the language necessary to do so had not yet been invented. The vocabulary I needed included such terms as: 'gender' (applied beyond grammar to social norms and identities); 'sex role;' 'sexism;' 'sexual harassment;' 'the double day;' 'sexual objectification;' 'heterosexism;' 'the male gaze;' 'marital, acquaintance and date rape;' 'emotional work;' 'stalking;' 'hostile environment;' 'displaced homemaker;' and 'double standard of ageing.' Because language is essentially public, creating new vocabularies is necessarily a collective rather than an individual project. In order that alternatives to dominant moral vocabularies may be developed, I have recently argued that, if discourses are to be open and inclusive for some, they may have to be closed to and exclusive of others.[31]

Feminist models of moral discourse are unusual in giving considerable attention to hearing as well as speaking; they have explained that hearing, especially hearing across diversity, is a complex and difficult activity in which people may fail for many reasons.[32] Laurence Thomas contends that, in an unjust society, there is no 'vantage point from which any and every person can rationally grasp whatever morally significant

---

[31] Alison M. Jaggar, "Globalizing Feminist Ethics," *Hypatia*, (1998) 13:2.
[32] Maria C. Lugones and Elizabeth V. Spelman, "Have We Got a Theory for You! Feminist Theory, Cultural Imperialism and the Demand for 'the Woman's Voice'." *Hypatia,* 1:1 (1983). Marsha Houston, "Why the Dialogues are Difficult or 15 Ways a Black Woman Knows When a White Woman"s Not Listening," in *Overcoming Racism and Sexism,* edited by Linda A. Bell and David Blumenfeld, Lanham, MD: Rowman and Littlefield, 1995.

experiences a person might have.'³³ For instance, he asserts, African Americans who have endured the pains and humiliations of racism experience an emotional vulnerability, anger and hostility, even a bitterness and rancour, which most white Americans cannot imagine. '(J)ust as a person does not know what it is like to be a bat by hanging upside down with closed eyes, (so) a person does not know what it is like to be a member of a diminished social category merely on account of having been affronted and insulted by a diminished social category person.'³⁴ In order that members of subordinated or stigmatized groups may be heard, Thomas recommends that more privileged persons should respond to their descriptions of their experiences with 'moral deference.'

The idea behind moral deference is not that a diminished social category person can never be wrong about the character of his own experiences. Surely he can, since anyone can... Rather, the idea is that there should be a presumption in favor of that person's account of her experiences. This presumption is warranted because the individual is speaking from a vantage point to which someone not belonging to her diminished social category group does not have access.[35]

Thomas did not develop his idea of moral deference in the specific context of feminist discourse but his concept captures the spirit of many feminist discussions of listening. As a defeasible presumption of a speaker's authority, moral deference may be viewed as a kind of discursive affirmative action necessary to achieving substantive rather than merely formal equality among participants in discourse.

Feminist models of moral discourse include a number of other characteristic features, in addition to their reinterpretations of equality, openness and inclusiveness. Among those features are a commitment to the collective moral evaluation of participants' emotions[36] and a conception of moral discourse as a nurturing rather than an adversarial practice.[37]

---

[33] Lawrence Thomas, "Moral Deference," *Philosophical Forum,* XIV: 1-3 (1992-3) p. 233.
[34] Thomas, "Moral Deference," op. cit., p. 240.
[35] Thomas, "Moral Deference," op. cit., p. 244.
[36] Alison M. Jaggar, "Love and Knowledge: Emotion in Feminist Epistemology," *Inquiry,* 32 (1989) 151-76.
[37] Patrocinio Schweickart, "Engendering Critical Discourse," in *The Current in Criticism,* edited by Clayton Koelb and Virgil Lokke, West Lafayette: Purdue University Press, 1987.

For feminists, moral discourses are not neutral procedures in which people withdraw from the real world to debate moral concerns; instead, they are activities within the world and themselves are liable to moral and political evaluation.[38] Done well, moral discourse has a value that is intrinsic and not merely instrumental.

3. Situating moral objectivity

Western philosophers have often construed moral justification as the attainment of 'the moral point of view,' a grandiose expression that hints heavily at a transcendent moral reality. In the twentieth century, they have interpreted the expression through such metaphors as a god's eye view, the perspective of an ideal observer or an archangel, an Archimedean point, a view from nowhere or a view from everywhere. These metaphors are paradoxical, of course, since their aim is to designate an imagined perspective that is precisely not a specific point of view, what might be called the father of all points of view.

Contemporary feminists typically regard these metaphors as misleading. For most feminists, moral justification cannot be achieved by an individual appeal to transcendent ideals or absolute principles; instead, it consists in the on-going evaluation of individual actions and social practices by people in actual communities of discourse who collectively construct historically specific ideals, norms and values. On this understanding, moral justifications are socially developed and contingently situated; 'the' moral point of view loses its transcendent status and becomes not single but multiple, rooted in the social world rather than floating above or outside it.

Rejecting moral realism, construed as the postulation of a mind-independent moral reality, does not commit feminists to embracing relativism, interpreted as the claim that all moral points of view are equally valid. Indeed, relativism is inconsistent with feminism's nonnegotiable moral commitment to opposing male dominance. The work surveyed here directs us to understand moral justification in terms of discursive processes that are open, inclusive and egalitarian. Since

---

[38] Linda Alcoff, "The Problem of Speaking for Others," *Cultural Critique,* 20 (1991-1992) pp. 5-32

openness, inclusivity and equality are moral and epistemic ideals that are only ever met imperfectly, to a greater or lesser extent, the warrant for accepting particular moral assertions will be stronger or weaker according to the degree to which the ideals are realized. The conclusions of moral dialogues thus are always provisional and fallible rather than final or absolute and always dependent on a discursive social context that determines what count as good reasons.[39]

IV. Who is authorized to define and interpret moral justification?

Feminist work on moral justification has revealed male and other biases lurking in common philosophical interpretations of ideals such as rationality, universality, impersonality, detachment, dispassion, neutrality and transcendence. It has not only challenged particular interpretations of those ideals but but also suggested that they should be abandoned as guides to moral justification. Feminism is not alone in its challenges to these ideals: as Margaret Walker notes, scepticism about them has been expressed by 'Aristotelians, Humeans, communitarians, contemporary casuists, pragmatists, historicists, Wittegensteinians, and others in the last several decades.'[40] Faced with such opposition, even Rawls has now abandoned his aspiration to achieve an 'Archimedean point' and substituted the notion of a specific community's 'overlapping consensus' about justice. However, whereas nonfeminist critics argue that Archimedean models of moral justification are simply mistaken, some feminists criticize them in terms that are explicitly moral and political.

Margaret Walker contends that the ideal of point-of-viewlessness fulfils an ideological function by concealing the specific, partial and situated character of views and positions that are put forward *'authoritatively*' as truths about "human" interest, "our" intuitions, "ra-

---

[39] On such a view, it is possible that autonomy should be thought of less as the first order ability to weigh impartially the interests of all those affected and more as the second order ability to accurately gauge the reliability of particular processes of justification.
[40] Margaret Walker, *Moral Understandings: A Feminist Study in Ethics*, New York: Routledge, 1998, pp. 53-4.

tional" behavior, or "the" moral agent.'[41] By discounting the effects of people's social identities on their moral thinking, the ideal of point-of-viewlessness insulates itself from any critical examination of its own social origins or functions. It denies that any philosophical significance attaches to the facts that few are authorized to define moral knowledge and that 'To have the social, intellectual, or moral authority to perform this feat, one must already be on the advantaged side of some practices of privilege and uneven distributions of power and responsibilities in the community in which one does it.'[42] That 'Western Anglo-European philosophical ethics as a cultural tradition and product has been until just recently almost entirely a product of some men's – and almost no women's – thinking' is, from 'the' moral point of view, dismissed as a matter of only historical, not philosophical, interest. Thus, traditional understandings of moral justification operate as a mystifying moral ideology that shields from view 'the historical, cultural, and social location of the moral philosopher, and of moral philosophy itself, as a practice of authority sustained by particular institutions and arrangements.'[43]

Some feminist critics thus charge that traditional conceptions of moral justification are more than simply expressions of a moral perspective characteristic of bureaucratic societies divided by class and gender. They are more than a deceptive rhetorical device that adds a ring of magisterial authority to philosophers' rationalizations of practices oppressive to women and members of other subordinated groups. They even have a function beyond invalidating criticism of such practices. Philosophical accounts of moral justification have been, finally, a means by which philosophers have promoted their own claims to define moral validity and to determine when its criteria have been met.

Perhaps uncomfortable in this authoritarian framework, some feminist philosophers have abandoned the traditional project of moral justification. Care theorist Nel Noddings writes:

> An ethic of caring does not emphasize justification. As one-caring, I am not seeking justification for my action; I am not standing alone

---

[41] Walker, ibid., p. 54.
[42] Walker, ibid.
[43] Walker, ibid., p. 56.

before some tribunal. What I seek is completion in the other... Thus, I am not justified but somehow fulfilled and completed...'[44]

Joyce Trebilcot insists that she speaks only for herself.[45] Postmodernist feminists insist on the multiplicity of possible narratives. Some feminists, however, are still concerned that feminism be able to justify its moral claims. Rather than abandoning the project of moral justification, we are working to reinterpret it in terms that are less covertly elitist and authoritarian and more transparent and democratic. Our accounts of moral justification operate at a lower level of abstraction than most philosophical accounts, and are in that sense less idealized and more naturalistic, but they are still explicitly normative. They link increased moral objectivity with the development of methods of justification that are increasingly open, egalitarian and inclusive.

Feminist challenges to canonical accounts of moral justification have pursued transparency by making visible what Walker calls 'the gendered structures of authority that produce and circulate existing moral understandings.' But even as it challenges the dominant tradition of Western ethics, feminism simultaneously contributes to that tradition. Its demand for transparency 'is embarrassing precisely because it exploits a tradition – its own – in which values of representation, consent, self-determination, respect, equality, and freedom are common currency.' The values it invokes 'are of specifically democratic, participatory, and emancipatory kinds, squarely founded on moral and political ideals of modern Western social thought.'[46] Rather than scrapping the master's tools, many feminist philosophers are working to transform them so that we may build a moral household that has neither head nor master.

---

[44] Nel Noddings, *Caring: A Feminine Approach to Ethics and Moral Education*, Berkeley: University of California Press, 1984.
[45] Joyce Trebilcot, *Dyke Ideas: Process, Politics, Daily Life*, Albany, NY: State University of New York Press, 1991.
[46] Walker, *Moral Understandings*, op. cit., p. 73.

Yvanka B. Raynova

HUMAN RIGHTS, WOMEN'S RIGHTS, GENDER MAINSTREAMING AND DIVERSITY: THE LANGUAGE QUESTION[1]

> *"The masculine gender will no longer be regarded, even grammatically, as the more noble genre, given that all genders, all sexes, and all beings should be and are equally noble."*[2]

Introduction

In a collective work that was published last year in Germany,[3] a special focus was set on the relation between gender, memory, and history and their impact on identity and subjectification. As my purpose here will be to relate this thematic with the problem of language, I want to recall briefly the essay by Christina Thürmer-Rohr, "The Faces of Silence: Feminism and the Cassandra-Syndrome,"[4] as far as it raises some very important questions.

---

[1] This article is an abbreviated version of a longer study in German which will appear soon at Peter Lang.
[2] *Women's Petition to the National Assembly* (1789), Engl. transl. online: http://chnm.gmu.edu/revolution/d/629/; in the French original it says: "Le genre masculin ne sera plus regardé, même dans la grammaire, comme le genre le plus noble, attendu que tous les genres, tous les sexes et tous les êtres doivent être et sont également nobles," *Requête des dames à l'Assemblée nationale* (1789), online: http://gallica.bnf.fr/ark:/12148/bpt6k426587.
[3] Jacob Guggenheimer, Utta Isop, Doris Leibetseder, Kirstin Mertlitsch (eds.), *»When we were gender...« - Geschlechter erinnern und vergessen: Analysen von Geschlecht und Gedächtnis in den Gender Studies, Queer-Theorien und feministischen Politiken*, Bielefeld: transcript, 2014.
[4] Christina Thürmer-Rohr, "Gesichter des Schweigens. Der Feminismus und das Kassandra-Syndrom," in *»When we were gender...,«* op.cit., pp. 171-190.

Christina Thürmer-Rohr begins by evoking Christa Wolf's book *Cassandra* (1979), which spurred in the past many expectations and fears about women's right to speak freely in public. Then she reminds us how, ten years later after Wolf's *Cassandra*, Barbara Sichtermann provoked the readers by saying: "Now that women are allowed to speak, men seem relieved because what they got to hear was not really different from what they were used."[5] Thürmer-Rohr explains this statement in the following manner: if women did not envisage another world, if they did not challenge the status quo, then the millennia of silence imposed to them would have been quite unnecessary. She draws on Sichtermann's provoking statement, which she interprets as a necessity of self-critique and self-reflection, in order to raise some fundamental questions, namely: What happened to women's own speaking? What has the women's movement achieved with the claims for freedom of speech and the rights to drive the prevailing discourses in other directions and to other contents? Is feminism today outdated, or futile as some claim?

Thürmer-Rohr describes the divide between the generations as a gap of silence and forgetting of women's history. Therefore she reminds us of the main issues of the second wave feminists fighting for women's rights:

> 40 years ago, it was [for us] about to break a silence: silence about a gender policy which waived the equal contribution of women; silence about a structural injustice that was enrolled in the institutions and consequently incorporated in people; silence over a place allocation which included and at the same time excluded women requiring of them loyalty (...); silence on a system justified by [unjust] gender relations (...) presented as a natural norm. The women's movement has called this logic patriarchal not only because of women's domination, but also because it is the reason for the destructive development of society. We were confident of women's unrealized potential which – if it would come to language – would fundamentally change the whole society. It was not just about correcting specific drawbacks, but about a radical break with a basic social understanding that had touched and damaged every sector of society.[6]

But today, for many young women the past is without interest, they are convicted that most women's issues are already solved. Many prefer

---

[5] Ibid.
[6] Ibid., p. 173.

to talk about success instead of discrimination and feel free, because they can speak about anything on social networks and the internet without any need "to go on the streets to yell and to protest." Thus, Thürmer-Rohr concludes, at the difference of Cassandra who had something to say but was not heard and was finally forced to silence, today we can be heard, but we have to raise new questions and approach problems which seem solved in a new way.[7]

In her essay "Against the Forgetting of the Others. Remembering as a Place of (feminist) Difference," published in the same collection, Birge Krondorfer points in a similar direction. In a time of destruction and crisis, where we often have to deal with repetitions and iterations, it is important to remember past alternative positions and to learn from:

> It is not about to thematize the past (as past), but to show the aspirations of the gone and, instead of handling it as historic "knowledge," to give voice to the silenced and muted. Only in this way tradition could warp from the conformism inherent of each epoch.[8]

In the following study I want to go back to the beginnings of the Women's Rights movements in order to pose anew some of these questions by taking a look at it through the prism of language as a powerful tool in human rights battles. This will permit me to show the deep interrelation between women's struggle for recognition and some particular women rights, like the "feminization" of professional titles and the implementation of a gender sensitive language. Hence I will argue the thesis that even in the most advanced European democracies, where freedom of speech, education, and scientific research seem to be legally guaranteed as universal rights, there is still a deep conflict in regard of the use of language and that we have throughout history backlashes, reproductions of past stereotypes, and a loss of women's rights that were previously acquired. Thus, the long women's fight for fundamental rights is far from being a closed chapter. Moreover, it has to be kept safe from forgetting, i.e. constantly re-contextualized, in order to clearly see where we are and what is still to be done.

---

[7] Ibid., p. 186.
[8] Ibid., p. 204.

1. Are Women's Rights Human Rights and Vice Versa?

Human rights, even when proclaimed as universal, have not always included women's rights as well. That is why, many times in history, they have been claimed separately, as Olympe de Gouges did, for example, in her famous "Declaration of the Rights of Woman and of the Citizen" (1791). When it comes to the history of the beginning of women's fights for equal rights, Olympe de Gouges is most often mentioned as the "mother" of modern feminism. But the idea of equality between women and men, which led finally to different declarations claiming the equality of rights for both sexes, has a much longer history. It goes back to the debates emerging since the 14th century, best known as *querelle de femmes*. In addition, one should not forget the role of French Enlightenment philosophers who defended the idea that women's rights are human rights before Olympe de Gouges. So, before taking a closer look at de Gouges' *Declaration of the Rights of Woman and of the Citizeness*, I want to refer briefly to some earlier documents and ideas which should also be remembered in this context.

1.1. Education as the Path to Women's Independence and Recognition

The first text to which I want especially draw attention is *The equality of men and women* (1622) by Marie de Gournay (1565-1645). Compared to other French *femmes de lettres*, who were born in noble families and had a good education and spent time with cultural activities, de Gournay's parents were not wealthy. Her father was an officer of low aristocracy and after his death the family came into financial troubles. Against an education preparing her for marriage, de Gournay refused to follow what was presented to her as "women's destiny." She chose to stay independent, began to educate herself (as she was not allowed to study like her brothers), learned Latin by comparing French translations to originals and gained success as writer, editor, and translator. She translated Tacit, Ovid, Cicero, Sallust and Vergil into French, edited the posthumous *Essays* of Montaigne, which contributed to her popularity, wrote several studies against the lingual purism of Malherbe and the Moderns, and took part in the foundation of the *Académie Française* in

1634. If I consider these biographical details, it is to emphasize, on the one hand, the importance which de Gournay attributed to learning, education and language. The fact that she was the first woman who wrote treatises on the French language should be kept in mind, as her lucid analyses accusing "the slavery of language"[9] and opting for a livid language, as well as her creative metaphors and neologisms are especially relevant in view of the recent debates on a gender sensitive language. On the other hand, it is important to highlight that her writings were in full accordance not only with her beliefs, but also with her own way of life. Today the address "Mademoiselle" may be seen as sexist and, indeed, there are enough reasons to claim its abolishment, but in the 17th century things were different. By proudly calling herself Demoiselle[10] de Gournay, it emphasized her own choice to live as an independent woman, rejecting the yoke of marriage and the oppressive social conventions of the position of women.

Due to the recent feminist interest in de Gournay, *The equality of men and women* (1622) as well as *The Ladies' Complaint* (1626) are actually some of her best known works, but they are only two of about forty essays, written when she was already almost sixty years old. So the (proto)feminism[11] of these two texts should be situated in a larger perspective which was previously elaborated, namely that of humanism and moralist critique, a perspective that she adopted from Montaigne and

---

[9] See Marie de Gournay, "Deffence de la Poésie, et du langage des Poètes," in *Les advis ou les presens de la Demoiselle de Gournay*, Paris: Toussainct-Du-Bray, 1634, p. 410.

[10] It is not an accident, but her will, that her collected works have been published as *Les advis ou les presens de la Demoiselle de Gournay* (Paris: Toussainct-Du-Bray, 1634; recently reedited in 2 volumes as *Oeuvres complètes*, Paris: Champion, 2002).

[11] Théodore Joran and Mario Schiff has been one of the first to call Marie de Gournay a "feminist" (see Théodore Joran, *La trouée féministe*, Paris, 1909, pp. 61, 63; Mario Schiff, *La fille d'alliance de Monteigne*, 1910, p. 49), yet many label her as "proto-feminist" [See f.ex. Anne R. Larsen, "A Women's Republic of Letters: Anna Maria van Schurman, Marie de Gournay, and Female Self-Representation in Relation to the Public Sphere," *Early Modern Women: An Interdisciplinary Journal*, 2008, vol. 3, p. 109; John J. Conley, "Marie Le Jars De Gournay (1565-1645)," in *The Internet Encyclopedia of Philosophy*, http://www.iep.utm.edu/gournay/]. There are also authors who emphasize the androgynous character of her oeuvre (see Tilde Sankovitch, "Marie Jars de Gournay: The Self-Portrait of an Androgynous Hero," in idem *French Women Writers and the Book*, New York: Syracuse University Press, 1988, pp. 73-100).

some classic authors but redesigned in her own way. It is in the context of her personal experience – being contested and even mocked as a woman writer – and her humanist ideals that de Gournay challenges the conceptions of women's intellectual and moral inferiority. What she aims to show is the deep interrelation between prejudices, ignorance and oppression, and hence the necessity of education and critical reflection – an approach quite similar to that what later will be called "Enlightenment" – as well as the rights of self-determination and free expression. To visualize the subjugation of women, de Gournay uses the icon of the distaff[12] in a quite similar way as Louise Labé, who opposed spinning, understood as an exclusion of women from culture and society, to writing, conceived as intellectual and creative work. But compared to Labé, who is promoting writing as a chance for the creative self-realization of women and a lasting self-contentment, de Gournay goes much further through a severe criticism of social customs, prejudices, and wrong ideas. Thus, at the beginning of *The equality of men and women* she explains that she rejects any conception that treats one of both sexes as inferior or superior:

> I am content to make them equal to men, given that nature, too, is as greatly opposed, in this respect, to superiority as to inferiority. But what am I saying? It is not enough for certain persons to prefer the masculine to the feminine sex; they must also confine women, by an absolute and obligatory rule, to the distaff – yea, to the distaff alone.[13]

Consequently de Gournay does not divide humanity into men and women, but rather wise ones and fools, honest and wicked.[14] Moreover, she attacks the uncritical reception of judgments and ideas:

> Because they have heard it cried in the streets that women lack value, as well as intellectual ability (…) their eloquence exults in preaching these maxims, and all the more richly for the fact that value, sufficiency, phys-

---

[12] An excellent analysis of the different interpretations of the icon of the distaff is given by Cathy Yandell ("The digressions of Louise Labé," in Kathleen P. Long [ed], *High Anxiety: Masculinity in Crisis in Early Modern France*, Kirksville, Missouri: Truman State University Press, 2002, pp. 1-17, especially pp. 2-4).
[13] Marie le Jars de Gournay, "The equality of men and women," in idem, *Apology for the Woman Writing and Other Works*, transl. by Richard Hillman and Colette Quesnel, Chicago: University of Chicago Press, 2002, p. 75.
[14] Ibid., p. 74.

ical make-up, and constitution are imposing terms. They have not learned, on the other hand, that the chief quality of a dolt is to espouse causes on the basis of popular belief and hearsay.[15]

Her second-guess of unreflected language as "popular belief and hearsay," which leads to prejudices, erroneous assumptions and defamation, is the basis of her skepticism and moral criticism. This is what places her, in my view, between Montaigne's skeptical self-reflection (*Que sais-je?*) and Descartes' method of doubt. Even de Gournay has not systematically elaborated on a philosophical method like Descartes, and one can find some similarities between her approach and Descartes' rationalist argumentation, in particular between her rejection of bias and his calling into question preconception and habitual opinion, between her assertion that men and women are equal by intellect because of their "rational soul"[16] and Descartes' famous statement that "good sense or reason, is by nature equal in all men"[17], as well as between her claim that sex differences are due to education, social environment, and nationality[18] and his belief that differences in opinions and character result from the social milieu and the country where someone is born.[19] More evident are the common points with Poullain de la Barre's Cartesian treatises *On the Education of Ladies* (1674) and *On the Equality of the Two Sexes* (1676) where, similarly to her, he declares that prejudices are the reason for inequality and that "mind has no sex"[20], that ignorance is slavery, that both sexes have the same capabilities and should have equal access to sciences and learning, and that women's flaws are caused by their education so they should receive a better one.[21]

De Gournay starts with a declaration that she does "not intend to prove the equality between the sexes with reasons, since the opinionated might dispute them, nor with examples, since they are too common, but

---

[15] Ibid., pp. 75-76.
[16] Ibid., pp. 82, 87.
[17] Rene Descartes, "Discourse on the Method or Rightly Conducting the Reason, and seeking Truth in the Sciences" http://www.gutenberg.org/files/59/59-h/59-h.htm
[18] Marie le Jars de Gournay, "The equality of men and women," op.cit., p. 81.
[19] Rene Descartes, op.cit.
[20] Francois Poullain de la Barre, "On the Equality of the Two Sexes," in idem, Three Cartesian Feminist Treatises, Chicago: University of Chicago Press, 2007, p. 82.
[21] Ibid., pp. 110 ff.

indeed only by the authority of God himself, of the Fathers – the buttresses of His Church – and of those great philosophers who have served as a light to the universe."[22] At first this seems to be a fundamental difference between her approach and the Cartesian method seeking for clear and evident knowledge; the reference to someone's "authority" also seems to contradict her appeal for critical and independent thinking as well the speaking of women with their own voice. But a closer look shows that she does exactly the contrary to her initial declaration: her entire approach is nothing but a logical argumentation, i.e. an argumentation by reasons advocating the equality between men and women and even in some points of women's superiority.[23] If she uses as proof some carefully selected ideas of the ancient philosophers and the Church Fathers as well as examples of the life and work of eminent women, it is to underpin and fortify her own arguments. Thus, she evokes Plato and Socrates, as well as Plutarch, Seneca and Aristotle, arguing that they attributed to women "the same rights, faculties, and functions in their Republics, and everywhere else," that women surpassed men as "they have invented a number of the finest of the fine arts, and even the Latin alphabet, they have excelled, they have instructed magisterially and with sovereign authority over men, in all sorts of disciplines and virtues."[24] De Gournay's presentation of the conceptions of ancient philosophers is often very stylized, omitting cautiously their misogynic assertions in favor of positive comments on women. She refers to Hypatia, to Themistoclea, the sister of Pythagoras, and to Theano, his wife, in order to show that there also were evolved women in philosophy. She reminds us that in antiquity there were brilliant women orators (Cornelia, Laelia, Diotima, and Aspasia) and women poets (Sappho, Corinna, Erinna)

---

[22] Marie le Jars de Gournay, "The equality of men and women," op.cit., p. 76.
[23] Various authors see the main merit of de Gournay in the fact that she was "the first woman theoretician of the equality between men and women," [Elyane Dezon-Jones, *Fragments d'un discours féminin*, Paris: José Corti, 1988, p. 11; cf. Claudia Opitz-Belakhal, "Anwältin der Gleichheit: Marie de Gournay und die französische Rechtskultur um 1600," in *Ein Platz für sich selbst. Schreibende Frauen und ihre Lebenswelten (1450-1700)*, Peter Lang, 2011, pp. 107-119]. And this is exact as she advocates for equal rights and recognition. But as I will show, there are text passages where she uses arguments to show that in some cases women have done even better than men.
[24] Ibid., p. 79.

equal to or even better than Pindar and Homer. So, if women attain excellence less often than men, it is not because they are less capable then men, but because they had no access to education: "it is a marvel that the lack of good education (...) does not do worse and prevent them from doing so entirely," she emphasizes.[25]

It is not certain from where de Gournay is taking all her references; some are received without doubt from Montaigne and her beloved ancient authors, other from the Church Fathers. However, she uses them in a very skilful way in order to show that there is no reason to exclude women even from public affairs and the exercise of supreme power:

> On the question of the Salic law, which deprives women of the crown, it applies only in France. And it was invented (...) solely because of the wars against the Empire, whose yoke our forefathers were throwing off, the female sex seemingly being physically less fit for bearing arms because of the necessity of bearing and nourishing children.[26]

De Gournay argues, on the one hand, that men's physical force is not a reason to exclude women from social and political life: the ancient Gauls did not disdain women, nor the Carthaginians who established the women of Gaul to serve as arbiters of their quarrels. On the other hand, physical force is not proof of men's superiority over women, because in this case some beasts would be superior to men also. Thus she emphasizes that "if men in many places rob the sex of its portion of the greatest advantages, they are wrong to make a right of their usurpation and tyranny."[27]

All these examples are just a prelude preparing the reader for the core statement of de Gournay, that is:

> ...the human animal, taken rightly, is neither man nor woman, the sexes having been made double, not so as to constitute a difference in species, but for the sake of propagation alone. The unique form and distinction of that animal consists only in its rational soul.[28]

In other words, against the essentialization of the sex difference de Gournay maintains that the *differentia specifica* of human beings is the

---

[25] Ibid., p. 81.
[26] Ibid., p. 84.
[27] Ibid., p. 86.
[28] Ibid., pp. 86-87.

rational soul as the "image of the Creator" and that it is equal in both sexes.[29] Thus she explains that man and woman are so thoroughly one that if man is more than woman, woman is more than man. In order to give her core statement an irrefutable foundation she refers to the Bible and the Church Fathers:

> Man was created man and female – so says scripture, not reckoning the two except as ones and Jesus Christ is called Son of Man, although he is that only of woman – the whole and consummate perfection of the proof of this unity of the two sexes. I speak thus according to the great Saint Basil in his first homily on the Hexameron: the virtue of man and of woman are the same thing, since Cod bestowed on them the same creation and the same honor: *masculum et feminam fecit eos*. Now in those whose nature is one and the same, it must be concluded that their actions are so as well, and that the esteem and recompense belonging to these are equal, where the works are equal.[30]

From here she continues to the next audacious statement of the equal virtues and the capacities of women to held church offices, to preach and to administer the sacraments of Baptism, of Eucharist etc., and gives examples of women who have been prophets and apostles, using feminine nouns to designate these functions.[31] De Gournay is aware that it could be said that there are passages in the Bible where women are ordered to obey and accept the authority of men. That is why she argues that this was done, for good or the bad, in order to assure peace between the sexes. As for St. Paul who forbids the ministry of women and commands them to keep silent in the church, she adds that "this is not at all out of contempt but rather, indeed, only for fear lest they should arouse temptations by that display, so plain and public, that must be made in the course of ministering and preaching, since they are of greater grace and beauty than men."[32]

But one the most central moments in de Gournay's text, which was overlooked by her commentators, is the position of human dignity as the foundation of human rights and women's rights. This is partly due to the

---

[29] Ibid., p. 95.
[30] Ibid., p. 87.
[31] For example she uses the female nouns "Apostresses" (women apostles), or "maistresse" (woman master), "instructrices" (woman instructors) etc., which shows the importance of language gendering when it comes to functions and titles.
[32] Ibid., p. 89.

English translation where the notion of dignity (*la dignité*) is translated with "superior worth" and the adjectives "*digne*" and "*indigne*" respectively with "worthy" and "unworthy." So in her conclusion she states that she has proven the equality between the sexes and any objection that "submission was imposed on woman in punishment for the sin of eating the apple" is a nonsense, an absurdity, even a blasphemy and does not speak in favor of "the supposed superior worth of man (*dignité*)":

> If one supposed that scripture commanded her to submit to man, as being unworthy of opposing him, consider the absurdity that would follow: woman would find herself worthy of having been made in the image of the Creator, worthy of the holy Eucharist, of the mysteries of the redemption, of paradise, and of the sight – indeed the possession – of God, yet not of the advantages and privileges of man. Would this not declare man to be more precious and more exalted than all these things, and hence commit the gravest of blasphemies?

> Because both sexes have been created in the image of God, both have the same *human dignity* which is the base of the human rights of both sexes. With this bold declaration de Gournay appears not just as the first woman fighter for equality, but also as precursor of the contemporary understanding of Human Rights as grounded on 'the dignity of the human person.'[33]

De Gournay has been criticized by some contemporary feminists for not being radical enough.[34] But it would be wrong to depreciate her importance. At a time when women had no access to education, when women's writings were not taken seriously but mocked, her ideas for women's liberation through instruction and her claims for women's participation in intellectual and social life have been a bold challenge of men's order of discourse. Moreover, with her choice to reject the alternative "marriage or convent" and to invent her own life, she gave women an example of engagement (in the Sartrean and de Beauvoir's sense) and

---

[33] "The dignity of the human person is not only a fundamental right in itself but constitutes the real basis of fundamental rights. The 1948 Universal Declaration of Human Rights enshrined human dignity in its preamble: 'Whereas recognition of the inherent dignity and of the equal and inalienable rights of all members of the human family is the foundation of freedom, justice and peace in the world.'" ("Explanation relating to the Charter of Fundamental Rights," *Official Journal of the European Union*, 2007/C 303/02, 17).

[34] See f.ex. Michèle Farrell, "Theorizing on Equality: Marie de Gournay and Poullain de la Barre," *Cahiers du dix-septième: An Interdisciplinary Journal*, 1 (1988) pp. 67-79.

became the forerunner of important feminist works like the mentioned essays of Poullain de La Barre, Gabrielle Suchon's *Treatise on Ethics and Politics* (1693), Condorcet's *On the Admission of Women to the Rights of Citizenship* (1790), Margaret Fell's *Women's Speaking Justified, Proved and Allowed by the Scriptures* (1666/67), Mary Wollstonecraft's *A Vindication of the Rights of Woman* (1792), John Stuart Mill's *The Subjection of Women* (1869) and many other.

1.2. The use of Feminine Language as Visibilization and Legalization of the Claims for Women's Rights as Human Rights

According Hannelore Schröder, the German translator and commenter of Olympe de Gouge, the fathers of French Enlightenment "defined women as being non-rational *a priori*, thus they were classified as non-human so that 'human' rights and civil rights did not apply to them."[35] This is maybe true in some regards to Rousseau and Diderot – and even here one should be careful – to which she refers more in detail; but it cannot be said about French Enlightenment as a whole, which was a quite heteronymous movement. One should not forget that prior to de Gouges there were philosophers of Enlightenment like Baron d'Holbach, who criticized the government that it does treat women as "a nothing," that their bad education leads to moral corruption of the whole society, and that men's tyranny over women seducing and exploiting them as objects of sexuality should be punished by law.[36] Yet, by remembering that according Plato women could be wise governors and even army leaders, d'Holbach did not request explicitly these rights for women, but rather a better education and the right to divorce, which would improve the moral health of society.[37] It was Marquis de Condorcet, another peer and philosopher of Enlightenment, who became advocate of women's political and civil rights in France. He argued on differ-

---

[35] Hannelore Schröder, "Olympe de Gouges' Erklärung der Rechte der Frau und Bürgerin (1791)," in Herta Nagl-Docekal (ed.), Feministische Philosophie, Wien, München: Oldenbourg, 1990, p. 215.
[36] Paul Henri Dietrich Baron d'Holbach, "Des femmes," in idem, *Système social ou Principes naturels de la morale et de la politique, avec un examen de l'influence du gouvernement sur les moeurs*, tome 3, London, 1773, pp. 122-136.
[37] Ibid., p. 130.

ent occasions the necessity to change the law in order to grant women equal rights and access to political life. I will refer here briefly on his essay *On the Admission of Women to the Rights of Citizenship* (1790) as it is an important bridge between de Gournay's struggle for the recognition of women's equality and de Gouge's explicit women's rights claims in all fields of social and political life.

The specificity of Condorcet's feminist ideas is that they are grounded on a conception of natural law, which is diametrically opposed to that of Jean-Jacques Rousseau's. According Rousseau there is a difference in the nature of the sexes which determines their different roles and duties, whereas woman's main predestination is to procreate and to care for husband and family. Thus, "woman is especially constituted to please man"[38], she has to be docile and "to endure the wrongs of a husband without complaint"[39]; women should be not ignorant, but their education must be planned in relation to men – to please them, to be useful to them, to make them happy, and thus their role is to be wife, mother, home guardian, and not to establish in house "a literary tribunal" becoming its president.[40] Condorcet too grounds his conception on the natural law, but he interprets the nature of women in completely different way. In his *Letters from a Gentleman of New Haven to a Citizen of Virginia* (1788) Condorcet explains that if the basis of human rights is their quality of being sensitive, capable of reason and moral ideas, so too should women have the same rights, including the constitutional right of citizenship[41]. This idea also constitutes the basis of his illustrious *On the Admission of Women to the Rights of Citizenship* (1790) where he declares:

> To show that this exclusion is not an act of tyranny, it must be proved either that the natural rights of women are not absolutely the same as those

---

[38] Jean-Jacques Rousseau, *Rousseau's Emile or Treatise on Education*, abridged, translated and annotated by William H. Payne, New York: D. Aplleton and Company, 1892, p. 260.
[39] Ibid., p. 270.
[40] Ibid., p. 303.
[41] Marquis de Condorcet, *Lettres d'un bourgeois de New Haven à un citoyen de Virginie, sur l'inutilité de partager le pouvoir législatif entre plusieurs corps, 1787*, in *Oeuvres de Condorcet*, publiées par A. Condorcet O'Connor et M. F. Arago, tome 9, Paris: Didot Frères, 1847, p. 15.

of men, or that women are not capable of exercising these rights. But the rights of men result simply from the fact that they are rational, sentient beings, susceptible of acquiring ideas of morality, and of reasoning concerning those ideas. Women having, then, the same qualities, have necessarily the same rights. Either no individual of the human species has any true rights, or all have the same; and he or she who votes against the rights of another, whatever may be his or her religion, colour, or sex, has by that fact abjured his own.[42]

Admitting for the moment that there exists in men a superiority of mind, continues Condorcet, then women's inferiority can only consist of two points. First, it is said that no woman has made any important discovery in science, or has given any proof of the possession of genius in arts, literature, etc.; but the rights of citizenship have never been accorded only to men of genius. Second, it has been said that there exists in the minds and hearts of women certain qualities which ought to exclude them from the enjoyment of their natural rights. Against this argument he gives examples of famous women who governed with courage and strength of mind – Elizabeth of England, Maria Theresa, and the two Catherines of Russia – or were capable of doing so, by evoking among others Marie de Gournay.[43] He refutes further the arguments that women are not conducted by reason, that they do not have sentiment of justice and therefore should be deprived from the right of voting; in fact women are conducted by other reasons than men and there is no reason to fear women of power, because they would gain only a better experience which would help to educate their children as better citizens:

> The principal source of this fear is the idea that every person admitted to exercise the rights of citizenship immediately aspires to govern others... And so it is scarcely necessary to believe that because women may become members of national assemblies, they would immediately abandon their children, their homes, and their needles. They would only be the better fitted to educate their children and to rear men.[44]

While Condorcet gave logical arguments for the equality of women in order to claim their rights as citizens, after the women's march on Ver-

---

[42] Marie-Jean-Antoine-Nicolas Caritat, Marquis de Condorcet, *On the Admission of Women to the Rights of Citizenship*, transl. by Dr. Alice Drysdale Vickery with preface and remarks, Letchworth: Garden City Press, 1912, p. 5.
[43] Ibid., p. 7.
[44] Ibid., p. 10.

sailles in October 1789 a more radical claim was addressed in the form of a women's petition to the National Assembly. This petition was done in response to the *Declaration of the Rights of Man and of the Citizen*, set up a few months earlier, which granted only rights to men without mentioning women. Hence, the *Women's Petition to the National Assembly* begins with the outrageous exclamation:

> It is altogether astonishing that, having gone so far along the path of reforms, and having cut down (...) a very large part of the forest of prejudices, you would leave standing the oldest and most general of all abuses, the one which excludes the (...) half of the inhabitants of this vast kingdom from positions, dignities, honors, and especially from the right to sit amongst you.[45]

The specificity of this petition is that it did not just demand for equality, but for a radical abolishment of all men's privileges. Thus, the first three of ten articles claim: 1) All the privileges of the male sex should be entirely and irrevocably abolished throughout France; 2) The feminine sex will always enjoy the same liberty, advantages, rights, and honors as the masculine sex does; 3) The masculine gender (genre) will no longer be regarded, even grammatically, as the more noble genre, given that all genders, all sexes, and all beings should be and are equally noble.[46] The third article is especially remarkable because it shows the clear awareness of a necessary deconstruction of the male's language and the introduction of feminine designations as well as the double-gender in legal documents. Indeed, the *Declaration of the Rights of Man and of the Citizen* used an obvious male language where the masculine gender was imposed as a generic and exclusive designation for the male sex; through the use of "*l'homme*" (man) and also of the plural "*les hommes*" (men), instead of "*les hommes et les femmes*" or the neutral "*les gens*" (people), all citizen rights were granted only to the male sex. Furthermore, the petition required equal authority in family and parenthood for women, the right to wear breeches as a symbol of freedom and independence, to have consultative and deliberative voices in assemblies, as well as positions, compensations, and even military dignities.

---

[45] *Women's Petition to the National Assembly* (1789), online: http://chnm.gmu.edu/revolution/d/629/.
[46] Ibid.

Yet, it was Olympe de Gouges who, two years later, applied the subversive lingual approach for the abolishment of the oppression of the "masculine gender."

The circumstances leading to de Gouges' women's rights writings are well known: at the beginning of September 1791 France adopted a constitution based on the mentioned *Declaration of the Rights of Man and of the Citizen*; it retained the monarchy, but gave all power to the Legislative Assembly and granted political and civil rights only to men, including suffrage. Against this deprivation of rights and the continuing oppression of women, Olympe de Gouges wrote her masterpiece *The Rights of Woman* (*Les droits de la femme*), published on 14 September 1791. It included the famous *Declaration of the Rights of the Woman and the Citizeness*[47] (*Déclaration des droits de la femme et de la citoyenne*) with a letter to the Queen, a prelude, a preamble and an important post-script. The *Declaration* was addressed and sent to the National Assembly as well, but nobody paid attention to it. This document is very important in many respects, although I want to draw attention only to a few points: de Gouges' defense of women's right to speech, her use of feminine language for the visibilization and legalization of women's rights as human rights, and the subtle application of a dialectic between equality and difference as a fundament of natural law.

Formally the seventeen articles of de Gouges' *Declaration* correspond by equal numbers to those of the *Declaration of the Rights of Man and of the Citizen*. Yet, this is neither a "pastiche" nor a "parody," as some authors allege,[48] but the negative of men's *Declaration*, i.e. a heavy accusation against its injustice of sex segregation. The Prelude of de Gouge shows that the men's *Declaration* that aimed to be an abol-

---

[47] There are different English translations for *citoyenne*; some scholars translate is as "female citizen" (see http://www.olympedegouges.eu/rights_of_women.php) other as "citizeness" (see https://chnm.gmu.edu/revolution/d/293/). I prefer to use *citizeness* as it better underlines, in my view, de Gouges' purposed feminization of "citizen" as a central notion.

[48] Lisa Beckstrand, *Deviant Women of the French Revolution and the Rise of Feminism*, Madison, NJ: Fairleigh Dickinson University Press, 2009, p. 17; Camille Naish, *Death Comes to the Maiden: Sex and Execution, 1431-1933*, New York: Routledge, 1991, p. 137; Susanne Sreedhar, "Constitutions and social contracts," in: Aaron Garteh (ed.), *The Routledge Companion to Eighteenth Philosophy*, New York: Routledge, 2014, p. 638.

ishment of the absolutist tyranny of the Ancien Régime and to grant all individuals as members of the nation equal rights based on natural law finally was nothing but another tyranny:

> Man, are you capable of being fair? A woman is asking: at least you will allow her that right. Tell me? What gave you the sovereign right to oppress my sex? Your strength? Your talents? Observe the creator in his wisdom, examine nature in all its grandeur for you seem to wish to get closer to it, and give me, if you dare, a pattern for this tyrannical power.[49]

By changing the grammatical gender, i.e. by replacing "man" with "woman," or by adding the word "woman" to "man," and by using a feminized language, de Gouges alters the subject of rights in order to grant women full citizenship, i.e. the civil and political rights that they have been deprived of, and to establish the legal equality between the sexes. This is articulated already in the title: *Declaration of the Rights of WOMAN and CITIZENESS* and especially in the Preamble, where the first phrase is a call for political participation through the institutions: "Mothers, daughters, sisters, representatives of the Nation, all demand to be constituted into a National Assembly."[50] As for Condorcet who reclaimed women's *citizenship*, "citizeness" – the subject and hence the central notion of de Gouges' women's right claims – means that women should not be just passive, muted spectators, not just *subjects of duties*, but become active actors climbing on the grandstand as *subjects of rights*. Thus, in the famous Article 10, amending the freedom of opinion, she declares: "Woman has the right to mount the scaffold, so she should have the right equally to mount the rostrum."[51] De Gouges was aware that as long as women are silenced they will remain citizenesses without citizenship, i.e. a wife or a daughter of a citizen subjected to his will and power. That is why in her dedication to the Queen she shows the importance of women's speech and articulation of the injustices of civil and political exclusion: "My aim is *to speak to you freely*: I did not wait for the era of Liberty to express myself thus but showed the same

---

[49] Olympe de Gouges, "The Rights of Woman," online: http://www.olympedegouges.eu/rights_of_women.php.
[50] Ibid.
[51] Olympe de Gouges, *The Declaration of the Rights of the Woman (September 1791)*, online: https://chnm.gmu.edu/revolution/d/293/.

determination at a time when blind Despots punished such noble audacity."[52] Thus, giving the Queen an example, she urges her as a woman and a mother to use her position so that women's claims could be heard: "Only one placed by chance in an eminent position can promote the Rights of Woman and hasten its success."[53]

The use of a feminine language is, without doubt, of central importance. But this can be fully understood only in the light of the specificity of de Gouges' *Declaration* which consists, in my opinion, of a new concept of natural law and natural rights that she offers; this concept is not just opposed to Rousseau's nor similar to that of Condorcet, but goes beyond these two alternatives. As I already outlined, Rousseau's concept of social contract and of natural law is based on a conception of *difference* in the nature of the sexes, which reduces women's role to procreation, i.e. to household and family, and legitimizes this way their exclusion from citizenship, whereas Condorcet's conception is based on a natural law which outlines the *equality* of women to men in their capacities of reason and moral ideas and advocates the necessity for them to be granted the same political and citizen rights. For her part, de Gouges presents – and this is my main thesis here – an ambiguous conception of human nature and hence of natural law and rights, which is founded on the dialectics of equality and difference.

The principle of equality, which represents, along with liberty, a fundamental value of the philosophy of Enlightenment, is essential for the men's *Declaration of the Rights of Man and the Citizen* as it defines its concept of natural rights. Natural rights, which are the rights of liberty, property, security and resistance to oppression (Art. 4), are "imprescriptible" (Art. 2). This means that they are not given by birth, social position or other privileges, as it was under the Ancient régime, but arise from (human) nature itself. Thus, they are "inalienable" and "sacred" (Preamble), i.e. they cannot be taken away from any human being – at least it should be so, but as we know women and slaves have been for long time treated as an exception. That is why in her *Declaration* de Gouges puts a focus on *natural law* and on the *sacrality of nature* in order to show that women's rights are *natural and sacral rights*, which

---
[52] Ibid.
[53] Ibid.

cannot be confiscated! And here she turns the tables on Rousseau's use of difference: yes, nature gave women the gift of procreation, but this is a special dignity, that of birth-giving and life-giving. So it is a proof not of inferiority, but of the superiority of women as contributing to the regeneration of nature and life. Further, nature blessed women with beauty and "every intellectual faculty."

That is why the prelude and the preamble make an apologia of *equality* – the cooperation of the sexes in nature, as well as of *difference* – the natural preeminence of women:

> Reconsider (…) sexual characteristics in the workings of nature: everywhere you will find them intermingled, everywhere cooperating harmoniously …Only man has cobbled together a rule to exclude himself from this system… he wants to command, like a despot, a sex that is blessed with every intellectual faculty; he feigns to rejoice in the revolution and demands its equal rights, to say nothing more (…) Given that ignorance, disregard or the disdain of the rights of woman (...), the sex that is superior in beauty as it is in courage during the pains of childbirth recognizes and declares, in the presence and under the auspices of the Supreme Being, the following Rights of Woman and the Female Citizen.

The dialectics of equality and difference is on the basis of de Gouges' claims of equal rights supplemented by some specific demands, as well as of her gender inclusive language, which makes a prudent use of feminine nouns. The first Article indicates not just the equality between individuals or male citizens ("Men are born free and remain free and equal in rights"[54]), but the equality between the sexes: "Woman is born free and remains the equal of man in rights." For the epoch making importance of this formulation speaks of the further history of struggle for women's rights, especially at the time of the elaboration of the *Universal Declaration of Human Rights* and the German Constitution after World War II, to which I will refer here after. In the second Article, de Gouges emphasizes the equality of "natural and imprescriptible rights" by using the gender equitable expression "Men and Women" outlining the need

---

[54] *Declaration of the Rights of Man and the Citizen (August 1789)*, online: http://www.historyguide.org/intellect/declaration.html.

of its institutional protection.[55] Consequently, all citizen rights should be given back to women:

> Liberty and justice consist in restoring all that belongs to another; hence the exercise of the natural rights of woman has no other limits than those that the perpetual tyranny of man opposes to them; these limits must be reformed according to the laws of nature and reason. (Art. 4)

In the men's *Declaration*, liberty was defined as "the power to do anything what does not injure others." De Gouges' reformulation of Article 4 puts liberty in relation to justice/injustice defining the deprivation of (women's) rights as tyranny. Moreover, as the Nation is but the Union of Women and Men (Art. 3), "the constitution is worthless if the majority that make up the Nation has not participated in its redaction" (Art. 17). De Gouges' call for political participation and suffrage is deeply related to the claims for social recognition, participation in administration, professional and economic rights: "All Female and all Male citizens, being equal in law, must be equally entitled to all public honours, positions and employment according to their capacities and with no other distinctions than those based solely on talent and virtue" (Art. 6). Because "woman shares all the labour, all the hard tasks; she should therefore have an equal share of positions, employment, responsibilities, honours and professions" (Art. 13) and "equal share not only of wealth but also of public administration" (Art. 14). Along these equal rights claims, de Gouges makes some particular requests for women as mothers, spouses, widows, and singles, which she did already and more extensively in her *Patriotic Observations* (1788). Thus, if Article 11 of men's *Declaration*[56] reclaims the right of "free communication of ideas and opinions," de Gouges transformed it in her *Declaration* as follows:

> The free expression of thoughts and opinions is one of the most precious rights of woman given that this liberty ensures the legitimacy of fathers

---

[55] "The purpose of all political organisations must be the protection of the natural and imprescriptible rights of Woman and Man: these rights are liberty, property, security and above all the right to resist oppression." (Olympe de Gouges, "The Rights of Woman," online: http://www.olympedegouges.eu/rights_of_women.php, Art. 2).

[56] "The free communication of ideas and opinions is one of the most precious of the rights of man; every citizen can then freely speak, write, and print, subject to responsibility for the abuse of this freedom in the cases is determined by law"[*Declaration of the Rights of Man and the Citizen (August 1789)*, Art. 11, op.cit.].

and their children. Any Female citizen can therefore freely declare 'I am the mother of your child' without a barbrous prejudice forcing them to hide the truth, unless in response to the abuse of this freedom in cases determined by the law.

In her Postscript she goes even further. Like Baron d'Holbach she condemns the exploitation of women's nature by men as the cause of the corruption of morals, of society and of women themselves. Women have for ages been nothing but sex slaves of men and, if being young and beautiful, they used men's weakness for their own interests: "The French government, in particular, depended for centuries on the nocturnal administration of women... the commerce of women was a sort of trade that was accepted in the highest circles." In order to illustrate this interdependence, where women are finally the losers, she uses a sort of master-slave dialectics, quite different from the one conceived later by Hegel and Marx. She compares women to slaves which can be purchased "like a slave on the coasts of Africa." But there is a great difference between an African slave who, if he becomes free, regains his human rights, and a woman who is set free when no longer needed: "The slave [woman] commands the master, but if the master frees the slave with no recompense at an age when the slave has lost all her charms, what becomes of this unfortunate woman? The plaything of scorn, even the doors of generosity close on her." De Gouges gives these examples not just to accuse men's abuse of women, but to awaken women who are still blind of their deplorable condition – "Woman, wake up... acknowledge your rights" – and so to request changes in law. It is principally in this point that she introduces sex difference: women as mothers, as spouses and as singles need special protection by the law. The "Frame for a social Contract between Man and Woman" that she proposes in the Postscript is nothing but a revolutionary revision of family and civil law:

> We intend and wish to combine our assets on the condition that they can be divided in favor of our children, (...) mutually recognizing that our wealth belongs to our children, directly, whatever their origins, and that all, without discrimination, have the right to carry the names of the father and mother who have recognized them, and we engage to accept the law that punishes those who renounce their own blood.

De Gouges' claims have been too radical for many. Her denunciation of women's oppression, of slavery, of corruption and many other injustices, her fight against the death penalty, her defense of the Girondists, her opposition to Robespierre, her support for the King and the Queen etc., generated serious enemies. After she printed a poster entitled "The three urns or the salvation of the fatherland" in the summer of 1793, where she required a referendum on the form of future government – monarchy, federalism or the Republic – she was put in jail, charged by the Revolutionary Tribunal on November 2, 1793, and executed the next day. Before being guillotined she declared to the Revolutionary tribunal: "Apostles of a massacring anarchy, I denounced you in the eyes of humanity long ago, that is what you cannot forgive... Shudder, modern Tyrants! My voice will be heard from the depths of my tomb."[57]

Like Cassandra's message, de Gouges' *Declaration* was not heard, at least not in her century. Even Condorcet decided to step back when he saw that women's rights claims had no chance of being accepted. Thus, in his report on February 1793, for the project of the new Constitution, he did not claim the suffrage for women anymore and reserved the question for oral debates in the Constitution Committee. It was another deputy, Pierre Guyomar, who then restarted Condorcet's arguments in his essay *The Partisan of Political Equality between Individuals* (April 1793). Guyomar's text had no impact on the decisions of the Assembly, but it is a very important document, which shows the deep interrelation between language and the claim for women's rights as human rights.

Guyomar starts his essay in defense of women's rights in explaining that he accepts the word "*l'homme*" in the *Declaration of Human Rights* of 1789 in the meaning of the Latin *homo*, as an individual of the human species who is man or woman, and hence the plural "*les hommes*" means "men of both sexes." On the question if the *Declaration* is addressed to women as well, he answers that the problem is "easy to be solved by right," but it still exists "as a fact."[58] In order to show the dis-

---

[57] Olympe de Gouges, "Olympe de Gouges at the revolutionary Tribunal," 1793, online: http://www.olympedegouges.eu/revolutionary_tribunal.php.
[58] Pierre Guyomar, *Le partisan de l'égalité politique entre les individus, ou Problème très important de l'égalité en droits et de l'inégalité en fait*, Paris: Imprimerie nationale, 1793, p. 102.

crepancy between the exclusion of women from the political rights and the universality of rights granted by the *Declaration* he refutes the distinction between sovereignty and nation, subject and citizen. The principle of all sovereignty resides essentially in the nation (Art. 3); any member of the sovereign is citizen of the nation and can participate in sovereignty by voting on the laws. If the nation is composed of men and women than men cannot be the sole citizens, as it would be against the spirit of Article 3. Moreover, women that have been counted in the metering of the French population (the social body) should be also part of the sovereign nation, i.e. of the political body, and therefore should have the right of suffrage. The fact that women do not have the right to vote is a usurpation of power, because half of the nation decides the laws for the other half; this is nothing but a reign of "the jungle law," a tyranny treating women as "helots of the Republic" and has nothing to do with natural law. And he concludes:

> In effect, they [women] will have no citizenship; if they do not have the right to vote in the primary assemblies, they are not members of the sovereign. These are two empty words for them. I observe, in passing, that the name of citizeness is more than ridiculous and should be struck from our language. We should henceforth call them either wives or daughters of a citizen, never citizenesses. Either strike the word, or bring reality in line with it...[59]

Some months later, in October 1793, all women's political activities and clubs were prohibited by decree.[60] Furthermore, Guyomar's challenging proposition to strike the word "citizeness" from language became reality at the end of the Revolution. Under the Consulate, which elaborated in 1799 a new Constitution, the word "*citoyenne*" was erased from the French language and replaced by the words "madame" and "mademoiselle." Thus, women were put anew in relation to men, i.e. to marriage and to husband's power, and the privileges of men became visible even in language where male generics became the norm and feminine nouns as designations of titles, functions and jobs disappeared.

---

[59] Cited here after the English translation at https://chnm.gmu.edu/revolution/d/597/.
[60] See *Discussion of Women's Political Clubs and Their Suppression, 29–30 October 1793*, online: https://chnm.gmu.edu/revolution/d/294/.

It took almost 150 years until French women could vote for the first time in 1944[61], and until equality became an explicit part of the *Universal Declaration of Human Rights* (Pr., Art. 1.3), adopted by the General Assembly of the United Nations on 10 of December 1948. All this happened with great efforts and struggles, as shown by Eleanor Roosevelt in her reports. She was one of those who insisted that in Article I of the *Universal Declaration of Human Rights* the phrase "all men are brothers" should be replaced by "all men are equal." Roosevelt explains how important the formulation of every word was and, especially, the significance of using a gender-neutral inclusive language that replaces the word "men" with "human being":

> The women on Committee III said: "'All men,' oh, no. In this document we are not going to say 'all men' because in some of our countries we are just struggling to recognition and equality. Some of us have come up to the top but others have very little equality and recognition and freedom. If we say 'all men,' when we get home it will be 'all men.'" So you will find in this Declaration – continues Roosevelt – that it starts with "all human beings" in Article I, and in all the other Articles it says "everyone," "no one." In the body of the Article it occasionally says "his," because to say "his or hers" each time was a little awkward, but it is very clearly understood that this applies to all human beings. (…) In Article I you will notice that instead of saying: "All men are created equal," it says: "All human beings are born free and equal in dignity and rights."[62]

Much more difficult was the task of Elisbaeth Selbert, a social democrat politician, who claimed equal rights for women in all fields of social and political life, insisting that the new German Constitution of 1948 should include as Article 3 §2GG the formulation: "Men and women have equal rights." She had to fight hard in the Parliamentary Council for this formulation to be accepted as a replacement of the old one given in the Weimar Constitution: "Men and women have the same civil rights and obligations." The reason why she insisted so obstinately on this formulation was that the formula given in Weimar Constitution

---

[61] While French men acquired all voting rights in 1848, French women had to wait until 1944. Finland was the first European country that gave women the right to vote, followed by Russia in 1917, Germany, Austria, Hungary and the UK in 1918, Italy in 1945, and Switzerland and Spain in 1971.

[62] Eleanor Roosvelt, "Making Human Rights Come Alive," March 30, 1949, online: http://gos.sbc.edu/r/eleanor1.html.

recognized women as equal only in respect to Criminal Law, but the reformulation by Selbert meant that deep reforms had to be made in marriage and family law as well in order to not contradict Article 3 §2GG. After Silbert's formulation was finally accepted, a resolution was made that the necessary reforms of the Civil Code should be done by 1953, but women had to wait until 1977 to see the abolishment of the oppressive marriage and family law.

Hence, in the next part of my study I will focus on the fight for a gender-neutral language, which still continues and which culminated in some cases that were taken up by the media in 2014.

2. Gender Mainstreaming, Gender Equality, and Gender-Neutral Language in Europe: Legal Regulations and Current Trends

2.1. The Legalization of Gender-Neutral Language

The incorporation of the principle of gender equality between women and men in the *Universal Declaration of Human Rights* was an important step in the struggle for recognition of women's rights as human rights. But the proposals of the UN Women's Commission were not really implemented and many gender-specific infringements and discriminations were not perceived as human rights violations. In many European countries, this situation did not improve. For example, till 1977 West-German women had to ask their husbands for permission if they wanted to pursue a professional activity, and women's property and money were also managed by the husband who had the say in all family affairs. The sexual exploitation and harassment of women in the workplace, in educational institutions and elsewhere, rape and mass rapes in wars, the trafficking of women, and forced prostitution etc., have long been treated as a "private matter" and not as human rights abuses. In order to make clear that Women's Rights are Human Rights, the UN Women's Commission proposed 1975 to be declared International Year of Women. From 1976, different World Conferences on Women took place around the world making women's rights a serious and constant topic within the United Nations. One of the most important legally binding documents was the Convention on the Elimination of all Forms of Discrimination Against Women (CEDAW) which was presented by the United Nations General Assembly in 1979 and signed in 1981 by 188 states. The same year in Quebec, which was the pioneer of francophone gendering, recommendations for femini-zation of the names of professions, official functions, ranks, and titles were compiled and adopted for the first time in the administration and in institutional texts. Special guidelines for a gender-equitable, non-sexist language in the administration were adopted subsequently by France in 1986, by Switzerland and Austria in 1988, by Germany in 1991, by Belgium in 1993, and finally in 1999 UNESCO published its own *Guidelines on Gender-Neutral Language*, which is still one of the most important documents on that topic. Since the beginning of the new millennium, almost all ministries of the EU countries adopted special regulations for Gender Mainstreaming and gender-neutral language. It should also be noted that in academia, the American Philosophical Association was one of the first to publish, already in 1986, special "Guidelines for Non-Sexist Use of Language."[63]

The gender focus on language is one of the results of the feminist struggles for recognition and the Women's Liberation Movement of the 60s. Thus, at the beginning of the 70s feminist linguistics emerged that began to challenge the use of generic masculine nouns as a sort of patriarchal occultation of women and women's faculties as sexist and androcentric. There are various arguments against the masculine generics, but the most important are the following:

- *The masculine generics are a male bias.* Different psycholinguistic research has proven that masculine generics are not perceived *as gender-neutral*, i.e. as including both sexes where women are "meant as well," but *as gender-specific*, i.e. more related to men than to women or to both sexes. Thus, women stay *invisible* in the public sphere and discourse.

- *The masculine generics lead to an occultation of women, which has social, economic and political disadvantages.* For example, when in jobs advertisements the generic "he" is used, instead of "he/she" or "they," many women does not feel concerned and do not

---

[63] "Guidelines for Non-Sexist Use of Language," in *Proceedings and Addresses of the American Philosophical Association*, February 1986, Vol. 59, Number 3, pp. 471-482.

apply for the job. They apply for jobs more frequently when the advertisement uses a gender-neutral language. A more significant example is the fact that until 1971, Swiss women had no right to vote, because one of the arguments against their political participation was that Swiss law used the word "Schweizer" (Swiss men) and not "Schweizerinnen" (Swiss women).

- *Language based on masculine generics is androcentric.* It favors men at the expense of women, because the masculine generics are understood as the norm in contrast to the feminine nouns, which in German, French, Slavic and other languages are often derived from masculine nouns, and are comprehended as a deviation from the norm, i.e. as an exception. In some languages, as f. ex. in French and English, the masculine nouns had not always a generic role, i.e. they did not occur "naturally" as generics, but have been instituted as such for political and economic reasons. Until the 16th century, in French language there was a symmetry of female forms corresponding to the masculine forms designating professions, titles, ranks and functions, because women were socially present in almost all social activities. The 17th century, dominated by the centralizing and eminently masculine image of the "Sun King" (le Roi Soleil) began to ignore feminized words, and successively, especially after the French Revolution, the male forms became generic. In English, the generic pronoun "he" has been required by normative grammar only since the 18th century. In previous centuries, the anaphoric pronoun was "they," such as in the phrase "anyone can do it if they try." "They," "their" and "them" have long been grammatically acceptable as gender-neutral singular pronouns in English, having been used in the singular continuously since the Middle Ages, including by William Shakespeare and Jane Austen. Generic masculine did not arise in a natural way, but was the result of efforts of various normative interventions in favor of an entirely masculine language. In 1850 the British Parliament instituted the use of "he" as the only anaphoric form in legal texts.

- *The masculine generics are equivocal and lead to misunderstandings.* There are many examples in different languages which show that by using male generics it is not clear if they mean "only men" or if they include women as well. This is embarrassing not only in everyday language, but also creates problems when understanding text, during interpretation and translation, and in particular, in reading some legal texts.

2.2. *Actual Trends and Academic Debates*

Although there are actually official European Union guidelines and legal norms for a gender equitable language, in Central and Western Europe there are still heated discussions in academia, in newspapers, as well as on social media, for and against gendering and what it has to look like, e.g. if it should apply only to women and men or to transsexuals, intersexuals and other persons as well. The main proposals written in German and French are outlined below:

- *The use of parentheses*: in German: der/die Autor(in), in French "l'auteur(e)." This practice, however, is mostly rejected, because it puts the feminine "in brackets" and thus makes it less important.

- *The gender gap* in German: "Autor_in," which is interpreted sometimes as a way to avoid the heterosexual binaries and include all genders.

- *The use of hyphen*, especially in French: "auteur-e," which underlines the union, the balance and the equality of the masculine and the feminine gender forms.

- *The use of a star* in diverse variations in German, f.ex. in the context of the both sexes: der*die Autor*in or in a context of multiple genders Autor_*.

- *The slash*, used in German and French as well: "Autor/in," "auteur/e."

- The use of a *capital I*, the so called "*Binnen I*" in German: "AutorInnen," which is very controversial but is still one of the most utilised gendering methods. Similar is the use of the *capital E* in French: "motivéEs."

- *The use of gender-neutral terms*, that is to say, common to both genres, which means in French f.ex. to speak of "persons" instead of "individuals." Thus in German the word students, "Studenten," which is a generic masculine noun, has been replaced with "Studierende" (studying people), and the word participants, "Teilnehmer" with "Teilnehmende" (participating people).

- *The creation of neologisms* for transgender, intersexual and other individuals. For example a German professor of Gender Studies, who does not want to decide between male and female gender, wants to be called "ProfX." In a similar way some French authors suggest using for "they" or "those" the neologisms "celleux" or "ceulles," or "chanteureuses," "chanteuseurs" for singers.

Protesting against some "new creations" and "lingual experiments," in many European countries antifeminist scholars, journalists, politicians, and masculinists actually reject any kind of non-sexist language and label it as "gender madness" ("Genderwahn"). An emblematic case in this regard is the "Open letter on the subject of lingual equal treatment" from 800 Austrian university professors, teachers, linguists, and journalists sent to the minister of Education and Sciences in June 2014, claiming "a return to the normalization of German language."[64] Their arguments express in a condensed form the common critiques against the gendering of language and could be summarized the following way:

- The German language not only has masculine generics, but also feminine and male generics include both sexes.

- The feminization of language is against the orthographic rules; it also leads to grammatical and logical errors, and destroys the German language. Feminine nouns are just malformed appendages, which distort the "normal," i.e. generic, masculine language.

---

[64] See "Offener Brief zum Thema 'Sprachliche Gleichbehandlung'," published by *Die Presse*, 14.07.2014, online: http://diepresse.com/files/pdf/Offener_Brief_Heinisch-Hosek_Mitterlehner.pdf.

- Language should serve primarily as a communication medium for understanding between people and not act just as promotion of feminist concerns.

- The majority of citizens, about 85-90%, prefer the generic language and not the divide between male and female forms.

- The feminist language has been imposed as politically correct from above, which is a sort of dictatorship.

The heated debates from the past year continue and will probably never end. They show, in my opinion, that there is consensus only between the enemies of gender sensitive language, who want to keep the generic masculine form and the male "order of discourse," while the proponents for a gender-neutral or gender-inclusive language are often divided. The solutions that the proponents for a gender sensitive language propose are manifold, but could be resumed, roughly speaking, in three groups or models:

- The use of the splitting method in order to make both sexes visible (or alternatively the use of the "*Binnen-I*").

- The neutralization of both sexes in order to build a gender-neutral language.

- The creation of neologisms and the experimentation with different typographic signs (stars, static and dynamic underscores, exclamation mark, slash etc.) in order to underline that there is not only two genders or sexes, but a multitude which should become visible as well.

All these models and suggestions have their strong and weak points. The use of the splitting method and the Binnen-I are suitable for making women and their activities more visible in society, politics, and mass media. This model is also very convenient as it helps to avoid the double, simultaneous use of female and male forms (e.g. "SchweizerInnen" instead of "Schweizer und Schwiezerinnen") which often makes texts difficult to read. But this method has been criticized, even by the proponents for a gender sensitive language, on the one hand for distorting the German or French language, and on the other, for producing new norms of oppression and exclusion.[65]

The use of a gender-neutral language, i.e. gender-neutral words, is conceived by some journalists, intellectuals, and academics as a more "elegant" form which does not distort language[66]. But, first of all, it is more complicated than the splitting method as it requires creativity and imagination. Second, it is not always possible to find or to form gender-neutral words. Third, this method may help to neutralize the dominance of the generic masculine, thus allowing one to be politically correct, but it does not help to make women more visible as it conceals, in fact, both sexes.

Finally, the creation of neologisms and the experimentation with different typographic signs may be helpful to break with the binary heterosexual matrix – at least this is the intention –, and it is therefore important for diversity and queer-theorists. But there are two problems within. Firstly, some feminists have emphasized that this language experiment eventually leads to a new occultation of women which ruins their long struggles for women's recognition. In addition, some exaggerations in this field make texts not only illegible, but also equality/difference issues derisory.[67]

All these difficulties show that none of these methods for the implementation of a gender sensitive language is perfect. Even though they have the same aim – the lingual deconstruction of the male "order of discourse" –, they are focused on different issues, which are to make women more visible, to neutralize the gender difference(s) or to emphasize gender diversity. Thus they offer different instruments which can be

---

[65] See the Spiegel Interview with Lann Hornscheidt, author of a queer guideline for gender sensitive language ("Gerechte Sprache an der Uni: Professix im Geschlechterkampf," ein Interview von Oliver Trenkamp, *der Spiegel* vom 24.04.2014, online: http://www.spiegel.de/unispiegel/wunderbar/gendertheorie-studierx-lann-hornscheidt-ueber-gerechte-sprache-a-965843.html).

[66] See the Swiss guide for gender equal language in German: *Geschlechtergerechte Sprache. Leitfaden zum geschlechtergerechten Formulieren im Deutschen* (hg. von der Schweizerischen Bundeskanzlei, in Zusammenarbeit mit der Zürcher Hochschule für Angewandte Wissenschaften. 2. Auflage, Zürich: BK, 2009, p. 29).

[67] Very sharp comments and analysis on this subject have been made, in particular, by the Austrian journalist Ingrid Thurnher who opts for a gender-neutral language (see Ingrid Thurnher, "Choreographie der Sonderzeichen," *Wiener Zeitung*, 30. 01. 1995).

efficacious or counterproductive depending on the socio-political or academic context.

2.3. Gender Equality and Gender Sensitive Language in Post-Communist Europe. A Case Study on the Example of Bulgaria

In the process of enlarging the European Union, the question about Gender Equality, which was declared by the Communist ideology as already achieved, came together with Gender Mainstreaming as a new social issue for the post-Communist countries. The situation and the problems in every country are quite specific, not to forget the lingual and cultural particularities. While it is impossible to present here an overview of the obstacles and the possibilities for a gradual introduction of a gender sensitive language in the whole region, I will try to illustrate some problems using the example of Bulgaria and Bulgarian, which is a Slavic language.

Bulgaria became an EU member in 2007. The equality between women and men is not explicitly mentioned in the new Bulgarian Constitution adopted in 1991, but it is implicitly included in Article 6 (al. 1-2), where it is said that "all persons are born free and equal in dignity and rights," and "there shall be no privileges or restriction of rights on the grounds of race, national or social origin, ethnic self-identity, sex, religion" etc. Equality between men and women is explicitly mentioned in other legal documents like the labor code (§ 243) and education law. In 2003 the Bulgarian parliament accepted the discrimination law, which is an enormous step forward as it includes some measures against sexual harassment, and in 2009 a law against domestic violence. Bulgaria has been a full member of the UNO since 1955 and EU member since 2007, which means that it is obligated to follow all their treaties, conventions and regulations, including the mentioned recommendations for a gender-neutral language. However, there are not any official guidelines for a gender neutral language as of yet. Moreover, a closer look at the translation of some official EU documents, not to mention the use of language in public space, will show that for Bulgarians this topic is still a *terra incongnita*. For example *The European Parliament's Rules of Procedure* (last version April 2015), begins with a statement that "In accordance with Parliament's decisions on the use of gender-neutral language in its documents, the Rules of Procedure have been adapted to take account of the guidelines on that subject approved by the High Level Group on Gender Equality and Diversity on February 2008."[68] This document is translated into all EU languages. That the Bulgarian translation does not employ gender-neutral language can be seen by the fact that it uses only generic masculine nouns even when a function or a title refers to a woman. So if the title "Vice-President" is translated in French as "Vice-présidente" and in German as "Vizepräsidentin," in the Bulgarian translation we read "zamestnik-predsedatel"[69] instead of "zamestnik-predsedatelka." The same errors can be seen in the Bulgarian translation of the EU *Manual for Gender Mainstreaming* (2008), which compared to the gender-neutral German translation only uses generic masculine nouns.[70] Much more problematic is the Bulgarian translation of the Eurochambres' toolkit on gender equality, *Break gender stereotypes, give talent a chance!*, where in addition to using masculine nouns in gender-specific contexts (!) there are some artificial word creations like "woman-director" ("zhena-direktor") instead of the existing feminine noun "direktorka," or woman-officer – "zhena-sluzhitel" instead of "sluzhitelka," or "women-mentors" – "zheni-mentori" instead of "mentorki," or "women-leaders" – "zheni-lideri" instead of "liderki" etc.[71] The only feminine nouns used in this translation are nouns for some "typically women professions" like – "medizinska sestra" (nurse), "domashna pomostniza" (household help), "akusherka" (midwife).[72] Thus, this toolkit, which should help to deconstruct gender stereotypes, is in fact a lingual cementing the criticized gender clichés through a bad translation. In general, Bulgarians use masculine and feminine nouns for

---

[68] See "Pravilnik za dejnostta na Evropejskiia parlament," online: http://www.europarl.europa.eu/sides/getDoc.do?pubRef=-//EP//TEXT+RULES-EP+20150428+RULE-130+DOC+XML+V0//BG.
[69] Ibid.
[70] Rykovodstvo za dzhendyr mejnstrijming posredstvom politikite na zaetost, socialno vkliuchvane i socialna zakrila, Liuksemburg: 2008, online: http://ec.europa.eu/social/BlobServlet?docId=2045&langId=bg.
[71] See *Razchupete polovite stereotipi, dajte shans na talanta. Instrumentarium za konsultanti i upraviteli na choveshki resursi v MSP*, Evropejski obshtnosti, 2008, pp. 9, 27, 28, availble online: http://www.businessandgender.eu/en/countries/bg/toolkit-bg.
[72] Ibid., p. 22.

professions, functions, titles etc. somehow voluntaristically, without any rules. Even on some Bulgarian feminist sites, which try to use a more inclusive language, one can see how chaotic it is. For example, in the report about the EU Project "Learning Partnerships against Social Exclusion: Mentoring for Women Enterpreneurs,"[73] organized by the Center for Women's Studies and Politics with the support of the European Commission, one can find words like "zheni predprie-machki," which is a literal and rough translation from the English word "women entrepreneurs" that does not make sense in Bulgarian, because " predpriemachki " is a feminine noun, so that the prefix "women," " zheni ," is confusing and tautological. In the same report, which is full of feminine nouns, suddenly appears masculine nouns like "uchastnici" instead of the feminine "uchastnichki" or a woman is presented as "koordinator" instead of "koordinatorka" and sometimes even the same word is used once in the feminine plural as "mentorki" (women mentors), and then again in the masculine singular as "mentor" instead of the "mentorka."

In the Bulgarian mass media we have the same chaotic use of masculine and feminine nouns to denominate professions, titles, official functions, etc. Moreover, in 2009 many newspapers even mocked the European Parliament's New Rules on a gender-neutral language. One could read the following headlines: "Euro-chiefs ban Miss and Mrs.," "Miss and Mrs. are said to be humiliating for women," "Women in the European Commission should not be divided into Miss and Mrs.," etc.[74] And most of the readers' comments have also been in the same scornful spirit – "In the EU Parliament they have no other problems," "What's that bullshit?!," "Who needs such idiotic language?," etc.

But if the Bulgarians are far away from a serious reflection about the connection between language and gender, this does not mean that some lingual uses and abuses always happen in a non-reflected manner. As mockery, sarcasm, and aggression are becoming the main style of Bulgarian "journalism," the use of feminine nouns for the designation of official titles and functions is becoming a popular means to humiliate

---

[73] See http://www.cwsp.bg/htmls/page.php?category=449&id=739&page=5.
[74] See http://dariknews.bg/view_article.php?article_id=339391; http://www.24chasa.bg/Article.asp?ArticleId=7066 ; http://www.dnes.bg/evrointegracia/2009/03/17/bez-quot-g-n-quot-i-quot-g-ja-quot-v-dokumentite-za-es.67735.

women in high positions and to make fools of them. This is easy to do because of some lingual particularities. Like in German, French or Slavic languages, Bulgarian feminine nouns are a derivative of masculine nouns, but the point is that in Bulgarian the feminine suffix "KA" is a diminutive form. Thus, it appears derogatory when used in some contexts or as a suffix of some official titles and positions, which are rated to apply usually to men, as for example director, minister, president, professor, doctor of sciences, etc. That is why, in government as well as in academia, women themselves prefer the generic masculine nouns when it comes to designating their official functions and titles. They do want to be called "direktorka," "ministyrka," "professorka," "doktorka," but to keep the masculine genus, in order to be recognized as equal to men in capacities, honor and position.

The resistance in the post-communist states against feminism, as well as the gender blindness due to diverse reasons, including the belief that gender equality is not the main problem of our society or not a problem at all, because it is already achieved, shows that it will not be easy to break with some stereotypes. Additionally, a society which is becoming more and more mafia-like and brutal, where the highest values are power and money, may accept in its legislation the principle of gender equality, but this does not mean that it will be implemented in reality. The point here is that Bulgaria first of all needs a deep transformation of the legal system and real mechanisms to restrict any kind of violence, including domestic violence, violence in the media, violence in language, etc. Without that, all social issues will grasp at nothing. This does of course not mean that we should wait until the restructuration of the legal system is achieved before we turn to the problems of gender equality and gender-equitable language. On the contrary, these problems cannot be solved without a transformation of our way of thinking, of our values, and that is why education and gender mainstreaming are so important.

What conclusions can be drawn from the stated trends and debates on gender-neutral language in respect to the situation in Bulgaria?

- As an EU member state Bulgaria needs to form an expert commission on gender-neutral language, which should elaborate spe-

cial guidelines to help the government and the institutions to formulate official documents more adequately and also to make better translations of the official documents of the EU. This commission should include not only linguists, but also psycholinguists and gender experts proficient in various languages, and it must take into account the social attitudes towards language and gendering in order to find publicly acceptable solutions.
- The Bulgarian translations of EU documents should not be made only from English as this leads to the use of masculine generics; they should consult the German and English translations as well.
- It is not advisable to impose from above a gender-neutral use of language in academia or in the public sphere, because it will lead to social tensions and create more problems than helping the implementation of gender equality. However, active steps are required to stop mobbing and violence in the media, including aggressive, harsh and derogatory language, which is becoming everyday use even in the Parliament. Because, as says Toni Morrison in her Nobel Prize Lecture:

> Oppressive language does more than represent violence; it is violence; does more than represent the limits of knowledge; it limits knowledge. (...) Sexist language, racist language, theistic language – all are typical of the policing languages of mastery, and cannot, do not permit new knowledge nor encourage the mutual exchange of ideas.[75]

3. (Re)defing the Subject of Feminist Discourse: Theoretical and Practical Issues

In this last, concluding part, I want to return anew to Christina Thürmer-Rohr's reflections on the Cassandra syndrome. What Thürmer-Rohr thematizes in her essay, as well as in another recent article, which I would like to refer to here, is the changed situation of feminism today:

> Like every new political movement feminism was inspired in his beginnings of uniting ideas and strove for a strategic and emotional We as a

---

[75] Toni Morrison, "Nobel Lecture December 7, 1993," online: http://www.nobelprize.org/nobel_prizes/literature/laureates/1993/morrison-lecture.html.

condition of a discourse of power that speaks with one voice and develops common objectives and public concerns. This unity of We was not intended as a representation of reality, but as an idea and a political postulate, and, of course, real differences were since the beginning a problem for the women's movement. But they were downplayed as "sister dispute" or blocked as "false consciousness," at least they were not theorized in the sense of plurality, as given diversity and political claim. Since then [the 70ies and 80ies] many things happened. First, "Women's Studies" were replaced by "Gender Studies," and then supplemented with "Gender Diversity"; consequently in some places "Gender Studies" were renamed in "Difference Studies" while Women's Centers became Centers for Gender & Diversity.[76]

Thus, on the one hand, there is no more a unified "We"-Subject that could say "We" as feminists or "We" as women claim this or that. On the other hand, feminist theory seems to be replaced by other disciplines and ways of thinking, especially by the "Gender Diversity" account. All this leads finally, as I will show, to the question of the place and the legitimacy of feminist theory in university and academia.

3.1. The Destabilization of Identity: Are the Man/Woman and Sex/Gender Categories still relevant for Feminist Theory?

Indeed, one of the main problems that feminists and women activists encounter today is not just the pluralism of life worlds, world views and life styles, but the problem of the multiplicity and the complexity of personal and collective identities that makes it, in some cases, difficult to capture the subject(s) of domination and exclusion, i.e. the subject(s) of human and women's rights and also, as we saw, their lingual gender articulation. However, without referring to a distinct subject of oppression, dominance and/or exclusion, one cannot prosecute any claim for human, women's, or/and LGBT rights, nor undertake a sustainable social and political critique. This is what even poststructuralists like Judith Butler, who claimed in the past that there is no stable subject, no preconstructed gender identity, have to agree with. Butler was conscious

---

[76] Christina Thürmer-Rohr, "Gender & Diversity - ein kritischer Blick auf feministische Traditionen und neue Entwicklungen," *Quer* 1/2013, p. 11, reprinted as "Gender & Diversity – gleich und verschieden" at the homepage of Heinrich Böll foundation, online: http://www.gwi-boell.de/de/2014/10/14/genderdiversity-gleich-und-verschieden.

that Foucault's central statement about the "death of the subject" could be hardly of use for a feminist theory, which aims at political action for sustainable social change. That is why she made clear:

> The critique of the subject is not a negation or repudiation of the subject, but, rather, a way of interrogating its construction as a pregiven or foundationnalist premise (...) To perform this kind of Foucauldian critique of the subject is not to do away with the subject or pronounce its death, but merely to claim that certain versions of the subject are politically insidious.[77]

So, no wonder if Butler actually "distances herself from her earlier conceptions of subjectivity," as noticed Seyla Benhabib.[78] Yet, it is not my intention here to enter into the debate about Butler's controversial concept of the subject whose merits and limits have already been discussed by various authors.[79] Rather, I want to call attention to some critical reflections about the evolution of feminist thought made fifteen years ago by Herta Nagl-Docekal which are still valid in my opinion; namely that the categories of "man" and "woman" as well as of "sex" and "gender," declared by many as outdated, have not lost their importance for feminist theory. On the one hand, Nagl-Docekal argues, the notions of "man" and "woman" continue to be used as categories of the "social order" so that sexual difference is still the base of different social norms and restrictions, which have an impact of women's lives. For example, the ascription of specific social roles to women on the basis of their "nature" and hence the legitimation of their exclusion from different social activities is still a matter of fact. This proves, consequently,

---

[77] Judith Butler, "Contingent Foundations," in Seyla Benhabib (ed.), *Feminist Contentions: A Philosophical Exchange*, London/New York: Routledge 1994, pp. 42, 47.

[78] See Seyla Benhabib, "Ethics without Normativity and Politics without Historicity On Judith Butler's Parting Ways. Jewishness and the Critique of Zionism," *Constellations*, Vol. 20, No 1, 2013, pp. 150-163, here p. 150.

[79] There are too many. Some of the most well-known critiques are those of Matha Nussbaum ("The Professor of Parody," *The New Republic*, 22.02.1999) and Seyla Benhabib ("Subjectivity, Historiography, and Politics," in idem (ed.), *Feminist Conten-tions*, op.cit., pp. 107-126). But I would like to refer here rather to the less known monographs of Isabell Lorey: *Immer Ärger mit dem Subjekt. Theoretische und politische Konsequenzen eines juridischen Machtmodells: Judith Butler* (Tübingen: edition diskord, 1996) and Christine Hauskeller: *Das paradoxe Subjekt. Unterwerfung und Widerstand bei Judith Butler und Michel Foucault* (Tübingen: edition diskord, 2000).

that sexual difference is still a subject of matter for feminist critique.[80] On the other hand, the distinction between the biological "sex" and the discursively constructed "gender" is still also a suitable instrument for feminist theory as it shows the dangers of a hasty dedifferentiation leading either to a biological reductionism, which uses the body as mono-causal explanation, or to a cultural reductionism, which over-rates the role of discourse. The sex/gender differentiation makes it possible to show that social norms are to be distinguished from physical conditions and that only on this basis a space can be created where options for action could be morally judged and justified.[81]

In other words, even feminists should be "self-critical about the processes that produce and destabilize identity categories" and also to reconsider the unity of the feminist "We,"[82] they should be able to designate the subjects of oppression, exclusion, and violence, in order to articulate the injustices and to justify new strategies of moral and political action. Moreover, the problems of language gendering that I described in the previous paragraph, show that while a (re)definition of the (feminist) subject is absolutely necessary for a gender sensitive discourse, which takes into account the real plurality of sexes and genders, this does not mean that the category "woman" should be dismantled. It just means that the category "woman," which is still basic in view of the world-wide violence against women and persisting discrimination practices, is no longer the only referent in a broader context of human rights and gender mainstreaming. The same is also true for Feminist Theory – even it is not the only discipline which focuses on gender oppression, it cannot be replaced or "suspended" (in the Hegelian sense) by Gender Studies or Diversity Studies without erasing the history of a long and still unfinished battle for women's human rights.

---

[80] Herta Nagl-Docekal, *Feministische Philosophie. Ergebnisse, Probleme, Perspektiven*, Frankfurt am Main: Fischer Taschenbuch Verlag, 1999, pp. 17-18.
[81] Ibid., p. 67.
[82] See Judith Butler, "Contingent Foundations," op.cit., p. 48.

3.2. The Precarious Situation of Feminist Theory and Gender Studies in Academia: A "Successful Failure" of Institutionalization?

In the first part of my article I showed the importance of language for the implementation of women's rights in society and law. In the second part I described how, though there are already legal regulations for the use of a gender neutral language in official EU documents, the fight against the feminization and gendering of language that culminated last year in Austria, France, and partly in Germany. In conclusion, I want to recall here some recent struggles about the place of Feminist Theory in Austrian academia which reveals similar problems to those depicted in the previous two parts of my article, and thus to argue the necessity of a precise lingual conceptualization in claims of academic and legal concerns.

Since the beginning of 2015 a series of articles, interviews, and comments were propagated in the media about the struggle for the Eva Kreisky chair on Political Theory at the University of Vienna and the precarious situation of feminist theory in academia. In an interview, published on the 8th of March, 2015, in the Austrian newspaper *Die Standard* – the woman's edition of *Der Standard* –, the well-known feminist Birgit Sauer, professor of political theory at the University of Vienna, disclosed:

> There are two levels in feminist science: feminist and gender research in the various disciplines and Gender Studies as an own discipline. In this regard a lot happened from 1970 to 1990. A Gender research unit was established at Vienna University and also different [feminist] chairs were created ... in philosophy, in history, and political science... But with the wave of retirements in the recent years it came to a struggle for these professorships. Unfortunately Feminist Studies at the Vienna University lost it often... In philosophy the chair [of Herta Nagl] was not filled by a feminist professor and the reappointment of the chair of Eva Kreisky, the pioneer of feminist political science, is uncertain. The University set a half-hearted signal even about the Gender Studies chair that was discontinued last week. Now we have a Master's Degree of Gender Studies which stands now without a professorship - that's a joke! At the Univer-

sity of Vienna there are more fights in this field than at other universities, because of the precarious financial situation.[83]

Furthermore, Sauer deplores the fact that there is no long-term strategy for the establishment of Gender Studies as academic discipline. Thus, not only is the institutionalization precarious, but also the gender thematic is in many disciplines marginal, especially in Austria. "The German Research Foundation, DFG, has since five years a gender program, so that a reflection on this theme must be present in all research proposals. At the Austrian Science Fund there is nothing like that and no one is committed to the issue," she says.

In another recent study Sauer gives a long analysis on the struggle for the institutionalization of Feminist Theory and Gender Studies in the German-speaking countries and comes to the conclusion that "On the one hand, the institutionalization of Women's and Gender Studies in the Political Sciences was relatively successful, but on the other hand, it would be justifiably to assert that it successfully failed."[84]

In their article "Feminist science is coming into trouble," published in the same edition of *Die Standard*[85], the authors – Sarah Yolanda Koss and David Tiefenthaler, freelance journalists and students at Vienna University – are deploring the same fact, namely that at Vienna University feminist critique is becoming unwanted and thus many feminist fields tend to disappear:

> With Herta Nagl-Docekal in philosophy, Edith Saurer in history and Eva Kreisky in political science a critical-feminist focus were created at the University of Vienna in the last decades which enjoyed international recognition. But currently the feminist researches have a strong counter-action – inside as well as outside of the university. With Kreisky's retirement in 2012, the chair of political theory was released. To date, it is open and the continuation of the feminist political studies introduced by

---

[83] See "Forscherinnen: 'Ich habe das Gefühl, ich bin in einem Dauerkampf," *Die Standart.at*, vom 8 März 2015, online: http://diestandard.at/2000012455589/ Forscherinnen-Ich-habe-das-Gefuehl-ich-bin-in-einem-Dauerkampf.

[84] Birgit Sauer, "Politikwissenschaftliche Frauen- und Geschlechterprofessorinnen im deutschsprachigen Raum. Zwischen Besonderheit und Besonderung oder auf dem Weg zur Normalität?," *Femina politica* 2015/1, pp. 126-134, here p. 127.

[85] Sarah Yolanda Koss, David Tiefenthaler, "Feministische Wissenschaft gerät in Bedrängnis," *DieStandart.at*, 8 März 2015, online: http://diestandard.at/2000012466033/ Feministische-Wissenschaft-geraet-in-Bedraengnis.

her is unclear. In any case in the chair tender of 2013 this [feminist] focus was not mentioned.[86]

In other words the call for tenders of Kreisky's chair was for "Political Theory" without any further specification. Moreover, the rector rejected the nomination of the jury, which proposed two women and a man, saying that the women were "unqualified" and their professional specialization is "too narrow." Consequently, a new sequence of the nominations was done so that the man moved from third place to first. This procedure was contested as a violation of the principles of equal treatment and sent to the Arbitration Commission of the University. On the initiative of the students an international petition was started which was signed by renowned professors, including Judith Butler. In conclusion, the authors of the article invited the readers to sign the petition. But as we actually know, the 1000 professors' signatures could not help and the case is still unclear.

The Sauer interview and the article by Koss and Tiefentaler provoked strong reactions from some university scholars.

In his article "Vienna University: No gender leasehold properties," published in *Der Standard* (the men's edition of *Standard*) Stefan Brocza, lecturer in the same Faculty of Political Sciences, reminds that Kreisky was an internationally recognized representative of the critical feminist tradition, but her chair and the call for tenders were not about feminism:

> It's not about the reappointment of a relevant gender professorship or a theory with gender focal point. The tender stated simply 'political theory' without any addition. The successor should represent the entire field in its full breadth and depth. She or he should have 'outstanding achievements in research, international reputation and excellent publication activities and integration into the international scientific community.'[87]

Depicting the academic struggle, he criticizes the way that Kreisky got the chair, and then the actual nominations, and concludes that none of the struggling parties will receive glory; neither the Institute because in fact it did not support a feminist focal point of research, nor the rector

---

[86] Ibid.
[87] Stefan Brocza, "Uni Wien: Keine Gender-Erbpachten," *DerStandart.at*, 16 März 2015, online: http://derstandard.at/2000013013902/Uni-Wien-Keine-Gender-Erbpachten.

because he did not take a firm position by assuming the consequences and appointing the best candidate (probably the male professor).

Another impassionate reaction, which is of special interest here, is the article by Elisabeth Nemeth, professor at the Department of Philosophy and Dean of the Faculty of Philosophy and Education at the University of Vienna, "Fog over the Gender Studies?"[88] It is striking that her text was printed in *Der Standard* and not in *Die Standard* even though it was a direct response to the interview of Birgit Sauer and the article by Sarah Yolanda Koss and David Tiefenthaler.

Nemeth begins with a firm statement, that "in the debates about an alleged feminist claim to professorships at Vienna University, it came to cheap misstatements" and that "it is time, to let populism aside in order to comply with already achieved standards of argumentation."[89] She recalls that the conditions for women's careers and gender research at the University of Vienna have recently been critically discussed often, which is a good thing, however incorrect points were publicly claimed: "It is wrong to claim that in the past a chair of Feminist philosophy was created, which had not been filled," referring to the chair of Herta Nagl. This professorship did not contain any sub-specification of philosophy. "Herta Nagl's research and teaching were about philosophy in all its breadth," and she dealt with feminism and gender intensively. In the 1980s and 1990s, the Institute of Philosophy created an environment that promoted feminist concerns. Nemeth also emphasizes that the University's policy at that time included three points: First the viewpoint that a clear distinction must be made between the promotion of academic careers of women and the promotion of feminist research; women should not feel forced, directly or indirectly, to pursue more feminist theory as other scientific interests. Second, it was clear that moving away from the term "women's studies" to "gender studies" contributed in a theoretical and political way. Thus, the criticism of the essentialist dualism "man/woman" made feminism politically questionable as women could no more claim the sole representation in terms of gender. Third, there was the viewpoint that chairs of feminism or gender studies

---

[88] Elisabeth Nemeth, "Nebel über der Genderforschung?," *Der Standart*, 27. April 2015, online: http://derstandard.at/2000014944819/Nebel-ueber-der-Genderforschung.
[89] Ibid.

are not the wisdom's last word. That is why neither philosophy nor feminist gender theory should be established as a closed area in itself for filling a niche. Even when few women could anchor at the University in this way, gender issues should not been isolated to research and teaching. Regarding these questions, outlines Nemeth, feminists never absolutely agreed and such an agreement is not desirable. Yet, what is desirable is to keep the academic reputation which Herta Nagl gave to feminist philosophy. Her work in feminist theory responded to the same systematic standards as demanded in other areas of philosophy, and this was of highest value for feminist philosophy. A gender specialization of her chair would not be of help to feminism in philosophy. Given the thematic breadth of Herta Nagl's internationally recognized and highly respected research, after her retirement in 2009, the tender of the chair was called "Political Philosophy and Social Philosophy," i.e. with a range in which gender issues could be, but must not be integrated. The jury nominated an internationally highly respected philosopher for first place, a man without specialization in feminist research, which was a legitimate option for the Institute. Hence, the cheap misrepresentation of the dedication of the chair as a feminist one, and the critique that it was given to a non-feminist, is highly inappropriate. In conclusion, Nemeth states:

> Historical reminiscences cannot answer the questions we ask ourselves today: What are the institutional and structural causes of the "glass ceiling"? How gender research will be further developed in philosophy? The debates will - as usual - have to be based on international research and quality standards.[90]

Let us a take a closer look at the presented positions and debates. Stefan Brocza is absolutely right – and this is, of course, the main problem – that the call for tenders of the Kreisky chair was for Political Theory at large, without any mention of a feminist focal point. If the call were with a specification then the rector could not so easily say the first two nominated women are not qualified for the professorship. The proof is that the second one nominated, Nikita Dhawan, got a professorship in late 2014 at the University of Innsbruck for "Political Science, Political

---

[90] Ibid.

theory with a thematic emphasis in the field of Women's and Gender Studies."[91] So much for her qualifications.

As for Herta Nagl's chair, Elisabeth Nemeth insists that the call for tenders was "Political Philosophy and Social Philosophy" without any sub-specification. But in the online comments, a person under the pseudonym of "dobiezki," obviously an ex-member of the Institute of Philosophy, accuses Nemeth of giving incorrect information and being perfidious:

> The chair of Nagl was called as follows: 'Political Philosophy and Social Philosophy with implication of Philosophy of Law and Philosophical Gender Studies.' The current chair-holder is not competent in the field of Gender Studies; so when Nemeth was asked about, she replied that the Institute took decision against the Gender Studies. There is falsity and falseness. Years ago the same Institute for Philosophy at Vienna University took a similar decision: as the Peers in the course of an evaluation of the Institute apprised the Working Group of Feminist Philosophy as outstanding and recommended to expand it, it happen exactly the same, namely nothing.[92]

As I'm neither a member of the Institute nor do I work at Vienna University, so I cannot say anything about the exact formulation of the call for tender. But years ago, when I was a guest researcher there, I was an associated member of the aforementioned Working Group and I remember the evaluation quite well. So this last part of the above comment is correct. For the rest, no matter how the call was formulated, it is clear that the Institute of Philosophy at Vienna University, similar to the Institute of Political Sciences which did not support a feminist focal point of research, decided against the fields of Feminist Philosophy and the Philosophical Gender Studies. I suppose that the whole procedure is done in a legal way so that no one can complain or rebut it. But does this mean that there is only "populism," "cheap misstatements," and "fog over the Gender Studies" in the testimonials of Sauer, Koss, and Tiefenthaler, as Nemeth suggests? What all three authors deplore is the fact that, after the retirement of such personalities like Eva Kreisky and

---

[91] See the chair at: http://www.zefg.fu-berlin.de/Datenbanken/Professuren-mit-Teil-oder-Voll-Denomination-fuer-Frauen--und-eschlechterforschung/datensaetze_oesterreich_schweiz/oesterreich/dhawan_nikita_nachfolge_werlhof_innsbruck.html.

[92] See the comment of dobiezki to Elisabeth Nemeth, "Nebel über der Genderforschung?," op.cit.

Herta Nagl, feminist research in Political Sciences and in Philosophy risks being lost in the case that there is no more recruitment of professors working in these fields. Sure, there are "no gender leasehold properties" on professorships which are on "Political Theory" at large or on "Political Philosophy and Social Philosophy" at large. But there is something very curious in the arguments against the "narrowness" of Feminist Political Theory and the Philosophical Gender Studies used against some candidates labeling their professional field of specialization as "too narrow." When Brocza underlines that, according the call for tenders, Eva Kreisky's successor "should represent the entire field in its full breadth and depth" than it follows, no more no less, that he/she should also be a specialist on Feminist Political Theory as a part of Political Theory. The position of Elisabeth Nemeth is more multisided, playing with open debates and concepts, but even she insists on "argumentative quality standards" her own argumentation is not exempt from inconsistencies.

As Nemeth knows, someone could object that Herta Nagl's successor is not competent in Philosophical Gender Studies, she underlines at the very beginning: "It is wrong to claim that in the past a chair of Feminist philosophy was created, which had not been filled," and explains later that since there was no sub-specification of the call for tender "gender issues could be, but must not be integrated." She is perfectly aware that it would be not plausible to directly argue the uselessness of feminist and gender issues which had a great impact in the past and contributed to the Institute's international reputation. So between her initial statement and the conclusion about the unrequired feminist chair in philosophy, she gives an extensive tutorial about high quality standards and policies of career advancement. In brief, she seems to advocate the promotion of women (as she herself is a woman who arrived, fortunately, to break the "glass ceiling" becoming a professor, then director of the Philosophy Institute and finally dean of the whole Philosophy faculty). But she does not insist on the promotion of Feminist Studies which is, she says, "something different," emphasizing that feminist chairs are not "wisdom's last word." In particular, Feminist Philosophy seems not to be needed. Evoking the move from Women's Studies to Gender Studies as a broader area, Nemeth *indirectly* suggests a move from Feminist Philosophy to the philosophical Gender Studies; I say "indirectly," because in fact she blends both terms at many points in her text. Yet, Feminist Philosophy[93] and philosophical Gender Studies are not the same pair of shoes; the one cannot replace or sublate the other. In the interview that I conducted with Herta Nagl in 1998 she explains why "Gender Studies in the area of Philosophy" is a term that cannot replace "Feminist Philosophy," and she underlines that there is not just a difference of terminology, but of thematics. Thus, both concepts have their legitimacy, according her, but we should be aware that the broad notion of Gender Studies bears the danger of losing the critical emancipatory impact inherent to the Feminist Studies.[94] Moreover, as I already mentioned, the professorship of Nikita Dhawan at the University of Innsbruck has a "thematic emphasis in the field of Women's and Gender Studies," which shows that both fields are still needed, something on what Herta Nagl also insists.[95] Nemeth, on the contrary, aims to prove that both fields are not needed either in Philosophy (as fields of Feminist Philosophy or philosophical Gender Studies), or as their own areas of research which should be institutionalized as chairs.

For the devaluation of Feminist Philosophy – one of Herta Nagl's main fields of contribution – and hence of a chair of philosophical Gender Studies, Nemeth uses her most sophisticated argument about the international academic reputation of Herta Nagl:

> Herta Nagl gave feminist philosophy an academic prestige that it never enjoyed before. Her work is the proof that she used in Feminist Theory the same systematic standards as demanded in other areas of Philosophy. This was for Feminist Philosophy of highest value. A gender-specialization of her professorship would not have helped Feminist Philosophy to arrive to such reputation. Given the thematic breadth of Herta Nagl's internationally highly respected research, after her retirement in 2009 the call for tender of her chair was for "Political Philosophy and

---

[93] She defines Feminist Philosophy as "philosophizing guided by the interest of woman's liberation," see Herta Nagl-Docekal (ed.), *Feministische Philosophie*, Wien: Oldenbourg, 1994, p. 13.

[94] See "Feministische Philosophie – Frauenforschung – Gender Studies. Ein Gespräch mit Herta Nagl-Docekal," in Yvanka B. Raynova, *Feministische Philosophie in europäischem Kontext: Gender Debatten zwischen "Ost" und "West,"* Wien/Köln/ Weimar: Böhlau, 2010, p. 182.

[95] Ibid., p. 181.

Social Philosophy" – that is, with a range in which gender issues can be, but must not be integrated.[96]

But what does this statement really mean?

Firstly, Nemeth insinuates that Feminist Philosophy is something less then all "other areas of Philosophy" which, as everybody knows, were created by men and are still dominated by men who define its standards of excellence. Second, this permits her to claim that "a *gender-specialization of her professorship* would not have helped Feminist Philosophy to arrive to such reputation" (sic!), i.e. that if the denomination of the chair was on feminist or gender issues in Philosophy, and if Herta Nagl had worked only on Feminist Philosophy, no matter how excellent her work may be, she would never have earned the same recognition nor arrived to give prestige to the field. (This is also the logic of the rector – Feminist Studies are too narrow.) Besides the fact that you cannot be good in Feminist Philosophy without being a good philosopher, i.e. without competences in "other areas of Philosophy," here we must deal with similar prejudices as in the time of Marie de Gournay and Poullain de la Barre; the difference is that it actually is not (just) about the intellectual capacities of women, but about the area of their research and methodology. Sure, Feminist Philosophy does not have the same "prestige" as, for example, Analytic Philosophy because it is not a dominant discourse and never will be. Moreover, as a critical methodology it is quite inconvenient – it calls into question the "order of discourse," power relations in society and philosophy, "grand narratives," ways of speech and argumentation which produce oppression and exclusion. Therefore, it is very convenient to say that Feminist Philosophy became prestigious only because of Herta Nagl (a nice way to flatter her) and thus to suggest that this prestige is passé with her retirement, i.e. that Feminist Philosophy has no own "scientific" value or theoretical impact. Third, all this permits Nemeth to propose that a special chair in Feminist Philosophy/philosophical Gender Studies is not needed.

Without a doubt, Nemeth's arguments go hand in hand with the decision of the Institute against Gender Studies and Feminist Philosophy. The future will show if this was an academic gain, advancing Philosophy to the highest international standards praised by her, or a loss that

---

[96] Elisabeth Nemeth, "Nebel über die Genderforschung," op.cit.

will maybe never be recouped. In any case, there is an obvious inconsistency in her argumentation and evaluation standards. On the one hand, if the Institute really wanted to keep the academic reputation and topical breadth that Herta Nagl gave to the chair, as Nemeth pretends, then the call for tenders should be *uncut*, i.e. it should be "Political Philosophy and Social Philosophy with implication of Philosophy of Law and Philosophical Gender Studies" in order to make sure that these fields will be covered. On the other hand, the areas of "Political and Social Philosophy" are so broad, when unspecified, that it would be hard to find a scholar who is competent in their whole. Today, almost every scholar specializes in some topic, thus everyone who applies for such a position could be rejected with the argument that he/she lacks of "thematic breadth." On the contrary, if there were specifications or sub-specifications of the academic field, the argument of "narrowness" could not be used as easily. So there are (good) standards and (bad) standards, and it is not just about argumentation, but about the hidden interests behind it, i.e. about power relations and legal ways of marginalization and obliteration of inconvenient fields of education and research. If there is a "fog over the Gender Studies," as Nemeth claims, then there is no less "fog over call for tenders" based on shady arguments about "thematic breadth" and "narrowness."

Concluding Remarks

What can we conclude from all these debates?

First of all, the history of women's movements shows that by changing the grammatical gender and the feminization of language, women were able to articulate themselves as a *subject of rights* and not just of duties. (Women) philosophers may dispute the meanings and ambiguities of the notions of "subject," "sex," "gender" etc., but in law, where every word counts, the univocal denomination of the subject is a *sine qua non* for any rights claims. This is important not only for women, but also for minors, people of color, GLBT, stateless persons, refugees, etc.

Second, those who pretend that equality between the sexes is de jure and de facto achieved are poorly informed or disingenuous. The fact that women have been granted suffrage as well as access to education and professional practice, that they do not need their husband's permission to work, that they have an own bank account etc., does not mean that equality is achieved, neither de jure nor de facto. One of the prime examples is the Equal Rights Amendment (ERA), which is a proposed amendment to the United States Constitution that would expressly prohibit discrimination against girls and women on the basis of sex. First introduced in 1923, it was passed by Congress in 1972, the deadline for state ratification ended in 1982, and since then it has been reintroduced in Congress every session. "Although polls indicate that more than 90% of Americans support the ERA, Congress has not once voted on it over the past thirty years," say official representatives.[97] And this is not a question about Yemen, Chad, Pakistan, Afghanistan, or Syria[98], but about the United States, which professes to be founded on the fundamental human rights and to protect them all over the world.[99] If a misogynistic politician like Donald Trump, who is "using women's periods not just to avoid a political question but also to insult ... all women's intelligence,"[100] will become the next US President, than it can be sure that the ERA will have to wait for many years to be voted on. But let us take another example that seems more favorable to women's rights. One of the greatest human rights acquisitions of the European Union is the *Charter of Fundamental Rights*, which became legal with the *Treaty of Lisbon* in December 2009. Although equality between the sexes is one of the main values and fundamental rights of the Charter and there are many other binding legal documents, gender mainstreaming and gender equality are still serious issues. That is why the European Union adopted a special *Women's Charter* in 2010 as well as a *Strategy for equality*

---

[97] "What is the ERA?," online: http://www.eracoalition.org/about.php; cf. Jessica Ravitz, "The new women warriors: Reviving the fight for equal rights," CNN International Edition, April 16, 2015, online: http://edition.cnn.com/2015/04/02/us/new-womens-equal-rights-movement/.

[98] See Alexander E.M. Hess, "The 10 Worst Countries for Women," 24/7 Wall St., November 28, 2014, online: http://247wallst.com/special-report/2014/11/28/the-10-worst-countries-for-women/.

[99] "Human Rights" article on the US Gouvernement site: http://www.state.gov/j/drl/hr/.

[100] I'm citing here Sarah Levy's statement about Donald Trump's disparaging remarks about Fox News anchor Megy Kelly (see "Portland artist uses period blood for Trump portrait," *USA Today*, September 16, 2015, online: http://www.usatoday.com/story/news/nation-now/2015/09/15/ period-blood-donald-trump/72339462/).

between women and men (2010-2015), which is now included for implementation in the *Europe 2020 Strategy*.[101] A brief look at the latest Eurostat Gender statistics gives us an idea about the persistent "gender gaps" in the fields of education, labour market, earnings and health.[102] In addition, the latest survey on violence against women shows extensive human rights abuse across Europe, which is underreported to the authorities and therefore not reflected by official data.[103]

Third, even though many women's rights seem to be achieved, at least in the Western world, history and recent events show a number of backlashes. This is what I have tried to demonstrate, among other things, in the three parts of my study. In the first part I sketched the struggle for women's equality in France from the early 17th century to the French revolution which ended in 1793 with the prohibition of women's organizations and women's political activities, and with the ban of feminine nouns, including the central notion of "citoyenne." Women had to fight for centuries for suffrage and to see equality inscribed in the *Universal Declaration of Human Rights* and the national constitutions; but even then, gender equality resolutions have not always been implemented. In the second part I outlined the legal steps toward the acceptance of a gender neutral language in official documents and in academia; these steps would suggest that the subject is closed, but recent events like the scandal in the French Parliament or the debates in the Austrian media show that the fight for an inclusive language still continues and that there is no end in sight. In the last part I have shown the ongoing debate about the Feminist Theory and Gender Studies chairs at Vienna University. The failed institutionalization of these fields of teaching and research is not only a backlash but also closes the doors for gender mainstreaming and diversity.

Today, the inconvenient women who fight for justice and rights are no longer executed by the guillotine as in the times of de Gouge, but

---

[101] See the Gender Equality page of the European Comission online: http://ec.europa.eu/justice/gender-equality/index_en.htm.
[102] See Eurostat's "Gender statistics up to may 2015," online: http://ec.europa.eu/eurostat/statistics-explained/index.php/Gender_statistics.
[103] See "Violence against women: an EU-wide survey. Main results report," online: http://fra.europa.eu/en/publication/2014/violence-against-women-eu-wide-survey-main-results-report.

language is still used to demonize and to silence them as Cassandras, to ridicule them as de Gournay once was, to fire them under some pretext, and to legally erase entire fields of feminist education and research. What "we" can hope is that there will always be not only Cassandras, but also women like de Gournay and de Gouge as well as honest men like Guyomar and that, when it comes to defend somebody's rights, "we" will not stay silent and look away.

Susanne Moser

THE CONCEPT OF RECOGNITION IN SIMONE DE BEAUVOIR'S *THE SECOND SEX*

When considered from a philosophical perspective, the concept of recognition has been introduced relatively recently. In *Multiculturalism and 'The Politics of Recognition'* Charles Taylor brings up the thesis that a connection exists between recognition and identity.[1] Identity as self-understanding of the human being, as consciousness of certain characteristics which make them human, depends at least partly upon recognition or non-recognition. Non-recognition or misinterpretation can cause suffering, some sort of repression and can leave his victims behind with tormenting self-hatred and painful wounds. Recognition is therefore a human basic need.

The philosophical concept of recognition originates in Hegel's work and its reference can be traced back to Fichte. Hegel's early works characterize the process of recognition still in an individual, intersubjective way, whereas this perspective is abandoned later increasingly in favor of a philosophy of the spirit. While Hegel's objective in his earlier works is to reconstruct the process of the formation of a universal consciousness through the struggle for recognition based on the actions and interactions of individual consciousnesses, in the *Phenomenology of Spirit* he concentrates on the experience and the manifestation of the spirit.[2]

---

[1] Charles Taylor, *Multiculturalism and 'The Politics of Recognition'*, Princeton: Princeton University Press 1992.
[2] This is the reason why Axel Honneth goes back to Hegel's earlier works, elaborating the thesis that social conflicts arise from the violation of moral claims leading to struggles for recognition. Axel Honneth, *Kampf um Anerkennung*, Frankfurt am Main: Suhrkamp 1994.

When dealing with the problem of the existence of the Other, Sartre refers in *Being and Nothingness* explicitly to Hegel's master-slave chapter in the *Phenomenology of Spirit*.[3] According to Sartre, "Hegel's brilliant intuition is to make me depend on the Other *in my being*. I am, he said, a being for-itself only through another."[4] Due to the fact that I must necessarily be an object for myself only over there in the Other, I must obtain from the Other the *recognition* of my being.[5] Thus, for Sartre, immense progress had been made: first of all, negation which constitutes the Other would be direct, inner and mutual and furthermore a negation that touches every consciousness deep within its being: "I find that being-for-others appears as a necessary condition for my being-for-myself."[6] However, Sartre also considers Hegel to be guilty of an epistemological optimism in assuming that through the authority of the Other's recognition of me and my recognition of the Other, an objective agreement is realized between the consciousnesses "I know that the Other knows me as himself."[7] But there is no common measure between the object-other and the I-subject. Furthermore, Hegel is also guilty of a more fundamental form of optimism, namely an ontological one, for in his eyes truth is the truth of the whole. Hegel himself assumes the perspective of truth, that is of the whole, in order to approach the problem of the Other: he does not put himself into an individual consciousness but moreover he forgets his own consciousness: he *is* the whole.[8]

1. The Master-Slave Dialectics in *The Second Sex*

In *The Second Sex* the Hegelian master-slave dialectics plays a pivotal role concerning the topic of recognition and the exclusion of

---

[3] A.V. Miller translates Hegel's chapter "Herrschaft und Knechtschaft" with "Lordship and Bondage" (see G. W. F. Hegel, *Phenomenology of Spirit*, Oxford: Oxford University Press 1977, p. 111-118).
[4] Jean-Paul Sartre, *Being and Nothingness*, transl. By Hazel E. Barnes, New York: Pocket Books, 1966above, p. 237.
[5] Ibid., p. 237.
[6] Ibid., p. 238.
[7] Ibid., p.240.
[8] Ibid., p.243.

women. Beauvoir writes that according to Hegel, the privilege of the master takes form when he risks his life in the struggle for recognition in order to gain and when he overcomes his fear of death and the spirit prevails over life. However, the one who surrenders, not having risked his life enough to succeed, emerges from this struggle as a slave. Nevertheless he had faced the same risk and therefore a sort of reciprocity can be seen between master and slave: in this struggle always being led by men, slaves are also granted a certain equality. "Whereas woman is basically an existent who gives life and does not risk *her* life; between her and the male there has been no combat."[9] For women had never entered this form of reciprocity, they became the absolute Other. Therefore, Beauvoir differentiates between the 'Other' and the 'absolute Other' where the latter can never acquire any sort of reciprocity. The misfortune on the part of the woman lies in the fact that she "is biologically destined for the repetition of Life"[10], whereas the modern women today rightfully demand "to be recognized as existents by the same right as men and not to subordinate existence to life, the human being to its animality."[11] Furthermore, Beauvoir writes in her historical overview in *The Second Sex* that the human race has always sought to escape its specific destiny. The support of life became for man an activity and a project through the invention of the tool, "but in maternity woman remained closely bound to her body, like an animal."[12] She maintains the life of the tribe by giving children their daily bread. "She remained doomed to immanence."[13] The woman was not creative in any field in contrast to the man who changed the world through his deeds, who transcended the given and brought forth the new: "He made conquest of foreign booty and bestowed it on the tribe; war, hunting, and fishing represented an expansion of existence, its projection toward the world. The male remained alone the incarnation of transcendence."[14]

---

[9] Simone de Beauvoir, *The Second Sex*, transl. by Howard M. Parshley, New York: Vintage Books, 1989, p. 64.
[10] Ibid., p. 64.
[11] Ibidem. p. 65.
[12] Ibid., p. 65.
[13] Ibid., p. 73.
[14] Ibid., p. 73.

The man gradually transformed his experience into action and the male principle triumphed in his imagination and his practical existence: "Spirit has prevailed over Life, transcendence over immanence, technique over magic, and reason over superstition."[15] The devaluation of woman represents – according to Beauvoir – a necessary stage in the history of humanity due to the fact that the woman based her prestige not on her own positive value but on the weakness of the man: "In woman are incarnated the disturbing mysteries of nature, and man escapes her hold when he frees himself from nature."[16] In his work he stands his ground against nature as a sovereign will and reinvents the world. At the same time he increases his access to the world. In this activity he puts his power to the test; he sets up goals and opened up roads toward them; "in brief; he found self-realization as an existent."[17] His only aim is not to sustain the world but to disrupt its limitations. Those nations though, Beauvoir surmises that are still under the influence of the mother gods and that have adhered to a matrilineal system remained at a primitive stage of civilization. Only after the man had started to dethrone the woman was he able to realize himself and to recognize the male principle of creative force, of light, of intelligence and of order.[18]

Beauvoir assumes that every society leans toward a patriarchal mode after man had acquired clearer self-consciousness, "once he dares to assert himself and offer resistance."[19] Even beforehand when still worshipping the magical powers of the woman, when he was still perplexed about the mysteries of Life, of Nature, and of Woman, he was never without his power. When, terrified by the dangerous magic of woman, he sets her up as the essential, it is he who poses her as such and thus he who really acts as the essential in this voluntary alienation. "In spite of the fecund powers that pervade her, man remains woman's master as he is the master of the fertile earth; she is

---

[15] Ibid., p. 75.
[16] Ibid., p. 75.
[17] Ibid., p. 63.
[18] Ibid., p. 76.
[19] Ibid., p. 73.

fated to be subjected, owned, exploited like the Nature whose magical fertility she embodies"[20].

The triumph of the patriarchate had neither been a matter of chance nor the result of violent revolution. "From Humanity's beginnings, their biological advantage has enabled the males to affirm their status as sole and sovereign subjects."[21]

Here, Beauvoir expresses the tension between humanity and the woman: humanity is not just a natural species that strives for sustaining its kind but wants to transcend itself. In setting himself up as the subject, man posits the woman as the Other, whereas the woman is placed as the Other by the man. "For the male it is always another male who is the fellow being, the other who is also the same, with whom reciprocal relations are established."[22]

Beauvoir points out, that we have to distinguish between two forms of alterity or Otherness.[23] One form of alterity – the category of the *Other* – is as basic as consciousness itself. A duality can be found in the most primitive societies and the oldest mythologies: "that of the Self and the Other."[24] The other form of alterity is the category of the absolute Other: "To be the absolute Other" Beauvoir points out means to be "without reciprocity."[25] To the degree at which woman is regarded as the absolute Other – that is to say, whatever her magic powers, as the inessential – it is impossible to consider her as another subject.[26] Because woman was made into the absolute Other she was excluded from the status of the subject. The woman, concludes Beauvoir, was not recognized by the man as equal because, for biological reasons, she remained subjected to reproduction. This in turn let her not participate in the struggle for recognition out of the initial *Mitsein* in order to place herself as a subject. She never shared man's way of working and thinking, because she remained in bondage to life's mysterious processes. The male did not

---

[20] Ibid., p. 73.
[21] Ibid., p. 77.
[22] Ibid., p. 70.
[23] Ibid., p. 71.
[24] Ibid., p. xxii.
[25] Ibid., p. 141.
[26] Ibid., p. 71.

recognize in her a being like himself. "What was unfortunate for her was that while not becoming a fellow work-man with the laborer, she was also excluded from the human *Mitsein*."[27]

Here Beauvoir argues again in a contradictory manner: whereas on the one hand *Mitsein* comprises the part of life from which the woman had failed to differentiate herself, namely the familial part, the area of reproduction, on the other hand Beauvoir considers *Mitsein* as the area of active work, the area of production where the master-slave dialectics gains importance. The slave is able to achieve recognition through work, for the master-slave-dialects have according to Beauvoir "its source in the reciprocity that exists between free beings."[28] A man can challenge and combat the sovereignty of the Other at any time. That is the reason why the master is always worried that the slave could rebel against him and challenge his dominance.

Even as a slave the man preserves his initial freedom that makes him challenge and combat the sovereignty of his master. The woman on the other hand does not represent any danger to the man because she does not challenge his sovereignty, nor does she combat it. Whereas the other man, even as a slave, is considered as equal inasmuch as he is freedom and transcendence, the woman does not dispose of this initial freedom. We are here confronted with a problem that has already been discussed in connection with *The Ethics of Ambiguity*. Beauvoir regards the human being as an ambiguous existence, as freedom and necessity, transcendence and facticity, being-in-itself and being-for-itself. In *The Second Sex*, Beauvoir makes a further step: man remains transcendence and being-for-itself even as a slave and from this position he is able to question the dominance of the master and fight against him. The woman however, represents the absolute Other, that is denied from any form of equality and reciprocity. In this case the woman is reduced to a passive victim, a relative being that had been set by men and that is dependent on them and only existing through them.

---

[27] Ibid., p. 77.
[28] Ibid., p. 141.

Beauvoir, however, had always resisted seeing the woman solely as a victim. In her work, we are therefore apparently confronted with two contradicting lines of argumentation. One showing that the woman was set as the absolute Other by the man and thus condemned to immanence. That is the reason for her being unable to participate in the struggle for recognition and therefore never accomplishing the status of a subject. But without the participation in the struggle for recognition, no independent existence as a subject can take place. The condition for participation is defined according to gender: while slaves are able to participate, women are excluded from participation due to their biological determination. When adhering to this argumentation, the process of recognition represents the necessary prerequisite for being a subject. Thus, every exclusion means remaining in the state of being-in-itself, of immanence, and to be unable to realize being a subject, being-for-itself and freedom. In this approach the environment, the corresponding situation, the Other and the general conditions in society play a decisive role: they determine whether I am a subject or whether I am able to become one. Therefore, I am dependent upon factors that I cannot control. Beauvoir, however, also attempts another direction in her argumentation: every human being is an autonomous freedom, regardless of his or her situation. Every human being is transcendence and freedom from the beginning of his/her life. The woman discovers and chooses herself as an autonomous subject even if men force her to adopt the role of the Other. What particularly signals the situation of woman, Beauvoir points out in the introduction to *The Second Sex*, is "that she – a free and autonomous being like all human creatures – nevertheless finds herself living in a world where men compel her to assume the status of the Other."[29] Thus, it looks as if Beauvoir would develop two different models of recognition. On one side, the model of recognition serves the purpose of bringing forth subjects and on the other side, already constituted subjects and autonomous freedoms come together.

Yet Beauvoir does not make this distinction. Her interpretation of the Hegelian master-slave dialectics and the focus on work as a rele-

---

[29] Ibid., p. xxxv.

vant aspect of liberation is strongly determined by Marxist ideas. Both Beauvoir and Sartre turned toward and tackled Marxism after World War II. Additionally it shall be noted that the Hegelian master-slave dialectics would never have assumed such a central position in the history of ideas as it later did without Karl Marx. Beauvoir's master-slave dialectics have to be interpreted therefore by taking the Marxist thesis of liberation through work into account without however, losing track of Beauvoir's individual approach to Hegel.[30]

Besides this, exclusion from work is not the only reason for transforming the woman into the absolute Other, rather the worst curse that was laid upon woman, was "that she should be excluded from these warlike forays. For it is not in giving life but in risking life that man is raised above the animal; that is why superiority has been accorded in humanity not to the sex that brings forth but to that which kills."[31]

Recognition is therefore only given to those that overcome life and do not fear death. The master risks his life in such a way that he prefers death to surrender, while the slave is not ready to risk his life and prefers a life in servitude as opposed to death. Femininity however is confronted with the inverse problem: it does not celebrate death as overcoming life but gives life by overcoming death. The woman risks her life every time she gives birth; and despite that she

---

[30] There is no doubt that a whole generation of left-orientated French intellectuals was influenced by Hyppolite's and Kojève's interpretations of Hegel. The thesis of Eva Lundgren-Gothlin that "the influence of Hegel evident in *The Second Sex* is mediated via the French tradition of Hegelianism, and particularly by the interpretation of Kojève" seems to me to be problematic. Eva Lundgren-Gothlin, *Sex and Existence. Simone de Beauvoir's the Second Sex*, London: Wesleyan University Press 1996, p. 67.
Beauvoir was very sceptical about all concepts of salvation – either through history or through Spirit. Beauvoir reports in her memoirs that she had a discussion with Queneau about the 'end of history': Queneau, who had been initiated into Hegelianism by Kojève, thought that one day all individuals would be reconciled in the triumphant unit of Spirit. 'But what if I have a pain in my foot?' I said. '*We* shall have a pain in your foot,' Queneau replied. While, as we can see, Beauvoir refers here explicitly to Queneau, she never refers to Kojève in any of her works. Simone de Beauvoir *Force of Circumstances*, transl. By R. Howard, Harmondsworth: Penguin Books, p. 43.
[31] Simone de Beauvoir, *The Second Sex*, op.cit., p. 64.

is excluded from the entitled recognition – at least in a model of war ethics as espoused by Hegel. She gives life, she does not take it. Far from receiving recognition for the production of new life this is rather, at least in a society that considers overcoming life as being of higher importance than life itself, the starting point for female suppression. In a patriarchal society the exclusion of the woman is based on her biological ability to give life. The power and recognition that she deserves due to her ability to give life is taken from her in the patriarchate: she is reduced to an instrument of reproduction, to an object. She is under the dominance of the man who seizes control over the female body. However, it was to take several years after the first publication of *The Second Sex* for Beauvoir to regard herself as a radical feminist and fight for birth control and abortion.

Due to the fact that the woman does not engage in a hostile confrontation with the man she represents, according to Beauvoir, the embodiment of a male dream: "She is the wished-for-intermediary between nature, the stranger to man."[32] She opposes him with neither the hostile silence of nature nor the hard requirement of a reciprocal relation. Thanks to her, there is a means for escaping that implacable dialectics of master and slave which has its source in the reciprocity that exists between free beings.[33] This is the tragedy of the "unfortunate human consciousness": each separate conscious being aspires to set himself up alone as sovereign subject. Each tries to fulfill himself by reducing the other to slavery. But the slave, through his works and fears, senses himself somehow as the essential and by a dialectical inversion, it is the master who seems to be the inessential.[34] In the case of the woman, however, man hopes to be able to escape these relentless dialectics by setting the woman as the absolute Other. "Woman thus seems to be the inessential, who never goes back to being the essential, to be the absolute Other, without reciprocity."[35]

Yvanka B. Raynova shows very clearly that Beauvoir supplements Sartre's initial project of the human being, i.e. to want to make

---

[32] Ibid., p. 140.
[33] Ibid., p. 141.
[34] Ibid., p. 140.
[35] Ibid., p. 141.

himself into God, with a gender specific aspect: Sartre's initial project does not include everyone but only men. In the case of the women, we encounter the complementary initial project of being-for-others It was Sartre's merit to point out that the fundamental project of being-for-itself, namely an in-itself-for-itself, that is God and thus grounding for itself, to want to become its being, is doomed to fail. Yet it was Beauvoir who brought the initial project of women into the open, namely the female project of being-for-men.[36] This project – according to Beauvoir – is however, just as inauthentic: "Woman is pursuing a dream of submission, man a dream of identification."[37] Beauvoir emphasizes that women, in never having set themselves as a subject, have never created any religion or literature of their own: "Woman do not set themselves up as Subject and hence have erected no virile myth in which their projects are reflected: they have no religion or poetry of their own: they still dream through the dreams of men. Gods made by males are the gods they worship."[38] The Woman sees herself and makes her choices not in accordance with her true nature in itself, "but as man defines her."[39]

The Myth of Femininity

Beauvoir explores in *The Second Sex* the role of male ideas and myths regarding women which form the basis for her exclusion as a sort of simulacra. In order to gain better understanding of the nature of the myth, Beauvoir proposes to take a look at what it was used for.[40] For it is difficult to describe a myth; "it cannot be grasped or encompassed; it haunts the human consciousness without ever ap-

---

[36] Yvanka B. Raynova, *Das andere Geschlecht im postmodernen Kontext*, in *L'Homme. Zeitschrift für feministische Geschichtswissenschaft*, 10. Jg. Heft 1, Wien: Böhlau 1999, p. 89. See also: idem. *Le deuxième sexe: Une lecture postmoderne*. In: *Le deuxième sexe: Une relecture en trois temps, 1949-1971-1999*, sous la direction de Cécile Coderre et Marie-Blanche Tahon, Montréal : les éditions du remue-ménage, 2001, p. 141.
[37] Simone de Beauvoir, *The Second Sex*, op.cit., p. 719.
[38] Ibid., p. 142.
[39] Ibid., p. 137.
[40] Ibid., p. 260.

pearing before it in fixed form."[41] For example, women can be seen as: idol, slave, source of life and power of darkness, the elemental silence of truth and deceitfulness, chatter and lie; healer and witch; prey of the man and his downfalls. This comes from not regarding woman positively, such as she herself considers herself to be, but negatively, such as she appears to man.[42] Beauvoir points out that the myth of woman, sublimating an immutable aspect of the human condition – namely, the "division" of humanity into two classes of individuals – is a static myth. "It projects into the realm of Platonic ideas a reality that is directly experienced or is conceptualized on a basis of experience; in place of fact, value, significance, knowledge, empirical law, it substitutes a transcendental Idea, timeless, unchangeable, necessary.[43] The myth is a transcendent idea that escapes the mental grasp entirely. Thus, as against the dispersed, contingent, and multiple existences of actual woman, mythical thought opposes "the eternal feminine, unique and changeless."[44] If the definition provided for this concept is contradicted by the behavior of women in flesh and blood, it is the latter who are wrong: we are told not that femininity is a false entity, but that the women concerned are not feminine. The contrary facts of experience are impotent against myth. "To pose Woman is to pose the absolute Other, without reciprocity, denying against all experience that she is a subject, a fellow human being."[45]

Beauvoir demonstrates that only few myths have proven to be of such advantage for the ruling caste as that of the woman: it justifies all privileges and even authorizes their abuse.[46] The woman is necessary for the joy of the man and his triumph to the point where it could be said that if she had not already existed, men would have invented her. And indeed, Beauvoir writes: "They did invent her."[47] The representation of the world, like the world itself, is the work of men; they describe it from their own point of view, which they con-

---

[41] Ibid., p. 143.
[42] Ibid., p. 143.
[43] Ibid., p. 253.
[44] Ibid., p. 253.
[45] Ibid., p. 253.
[46] Ibid., p. 255.
[47] Ibid., p. 186.

fuse with absolute truth. "Thus humanity is male"[48] Beauvoir follows, and man defines woman not in herself but as relative to him; she is not regarded as an autonomous being. Her determination and differentiation is based on the relation to man, whereas his is not in reference to her. "She is the incidental, the inessential as opposed to the essential. He is the Subject, he is the Absolute, she is the Other."[49]

Men wanted to sustain their male predominance. That is the reason they had invented the separation in society between immanence and transcendence: "Men have presumed to create a feminine domain – the kingdom of life, of immanence – only in order to lock up women therein."[50] The man likes to make reference here to Hegel who legitimized these two separate areas through his philosophy: "With other men he has relations in which values are involved; he is a free agent confronting other free agents under laws fully recognized by all; but with woman – she was invented for the purpose – he casts off his responsibility of existence, he abandons himself to the mirage of his *en-soi*, or fixed, lower nature, he puts himself on the plane of inauthenticity."[51] The woman on the other hand does not only believe that truth is something *other* than what men claim it to be. She recognizes, rather, that there is not *any* fixed truth.[52] Not only the becoming of life, not only the magical phenomena that surround her and undermine the idea of causality prompt her suspicion against the principle of identity: in the midst of the male world that she herself belongs to, she perceives in herself the ambiguity that is innate in every principle, each value, everything that exists. She is aware of the fact that male morality is a deception in respect to the woman. Art, literature and philosophy all represent attempts "to found the world anew on a human liberty: that of the individual creator; to entertain such a pretension, one must first unequivocally assume the status of a being who has liberty."[53] The ability to set oneself as autonomous freedom was however explicitly denied to women. In order to enable the

---

[48] Ibid., p. xxii.
[49] Ibid., p. xxii.
[50] Ibid., p. 65.
[51] Ibid., p. 613.
[52] Ibid., p. 612.
[53] Ibid., p. 711.

woman to become a creator herself, all the restrictions that have been imposed on women would have to be eliminated.

Beauvoir notes here that Hegel's philosophy produces the exclusion of women. However much Hegel's philosophy implies a potential for emancipation and change, it creates the areas of immanence and transcendence in the first place thus enabling the legitimization of the dominance of man over woman. The areas of family-immanence and public-transcendence are not complementary in Hegel's work but rather, as has already been shown, outlined in a hierarchical way. The status of the subject can be attained only through participation in public life, i.e. in transcendence.

Beauvoir demonstrates that Hegel's philosophy implies an irresolvable contradiction in respect to gender relations. On the one hand, Hegel's philosophy could be seen as the philosophy of freedom par excellence, as its aim is the gradual realization of freedom and transcendence in the world and not merely a shifting of transcendence into an afterlife. On the other hand however, women are excluded from access to transcendence because of their nature. They are kept in immanence including the entire areas of reproduction, education, care and interpersonal relations that make a society viable in the first place. If women, for example, would break out of these areas and leave them behind in order to set themselves as subjects in the area of transcendence, this would inevitably cause a lot of troubles. Thus, the myth of woman is utilized for imprisoning women in the private sphere. This implies several benefits: firstly, the provision of the vital area of reproduction is secured, secondly, it enables the exclusion of women from recognition and competition. In this conception that is neither based on complementarities nor on mutuality, immanence represents a hierarchically lower level that is to be transcended and that is equated with femininity. Thus it is not surprising that all activities connected to this area not only have no value but that femininity itself is regarded as something that is without any value and that needs to be transcended. Only to take part in the struggle for recognition will enable women to attain the status of a subject. If one is to adhere to this conception then femininity has to be given up, in order to be able to become a subject.

Even though Beauvoir is aware of the pitfalls within the Hegelian system, she partly follows the same misogynous tendency in *The Second Sex* by equating the nature of the woman, her biological determination, as well as the activities connected to reproduction, with immanence, in order to depreciate them and to contrast them to transcendence. Consequently, such activities are not considered as projects. Here Beauvoir adheres to the nature-culture-problem encountered in modernity: modernity judges humans on what they do. Modernity assumes a depreciative position toward all processes that occur by nature, without creation by humans, as nature is as a stage that requires transgression and dominance by the human being.

Beauvoir assumes that the myth of woman can emerge only in those cultures that have attained a certain level of prosperity: "The myth of woman is a luxury. It can appear only if man escapes from the urgent demands of his needs."[54] According to Beauvoir the fellah of ancient Egypt, the peasant Bedouin, the medieval artisan and the contemporary worker has in the requirements of work and poverty relations with his particular woman companion which are too definite for her to be embellished with an aura either auspicious or inauspicious.[55] Here Beauvoir addresses an issue that is essential for the understanding of *The Second Sex*: that is the limitation of the thesis of the woman as the absolute Other from a regional and historical perspective as well as from a sociopolitical perspective. The woman was not excluded at all times and in all nations from the active *Mitsein,* from work. Amongst the medieval artisans, work still took place within the domestic area where the woman still played an essential economic role. Also, in the case of the fellah in ancient Egypt, the women were responsible for the economic provision of the household. Beauvoir furthermore points out that the myth of woman did not find its adequate place in the working classes: it was poverty that forced women to work and prevented them to be turned into the absolute Other.

---

[54] Ibid., p. 260.
[55] Ibid.

Mutual Recognition: Friendship

In *The Second Sex* Beauvoir seeks a way out of the endless struggle for recognition, she looks for "a means for escaping that implacable dialectic of master and slave."[56] Beauvoir attempts to find a possibility to encounter another subject as a subject, without necessarily having to oppose it from the start. She sees this possibility in friendship. In friendship it is possible to rise above this conflict "if each individual freely recognizes the Other,"[57] each regarding himself and the Other simultaneously as object and as subject in a reciprocal manner.

It is striking that Beauvoir considers this reciprocity realized specifically in the case of lesbian women: "in exact reciprocity each is at once subject and object, sovereign and slave."[58] However, it is not the refusal of wanting to make oneself into an object that leads the way for women into homosexuality. Most lesbians rather try to cultivate the treasures of their femininity. A man would be able to reveal the existence of her flesh *for herself*, not however for what it represents *to others*. "It is only when her fingers trace the body of a woman whose fingers in turn trace her body that the miracle of the mirror is accomplished."[59] Caressing is not a means for appropriating the partner but rather to gradually find oneself through her. The possibility exists to try out different roles and to follow new paths where both partners can remain autonomous subjects. In spite of her appreciation of female homosexuality Beauvoir does not draw any conclusions for a political strategy. Beauvoir thus in her theory does not elaborate further on the concept of female homosexuality as an expression for mutual recognition.

The concept of friendship is only mentioned briefly by Beauvoir in order to make way for the master-slave dialectics thereafter. For friendship, she points out, is not an easy virtue. It is moreover the highest achievement of the human being that paves his way to the

---

[56] Ibid., p. 141.
[57] Ibid., p. 140.
[58] Ibid., p. 416.
[59] Ibid.

truth. "But this true nature is that of a struggle unceasingly begun, unceasingly abolished, it requires man to outdo himself at every moment."[60] This authentic moral attitude, however, can only be achieved by the human being "when he renounces *mere being* to assume his position as an existent."[61] Through this transformation he/she also renounces all possessions, for possession is one way of seeking mere being. It is the existence of other men/women that tears each man/woman out of his/her immanence and enables him/her to fulfill the truth of his/her being, to complete himself/herself though transcendence, through escape toward some objective, through enterprise.

Even if not completely elaborated on, a new concept of the subject is proposed by Beauvoir in a few short lines: the subject does not set himself/herself by opposing and proving his/her only authority against the Other, moreover the subject is formed only through the existence of another human being, who enables him/her to live his/her transcendence and his/her project. Without the help of other people, without the recognition through others, I may remain helplessly in the state of immanence. Only the encounter with other humans who support me, open up to me the joys of transcendence and offer me the possibilities for realizing my projects, who actually open my eyes to the fact that I am able to create my own projects; only this makes it possible for me to fulfill myself as transcendence. The freedom of the other that confirms my freedom can in turn be confirmed in his/her freedom as well, however this does not have to necessarily happen. Another possibility would be to arrive at a conflicting situation with one another. Inasmuch as the subject actually sets himself/herself through his/her projects as transcendence, conflicts can arise. However this is not imperative, moreover a project could also be enabled through the Other in the first place. Friendship, therefore, is according to Beauvoir "a true alterity."[62] I recognize that there exists a consciousness separate from mine and substantially identical to mine.

---

[60] Ibid., p. 140.
[61] Ibid.
[62] Ibid.

Thus we can differentiate between three types of alterity in Beauvoir's work:

1. Alterity as the absolute Other: this conception determines Beauvoir's thesis of the woman as the absolute Other. It is the man who is the subject positing the woman as the absolute Other, without her being able to reverse this position.

2. Alterity as the constituting characteristic of identity: the subject is only able to set himself/herself by opposing an existing Other and attempts to dominate this Other that stakes the same claim. In the struggle for recognition, a common level is now sought where the Otherness can be transformed in favor of sameness, for Otherness basically represents danger. This concept determines Beauvoir's master-slave-dialectics;

3. Alterity as the condition for friendship where each individual freely recognizes the Other, each regarding himself/herself and the Other simultaneously as object and as subject in a reciprocal manner, without seeking to dominate the Other.

Here, Beauvoir attempts in a few lines to contrast the absolute claim of the subject of dominance with a new subject relation, namely that of friendship. While the subject of dominance requires the Other for limiting and negating it in order to be able to set himself/herself as a subject, in friendship I recognize that the Other has a consciousness as well, which is coequal with mine, that he or she is also freedom and transcendence and thus I do not try to set myself as the only sovereign consciousness. It is not attempted to abolish this alterity, but rather the real, concrete alterity is the prerequisite for real friendship.

Beauvoir introduces here a concept of alterity and mutual recognition that unfortunately she fails to develop any further. Therefore many questions remain unanswered. When she says in reference to Hegel that in every consciousness a fundamental hostility against any other consciousness can be found and it stakes the claim to set itself as the only sovereign subject, how is then such an alterity possible? How can it develop? Is the only possible way to become a subject to be involved in the struggle for recognition? Is this a necessary condition for a moral attitude? Does humanity have to transgress this process in order to be ready for true friendship? Does this imply for women that they have to enter the struggle for recognition, or is another way possible as well?

As we can see, Beauvoir does not reserve as much room for positive solutions as she does for conflicts. This is not only found in the case of friendship but also in that of recognition in general. However, the key to all positive solutions can be found in the problem of the subject, as I have already shown.[63]

---

[63] See Susanne Moser, *Freedom and Recognition in the Work of Simone de Beauvoir*, Frankfurt am Main, Berlin, Bern, Bruxelles, New York, Oxford: Peter Lang, 2008, pp. 162-213.

4

Sonia Kruks

BEAUVOIR, FOUCAULT, AND "POSTMODERN FEMINISM"

The best of what "postmodern feminism"[1] has so far developed is a series of radical glosses on Simone de Beauvoir's now classic starting point: "one is not born a woman: one becomes one." For, like the work of Beauvoir, postmodern approaches enable us to de-essentialize and de-naturalize the concept of "woman." In particular, creative appropriations of Foucault's genealogical methods have enabled feminist scholars to explore the ways in which representations of "woman" have shifted over time. His insights into the inseparability of power and knowledge, and his explorations of the disciplinary practices that produce "subjectified" subjects, have also made his methods a valuable resource for a wide range of feminist analyses of women's subordination.

But there are also difficulties for feminism – and other emancipatory movements – in appropriating Foucault too fully or too uncritically. In reading Foucault both through and against Beauvoir in this paper, I seek to illuminate and address some of these difficulties. By pointing not only to the divergences but also to the striking complementarities between the two thinkers, I aim to challenge views of Beauvoir and Foucault as advocates, respectively, of "Enlightenment" and "post-Enlightenment" philosophies that are starkly antithetical. For the binary oppositions between Enlightenment and post-Enlightenment thought, between modernity and postmodernity, that too many pro-

---

[1] I use this term somewhat reluctantly since it can cover such a diversity of positions. However, it does connote an intellectual style and a cluster of loosely shared assumptions and, given also its extensive utilization within feminist (and other social) theory, it seems necessary to employ it.

tagonists on either "side" of recent debates have accepted, are themselves highly problematic.

More specifically, I argue that Foucault's insightful account of the production of "subjectified" subjects is, as it stands, still inadequate and incomplete. It either remains at the level of description or else, at an explanatory level, falls into a version of crude functionalism. In reading Foucault through the lenses of Beauvoir we can find means more adequately to explain what Foucault describes. I also argue that reading Foucault through Beauvoir enables us to reintroduce into his analyses notions of personal agency and moral accountability that remain important for any project of emancipatory politics. Foucault claims to deny the importance of such notions, yet his work still tacitly presupposes them. Beauvoir's concern with the ethical aspects of subjectification can be used to bring both greater intellectual coherence and explicit moral import to Foucault's work.

Foucault's work is, of course, far from monolithic. In what follows I am concerned with the Foucault of the mid-1970s; that is, the Foucault whose focus is less on the "care" of the self than on the anatomopolitical production of the self. For this is the Foucault with whom feminist theory has most pervasively engaged: the Foucault of *Discipline and Punish* (1975), the first volume of *The History of Sexuality* (1976), and the essays published in English in *Power/Knowledge* (1980), a thinker whose focus is on the inseparability of power and knowledge, and on their constitutive role in the production of the subjectified subject through disciplinary and normalizing practices. This is a Foucault for whom subjectivity is so thoroughly produced "from the outside in"[2], by the micro-practices of power, that to ask questions about the degree to which freedom or moral capacity might be attributes of subjecthood appears simply irrelevant.

It is also the Foucault whose work has a distinctly functionalist, even a teleological, cast insofar as disciplinary practices are said to take on purposive attributes that have traditionally been ascribed to the individuated human subject. Discipline is frequently personified or anthropomorphized. It knows what it is doing; it acts in an intentional,

---

[2] Elizabeth Grosz, *Volatile Bodies: Toward a Corporeal Feminism*. Bloomington: Indiana University Press, 1994.

goal-oriented, rational manner, to perform necessary social functions. For example, Foucault writes: "discipline *had to solve* a number of problems for which the old economy of power was not equipped (...) *it arrests or regulates* movements; *it clears up* confusion (...) *It must also master* all forces that are formed from the very constitution of an organized multiplicity; *it must neutralize* the effects of counter-power that spring from them and which form a resistance to the power that wishes to dominate it"[3] (emphases added).

This is not to deny that one can still find reflections on freedom in Foucault's work; but freedom is not an attribute of the subject, or of individual agents. Rather, freedom is cast as the "insurrection" of subjugated knowledges[4], or as the emergence of "transgressive" discourse that has purpose of its own: transgression too has agency, but no specific authors. One might talk not only of a history without a subject, or of a text without a subject, but also of agency and freedom without a subject. As with discipline, Foucault personifies transgression attributing to it intentional agency rather than attributing such agency to persons. He writes, for example, that "transgression does not seek to oppose one thing to another (...) its role is to measure the excessive distance that it opens at the heart of the limit and to trace the flashing line that causes the limit to arise."[5]

"What difference does it make who is speaking?" In his essay, "What Is an Author?" Foucault suggests that the notion of individual authorship emerged at a particular moment in the history of ideas: a

---

[3] Michel Foucault, *Discipline and Punish. The Birth of the Prison*. Transl. by Alan Sheridan. London: Penguin Books, [1975] 1977, p. 219.

[4] Michel Foucault, *Power/Knowledge: Selected Interviews & Other Writings, 1972-1977*. New York: Pantheon, 1980, p. 84.

[5] Michel Foucault, *Language, Counter-Memory, Practice. Selected Essays and Interviews*. Edited and translated by David E. Bouchard. Ithaca: Cornell University Press, 1977, p. 35. The most sustained attempt to date to extract a theory of freedom from Foucault is perhaps Dumm's. Dumm makes a strong case that Foucault effectively challenges the "liberal" notion of the "democratic individual" as "the exclusive site of freedom" (Thomas Dumm, *Michel Foucault and the Politics of Freedom*. Thousand Oaks: Sage Publications, 1996.

1996, 5). However, his work does not explore issues of freedom raised by an alternative conception of the self, such as Beauvoir's, that does not neatly correspond with the liberal model.

moment when "individualization" came to be privileged. That moment, he argues, has now passed: "it is a matter of depriving the subject (or its substitute) of its role as originator, and of analyzing the subject as a variable and complex function of discourse"[6]. The issue of authorship, then, is part of a wider debate about the status of "the subject," about whether human actors are knowing and volitional subjects, and about freedom. But above all, for Foucault (and here we must focus on his particularity) "the subject" in question is the subject of French phenomenology. For there is (to psychologize in a way he would have detested) something obsessive in Foucault's relationship to phenomenology: the Sartrean Father has to be killed over and over again. Long after we might have thought phenomenology to be dead in France, Foucault continued to feel the necessity repeatedly to exterminate it. For example, in a 1977 interview he stated:

> I don't believe the problem can be resolved by historicizing the subject, as posited by the phenomenologists, fabricating a subject that evolves through the course of history. One has to dispense with the constituent subject, to get rid of the subject itself, that's to say, to arrive at an analysis which can account for the constitution of the subject within a historical framework (...) genealogy (...) is a form of history which can account for the constitution of knowledges, discourses, domains of objects etc., without having to make reference to a subject which is either transcendental in relation to the field of events or runs in its empty sameness throughout the course of history.[7]

This statement opposes as stark alternatives, on the one hand a conception of the subject as "constituent" (or constituting) and as "transcendental" to history, that is, unsituated; on the other a conception of

---

[6] Michel Foucault, "What is an Author?" *The Foucault Reader*. New York: Pantheon Books, [1979] 1984, p. 118.
[7] Michel Foucault, *Power/Knowledge: Selected Interviews & Other Writings, 1972-1977*. New York: Pantheon, 1980, p. 117. Moreover the embarrassing evidence of Foucault's own youthful embrace of phenomenology has to be deliberately expunged from the author's presentation of his "work." Thus, in an interview published as late as 1983 (the year prior to his death) Foucault referred to *Madness and Civilization* as his "first" book ([1983] 1988, 23). In doing so this man, who claimed he wrote "to have no face" ([1969] 1972, 17), deliberately (mis)presented his "work" so as to exclude from it his earliest, and still phenomenologically influenced book, *Mental Illness and Psychology* ([1954] 1976).

the subject as constituted and to be analyzed (through genealogy) as no more than an "effect" of its historical framework. In it we find posed those overly simple dualities, between humanism and anti-humanism, between "Enlightenment" and "postmodernity," that we need to put into question. For in order to account (with Foucault) for the weight of social structures, discourses and practices in the formation of the subject, and yet still to acknowledge (against Foucault) that element of freedom which enables us also to consider the self as a particular and intentional agent that is to some degree responsible for what it does, we need a far more complex account of the subject than Foucault would appear to grant us.[8]

It is with this in mind that I return to Beauvoir and read Foucault through and against her. For much of her painstaking and detailed account in *The Second Sex* of the young girl's *formatio*[9] and the perpetuation of "femininity" could be re-told in the Foucauldian modes of "the political technology of the body," of "discipline," of "normalization," and of "panopticism." Yet Beauvoir still adheres to a notion of the *repression* of freedom that Foucault would not endorse. However suppressed, however "disciplined," it is still freedom-made-immanent, that distinguishes even the most constituted human subject from a trained animal. A real repression – or oppression – of the self is always possible for Beauvoir. For Foucault – at least as he expressly presents his position – this is not the case. I will pursue this divergence primarily through the notion of "panopticism" of the place of the gaze or look in producing docility, as Foucault and Beauvoir respectively treat it. For Beauvoir, "becoming a woman" also involves subjectification through what Foucault will call panoptic practices. But to understand this process of "becoming" we must also explore the ways in which subjectification is lived and taken up by the subject, be it in modes of

---

[8] Thus James Miller observes, in the Preface to his account of Foucault's life and work, that (perhaps contra Foucault himself) "I was forced to ascribe to Foucault a persistent and purposeful self, inhabiting one and the same body throughout his mortal life, more or less consistently accounting for his actions and attitudes to others as well as himself, and understanding his life as a teleologically structured quest" (Miller 1993, 7).

[9] The English translator of *The Second Sex*, Howard M. Parshley, has unfortunately translated Beauvoir's chapter heading, "*Formation*," as "The Formative Years," thus weakening the notion of an active production of the self implied by the French term.

complicity, of resistance, or both. This "lived" aspect of subjectification cannot be accessed through Foucault's explicit framework of analysis yet, I suggest, his own analyses actually require that we acknowledge and consider it.

Panopticism is, according to Foucault, the quintessential form of the method of "hierarchical observation" that is integral to much disciplinary power. It is a mechanism "in which the techniques that make it possible to see induce effects of power."[10] It is a crucial (though certainly not the sole) component of those modern disciplinary practices, which produce the normalized subject, both in formal disciplinary institutions and beyond. In Bentham's ideal prison, in which each isolated inmate lives – and *knows* himself to live – under continual inspection from the all-seeing (but anonymous) eye of the guard, the major effect of the Panopticon is "to induce in the inmate a state of conscious and permanent visibility that assures the automatic functioning of power."[11] Interiorizing the scrutinizing gaze to which he (or she) is subjected, the inmate becomes effectively (and efficiently) self-policing:

> He who is subjected to a field of visibility, and who *knows* it, *assumes responsibility* for the constraints of power; *he makes them play* spontaneously upon himself; *he inscribes in himself* the power relation in which *he simultaneously plays both roles*; he becomes the principle of his own subjection.[12] (emphases added)

Panopticism is not confined to particular institutions, such as the prison or the asylum. On the contrary, Foucault conceives it to be a general "modality of power" in normalizing societies such as ours. Moreover, women are subject to (and subjects of) what Foucault refers to as "the minute disciplines, the panopticisms of every day", in a particularly all-encompassing and complex manner that he does not himself explore. Indeed, Beauvoir's account of how one "becomes a woman" intriguingly anticipates Foucault's later account of panopti-

---

[10] Michel Foucault, *Discipline and Punish. The Birth of the Prison*. Transl. by Alan Sheridan. London: Penguin Books, [1975] 1977, pp. 170-171.
[11] Michel Foucault, *Discipline and Punish. The Birth of the Prison*. Transl. by Alan Sheridan. London: Penguin Books, [1975] 1977, p. 210.
[12] Ibid., pp. 202-203.

cism. As she describes it, becoming a woman requires developing an awareness of one's "permanent visibility," learning continually to view oneself through the eyes of the generalized (male) inspecting gaze and, in so doing, taking up as one's own project those "constraints of power" that femininity entails. But becoming a woman is, for Beauvoir, still an intentional process, even though it is en-acted within the constraints of power. Thus questions that Foucault leaves hanging in mid-air, concerning *how* this modality of power functions, are more adequately addressed by Beauvoir.

Foucault is (to put it politely) sometimes a slippery thinker. His previously cited claim, that we need "to get rid of the subject itself," and his affirmations that the subject comes into being as simply the effect of power, are tacitly put into question by passages such as the one I just quoted from *Discipline and Punish*. Such passages imply something else: an active, even, one could argue, a quasi-constituting subject; a conscious subject who "knows" that he is visible; one who "assumes responsibility" for the effects of power on himself, and who is active in playing "both roles," that of scrutinizer and scrutinized. But just how and why does the panoptic gaze induce such an active compliance? It is not clear. "Just a gaze," Foucault says. "An inspecting gaze which each individual under its weight will end by interiorizing to the point that he is his own overseer, each individual exercising this surveillance over, and against, himself."[13] But how and why does an individual interiorize the gaze? What kind of subjectivity is capable of such an interiorization? Or, most importantly, of resisting it? For, as Foucault acknowledges, there has also been "effective resistance" to various forms of panoptic scrutiny.[14]

But while Foucault's own analyses actually call for an account of the subject as both constituted and constituting, as playing "both roles," his concern to distance himself from his phenomenological fathers precluded him from acknowledging this. Thus his explicit pronouncements that "the subject" is produced through panoptic and other disciplinary "subjectifying" practices, and the implicit presuppositions

---

[13] Michel Foucault, *Power/Knowledge: Selected Interviews & Other Writings, 1972-1977*. New York: Pantheon, 1980, p. 155.
[14] Ibid., p. 162.

of his account come to be at odds with each other. Foucault claims that, "power relations can materially penetrate the body in depth, without depending even on the mediation of the subject's own representations. If power takes hold of the body, this isn't through its having first to be interiorized in people's consciousnesses."[15] Yet, we have seen, panoptic power *does* have to be interiorized in a way that engages consciousness; and if its interiorization can be resisted this implies also that, in some manner and to some degree, individuals may choose how to respond to it. Resistance cannot be explained solely as the result of the self-functioning of transgressive discourses, or of the deployment of subjugated knowledges (though it might be incited or invited by these). On the contrary, it also involves individual responses that imply some play of intentional consciousness, even of what we might call freedom.

Foucault reverses traditional forms of mind-body dualism by privileging the body as the site of the formation of the self, yet he is still caught up in this dualism. If the interiorization of power takes place through "the body," then it can of course bypass that – allegedly – distinct entity called "consciousness." But if, with Beauvoir (who here draws on Merleau-Ponty) we insist that the body is *not* distinct from consciousness but rather is the *site* of their interconstituency, and the site of a sentient and intentional relation to the world, then the modalities through which we interiorize and/ or resist the panoptic gaze can be explored more adequately.

Judith Butler has suggested that there are ways in which "the body" comes to be a substitute – and an inadequate one at that – for the psyche in Foucault's theories.[16] She rightly argues that Foucault leaves us with the problem of how to understand "not merely the disciplinary production of the subject, but the disciplinary cultivation of *an attachment to subjection*" in the modern self.[17] Butler turns to a psychoanalytic framework to address this problem, but in what follows I offer an alternate route. I return to Beauvoir and to her phenomenological

---

[15] Ibid., p. 186.
[16] Judith Butler, *The Pyschic Life of Power: Theories in Subjection*. Stanford: Stanford University Press, 1997, p. 94.
[17] Ibid., 102.

explorations of the look, or gaze, in order further to examine some of the issues of complicity and resistance to power that Foucault implicitly raises – yet never adequately addresses.

In Foucault's general discussions of power – of power as capillary and circulating – normalization proceeds through panoptical and other disciplinary practices in which, as subjectified subjects, as both the effects of power and the bearers of power, we are all implicated. As he puts it, "power is employed and exercized through a net-like organization. And not only do individuals circulate between its threads; they are always in the position of simultaneously undergoing and exercising power (...) The individual (...) is not the *vis-à-vis* of power; it is I believe, one of its prime effects."[18] However, in discussing the generalized masculine gaze, under and through which women become and remain women, Beauvoir suggests that men and women are not subjected to the same forms of power, nor subjected to power to the same degree. At one level Beauvoir agrees with Foucault: the generalized power of men over women is possessed by no specific individual. Thus, she points out, an individual man who wishes to cease participating in the privileges of masculine power finds that he cannot withdraw from it; it is not his to renounce. "It is useless to apportion blame and excuse (...) a man could not prevent himself from being a man. So there he is, guilty in spite of himself and burdened by this fault he did not himself commit."[19]

Even so, men and women, as socially distinct groups, are differently positioned within generalized networks of power in ways that Foucault does not recognize. Furthermore, as Beauvoir sees very clearly, their differential positionings may easily permit the actual "possession" of power by a particular man over a particular woman. In Beauvoir's France the marriage contract still brought into being a form of "sovereign" power, in which a husband unambiguously controlled his wife's finances, domicile, access to her children, and so on. Beauvoir was

---

[18] Ibid., 98.
[19] Beauvoir, Simone de. *The Second Sex*. Translated by Howard M. Parshley. Preface by Deidre Bair. New York, Vintage Books. [1949] 1989, p. 723. (Originally published as *Le deuxième sexe*. Paris: Gallimard. Original English edition, New York: Knopf, 1952).

acutely aware of the significance of what we might call the institutional dimensions of masculine power, as they mutually enabled and reinforced those more diffuse forms of power that Foucault describes as disciplinary or normalizing. For it was not the case that "power [was] no longer substantially identified with an individual who possesses or exercises it by right of birth."[20] On the contrary, in marriage, right of birth alone still conferred juridical grants of "sovereign" power to husbands in Beauvoir's world. Although such power does not formally exist today, at least in most Western liberal democracies, the institutional dimensions of continuing masculine privilege should not be underestimated.

If we are to understand women's complicity in sustaining those normalizing practices through which their subordinating "femininity" is perpetuated, we will need also to look at juridical, economic, and other institutional arrangements in which women find themselves located. For these often still produce *de facto* relationships of personal privilege and dependency that make compliance a rational survival strategy for many women.[21] We will need also to look at the ways in which women become invested in their femininity, not only as a material survival strategy but as a mode of lived experience that is integral to the self. It is in exploring the less calculating ways in which women become invested in their femininity that Beauvoir allows us to examine also "from the inside out"[22] Foucault's account of the disciplinarily constituted subject. When discussing the Panopticon, Foucault writes,

---

[20] Michel Foucault, *Power/Knowledge: Selected Interviews & Other Writings, 1972-1977*. New York: Pantheon, 1980, p. 156.

[21] These relationships may sometimes give rise to the quite explicit *interests* that certain women have in complying with the norms of femininity. For example, for a dependent or low-earning housewife, the economic costs of a broken marriage that might result from resistant behavior can be catastrophic. Likewise, the refusal docilely to submit to forms of sexual harassment by a male superior at work can jeopardize many a woman's career. In some instances, contra Foucault, we may reasonably posit a woman as an interest-maximizing agent, in order to account for her complicity in her own continued personal subordination.

[22] Elizabeth Grosz, *Volatile Bodies: Toward a Corporeal Feminism*. Bloomington: Indiana University Press, 1994.

"we are talking of two things here: the gaze and interiorization."[23] However, he does not ever explain how the latter, the interiorization of the gaze, is effected. Nor does he show how it brings into being the complicity of the self-surveilling subject; nor (more generally) does he reveal how the continuous and minute disciplining of the body that he describes produces its correlative "soul."

It is, on reflection, quite remarkable that in the three hundred or so pages of *Discipline and Punish* we get absolutely no sense of what it *feels* like to be subjected to the panoptical gaze; nor any sense of the experiential dimension of becoming a self-surveilling "subject" of panopticism.[24] Foucault's disciplinary subjects do not appear to feel fear, anxiety, frustration, unhappiness. Such emotions, not to mention pain, are strikingly absent from his account. It is here that Beauvoir's analysis adds another necessary dimension to Foucault's. We do not need to posit a Cartesian knowing subject, or a pure constituting consciousness to understand *how* the practices of power are taken up, or interiorized, by an individual self or "soul" that may inflect, deflect, accept, or resist them in multiple and idiosyncratic ways. However, we do need to posit a subject that is active and intentional to some degree. Beauvoir's account of an embodied and situated subject, a subject that while never being an absolute freedom or pure consciousness, has a view-point on the world and an intentional relationship with it, offers us what Foucault lacks.

Beauvoir's account of women's diverse interiorizations of the male gaze involves a creative reworking of Sartre's phenomenology of "the look" in *Being and Nothingness*. For Sartre, another's look is always experienced as a threat. For to be seen by another is to become an object in his world; and to be aware of myself as being seen by another is to be aware of myself as object-like. The look is thus always experienced as an assault on my freedom: on my ability to define for myself the meaning of my situation.[25] However, for Sartre, I am always free to

---

[23] Michel Foucault, *Power/Knowledge: Selected Interviews & Other Writings, 1972-1977*. New York: Pantheon, 1980, p. 154.

[24] It is, I think, this omission that Nancy Hartsock has in mind when she observes (following Edward Said) that Foucault is "with power" rather than against it (1996, 36).

[25] The French, "le regard" has conventionally been rendered as "the look" in Sartre translations and scholarship, and as "the gaze" in the case of Foucault. While the two

reaffirm my status as a subject by turning the tables on the Other, by in turn looking at him.

I have argued elsewhere[26] that Beauvoir radically modifies Sartre's account of self-other relations by insisting that, where there are relations of social equality, objectification can be superseded by forms of mutually validating "reciprocity."[27] The look can be a means of expressing friendship or love, of sharing, of validating another: it can, in short, be intersubjective, rather than objectifying. However, in those formal institutions that Foucault characterizes as panoptical – the prison, the asylum, the school, the army parade-ground, etc. – surveillor and surveilled are not equally positioned, and the look thus functions irreversibly to objectify. Indeed, in Bentham's design for the Panopticon it is essential that the in-mates are illuminated and visible to the inspecting gaze of the guard or overseer, but that he is not equally visible to them. Similarly, those assembled for inspection, such as soldiers on the parade ground, may not look back at those who inspect them.

To be subjected to a gaze that one cannot reciprocally return is, indeed, to experience objectification, or an alienation of one's subjectivity. I experience a loss of my immediate, lived subjecthood as I become fixed or immobilized *in my own eyes* as the object that I am (or believe myself to be) in the eyes of the one who looks at me. However, this experience is not *by itself* sufficient to account for the production of docility and of compliant self-surveillance that Foucault attributes to the power of the Panoptic gaze.

What is also essential here is what Sartre and Beauvoir call "shame": a relation to oneself, in the presence of another, in which one *evaluates* oneself negatively through the look of the other. Sartre begins his discussion of shame in *Being and Nothingness* with the well-known example of hearing somebody else approaching while, "moved by jealously, curiosity, or vice," I am peeping through a keyhole.[28] The

---

terms carry different resonances in English, these are the function of translation processes, and would not be present for French readers.

[26] **Sonia** Kruks, *Situation and Human Existence: Freedom, Subjectivity and Society*. New York and London: Routledge, 1990, p. 83-112.

[27] Simone de Beauvoir, *The Second Sex*. Translated by Howard M. Parshley. Preface by Deidre Bair. New York, Vintage Books. [1949] 1989, p. xxiii.

[28] Sartre, Jean-Paul. *Being and Nothingness*. Translated by Hazel E. Barnes. New

experience of shame in being "caught" in such a circumstance involves not only seeing myself as the object that the other sees, but seeing myself as the other will *judge* me: as reprehensible, faulty, inferior. Moreover, I do not just feel shame of my act, but of my *self*. For suddenly I *am* as I am seen to be: "shame (...) is shame of *self*; it is the *recognition* of the fact that I *am* indeed that object which the Other is looking at and judging".[29] Here, we have an initial account of how the power-effect of the look, which Foucault only observes, actually operates. We see how, in interiorizing the shaming look, I become not only the object of my own surveillance but also the judge of myself.

But Sartre's account of shame calls out for further elaboration – which Beauvoir offers in her descriptions of feminine experience. First, I can come to feel shame by virtue of such facticities as my bodily characteristics or my social status without having engaged in any specific act. I may judge myself to be ugly, for example, if my body does not conform to the norms of beauty in my society. Or, if I am a member of a class of people, such as women, that is deemed to be socially inferior, I may judge myself to be inferior.[30] Second, although I may come to judge myself through the look of a single individual, as in Sartre's example, I may also do so through an impersonal or anonymous, an entirely non-specific, or even in the long run absent, Other. In the panoptical institutions that Foucault describes, the look is impersonal but presumed present: continuous scrutiny on the part of designated officials is part of the disciplinary regime. But in other instances, the look is generalized or non-specific; "they," "others," "society," judge certain of my characteristics to be signs of my inferiority. And, in its most strongly interiorized forms, the look may become so integral to the self that it functions in a situation of total privacy – as when a woman carefully applies her make-up even if she intends to stay at home on her own the whole day and will be "seen" by absolutely nobody but herself. In these latter cases we might appear

---

York: New Philosophical Library. Originally published as *L'Etre et le néant*. Paris: Gallimard, [1943] 1956, p. 259.
[29] Ibid., p. 261.
[30] Frantz Fanon also powerfully developed Sartre's account of shame, to explore the lived experiences of black embodiment in a predominantly white society ([1952] 1967). I discuss Fanon's relationship to Sartre more fully in Kruks 1996.

to return to notions of panoptical power as circulating and capillary, to Foucault's "minute disciplines, the panopticisms of everyday," in which nobody possesses power. Yet, when we come to look more closely, contra Foucault and as Beauvoir realizes, some are more disciplined, more normalized, and less powerful than others – among them, women.

Woman, as Beauvoir depicts her, is not just man's Other, she is his *inferior* Other: "The relation of the two sexes is not like that of two electrical poles, for man represents both the positive and the neutral, so that in French [as in English] one says 'men' to designate human beings (...) He is the Subject, he is the Absolute – she is the Other."[31] Whereas Sartre argues that by returning the look one can always turn the tables on the Other, Beauvoir suggests that what distinguishes the situation of woman is precisely her *inability* to do so. "No subject," she observes, "immediately and voluntarily affirms itself as the inessential, "thus the question is "from whence comes this submission in women?"[32]

In answering this question Beauvoir offers us a series of descriptions of how women come to exist in the mode of inferiority and to subsume it into forms of subjectified feminine subjectivity. If "not every female human being is necessarily a woman,"[33] then we need to grasp the processes through which "one becomes one" as not only the exercize of power upon and its transmission through the subject, but also as it is interiorized, taken up, and lived. It is here that the panopticisms of daily life and the "interior" experiences of shame they induce are crucial.

Beauvoir begins by describing the multitude of small disciplines to which female children are often subjected and which still today induce passivity, timidity, and physical self-constraint.[34] But she suggests that

---

[31] Simone de Beauvoir, *The Second Sex*. Transl. by Howard M. Parshley. New York, Vintage Books. [1949] 1989, p. xxiv.
[32] Ibid.
[33] Ibid., p. xix.
[34] Although girls from most social strata in the USA today are less constrained than were the middle class women of Beauvoir's France, Beauvoir's observations generally still appear to hold. Iris Young has discussed a range of studies that show that girls (and women) still fail to extend their bodies, or to occupy space as fully as boys do;

it is at puberty that more profound experiences of shame usually begin. At that time, a girl often becomes the object of stares, whistles, derogatory remarks on the street (and at school in coeducational systems) and, simultaneously, is required to hide from view the newly acquired "secret" of menstruation. In the experience of menstruation (at least in Western society) a young woman's profound sense of herself as not only the Other but as the inferior Other is dramatically discovered. She must ensure that she does not appear soiled in public; must learn discreetly to dispose of bloodied pads, tampons and clothing; is warned that she might give away her "condition" by the smell of menstrual blood should she not keep herself sufficiently clean.[35]

In such ways, a young woman learns how to develop those practices of self-surveillance and self-discipline that Foucault attributes to the panoptic gaze. But they are not the *direct* effect of the gaze itself, so much as of the shame with which it forces her to see "herself." Shame, as what we might call a primary structure of a woman's lived experience, extends far beyond her relationship to menstruation, and it becomes integral to a generalized sense of inferiority of the feminine body-subject. A woman, Beauvoir writes, "*is* her body; but her body is something other than herself."[36]

As Beauvoir's account of women's lived experience proceeds, from early childhood, through girlhood, sexual initiation, marriage, childbirth, and motherhood, toward old-age, shame remains a primary structure of experience. Shame of an embodied self that is always marked as inferior, as defective, is instrumental to women's participation in the multitude of minute daily practices that induce docility and

---

they throw, sit, walk, and carry things in typically timid and constricted "feminine" modalities. Young suggests that these are not merely different from masculine modalities, but are indicative of women's oppression: "Women in sexist society are physically handicapped. Insofar as we learn to live out our existence in accordance with the definition that patriarchal culture assigns to us, we are physically inhibited, confined, positioned, and objectified"(Young 1990, 153).

[35] An astounding number of products are aggressively marketed today that promise women "protection" against the dread embarrassments of leaks and odors. Deodorant tampons, special cleansers, and other such products abound on supermarket shelves and are heavily advertized.

[36] Simone de Beauvoir, *The Second Sex*. Transl. by Howard M. Parshley. New York, Vintage Books. [1949] 1989, p. 29.

reproduce forms of normalized feminine behavior.[37] Nor does the woman who resists, the would-be "independent" woman whom Beauvoir describes in the final section of *The Second Sex*, escape from it.

On the contrary, Beauvoir points out, the would-be independent woman lives her femininity as a painful contradiction. Brought up (as most girls still are today) to see herself through the male gaze, enjoined to passivity, and to make herself desirable to man, she *is* her femininity. Her being-for-others is profoundly gendered. This is not a facticity that can be ignored, since it thoroughly permeates her being-for-herself. She cannot renounce her femininity, for it is constitutive of her selfhood even as it undercuts her struggle for self-affirmation. The "independent" woman thus lives divided against herself even more starkly than the woman who more fully accepts traditional feminine roles.[38]

Moreover, because Woman is not merely man's Other, but an inferior Other, Beauvoir is keenly aware that individual solutions are not fully realizable. This is not to say that individual women should cease to mount a personal challenge to normalizing femininity. But in challenging it they will disclose the radical inequality of their situation and encounter the limits to what can be individually achieved. Beauvoir is far from affirming the untrammelled capacity for freedom, or "transcendence," of which she is often accused. On the contrary, she would agree with Foucault that it is through subjection to disciplinary and

---

[37] The *content* of normalized femininity has, of course, shifted dramatically since Beauvoir's time, especially in the USA. But normalizing demands are no less intense today. Indeed, if the corset once constricted the body from without, today the demands not merely for slenderness but for a well "toned" body necessitate an ever greater interiorization of discipline (Bordo, Susan. *Unbearable Weight: Feminism, Western Culture, and the Body*. Berkeley: University of California Press, 1993). Sandra Bartky has suggested, with some plausibility, that women "have their own experience of the modernization of power, one which begins later but follows in many respects the course outlined by Foucault" (Sandra Bartky, *Femininity and Domination*. New York: Routledge, 1990, 97). As women have achieved more freedom of movement, and as juridical male power over them has diminished, they have become subject to ever more demanding normalizing practices.

[38] Beauvoir suggests this is also the case for lesbians who, while refusing to engage in "normal" heterosexual behavior, still find themselves trapped in normalizing femininity (Simone de Beauvoir, *The Second Sex*, 404-24).

normalizing practices that subjectivity comes into being. The feminine subject cannot simply shed her femininity, for there is no "inner" subject that can, in absolute freedom, transcend its body and its situation; there is no pure constituting consciousness. But to acknowledge this is not to deny all freedom to the subject. For most women, a range of choices are still open as to *how* one interiorizes, assumes, and lives normalized femininity. Thus, issues of personal agency, ethics, and responsibility, that cannot consistently be posed within Foucault's explicit framework, emerge as central for Beauvoir.

Beauvoir posits a continuum of situations. At one end of the continuum, she offers an account of the subject that could be re-cast in Foucault's starkest terms. She talks of the woman who lives in a situation of such extreme subjection that freedom is made immanent, is no more than a suppressed potentiality. Here a woman *is* so thoroughly her situation, so thoroughly its product, that no effective choice as to how it is to be lived is possible. Such a woman is, as Foucault had put it, a constitut*ed*, not a constitut*ing* subject.[39]

But while immanence marks one end of a continuum of theoretically possible situations, it is doubtful if many women actually live in such a condition. At the other end of the continuum is the "independent" woman, who struggles doggedly against the constraints of her situation and in so doing reveals the impossibility of fully transcending it. Most women, however, live neither in total immanence nor in a mode of continuous revolt. They live somewhere between, embracing various modes of complicity, compromise, or resistance, each of which has both rewards and costs attached to them. Here we return, with Beauvoir, to those issues of complicity with subjection; and to those questions of individual resistance that Foucault's account of subjectification tacitly poses but does not adequately address.

Near the end of *The Second Sex* Beauvoir observes that men find in women "more complicity than the oppressor usually finds in the oppressed."[40] The term "complicity" for Beauvoir connotes a moral register, absent in Foucault's account of the subject's "compliance" in

---

[39] Michel Foucault, *Power/Knowledge: Selected Interviews & Other Writings, 1972-1977*. New York: Pantheon, 1980, p. 117.
[40] Simone de Beauvoir, *The Second Sex*, p. 721.

disciplinary power. What both Beauvoir and Foucault share is the insight that the subject of disciplinary power actively participates in it: power is not unidirectional, nor simply top-down. We have already seen that Beauvoir accounts more fully than Foucault for *how*, through self-objectification and shame, disciplinary power is internalized so that its subject comes also to be its agent.

But, beyond the "how," there are also questions of "why." For Beauvoir also suggests that in many instances complicity could be more fully resisted. The subjectified subject who takes up those practices of power through which it is both constituted and self-constituting, still enjoys a degree of freedom as to how it assumes them. Here, ethical issues begin to arise: for if the subject enjoys a degree of freedom, complicity is not just a fact to be described, but a choice, a project, that is open to moral evaluation. It is a matter of what, following Sartre, Beauvoir will call "bad faith," "flight," or the choice of "inauthenticity."

After decades of popular self-help manuals, the term "authenticity" often connotes today a highly psychologized notion of the search for "inner meaning" or the quest to get in contact with one's "real self." But for Beauvoir – as for Foucault – there is no real or inner self "there" to be discovered. Rather, what is at issue here is the choice of an ethical stance in the face of one's situation and its facticities. In inauthenticity, a woman affirms her selfhood to be constituted by exterior conditions and forces even when this is not wholly the case. The "bad faith," or self-deception, lies in the fact that one is still making choices and exercising a degree of freedom, while claiming to be unable to do so. For (very rare circumstances apart), one is not free not to choose how one takes up one's situation. To "become a woman" is not to be sculpted by exterior forces like a lump of clay. To claim an analogously inert status, to claim that one is "constituted" through and through, is in bad faith to flee one's freedom.[41] Beauvoir thus insists

---

[41] It is also to live in what Beauvoir (following Sartre) calls the mode of the "serious." As she wrote in *The Ethics of Ambiguity*,"the characteristic of the spirit of seriousness is to consider values as ready-made things" (Simone de Beauvoir, *The Ethics of Ambiguity*. Transl. by Bernard Frechtman. New York: The Citadel Press, 1967, p. 35) and so to refuse to accept responsibility for the values implicit in one's own actions. "The serious man's [sic] dishonesty issues from his being obliged ceaselessly to renew his

that, however constrained our situation, we can almost always still take it up in different ways, and that we must accept responsibility for our own choices and values.

Today, few Western women fit the details of Beauvoir's outdated portrait of the inauthentic housewife in *The Second Sex*. Yet surprisingly many of her insights remain pertinent. Self-abnegation and denial; deference to the opinions of others and failure to assert one's own; limiting one's goals and ambitions, particularly to fit in with those of a lover or husband or child: all of these typically "feminine" forms of behavior still endure among a diverse range of women today. They can, of course, often be explained as rational, even self-interested, strategies on the part of those who are still, to a significant degree, economically dependent on men. In Foucaultean vein, one can also account for them as strictly the effects of those disciplinary and normalizing practices through which women are constituted as subjects. But if neither explanation is wrong, neither is by itself adequate. For "feminine" behavior is more than either a calculated strategy or a discursively produced effect. It is more than a strategy because being a woman is not an identity that an "inner" self could pick up or shed at will. It is more than a discursive effect because it is interiorized and taken up in ways that are both constrained and yet still indeterminate, and open to moral evaluation.

It is from this indeterminacy that feminism, as a political project, begins. It must start by recognizing the existence of that margin of freedom that enables us to struggle against our complicity in subordinating and subjectifying practices – as well, of course, as to struggle against the institutional dimensions of subordination, such as legal lack of control over our own bodies, or unequal pay. Beauvoir's message is clear: feminism must not be shy to affirm its values, for any emancipatory project implies an ethical stance. And, indeed, given even the smallest margin of freedom, we cannot avoid affirming values in all that we do. To deny this is to act in bad faith, and lay claim to an irresponsibility we do not enjoy.

---

denial of freedom (...) The serious man must mask the movement by which he gives [values] to himself, like the mythomaniac who while reading a love-letter pretends to forget that she has sent it to herself" (ibid., p. 47).

It is also true, of course, that no emancipatory project is entirely innocent. As Foucault has so clearly pointed out, all claims to truth, or affirmations of values, are also productive of power effects. However, this does not mean that we should endeavor not to affirm our own values lest, in the name of truth, we become yet further complicit with power.[42] On the contrary, the better safeguard is to make explicit the values implied by our actions, while also recognizing our responsibility for the power effects they produce.

Thus to write, with Foucault, "to have no face," to insist that there are not authors (be it of texts or of deeds), to attribute to disciplinary practices their own purposes and intentionality, and to claim that each of us is equally constituted by a power that none possesses, amounts finally to a flight into the self-delusional and irresponsible world of bad faith. To conclude, Foucault offers us a new version of "the temptation to flee freedom and constitute oneself a thing"[43] – a temptation we should resist, even as we continue to draw on his rich insights into the operations of power and subjectification.

---

[42] Although his failure to make his own values explicit invites such a reading, I don't think Foucault himself draws this conclusion from his analyses. However, it is the demobilizing consequence drawn from his work by many feminists and other radicals, who fear to speak on certain topics lest they become implicated in power. Silence, it should be remembered, can equally implicate one in power.

[43] Simone de Beauvoir, *The Second Sex*, p. xxvii.

5

María Luisa Femínias

JUDITH BUTLER AND THE "GENDER" QUESTION

The emergence of the North American post-modern Sex Theory in the 1990s destabilizes the category of sexual difference. The sexual theorizing impact results – in Judith Butler words – in a renewed interest on questions of sex and gender ontology and fundamentalism. Some new writers challenge the stability of binarian sex/gender categories from transgender-identified perspectives. They say that sex/gender categories are becoming more fluid and less able to be sustained on essential and monolithically based sexual differences in terms of binarian sexes. The distinction between hetero and homosexuality develops a strong current of feminist critique of normative sexuality, focusing on alternative readings of sex/gender accounts.[1]

Discursive differences are being examined creating new philosophical questions about the matter of bodies and the materialization of sexualities, where Judith Butler is perhaps one of the most influential radical philosophers. Her insights of gender essentialism as a tendency to be suspected firstly, leads her to identify – wrongly as we will attempt to show – Beauvoir as one of the first feminists to use that category and ascribes her an essentialist condition indebted to Sartre's ontology. So, while arguing that gender is a cultural/discursive configuration of the body she ascribes to Beauvoir the concept of "gender" as a "natural kind," and in so doing she reaches some crucial and controversial conclusions ignoring Beauvoir's contributions to dismantling the lure of normative sexuality in heterosexual relations. A dismantling from the prevailing normative constructs of sex and gender – as

---

[1] See Ofelia Schutte, "A critique of Normative Heterosexuality: Identity, Embodiment, and Sexual Difference in Beauvoir and Irigaray," *Hypatia*, 12, no. 1 (Winter 1997): 40-62. I am in debt to Victoria Costa and María Spadaro for their helpful suggestions.

Ofelia Schutte explains – is necessary for the construction of any feminist social and political order.²

1.

Simone de Beauvoir's *Le Deuxième Sexe* is perhaps the most influential work of feminist theory in the Twentieth Century, and in the United States it inspired radicals such as Shulamith Firestone and Kate Millet, as well as liberals such as Betty Friedan or socialists such as Juliet Mitchell. Beauvoir based her understanding of the *situation* of women on descriptions of *women's own experience*, confirming the priority of the concrete and experiential over the abstract and the ahistorical. She locates her ethical enquiry within the context of specific historical relationships, given man's historical definition of women as the Other, and in doing so criticizing traditional philosophy, religion, psychoanalysis and even Marxism.

She opens her analysis of normative constructions of heterosexuality with the goal of reinforcing the wide range of non-normative gender and sexual options available to feminist women because there is an assumed identification or overlap between heterosexuality and normativity ignoring the fact that "normative sexuality [is] a type or form of sexual activity that is marked by a coincidence between socially privileged sexual acts and privileged gender constructs".³ Any heterosexual woman can break normative gender stereotypes by succeeding economically, being unemotionally dependent, or refusing to be a mother. When Simone de Beauvoir poses her most famous question *qu'est-ce qu'une femme?*⁴ she places the categories of *woman* and *man* on the stand. And from the morals of the existential framework she answers that "one is not born, but rather becomes a woman because "every subject plays his part as such specifically through exploits or projects that serve as a mode of transcendence; he achieves liberty only through a continual reaching out toward other liberties."⁵

---

[2] Judith Butler, "Sex and Gender in Simone de Beauvoir's *The Second Sex.*" *Yale French Studies* 72 (Winter 1986): 35-49.
[3] Ofelia Schutte, "A critique of Normative Heterosexuality..", op.cit., 41-42.
[4] Simone de Beauvoir, *The Second Sex*. New York: Vintage Books, 1989, 13.
[5] Ibid., xxiv.

So, to be is to become to being, but the drama of the woman is the conflict among the essential aspirations she has the rights to, as an autonomous being, and "a world where men compel her to assume the status of the Other. They propose to stabilize her as object and to doom her to immanence since her transcendence is to be overshadowed and forever transcended by another ego (*conscience*) which is essential and sovereign."[6] The woman's drama consists of the paradox between her rights and aspirationsas a subject (the nominalistic universal subject that Enlightenment proposes and Beauvoir is thinking of) and her facticity where she is constituted as inessential.[7] Moreover, much as European Sexual Difference theorists do current day, Beauvoir states the obvious and focuses at first on the difference between masculine and feminine normative subject positions: sex is not only a biological fact and does not denote only a chronological episode in human history. This also concerns women's reproductive functions. Beauvoir seems to consider women's reproductive function as the main obstacle to their realizing the radical freedom existentialists believe humans have to determine themselves as their own essence, so it seems she understands motherhood as an obstacle to have a share in the human *mitsein*. No woman can evidently forget what she is, "*no woman can pretend to live beyond her sex*"[8] because the body is important as the *locus* of concrete "lived experiences," the body is not "the body-object described by biologists that actually exists, but the body as lived in by the subject," for women (likewise men) are subjects *in situation*.[9] So far about Beauvoir's central assertions. Let us examine now Butler's discussion.

2.

Rosi Braidotti describes the North American reception of Poststructuralist Theories of Sexual Difference in terms of a "Transatlantic Disconnection," which I will rewrite now in terms of "Butler Disconnection," as she basically misinterpreted the main contributions in

---

[6] Ibid., p. xxxv.
[7] Ibid., p. 31.
[8] Ibid., p. 13.
[9] Ibid., p. 38.

Beauvoir's *Le Deuxième Sexe*. By discussing the ideas of Beauvoir, a theory of gender was mistakenly endorsed by Butler which does not provide enough support to her oversimplified reading. Unfortunately, such a reading has been uncritically assumed by many North American (post)feminist (post)structuralist thinkers.[10] This means that I do not share her critiques though I recognize the sharp implications of her analysis.

According to Butler, Beauvoir's contribution in *Le Deuxième Sexe* appeals, at least, to 1) a voluntarist theory of gender, 2) a Cartesian (dualistic) view of the self (*moi*), identified with Descartes' *cogito* and with Sartre's "being-for-itself" (*être-pour-soi*), 3) an ontological hang over, 4) an abstract universal subject, 5) a biological essentialism. Butler's misinterpretation is basically directed by her claim that Beauvoir *has* a theory of gender. Even though Beauvoir's latter experience of the contemporary women's movement in the 1970s changed her perspective on the sex/gender question, she never understood gender in the way that Butler does when she endorses her concept of "gender" to be the "most distinguished contribution of Simone de Beauvoir."[11]

3.

Judith Butler seems to start her reading of Beauvoir with the assumption that *Le Deuxième Sexe* is based on a thesis about the sex/gender relation, but not from the Existentialist Ethics and a non Husserlian Phenomenological description of the place women hold in society due to their sexual difference.[12] Butler's strategy reminds one strongly of her own comments about "the foundationalist fictions that

---

[10] Butler cites Howard M. Parshley's translation into English that was extensively critised (Cf. Margaret A. Simons, "Two Interviews with Simone de Beauvoir," *Hypatia* 3, no. 3, 1989, 12 and Simons 1999, 61-91).

[11] Judith Butler, "Sex and Gender in Simone de Beauvoir's *The Second Sex*," *Yale French Studies* 72 (Winter 1986): 35-49; Judith Butler, *Gender Trouble: Feminism and the subversion of identity*. New York: Routledge, 1990.

[12] Linda Nicholson considers that English language-speakers started to use the word "gender" technically in the late 1960s. (See Linda Nicholson, "Gender", in Jaggar-Young, 1998, 289-297). Spanish and other Latin languages use "gender" in a non-feminist way till North-American literature introduced it in the early 1970s, and the use of this expression is quite resistant.

support the notion of subject," and although she criticizes Beauvoir's conceptualization of "women" and the representationist theory that supports her political theory of the body, she suggests that in "one is not born a woman, but rather, becomes one," is where gender is "constructed" in a strong voluntaristic way.[13] So, being a woman is a voluntaristic cultural construction and "woman" only designates a variety of modes in which the facts acquire cultural meaning or intelligibility, as a process of gender self-construction, where "women" is *that* what we finally *become*.

Although, how can a certain sex become a certain gender, asks Butler. According to her reading of Beauvoir, nothing can designate a "female" as the fixed and self-identical set of cultural presumptions that "women" fulfill.[14] Thus, Butler strongly suggests that Beauvoir's "to be a woman" is a cultural interpretation of "to be a female," where the female body is the arbitrary *locus* of "women" as gender.

So Butler considers that to become a "woman" is a "process of constructing ourselves (...) is a purpositive and appropriative set of acts, the acquisition of a skill, a 'project,' to use Sartrean terms, to assume certain corporal style and significance."[15] Butler takes "to become" as "purposefully assumed or embodied" and makes use of Sartrean categories to support the striking claim that endorses Beauvoir in a voluntaristic account of gender as a self-reflexive process to become our genders, previously determined by the very system of representational politics that Beauvoir's feminism itself was combating, in its struggle for women's emancipation. At least with regard to the first issue, Butler reads the "Sartrean Project" in terms of the performative, and so in a consciously voluntaristic way. So woman's submission designates her true vocation of male dominance. But this does not seem to be the best standpoint to judge Beauvoir's position.

This is to say that, on the one hand, sex is taken to be natural, biological and bodily in ways that are not politically or culturally cir-

---

[13] Judith Butler, *Gender Trouble*, op.cit., p. 3; idem. "Sex and Gender in Simone de Beauvoir's *The Second Sex*," op.cit., p. 36.
[14] Judith Butler, "Sex and Gender in Simone de Beauvoir's *The Second Sex*," op.cit, p. 37.
[15] Ibid., p. 36.

cumscribed, and that (sex) fully imposes its effects on the normative construct of women while it marks her subordination. On the other hand, Butler points out that Beauvoir misses the *performative* point; sex is constituted by way of exclusionary claims that may be more or less invisible to those of us who are caught up in the socially varied discourse which itself is not immune to the heterosexual, racial, and class prejudices that help to structure and maintain the *status quo*.[16] "Becoming" a gender has to be understood to be both, a choice and an acculturation process. It seems to Butler that Beauvoir formulates "gender" ambiguously because she misses the performative point. In other words, Butler's own construction of gender as performative and citational provides Beauvoir with an "ambiguous discursive trend" that she in fact lacked. This system unilaterally imposed on Beauvoir also engages Butler in the claim that we need to understand the term "woman" *as the site of permanent openness and resignifiability* ignoring that Beauvoir can both acknowledge the weight of social construction and the autonomy of the self, because women are subjects "in situation," a category she posed (not Sartre) to explain the particular position human beings – especially women – have. Beauvoir is certainly an existentialist, but her position is not simply that of Sartre's. She is not a Sartrean epigone. One can be interested – as Butler is – in Sartre's influence on her philosophy but, on the contrary, her philosophical differences from Sartre's can be richly explored.[17]

This means that Butler understands that "gender" also entails a critique of "woman" as possessing any "essential" or unitary meaning. She suggests in *Gender Trouble* that there is a parallel to be drawn between the way we think of sex, and the tendency to naturalize, or posit foundational and unchanging biological grounds to the fictional or discursive category of women. The idea of women as unitary is

---

[16] Judith Butler, *Gender Trouble*, op.cit., p. 4; Jaggar, Alison and Young, Iris. M. *A Companion to Feminist Philosophy*. London: Blackwell, 1998.

[17] Simons, Margaret A. *Beauvoir and the Second Sex: Feminism, Race, and the Origins of Existentialism*. Lanham, MD: Rowman & Littlefield, 1999, p. 41ff; Sonia Kruks, "Gender and Subjectivity: Simone de Beauvoir and Contemporary Feminism." *Signs* 18, no. 1 (1992): 89-97, here p. 92; Maria Teresa López-Pardina, "El feminismo de Simone de Beauvoir." *Historia de la Teoría Feminista*. Edited by Celia Amorós. Madrid: Universidad Complutense, 1994.

fiction in the service of the very oppressive regime that feminism seeks to overthrow. This is to say – in Butler's own words – that the belief that "women" does have some common meaning serves to coerce individuals into a behavior aimed to exhibit such a meaning. In other words, the idea of "women" as unitary operates as a policing force which generates and legitimizes certain practices, and experiences and delegitimates others. Moreover, the idea of the "woman" as a unitary situated human being in opposition to "man" works to sustain the *status quo* by supporting the norm of heterosexuality. The idea of "woman" and "man" as possessing an unitary meaning in opposition to each other supports the idea of sexual desire as the "attraction of opposites," where Butler understands heterosexuality and normativity as synonyms. Butler considers that there is no sexed body prior to its construction by phallocentric signification. So any feminist project which assumes such unitary meanings ends up therefore by reproducing both, the very sexist and heterosexist social order it aims to eliminate, as Beauvoir does.[18] So Butler blames Beauvoir of cutting into her analysis of gender and to assume a fixed ontological status of woman and the body. As we can see, she criticizes Beauvoir's work as heterosexist, masculinist and Sartrean.

This means to ignore at least that Beauvoir challenged the normative elements that delimit the senses of woman (mainly the heterosexual canon, but also the lesbian one). When Beauvoir uses the category of *femme indépendante* it is suggested that she draws a distinction between woman as "the Other" (the normative description of women, as placed in a position of subordination to man) and woman as an agent in pursuit of freedom.[19] Beauvoir's rejection of normative femininity and sexuality plus her ascription to an Existential Philosophy prevents her from any assumption of a fixed ontological status of woman and this opens into revolutionary feminist potential. It is true that Existential Philosophy carries a recognizable masculine-

---

[18] Alison Jaggar and Iris M. Young, *A Companion to Feminist Philosophy*. London: Blackwell, 1998, p. 293.
[19] Margaret A. Simons, *Beauvoir and the Second Sex: Feminism, Race, and the Origins of Existentialism*. Lanham, Md.: Rowman & Littlefield, 1999, p. 115; Simone de Beauvoir, *The Second Sex*, op. cit., p. 597.

centered focus on existence, but at the same time nourishes a spirit of rebellion against any constraints on one's freedom and this spirit is extraordinarily helpful for feminists.[20]

Butler is also critical of philosophy's tendency to ignore the body or worse, to write against it. Drawing on Lacan and Foucault, she attempts to theorize the materiality of the body and the ways in which *bodies are materialized as sexed* in the light of a critique of heterosexism. In other words, "sex" is an ideal construct which is forcibly materialized through time. It is not a simple fact or "static condition of a body but a process whereby regulatory norms materialize 'sex' and achieve this materialization through a forcible reiteration of those norms; this means that there is no reference to a pure body."[21] Neither Beauvoir nor Merleau-Ponty would deny this statement. But Butler wishes to go beyond the conventional limits of constructionist theories to consider "how such constraints not only produce the domain of intelligible bodies, but produce as well a domain of unthinkable, abject, unlivable bodies."[22] From her hyperconstructivist point of view, she pretends to show that sex is the regulatory norm which qualifies a body for life within the domain of cultural intelligibility.[23] Gender identity – Butler argues – is a performance not determined by a fixed biological nature, but it is not a performance at will; the conventions by which we are named "girl," "boy," "queer," "gay" are constituted in language. So Butler goes on to use the resources of the speech act theory and reference theory to understand how the linguistic mechanisms that produce normal and abnormal bodies, normal and queer subjects, might be cooptable or interruptible to produce new sexual/social identities.[24] Butler's concept of performativity is useful here (but it is not Beauvoir's). She focuses on genders' performance analyzing in detail the cultural production of gender transgression especially in terms of hetero/ homosexuality. But, might performativity (in the sense of literal perfor-

---

[20] Ofelia Schutte, "A critique of Normative Heterosexuality...," op. cit. 47ff.
[21] Judith Butler, *Gender Trouble*, op.cit., p. 80.
[22] Ibid.
[23] Judith Butler, *Bodies that matter*. New York-London: Routledge, 1993, p. 2.
[24] See Jaggar, Alison and Iris M. Young, *A Companion to Feminist Philosophy*, op.cit, p. 155.

mance, whether or not to do with gender) itself also influence the way the body works its interiority?[25]

Butler's suggestion – as we have already seen – that we "choose" or "build up" our gender moves to perplexity as it implies an ontological puzzle: a *res cogitans*, prior to the gender constructed, is needed as a pre-genderized *locus* to build a gender up. This means that Beauvoir would have considered – according to Butler's reading – that a kind of self-constituent agent is needed previous to the gendered body. This is what Butler identifies as *Cartesian Ghosts* in the *Sartrean Bodies* and "Beauvoir's becoming a gender seems both an extension and a concretization of the Sartrean formula."

Butler, by the way, explores themes in Sartre's philosophy that had an influence on Beauvoir's (or so she says), but she is not interested in her influence on him, probably believing in Beauvoir's statement that she does not consider herself a philosopher.[26] But her perspective in *Le Deuxième Sexe* and Sartre's perspective in *L'être et le néant* are not the same. He writes an *essai d'ontologie phénoménologique* where Beauvoir places her critique more on a moral plane, as a human activity.

So, Butler reads Beauvoir as if in "transposing the identification of corporal existence and becoming onto the sense of sex and gender, she appropriates the ontological necessity of paradox" where the tension moves from natural to an acculturated body.[27] Butler concludes that Beauvoir's thesis is tautological for the *ego* lives prior to discourse and consciousness comes before being apart from the body. This is why Butler considers that she could not avoid a dualistic conception of the human being. So understanding Beauvoir's philosophy, Butler can claim that "we do not become our gender from a place prior to culture or embodied life, but essentially within their terms." And Beauvoir surely would have agreed with her as she nev-

---

[25] Ibid., p. 200.
[26] Margaret A. Simons, "Two Interviews with Simone de Beauvoir." *Hypatia* 3,no. 3 (Winter 1989): 11-27, here 13.
[27] Judith Butler, "Sex and Gender in Simone de Beauvoir's *The Second Sex,*" op.cit., p. 39.

er believed in *human nature* as a predetermined site, but in *human reality*, a Heideggerian term, meaning man's presence in the world.

On the other hand, Butler recognized the importance of Merleau-Ponty's strength in Beauvoir's conception of the body, particularly in its sexual aspect, as above all a historical and cultural modality of existence. Both of them consider sexuality as coextensive with existence and not as an isolated sphere of drives, or a natural given. However, the account Merleau-Ponty gives of the body in its sexual being is actually an account of the heterosexual male body and while he claims to talk of concrete "lived experiences," paradoxically, he refers only to the experiences of male-bodies. Again, Butler considers that this is a biased heritage, as Merleau-Ponty opposes "male" to "female" as discrete units. Biology rests a bound, biological essentialism is not put into question; "the body is understood in the sense of "limit" or "essence" [not as] a field of interpretative possibilities, the locus of a dialectical process of interpreting anew a historical set of interpretations which have become imprinted in the flesh."[28] This biological dimorphism becomes the significant of the cultural order, as Lacan posed, though her "perspectivism" or "situationism" does not recover the body as another institutional construction, as Butler's states it.[29] So it makes perfect sense to Butler that Beauvoir does not challenge the notion of natural body (sex) and exposes herself to the political uses of biological discriminations accepting a dyadic gender system. Butler assumes that Beauvoir also emphasizes that the demarcation of anatomical difference does precede the cultural interpretation of that difference and the normative assumptions it carries.

But it is noteworthy that for Beauvoir *The Data of Biology* is subjected to non-natural systems of interpretation, the body as a natural fact never exists without a human experience, so it cannot be found to be "pure," but situated, as the *locus* of cultural interpretations and – like Butler's – "it is not merely a body, but rather a body subject to taboos, to laws, conscious of him/herself and attains fulfillment."[30] Beauvoir wrote freely that she was completely against the searching

---

[28] Ibid., p. 45.
[29] Ibid., p. 48.
[30] Ibid., p. 46.

for woman-identity as a feminist aim. She considered searching women-identity as a part of men's mythology that is as if women were essentially apart. On the contrary, she finds everybody's duty to identify themselves as "a human being who happens to be a woman," a different situation, which is not the same as men's situation.[31] Beauvoir does not suggest the possibility of other genders besides being a "man" or a "woman," yet she insists that these are historical constructions and either her bisexual orientation or her fictions about female sexuality (for example *Les Mandarins*) correspond to her critique of normative femininity (or any other forms of orthodoxies) as much as her notion of sexual pleasure is surely an ethics of transgression and an appeal to imagination *to repopulate the future*.

4.

On the one hand, Butler's approach seems fruitful enough to call attention and her *Performative Theory of Gender* is interesting and provocative. But her framework seems to not be the right one for interpreting Beauvoir. So why does she critique Beauvoir on the basis that the French philosopher did not support? Whatever her motivations were, Butler seems to work on at least three preconceptions:

- She considers the notions "subject" and "he/man" to be equivalent (Susan Bordo's thesis), and in this way she takes into consideration both extensional and intentional strokes;
- She rejects feminist theories based on the acceptance of the biological sexual difference (which entail normativeness, ontological hang over) in order to establish post-feminist foundations;
- She thinks that the body is not a biological *data*, but also a performative cultural-discursive construction.

On the other hand, in *Le Deuxième Sexe*, Beauvoir ignored gender as an analytical category. Her perspective of "sex" (female / male) cannot be conceived as the natural basis for a "gender" construction, and "gender" should not be viewed as the cultural interpretations of a pre-given sex – even though her experience of the 1970s movement

---

[31] Judith Butler, "Variaciones sobre sexo y género: Beauvoir, Wittig, Foucault," in *Teoría feminista / Teoría crítica*. Edited by Seyla Benhabib and Durcilla Cornell. Valencia: Alfons el Magnànim, 1989, p. 19.

of women led her to accept the notion of "gender" without many of Butler's theoretical implications. The body is not a choice, it is the point of departure from *which I am*; to be present in the world implies strictly that there exists a body which is at the same time a thing in the world and a point of view of the world. Subjectivity and corporeality are co-extensive. For choices are always made in a certain situation and starting from the same situation one can choose this or that. So one can have different choices in a single situation and one can choose to accept it or escape it.

So, there is theoretical tension in *Le Deuxième Sexe* on the question of choice and oppression: women are an oppressed group, but in a way each girl chooses to be the Other so she is in complicity with her oppression. Beauvoir knows that it is convenient for bourgeois women within this kind of oppression, but she appeals all the same to the possibilities of each human being having to refuse her/his situation.

In brief, as Heinämaa insists "bel et bien, when Beauvoir asks how does one become a woman, she in fact asks how it is possible that a body, intertwined with the world and other bodies, can both repeat certain postures, gestures and expressions, and change and modify them."[32] This is to say, we need to explore the strange ambiguity of existent bodies. In so doing, Butler needs an *interlocutor,* not to read her works, but to follow her own reflections: Beauvoir remains there richly suggestive.

---

[32] Sarah Heinämaa,"What is a woman? Butler and Beauvoir on sexual difference," *Hypatia* 11, no. 1 (Winter 1997), p. 37.

6

Tatyana Batuleva

RETHINKING IDENTITY AND OTHERNESS: LUCE IRIGARAY'S SHARED WORLD

1. The Other's Difference: Readings and Interpretations

The different generations of feminists have constructed their narratives about otherness in different ways. In the narratives, the otherness's difference may be perceived in some cases as synchronous, in other cases as polyphonous, in still others, as oppositionary; it can be conceived as a value in itself or, on the contrary, as a shortcoming; but invariably, the little narratives in question have striven for recognition and preservation of otherness, for overcoming the coercive nature of logos and of the universal subject. In fact, the relation towards otherness is precisely the point that most clearly distinguishes the separate stages of the philosophy, history, and struggles of various generations of feminists.

As theory, feminist philosophy has also had different stages of development. For instance, the first type of feminism, "equality feminism", derives from Simone de Beauvoir's *The Second Sex*. In the perspective of this work, women's otherness is perceived as a sign of inferiority. It chains women to the immanent and is linked to various restrictions. The implication is that overcoming otherness can become a basis of gender equality. Thus, women's otherness is seen as the source of their unenviable fate and is viewed in the negative aspect. It is not coincidental that this First-wave feminism has been defined as "androcentric".

According to Sylviane Agacinski, for instance, the first feminism's striving for equality "would practically lead to obliterating the difference between genders".[1] For, by associating activeness with the positive pole and viewing woman's otherness as passive and tied to immanence, this feminism in fact reproduces the laws of Western metaphysics. Agacinski offers her own deconstructivist reading of the role of the subject and otherness and her critique of the kind of androcentric feminism that aims to neutralize cultural and natural differences. For Agacinski the difference between sexes is an "irreducible anthropological given": "I believe in the value of difference, not in its obliteration", she writes.[2] In the interpretation she gives of motherhood we see yet another difference between her and Beauvoir. For Agacinski giving birth is not simply a personal destiny. On the contrary, it exalts even the most trivial subjective project, it transcends individuality and creates a future outside one's own life. Motherhood is a freedom that ressembles the freedom of one who is in love. It is a call to responsibility, because it sets the beginning of an existence that must be given the possibility of access to meaning. The mother's behavior does not enclose her within immanence: on the contrary, it is a model of relationship toward the other, a universal model of openness and care.

Of course, this thesis is not unambiguous and is liable to different interpretations. Unlike Agacinski, Susanne Moser, in her book *Freedom and Recognition in the Work of Simone de Beauvoir*[3], dissociates herself from the traditional interpretation of Beauvoir's views and assumes that her project exemplifies a way of thinking beyond all totalizing ideology. It is true, however, that Moser also finds internal inconsistencies in Beauvoir, who, on one hand, makes a critique of the negation of the feminine, but on the other hand, falls into this same negation, as illustrated by her attitude to feminine values.

But the important point in Moser's book is its analysis of the three types of subject proposed by Beauvoir: the subject of existence; the subject of domination; and between them is the subject of morality, a concept in which Moser finds proof that Beauvoir went beyond Sar-

---

[1] Sylviane Agacinski, *Politique des sexes*. Paris: Le Seuil, 2002, p. 85 [Engl. *Parity of the Sexes*. Translated by Lisa Walsh, New York: Columbia University Press, 2001].
[2] Ibid., p. 64.
[3] Susanne Moser. *Freedom and Recognition in the Work of Simone de Beauvoir*, Frankfurt am Main: Peter Lang, 2008.

tre's ontological notion of freedom. Moreover, according to Moser, Beauvoir developed the concept of moral freedom, thus paving the way for the next generations of feminists.[4] But regardless of these nuances, it is true that, in the framework of this first feminism, interwoven with ideas of existential philosophy, woman's otherness is seen as something negative that should be surmounted in order for the desired equality of women to be achieved. The aim of the following essay is to present Luce Irigaray's conception of otherness as an alternative to Beauvoir's and also to that of other French philosophers, in particular Emmanuel Levinas and Jacques Derrida.

2. Subject and Otherness: The Ethics of Difference

Luce Irigaray (who is one of the most important contemporary thinkers, a leading figure in feminist theory and, more generally, in continental philosophy; and whose fertile works are situated at the intersection of philosophy, feminism, linguistics and theory of culture) takes a different approach. In her "ethics of difference" she places foremost the positive aspects of feminine otherness.

In her first works, which are closely related to deconstruction, Irigaray critiques the psychoanalysis and the history of philosophy: the universal subject, as defined in the Western philosophical traditions, in fact reflects the interests of the male subject and sanctions the exclusion of the feminine from the sphere of being a subject. As Luce Irigaray puts it with precision: "Any theory of the subject has always been appropriated by the masculine."[5] Built according to the model of Western rationality, this autonomous subject takes over discourse and pushes away everything connected with feminine contents, declaring them to be of little value.

But not only does the feminine lack access to subjectivity – it is likewise excluded from the symbolic order of things. The so-called universal subject actually effaces the specificity of the feminine other-

---

[4] Ibid., p. 121.
[5] Luce Irigaray, *Speculum, de l'autre femme*. Minuit, 1974, p. 133 [Engl. *Speculum of the Other Woman*. Translated by Gillian C. Gill. New York: Cornell University Press, 1985].

ness, of the feminine experience, and turns the masculine and its related values into universal norms. This model provides a pattern upon which are built epistemological, social and political theories. In the framework of this understanding, the feminine is presented not only for itself but also as an alter ego, as the reverse, negative side of the masculine. It is a lack, an insufficiency, an undeveloped and unperfected masculine.[6] For her part, Sylviane Agacinski also points out this fact. In emphasizing that each of the two sexes should be evaluated in terms of its own specificity, potential and insufficiencies, Agacinski raises the question: in case we follow the logic of insufficiency, why not define the masculine in terms of the inability to give birth.[7] In the traditional Western philosophical and psychoanalytical discourse, the feminine, apart from being an insufficiency and the reverse side of the masculine, is also the locus of the appearance of masculine desire. All these strategies deprive the feminine of the possibility to be viewed in itself. Its otherness is lost, it is not an absolute value but a relative magnitude that exists only in relation to the masculine. Deprived of an identity of its own, the feminine turns into an addendum and reverse side of the dominating male subject.

Moving from critique of the dominant tradition, centred on the universal subject, Irigaray goes on to affirm the double, male-female, subject. Importantly, she does not limit herself to refutation, but shows the paths by which the male and female subject may establish non-hierarchical relations, and how the ethics of difference may serve as a foundation for a new type of social organization.

Starting from her earliest works, Irigaray proceeds from different levels of effacement of the feminine: in philosophy, politics, psychoanalysis. Since in the framework of paternalism feminine nature is viewed as live matter meant to serve the desires of others and the function of reproduction, a woman cannot live in the framework of the "in-itself" and "for-itself" dialectics; she cannot use them as a path to spirituality. Irigaray draws a distinction between the domination of the

---

[6] Luce Irigaray, *Ce sexe qui n'en est pas un*. Paris: Minuit, 1977 [Engl. *This Sex Which Is Not One*. Translated by Catherine Porter and Carolyn Burke. New York: Cornell University Press, 1985].
[7] Sylviane Agacinski, op.cit., p. 103.

male subject, which is already encoded in culture, and what women continue to create by themselves every day. But both aspects affirm the hierarchy of the genders and contribute to the permeation of the established patriarchal order throughout everything.

Already in her work *This Sex Which is Not One,* Irigaray points out that the patriarchal foundations of sociality are even part of contemporary politics as well, and she concludes that no politics have called in question phallocratic power. This engenders a contradiction: when emancipation has achieved one of its aims, when women have fallen in the trap of power and accepted to play the game of dominator and dominated, they lose the possibility of "speaking as women", of expressing the feminine. That is why her aim is not to create a theory, a concept of woman, but to preserve the place of the feminine within gender difference, a difference that has so far always functioned within the self-presenting systems of the male subject.

Irigaray's strategy to include the feminine in the conceptual construction of subjectivity does not imply a return to the systems that are dominated by the male subject. To the contrary, she proposes the thesis of the double, male-female, subject, which includes both the male and female specific experience. Only thus will the voice of the feminine find its place, and gender difference will not be effaced but will receive its due status. Irigaray not only critiques the dominant forms of subjectivity; her "deconstruction" has a positive meaning because it defines the paths that ensure "the construction of an intersubjectivity respecting sexual difference".[8] She looks for mediations that permit the feminine subjectivity.

The important is that the perspective offered by Irigaray is not only overcoming the subject-object relation. The question is to unite the energy of two human beings, two subjects (the same and the other): "to reach samadhi without destroying either myself or the other".[9] This point of view is important, because doesn't create an opposition be-

---

[8] Elizabeth Hirsh, Gary Olsen, "Je-Luce Irigaray: A Meeting with Luce Irigaray. Interview," *Hypatia* vol. 10, No. 2, (1995), 93:114, here, p. 97.

[9] Luce Irigaray, "Thinking Life as Relation: An Interview with Luce Irigaray", by Heidi Bostic and Stephen Pluháček, in: Luce Irigaray, *Conversations.* London: Continuum, 2008, p. 41.

tween sameness and otherness. The difference requires the sameness and the sameness requires the difference. As she explains the "to" in *I love to you (J'aime à toi)* is the guarantor of indirection", it signifies that you has not become an object for I. This kind of expression transforms the usual subject-object relation into a relation between two subjects: it is the indication of the passage from the discourse of only one subject to the discourse of two subjects belonging to two different worlds.[10]

One of the reasons why the hierarchic relation is rejected is that reciprocity cannot flourish in it. But in this case it is not a question of overcoming hierarchy in the name of social equality. She stresses that for Hegel and Marx, for instance, difference is based on a quantitative relation (the transformation of quantitative changes into qualitative); a similar structuring characterizes Freud's psychoanalysis, which, to a great extent, reduces the differences between sexes to presence or lack. But the difference between masculine and feminine is of another type; the two are irreducible to each other due to their different quality, not quantity. She believes such an understanding of difference (as something qualitative, irreducible, engendering horizontal relations, and not included in a hierarchic structure) would meet, among others, the new requirements of education, which is also under the sway of the oppositions "personal vs. public", "nature vs. culture", "male vs. female", "instinctive vs. abstract".

From an early age, children are torn away from their "relational context". According to Irigaray the cause of this is that the male subject is in need of objects and prefers to establish relations with what is similar, privileging group structure over the "between-two" of two independent othernesses, of two subjects that are different from each other. And such conditions do not permit the happening of the feminine subject; that is why the so-called "women's values" should find a place in the educational system. This is important not only for the rehabilitation of the feminine but as a preparation for the encounter with difference in general.

---

[10] Ibid., p. 42.

3. The birth of the feminine subject

"Sexual difference probably represents the most universal question we can address. Our era is faced with the task of dealing with this issue, because, across the whole world, there are only, men and women", writes Irigaray (Irigaray, 1992). For centuries, gender difference has been included in a bi-polar hierarchic structure of a supposedly unified subject, in which the woman plays the role of matter-nature-mother, while the man embodies the active principle. That is why, in order to attain recognition of gender equality it is not enough to overcome the hierarchy; something more is needed: to accept that there are two different subjects, male and female, each with its internal space, boundaries and weaknesses. According to Luce Irigaray, every "theory of the subject" has always been appropriated by the male principle. Hence, it is necessary to overcome the "omnipotence of the subject". She repeatedly points out that this does not refer to the absolute Hegelian subject but to the subject that has usurped language that has forced out "the other face of discourse". For Irigaray this is the speaking subject. She writes: "The fact that you no longer declare yourself an absolute subject changes nothing. The breath that animates you, the duty and the law that guide you, are also your quintessence as a subject. You no longer care for your Self. Yes, but your Self cares for you.[11]

In Irigaray's view, the birth of the feminine subject implies several strategies. One of these takes the path of "feminine speech" and "feminine writing" ("le parler-femme" and "l'écriture féminine"). Irigaray considers woman's otherness to be a value and a basis for new types of relationships. That is why becoming a feminine subject does not entail access to the universal subject. On the contrary, the aim is for the feminine to achieve its otherness, to inscribe its irreducible experience within the symbolic order, to create a language of its own.[12] She proceeds in the framework of the deconstructivist approach, which views

---

[11] Luce Irigaray, *Passions élémentaires*, Paris, Minuit, 1982, p. 101 [Engl. *Elemental passions*. Translated by Joanne Collie and Judith Still, London, New York, New Delhi, Sidney: Bloomsbury Academic, 2000.].

[12] Luce Irigaray, *L'éthique de la différence sexuelle*. Paris: Minuit, 1984, pp. 60-65 [Engl. *An Ethics of Sexual Difference*. Translated by Carolyn Burke, Gillian C. Gill, New York: Cornell University Press, 1993].

difference (including that between sexes) as something mobile, and situates it in the space of reading. Her similarity to Derrida is obvious, as the latter called for a debiologization of difference, i.e. for interpreting difference beyond the visible, beyond the anatomical, by effectuating a shift from seeing to "reading". "Let us leave the hall to which we are summoned as witnesses to the truth. And let us pass on to the hall of reading of gender difference. And it, gender difference, lies precisely in this − to ask questions, because there is no meta-sexuated reading".[13]

Irigaray aims to achieve a double effect: to deconstruct the fundamental elements of this alienating, assimilating hierarchy that pushes otherness away; and also to reveal the mechanisms of preservation of feminine otherness. We could call Irigaray's approach *deconstructivist-constructivist*. Irigaray defines another style of writing that does not lend itself to the "masculinizing syntax". In this style the images spring out of verbal associations. Other scholars, such as Hélène Cixous, also look for a specific reading of gender difference within the area of texts. Cixous gives an example of a reading that makes us aware of the difference between male and female writing. She bases her analysis on texts by the Brazilian poetess Clarice Lispector and by Jacques Derrida. According to Cixous, Derrida's texts are constructed through "an exceptional mobilization of the word". In them the word deals a blow, turns into a unit that ensures the advance of the text and that gradually grows in power; brought to an apocalypse, the word triumphs. Unlike the distance and transcendency typical of male writing, in feminine writing the world is made inward; this is a writing that has become an ear, a rhythm, which remains stretched between intimacy and infinity, between the present moment and eternity.[14]

Luce Irigaray not only calls in question the universal subject, but she proposes alternative solutions. In this case, her disagreement is with the way in which the connection between male and female takes place, happens; it is disagreement with the hierarchy, explicit or im-

---

[13] Jacques Derrida, "Fourmis". In: *Lectures de la différence sexuelle*. Paris: Des Femmes, 1994, p. 73.
[14] Hélène Cixous, "Contes de la Différence sexuelle", in *Lectures de la différence sexuelle*. Paris: Des Femmes, 1994, pp. 59-60.

plicit, that has led to subordination of the otherness to the "One". By force of this hierarchy, otherness acquires meaning only by its inclusion in opposed couples. For Irigaray the universal, constructed on the basis of a hierarchization that takes into account only part of reality, should be replaced by the universal that respects all aspects of this reality. The deconstruction of this hierarchy should not be reduced to a logical operation. On the contrary, it should be based on the fact that there exist two genders, two subjects, male and female, that are irreducible to each other. The irreducibility of the two genders serves as a point of departure for deconstruction. It sanctifies their independence as well as the significance of the difference between the genders.

Irigaray proposes her own reading of the possibility to overcome the universal subject by opposing it not with diversity but with a different subject that is its equal and yet different from the universal subject. Unlike contemporary thinkers who stress multiplicity and diversity, she affirms "bi-subjectness". Her approach pursues two basic goals. *First*, in this way she avoids the possibility that the universal subject might reappear under the guise of multiplicity. *Second*, by positing the double, male-female subject and the bi-subjective culture, deconstruction avoids the risk of bringing about a new hierarchy of values. Elimination of the domination of the universal, absolute, transcendent over the single, relative and immanent should not lead to a reversal of oppositions whereby the negative, subordinate term is transformed into a new transcendental signified. The deconstruction of the subject ought to be tied to new values, and surmounting the hierarchy should not lead to chaos or to a veiled, implicit, but no less dangerous, hierarchy.

4. Relational Identity and Two-Subject Culture

As mentioned, for Luce Irigaray the difference is of central importance: she builds her ethics on its basis. She also stresses one other thing: the recognition of woman's otherness cannot be achieved without correcting the impaired symmetry between paternal and maternal authority. In patriarchal society the maiden bride must tear herself away from her roots, must inscribe herself within her husband's family. The source of this asymmetry is the obliteration and the devaluation of the feminine deities, usually related to earth fertility. Thus, the other face of discourse is doomed to oblivion, repression, censorship. The subject effaces woman's otherness in order to project its own image upon that otherness, as in a mirror.

That is why she attaches special importance to women's mediation for the preservation of difference. According to Irigaray, the preservation of women's otherness must pass through inclusion in the feminine community, in the space in which women's otherness is preserved, beyond the hierarchic structures. But the question arises: is there not a risk that women's mediation, instead of being an advantage, might become a shortcoming, might lead to excessive caution about encountering otherness (the man's otherness), and thus to the establishment of a new realm of similarity and uniformity?

Some authors (Agacinski), however, think that the differential feminism attaches too great a value to difference – it thereby turns value into an essence and returns it to the tracks of the greatly disputed metaphysics. She stresses that the merit of differentialism is its attempt to rediscover women's otherness and the specificity of the feminine subconscious. Its shortcoming, on the other hand, is that it focuses too much on bodily differences. Second, she does not accept the separatism of the differentialists, for the strategy of separatism, or of the non-mixed, implicitly calls for the creation of a homosexual culture, a unisexual world, which is to serve as a response to the totalizing male universe. She stresses the difficulty of attaining a philosophical understanding of difference: it does not reside in only one of the two, but is situated between-the-two and is interplay of elements. That is why there cannot be absolute cognition of gender difference. Yet difference itself is a constant in which the male and female principles are of equal status. The question is not to define difference, but to accept this difference without rejection.[15]

It is true that Irigaray talks about the need to build a feminine space ("between them"), in which the traditional model of rivalry between women is overcome. But, *first*, this refers not to enclosure but to making personal experience meaningful and sharing it, which should be the basis of viable politics that correspond to the interests of women –

---

[15] Sylviane Agacinski, op.cit.

politics that would foil the appropriating strategy applied towards women by many political parties in pursuit of their own aims. *Second*, this "women's space" is only a necessary stage, part of what Irigaray recommends. Her thesis is related to the need to build a *relational identity* that would preserve the masculine and feminine, the need to make this relation a basis for interpersonal and social relations, to build a two-subject culture. No one has stressed more strongly than Irigaray the possibilities and ways to preserve otherness and to make sexuated difference serve as the foundation of a new type of sociality. Irigaray argues that it is possible for two different human beings to exist and create together. Moreover, the sexuated difference, as a foundation-setting otherness with a much larger scope of action than the physical aspect, involves different models of thinking and a different type of creativity. The fact that this difference becomes a focus for building horizontal relations leads to awareness of other types of difference and contributes to the opening to otherness, to cultural diversity, to a world built beyond the model of rivalry and rejection.

In *An Ethics of Sexual Difference* Irigaray describes the two kinds of relationship between women. The first, horizontal kind develops between women as a relation between sisters – this is a relationship with another woman. The second, vertical kind refers to a mother-daughter type of relationship. Here we may ask: how certain can we be that the vertical relationship does not potentially carry an obvious or concealed hierarchy? Irigaray's answer is that this type of vertical relationship cannot be conceived after the model of relationships with a father or with God as a father. In her view, the mother-daughter relationship remains much closer to nature and does not risk falling captive to the abstract.

Irigaray writes about relational identity and sexuated difference as opposed to hierarchy. In her view, a woman's vocation is to have greater respect for otherness due to the fact that she herself is already two people (because of pregnancy) and because motherhood requires deep respect for otherness. She supports this thesis with the following argument: she regards the placenta in the mother's womb as a "third presence", as the difference between two living beings. She considers the opposite of the closed hierarchic structure to be the "copula", i.e., the living relationship with the other, which preserves that otherness and remains open to new configurations. The imposition of the same, of the identical, of what corresponds to the law of non-contradiction, tends to destroy life. Obviously, Irigaray is attacking the prevailing interpretation of identity, which, she believes, follows the model of traditional logic and amounts to fixedness in similitude. It is an identity not susceptible to any variation, not changeable by an event or by the encounter with otherness.

5. Breathing (and) Subject

In *Between East and West* Irigaray uses the concept of "breath", borrowed from Yoga practices, and through it, grounds the possibility of a new form of subjectivity incarnated or rooted in the body. Through "breath", she connects the non-hierarchic modes of relation between two unequal subjects. The new idea of a relational subjectivity connected to the body can cast doubt upon the dichotomies that structure the Western culture. Breathing and air become mediators for overcoming the binary oppositions. Humankind must return to those forgotten mediators, whose suppression (by the leading texts of Western philosophy) is disastrous not only for feminine otherness but for otherness in general, including that of marginalized groups and of nature. According to Irigaray, we are not really aware of the enormous importance of breathing and underestimate the possible connections between the process of breathing and other spheres of life. She writes: "As we move farther away from our condition of human beings, we tend to forget the most indispensable element in life: air. The air we breathe, in which we live, speak, appear; the air in which everything 'enters into presence' and can come into being. This air that we never think of has been borrowed from birth..."[16] Air determines "the possibility of his coming into the world and the potential opening of a horizon of thought, of poetry..."[17] It is not only an element of nature, but also a mediator between nature and culture that ensures their mutual connection and interaction. Being a basic element of life, air is what

---

[16] Irigaray, Luce. *Speculum,* op.cit, p. 127.
[17] Ibid.

two subjects share. In her book *The Forgetting of Air* (1983) she draws an analogy between one's connection with air and a child's with the mother, who, through her body, gives oxygen to the child and thus provides it with life. As mediator, the air is something necessary not only for the encounter between the subject and the other but also for the connection of the subject with itself. So, on one hand, air provides dialogue, ensures speech with the other, the acceptance of otherness; on the other, the cultivation of breathing ensures the autonomy of the subject, the preservation of its own otherness. She has turned her attention to Eastern practices such as Yoga, which cultivate breathing as an act of the integral Self, in which body and soul are combined. In her words, "In the East it is more common to remember that living is equivalent to breathing. And the Sages there care about acquiring a proper life through practicing a conscious breathing".[18] She points out that the first thing she learned from Yoga was "to breath", which corresponds to "assuming responsibility for your own life".[19] Without autonomy, there can be no life or relation, and without air, there can be no autonomy. Irigaray connects breathing to our duty to nature and to the mother (we all have an "unpaid debt to the maternal", because, before being born, the child receives oxygen from its mother): "Breathing is thus a duty toward my life, that of the others and that of the entire living world".[20] Only two autonomous subjects are in a condition to create a connection outside the negative projection or appropriation. If we fail to gain from breathing all that which grants us autonomy and makes us assume responsibility for our lives, then we risk remaining passive in a socio-cultural placenta that envelopes us in already breathed-out, used, impure air. In that case, it is as if we had refused to be born, to leave the womb and to start out on our road.

Here Irigaray suggests that maternity can be a model for a connection, a relation that, while preserving its own autonomy, also provides autonomy for the other. "The mother gives her breath and lets the other

---

[18] Luce Irigaray, *Entre Orient et Occident*, Grasset, 1999, p. 74 [Engl. *Between East and West: From Singularity to Community*. Translated by Stephen Pluhácek. New York: Columbia University Press, 2002.].
[19] Ibid., p. 50.
[20] Ibid.

go; she gives the other life and autonomy". Air is the environment in which the lives of people, animals and plants develop, in which autonomy is born – the autonomy of two subjects on an equal standing; air provides possibilities for creativity and for a new type of non-hierarchic relation beyond the subject-object connection and the market economy ESD.[21]

6. Body and Transcendence

"What is spirit if it forces the body to comply with an abstract model that is unsuited to it", asks Irigaray in *I love to you*.[22] For Irigaray, sexual difference combines the natural and the cultural – that is why she argues against the erroneous division between body and soul. She argues also that our cultural tradition does not take into consideration transcendence in the relations *to* and *with* the other. In the Western culture the transcendence is projected into an Absolute extraneous to our daily life, an ideal that we could not reach and the philosophy is understood as a love of wisdom.[23] The philosophers progressively forgot the figure of the Goddess and transformed her into emptiness. The wisdom of love is substituted by the love of wisdom.

Irigaray attempts to create a space of difference in the realm of the spiritual; to this end she critiques that other well-established hierarchy in Western culture, the connection between mind and matter, soul and body, in which one of the two terms is declared to be inferior to the other. Here too, in place of the traditional hierarchy, she prefers the transformation of the body from live matter into *spiritual matter*. The aim is to attain a sensory-transcendent unity that overcomes the division between mind and matter and leads to a progressive spiritualization of the body. For the female gender the conquest of the spiritual passes, also, through the relationship towards the body, something that Irigaray calls "virginity". But this virginity is different from the physi-

---

[21] Ibid., pp. 12, 80, 128.
[22] Luce Irigaray, *J'aime à toi*, Paris: Grasset, 1992, p. 25 [Engl. *I Love to You: Sketch of a Possible Felicity in History*. Translated by Alison Martin. New York: Routledge, 1996].
[23] Ibid., p. 40.

cal one. It cannot be described negatively, does not rest upon some lack or some prohibition for certain body-related experiences; it integrates those experiences, thereby building the specificity of women's acquired experience. The body becomes a pathway towards the spiritual; and virginity, as Irigaray uses the term, is synonymous with spiritual integrity (conquered and preserved). Unlike the physical kind, this paradoxical virginity does not come at the beginning but later on, as a result of long initiation. It leads to expanding horizons for the self beyond the notions imposed by routine. On one hand, this virginity is part of the specific dimensions of female spirituality; but, on the other hand, in a more general perspective, and outside the feminist context, we will find that it does not lose its meaning and fits very well in the area of almost forgotten but always topical practices of initiation in the framework of the relationship between disciple and spiritual teacher.

7. Between-two: being-for-the-Other (Levinas), the possibility of the impossible (Derrida), and the two-subject shared world (Irigaray)

Here we should make a comparison between Irigaray's two-subject, shared world, and Levinas's "being-for-the-Other". Unlike the latter, which is non-symmetrical, non-reciprocal, since the Self that has given up its own boundaries attains complete hypostasis in the Other, Irigaray's relation between two equal subjects is *symmetrical and reciprocal*; it preserves the otherness of *both* subjects; and it is reminiscent of Ricoeur's reciprocity in dissymmetry.[24] "Being-for-the-Other" and the relation of two subjects are similar in that they both form a space of spirituality in which humaneness is not only preserved but expands its boundaries. Levinas refers to a space of immediate closeness. Such a nuance is not absent in Irigaray's terms either. When she writes about the connection to the mother, she points out that "the customs in the mother's world are usually set in motion by closeness"; while in the father's world the law of property functions predominantly. For Irigaray and Levinas alike, the transcendent springs from hu-

---

[24] Paul Ricœur, *Parcours de la reconnaissance*. Paris: Stock, 2004, p. 236 [Engl. *The Course of Recognition*. Cambridge and London: Harvard University Press, 2005].

maneness, from the *"between-two"*, from the intersubjective tie. Levinas refers to hypostasis of the self in the other, while Irigaray asserts that each of the two independent and different subjects has its own boundaries, and precisely these boundaries contribute to their drawing close together. In the framework of Levinas's ethics of responsibility the hypostasis of the self is final, while in Irigaray's ethics of difference, the transgression of the self is temporary and counterbalanced by loyalty to oneself; *the two subjects remain open to new configurations, new shared worlds and new returnings to oneself.* Both thinkers believe that genuine, live contact between the two people is achieved outside intentionality; but while Levinas accepts that the recurrence (or hypostasis) of the self is a movement contrary to intentionality (which has a voluntary element), Irigaray holds that no real contact occurs where the predominant relation is between subject and object, or between two similar subjects. Levinas builds the "between-two" as an overcoming of verbiage: "at times the very act of persuasion is violence", he writes. For him, encounter-parting is not built through dialogue, because "the demand of the opposite side is tacit". For her part, Irigaray sets in contrast breathing and speaking. Even when she writes about dialogue, she has in mind a kind of dialogue that is different from the speech of philosophers (which she characterizes as monologue, and stresses that philosophers either speak to themselves or to disciples who are not their equals). This way of speech produces a partial truth, which lies outside of life, does not include inner experience, constantly refers to a logocentric order, and deals with the limited world of concepts. To the contrary, the ability to listen to the other, to speak "with" subjects, not "to" objects, is part of the cultivation of a true relation between two different subjects, two independent persons; this relation does not turn into a subject-object relation based on the characteristics of the male world.

For both thinkers, otherness is not repressed or appropriated, but preserved; but unlike Levinas, Irigaray sees the balance of the two othernesses as fully preserved. Both Levinas and Irigaray derive the pathos of relationship not from the community but from the "between-two" relation with the other – here, the other is not someone similar, not "my neighbor", but has the quality of being impenetrable, vast, and absolutely other. Both Irigaray and Levinas make this "between-two" a model for a new social organization. In the case of Levinas, this can be achieved by the appearance of a "third person" and the action of justice (the horizon of which is, after all, care and responsibility for the other), while for Irigaray this happens through the value of sexuated difference, which becomes a focus and model of acceptance of difference in general, including religious and cultural difference. It is hard to believe that Levinas's ethics, even though they are balanced by the third person and justice, can serve as a foundation of a new type of sociality. Whereas Irigaray proposes a positive strategy for a new type of sociality, built precisely upon the relation between two subjects of equal value. For Levinas, ethics comes before any ontology and, also, before any religious doctrine, because morality has no need of prescriptions. In Irigaray we find a new type of spirituality that makes of the human body a gateway to spirituality.

Luce Irigaray's deconstructivist project rests not upon the reversal of opposites but upon the distance and balance between them; similar to Derrida's deconstruction, she builds a paradoxical unity between two opposite terms. Irigaray points out that, under certain circumstances, deconstruction could turn into nihilistic folly, and Derrida calls for preserving the aporia. Irigaray writes about sharing while maintaining differences and the unique encounter between subjects – this encounter is never a repetition of something that has already happened before. Derrida accepts that authentic responsibility is a "testing of the aporia", "a trial of the possibility of the impossible", because to remain within the boundaries of the possible means to leave the sphere of ethics, and the all-too-pure conscience is another name for irresponsibility. We may regard sexuated difference, as Irigaray sees it, as a foundation and pathway to the conditional and unconditional hospitality in Derrida. Irigaray points out that sexuated difference can develop a culture of difference. On the other hand, it sets boundaries to our relations with the other, boundaries that we may open but also reclose.

For instance, Irigaray's views regarding woman's otherness have become a basis for the search of a new type of universality, resting on addition, not exclusion (universality with a plus sign). This universality of addition rejects the negative projection typical of the universal based on abstraction and exclusion. In the context of the deconstructionist paradigm, the ethics of difference represents an attempt at a new reading of woman's specificity that avoids the traps of an imposed patriarchal model. This ethics is constructed as a theory of recognition of otherness; it is a new interpretation and new appreciation of the value of all the forms otherness may assume.

The purpose of such a theory is equally to preserve feminine otherness and male otherness. This change of perspective is not based on a reversal of oppositions and does not declare the feminine to be in the lead. It is also a critique of abstract universality, which preserves only the formal aspect of human beings and neutralizes the differences between sexes. For the time has come to attain such a way of thinking universality that would include the interplay of differences as well; the time has come for life to be preserved in its male-female definedness. Irigaray offers a most balanced perspective. On one hand, this relational subject is obviously in constant dependency on otherness; on the other, its preserves its autonomy. Unlike other philosophers of difference, who no less forcefully call in question the hierarchized structures and the domination of the One over diversity, Irigaray draws a dividing line that passes not between One and diversity but between two subjects in positions of equality, who preserve their irreducible otherness. She seeks projections of philosophy in the fields of ethics and politics, and traces paths by which the feminine and the masculine subject might establish non-hierarchic relations in the name of love and sharing, and create a space of reciprocity.

7

Mary-Kate G. Smith

WESTERN LIBERAL FEMINISM, LIBERAL VALUES, AND THE DIVERSITY OF WOMEN'S SITUATIONS

1. Globalization, liberal values and post-colonization

The world's boundaries have continually been challenged and reshaped throughout history yet more recently they seem to be undergoing notable pressure particularly from economic, political and cultural forces. The processes of so-called globalization have taken on new dimensions of late with increased technologies, speedier communications, and the increased desire for economic expansion.[1] And, the "benefits" of the current system of globalization are not enjoyed by all parties involved. For some, entire ways of life have been devastated without the consent of the community members, some have been thrust into even more dire poverty and lack of agency, and some once sustainable communities have been forced into dependency on other, more powerful states.

Within the interplay of this process of globalization and post-colonization, some institutions and states, mainly focused in the West and/or North, continue to retain hegemony around the globe. The West has arguably accumulated the most influence and power in defining the economic, political and social processes that contribute to globalization. And, it seems apparent that women and children have been most harshly effected by such processes and lack equal bargaining power. In such an unequal balance of power relations and structures of authority, a universal system of just standards and values seems most urgent in order to have a systematic way to regulate and judge

---

[1] See Takis Fotopoulos, *Towards an Inclusive Democracy*, New York: Cassell, Wellington House, 1997, 33-55.

moral and political processes that are occurring exponentially on a transnational level. Yet, is a universal theory of justice possible that can be applied to all human beings everywhere possible? Or would such a universal theory somehow be a bit oppressive by being inherently exclusive to some? Who has the authority to establish such a theory and how would it be developed? Can a feminist perspective inform such a theory to level out power differentials and domination? It seems to me that the trend, in the political arena at least, has been to look to democratic values and human rights as way (at least superficially) to secure a transnational or universal just standard. But, are democratic values the ideal values which should and can be embraced by all? Can espousing liberal democratic values on to the world, in effect, decrease women's voice and political agency? Should we revise democratic values to include a dialogic ethic based on free and open speech? And if so, how should it be done?

Although developing moral and political just standards that can guide transnational judgments is an urgent issue, we approached a moral and/or political dilemma in trying to formulate and establish such standards. For, on the one hand, there seems to be an urgent need for universal standards in order to make moral and political judgments that affect the lives of so many. However, any universal theory seems bound to rely on specific values and/or certain specific human capacities that are construed as universal but in fact are not. Universal theories are usually bound to the idea that all humans are basically alike. Thus, universal theories are incapable of taking into account the plurality and difference that explicitly exists throughout the world. On the other hand, making room for difference seems to require taking into account billions of concrete contextual points of view. And in so doing, the ability to form standards, make judgments and criticize actions seems compromised because no criterion of judgment seems applicable. Paying attention to particularity and to socially and historically located individuals or cultures seems to risk falling into dreaded relativism through which an unjust system of standards can conceivably be supported equal to that of a just system. Should we surrender completely our attempts to establish universal standards or is it possible to pursue a somewhat more innocuous avenue that balances the particular with the universal? These questions are imposing and need continual reverent attention which means that they cannot be adequately answered or even discussed within an article, but demonstrate the backdrop in which the focus of this essay rests[2].

These questions resonate with the phenomenon of Western liberal feminists' preoccupation with liberating and helping the "poor oppressed" women who live in non western and so-called "Third World"[3] cultures in order to bring justice to their lives. According to some liberal feminists, most women in so-called non-western traditions are oppressed because they are denied liberty, justice and/or equality on the basis of their sex or qua being female. And in this light, they believe that it is possible to critique "other" cultures on the premise that these cultures victimize and hurt women by denying them their human rights or ability to decide for themselves how to lead their lives. They believe that these cultures ought to uphold and to instill feminist liberal and democratic principles. For they obtain that these principles are universally applicable and beneficial to all women and all persons.

I would agree that this pursuit may be a helpful one. Yet, arguing for liberal and democratic values, and speaking for these women raises many difficulties. For, are western feminists or western liberal feminists actually harming those women they are intending to "help" or "save"? For example, liberal feminists who take this position might be assuming that their principles are more developed than the "others'" and they be assuming prematurely that their principles would suit these women and their ways of being. So, even with well-meaning intentions, trying to help so-called other, non-western "Third World" wom-

---

[2] See David A. Crocker, "Insiders and Outsiders in International Development" *Ethics & International Affairs* 5 (1991): 149-172.

[3] I use the term, "Third World", carefully to signify the traditional use of the words and to show that they are denigrating terms. These words typically refer to parts of the world that are generally poorer and less industrialized than Europe and the United States or the West/North. I do not assume that all countries that are often subsumed under this heading actually have any intrinsic value that is less than any other country in the world as might be signified by the word "third". Nor am I assuming that all of the countries within the "Third World" are alike and have similar problems or similar solutions to their problems. In fact, it is the universalizing use of this term which is criticized in this paper. I use the term with critical cynicism and in order to argue against it.

en is problematic, even if it is in the name of supposedly neutral liberal democratic ideals of liberty and equality. In her essay, "The Problem of Speaking for Others", Linda Alcoff puts this point clear when she writes that, "certain privileged locations are discursively dangerous. In particular, the practice of privileged persons speaking for or on behalf of less privileged persons has actually resulted (in many cases) increasing or reinforcing the oppression of the group spoken for."[4]

In this essay, I will focus on two of Susan Moller Okin's works as a liberal feminist perspective. I do not claim that her work is wholly representative of liberal feminist thought or that all liberal feminists agree with her and her methods. Instead, I use her work as a focal point because it is compelling yet provocative and to demonstrate the manifold difficulties in trying to speak for others on their behalf, in ending the so-called global subjugation of women, and in developing a universal theory of justice.

I will begin with a brief discussion of what liberal values are and what liberal feminists often advocate. This is not intended to be an all encompassing detailed discussion of liberalism and liberal feminism, but instead one that provides background information in order to guide our thoughts on these terms through the upcoming sections.

2. Liberalism, Liberal Feminism and Democracy: Background[5]

Liberalism is a tradition that has been born out of many ideas of several thinkers and of several social situations, but is most often characterized as part of the "western" tradition. Liberalism can be seen as a reaction and attempt to reverse oppression which restricts people's freedoms.

According to this tradition, human beings are autonomous and individual rational thinkers. Reason is a specifically human capacity

---

[4] Linda Alcoff, "The Problem of Speaking for Others", in *Cultural Critique,* No. 20 (Winter, 1991-1992), pp. 5-32.
[5] Most of the discussion in this section should be seen in the context of Alison Jaggar's *Feminist Politics and Human Nature* (Totowa, NJ: Rowman & Allanheld, 1983), but it is also a result of my formation and experience over the years.

which distinguishes humans from animals and all else. Humans, according to liberalism, are basically unencumbered selves with the ability to think rationally and make choices about their "own" beliefs about the good life. Within this tradition, the self is viewed as a predominantly atomistic and individual entity rather than an entity that is fully encumbered in particular and community based and familial attachments. And so, fulfillment in life is achieved by thinking for one's self and developing one's own rational capabilities.[6] According to liberalism, all humans have an inherent equal worth or value based on their basically equal capacity to think rationally. And it is this basic equality of rational capacities justifies claims to equal rights.[7]

Liberty is also a traditional value with which liberalism in concerned. Liberty, within a liberal framework, ensures that individuals are free to seek to attain their own ends without interference from others or the state. So, liberal governments in theory limit intervention into the private lives of individuals and attempt to remain neutral on ideas of the good life. Of course, the distinction between the public and the private is not so clear and often overlaps.[8] The state is to only regulate the so-called public or political sphere because advocating certain collective goals or ideas of the "good" may be oppressive toward those who do not agree. For, advocating one form of the good

---

[6] The liberal idea of the self is most often contrasted with the communitarian view of humans as encumbered selves whose fulfilment is based on communal and cultural connections and interactions.

[7] Alison Jaggar, *Feminist Politics and Human Nature*. Totowa, NJ: Rowman & Allanheld, 1983.

[8] This is often a point of contention for feminists. Where one's political or public life ends and one's private life begins is unclear. The division of public and private is evolving and changing and no clear boundary exists. For a beneficial discussion of the division of the public and private and the effects on women, see Nancy Fraser, "Rethinking the public sphere" (in *Justice Interruptus*. New York, London: Routledge, 1997), as well as Martha A. Ackelsberg and Mary Lyndon Shanley, "Privacy, Publicity and Power: a Feminist Rethinking of the Public-Private Distinction" (in *Revisioning the Political: Feminist Reconstructions of Traditional Concepts in Western Political Theory*. Eds. Nancy Hirschmann and Christine Di Stefano, Boulder: Westview Press, 1996).

denies validity to other forms of the good which in turn denies the individual's right to choose for her or himself.[9]

Individuals are granted civil and political rights to protect them from oppressive government intervention and gain formal equality. Political or human rights are ideally to be universally and impartially applied, for the state to remain neutral and so everyone basically enjoys the same rights. Rights that are usually supported by liberalism are freedom of speech, information, conscience, association, expression and privacy. These political rights are supposed to be available to all individuals regardless of group affiliation. Claude Akes definition of human rights is very helpful; he writes that, "It is that human beings have certain rights simply by virtue of being human. These rights are a necessary condition for the good life. Because of their singular importance, individuals are entitled to, indeed, required to claim them and society is enjoined to allow them. Otherwise the quality of life is seriously compromised."[10]

Democracy can be identified as a form of government which, at least ideally, is controlled by all the people, each having equal access to the privileges of the state and sharing equally in duties and responsibilities. Each individual is supposed to participate in the governing and decision making process, whether directly or through representation. Democratic values focus on political, legal and social equality and respect for the individual. Such values are supposed to relate to and/or promote the peoples' interests.

A democracy that encompasses the ideal has yet to be realized and is most likely an impossible goal. Thus, in a not so ideal world, individuals obtain formal equality through a representative democracy, where politics are instrumental to private ends. The hope is that representatives will serve the ends of individuals and represent their interests without every individual having to serve time in the legislature or having to make policy decisions. And, a just representative democracy should also seek to justly distribute society's goods and services so to

---

[9] See Alison Jaggar, *Feminist Politics and Human Nature*, op.cit.
[10] Claude Ake, "The African Context of Human Rights," *Africa Today*, 34:1-2 (1987), 103.

as secure equal opportunity. Through fair and democratic procedures, the liberal state is to ensure toleration, equality and freedom.

Liberal feminists agree with these concepts in principle but argue that all societies, even those that are traditionally based on liberal values, have often excluded women from participation in society and the fulfillment of their rights. Therefore, they argue that these societies have oppressed women by restricting their freedom and their political rights. Liberal feminists have embraced liberal principles, but argue that women should receive equal political rights and status with men. They argue that women have the ability to reason equal to that of men and so have equal moral worth as individuals. Since they are basically equal to men they are just as deserving of such rights. According to them, women have been oppressed as a group and been limited and restricted because of their sex. Women have traditionally been discriminated against in all areas of life especially the economic and political realms. And so, liberal feminists advocate such things as pay equity across the sexes and women's economic independence, because without these, women are unable to exercise and enjoy their full political rights and to obtain equal bargaining power with men.[11] Alison Jaggar describes liberal feminists in, *Feminist Politics and Human Nature*, and writes that they, "…want to eliminate sex-based discrimination in all areas of life and guarantee women equal opportunities with men to define and pursue their own interests."[12]

To end sex-based discrimination and for women to achieve real equality, many liberal feminists argue that there are preconditions for this equality that must be secured by the state. Some of the preconditions for equality that are often cited are the elimination of poverty (women are disproportionately poor), strict laws against domestic violence, state shelters for domestic violence victims, child care and child care centers provided by the government, and more education and training for women. These types of state supported programs are hoped to bring women to an equal starting point with men or to help establish and ensure equal opportunity.[13]

---

[11] Alison Jaggar, *Feminist Politics and Human Nature*, op.cit., pp. 173-180
[12] Ibid., p. 181.
[13] Ibid., p. 183.

Advocating equal rights for women, equal opportunity for women and liberal values in general might be a beneficial beginning to creating a more just society and world. Yet, advocating liberalism as a universalizable standard to guide international relations is problematic and depending on the type of method employed, the project's original purpose of instantiating justice can be contradicted or debilitated.

3. Liberal feminist critique of third world countries and an argument for human rights of women: Susan Moller Okin

Since Susan Moller Okin believes that liberal values are universalizable to all women and people regardless of their culture, historical situations and situated positions, she argues against the universal oppression of women from men. She argues that women experience a similar subjugation that is universalizable to all women regardless of race, culture or socioeconomic status. And so she believes that women in the "First World" can legitimately speak for all women and especially for the women in the Third World in speaking out against this oppression. I argue that, although we might have a duty to speak out against oppression, I question whether Okin's method of speaking for women in the "Third World" and making vast generalizations over the entire "Third World" which I presume includes at least three continents, namely Africa, Asia and South America. Her method might actually serve to silence the women for whom she is speaking and in turn decrease the likelihood of establishing real democracy and liberal values throughout the world. In effect Okin's project might end up contradicting itself.
Susan Moller Okin, in her essay, "Gender, Inequality and Cultural Difference", is skeptical of some feminists' claims that any universal theory, even universal feminist theories, inevitably excludes certain people. She doubts that listening to every concrete voice is a viable avenue to creating moral and political standards or a coherent theory of justice. She argues that women's experience of oppression is generalizable and argues that the conditions which women endure in poorer countries are similar to, but worse than, the experiences of western women in richer nations; she claims their problems are, "similar to

ours but more so."[14] Okin believes that she can provide comparative evidence to this end and substantiate the claim that western accounts of gender inequality are universalizable to women across the world even in light of tremendous cultural, political and economic difference.[15] In so doing, she addresses four issues which will purportedly provide the evidence to support her argument. She discusses the issues of attention to gender as comparatively recent, the importance of paying attention to gender inequality, justice in the family (or lack thereof), and the policy implications of her findings.

Okin argues that issues regarding gender inequality have been neglected because the unit analysis for development studies and the like has been the head of the household which has typically been the male. The distinction between the public and private is assumed correct so that development studies and theories of justice only make reference to the public sphere and have tended to ignore the private. And, development and justice theorists have employed so-called gender neutral terms assuming them to be applicable to all people. The difficulty is that these development and justice theorists have used these terms even in relation to issues that are not relevant to women. And in this way women are not taken specifically into account and have become invisible because their concerns are equated with men's or with families' and their concerns are never explicitly the focus.[16]

Attention to gender is important, according to Okin, and this is undeniable, because inequalities exist between the sexes and women matter just as much as men. In order to balance out the inequalities, one has to pay attention to gender related issues, especially since the inequalities many times have fatal consequences for women. Gender inequalities have compromised equality of opportunity for women and girls and so needs to be addressed. She argues this is the case for women of the "Third World" as well as for "First World" women, but just that it is a much direr situation for women in the "Third World". I would argue that here Okin unfortunately does not question the values

---

[14] Susan Moller Okin, "Gender Inequality and Cultural Differences" *Political Theory*, 22:1 (February 1994): 5-24, here p. 8.
[15] Ibid., p. 9.
[16] Ibid., p. 10.

of equal opportunity and her own ideas of equality. She assumes that these values are good and necessarily universalizable. Arguably, women facing unproportionate deaths is wrong. But, Okin's more general assumptions about the value of equal opportunity and equality are values that she should be defending against her critics instead of assuming them. This is the case because these are questionable values to many people in the world, and possibly to many women. That is why Okin had to incorporate an argument for these values rather than merely presuming them as goods. She is speaking from a liberal feminist point of view and so to some extent does believe these values to be true. But much of her point in her essay is to defend these values in light of her critics and so she ought not to assume that all these values are necessarily good for all women and all people, but rather ought to demonstrate how this is the case.

Okin also points out that the family unit should be focused on in development studies and theories of justice, because it is "the first and arguably the most influential, school of moral development." According to her, people first learn how to interrelate with others and how to be just or unjust within the family unit; children witness the power differentials within the family and will then go on to replicate them, which usually means that males will wield the power over the females. She explains:

> They are likely to learn injustice by absorbing the messages, if male, that they have some kind of "natural" enhanced entitlement and if female, that they are *not* equals and had better get used to being subordinated if not actually abused.[17]

Thus, she goes on to accuse many "Third World" families of being worse than, "their *developed* world equivalents",[18] [emphasis added], at schooling their children in values of justice.

It seems that Okin is somewhat condescending to these communities by generalizing over vast differences and by employing negative stereotypes directed at various communities without any direct evidence. One wonders exactly about whom or which communities she is

---

[17] Ibid., p. 12.
[18] Ibid., p. 13.

actually speaking. She paints a denigrating picture of the whole of the "Third World" without real evidence to support it. She assumes the privileged position as the norm and ethnocentric universality of her culture and cultural norms while she condemns whole communities, wielding blanket judgments of many "Third World" families as if no difference in contexts and historicities exists.[19] She explicitly says that the Western world is better at schooling their children in morals and this also seems to imply that the West has better morals than the whole of the "Third World". These statements are extremely difficult to substantiate and so stand as biased judgment that supports negative stereotypes of "Third World" countries. I am not arguing that women are not often abused in the countries that are named as "Third World", nor am I arguing that the abuse does not occur at a greater extent than in the "First World". Rather, I am arguing that Okin should be careful in stating such accusations without substantiation, especially when it can incur such negative stereotypes of countless communities throughout the world invoking an air of post-colonial condemnation of these communities as uncivilized or even backwards. Okin might therefore be accused of ethnocentricism.[20]

---

[19] See Chandra Talpade Mohanty, "Under Western Eyes: Feminist Scholarship and Colonial Discourses" in *Third World Women and the Politics of Feminism,* eds. Chandra Mohanty, Ann Russo and Lourdes Torres, (Bloomington IN: Indiana University Press, 1991): 51-80.

[20] David Crocker distinguishes between two senses of ethnocentrism and I think Okin can be accused of being ethnocentric in both senses, but this is debatable. He writes that, "It is widely believed, especially by those living in rich and powerful countries, that appropriate Third World and global development models, policies, and projects should reflect Northern/Western development experience. Increasingly this belief is seen, especially by those living in the Third World, as ethnocentrism. Here "ethnocentrism" means two things. First, Northern/Western ethnocentrics employ their own cultural norms in evaluating foreign practices. In this firs sense, ethnocentrism is 'a habitual disposition to judge foreign peoples or groups by the standards and practices of one's own culture or ethnic group'. Second, these ethnocentrics employ their standards to make *invidious* comparisons. Foreign standards and practices are judged to be inferior to those of the evaluator. In this second sense, ethnocentrism is 'a tendency toward viewing alien cultures with disfavour and a resulting sense of (one's own) inherent superiority'" (David A. Crocker, "Insiders and Outsiders in International Development" *Ethics & International Affairs* 5 (1991): 149-172, here pp. 150-151).

As an example of injustice in the family, Okin uses the fact that most of the work that women perform is unpaid household work and that women face discrimination and segregation in the workplace.[21] She argues that this is the case for both Western women as well as their "Third World" counterparts. For, women's work is most often less valued which devalues women, gives them less power and are paid less than men. So, they are often economically dependent on men. This lack of power and their dependency on men lends women extremely vulnerable and subject to, "physical, sexual, and/or psychological abuse by the men they live with."[22] And, according to her, the situation is much worse in the "less developed" regions of the world. Again Okin assumes that generally "Third World" men systematically abuse "Third World" women and this adds support to the stereotype that "brown" men abuse "brown" women more than white men. She makes this generalization, which is most likely an exaggeration, across numerous regions of the world without any real justification. I think evidence is necessary for such a grand statement. She also does not take into consideration the possible effects of her position which can be understood as equal to a colonizing gaze treating "Third World" people as more barbaric than their Western "counterparts" because the people of the "Third World" are less developed and uncivilized.[23] Problematizing and speaking out against the abuse of women and the barriers to women's agency is necessary to establish a more just global system, but Okin's particular method may not prove to be beneficial to the women she is trying to assist.

Okin does not mention that work done by some women in some communities of the "Third World" is not necessarily less valued and that many times it is the instillation of a western system of a cash economy and capitalism that has created, or at least exacerbated, the inequality. Western institutions like the World Bank and International Monetary Fund have disrupted and distorted some self-sufficient

---

[21] Susan Moller Okin, "Gender Inequality and Cultural Differences" *Political Theory*, 22:1 (February 1994): 5-24, here p. 13.
[22] Ibid., p. 14.
[23] See Chandra Talpade Mohanty, "Under Western Eyes: Feminist Scholarship and Colonial Discourses", op.cit.

communities and have had great influence in creating the value system which values the male bread winner as the worker who goes out to make the money.[24] Although it is true that in some places women are forbidden to seek outside work, Okin forgets to analyze the West's possible complicity in this phenomenon. Jane Flax, in "Ethics of Difference" writes that, "Okin's argument relies on the assumption that First World women *are* outside the social relations that produce poor ones. This mistaken belief functions as a defense against acknowledging the social practices that constitute the Western observer and the relations between observer and observed. It obscures 'the complex interconnection between first and third world economies and the profound effect of this on the lives of women in all countries'."[25]

Often, non-Western cultures hold tight to certain value systems as part of their tradition in attempts to keep Western influences at bay, even if it might mean constructing relatively new values held as traditional or devaluing women and their work.[26] One could argue that the West is therefore partly responsible for the devaluation of women's work in certain places, due to colonization and imperialism. This is something that must be taken into consideration before Okin passes broad negative judgments solely onto the "Third World". This point also illustrates the difficulties of Okin's generalization over the entire "Third World" and her lack of attention to contextual or specific histories and cultures.

The policy implications or solutions Okin suggests are to challenge the public and the private dichotomy and to focus on individuals instead of households in theory and policy making. In dividing the public and private spheres, Okin argues that the oppression and inequality that occurs within the private sphere has been obscured. For, it has been assumed that the public spheres of the political or economic areas of social life are the true objects of theories of justice and state inter-

---

[24] See Takis Fotopoulos, *Towards an Inclusive Democracy*, New York: Cassell, Wellington House, 1997.

[25] Jane Flax, "Race/Gender and The Ethics of Difference: A Reply to Okin's 'Gender Inequality and Cultural Differences'," *Political Theory* 23:3 (August 1995): 500-510, here p. 504.

[26] See Uma Narayan, *Dislocating Cultures: Identities, Traditions, and Third World Feminism*. New York: Routledge, 1997.

vention. Okin questions this and argues that we need to look to domestic areas of the private life and realize the tremendous injustice that often occurs within it. She also urges that we should focus on the individual and not the household for studies and policy making so that women receive equal treatment and that their inequality is recognized.

Okin is correct to investigate, problematize and draw attention to the way women and other persons who have less power within different cultures are treated and how their freedom might be compromised within the group. I thank her for drawing our attention to the fact that many injustices do take place in the private sphere, most often against women, and so that state intervention may be required to intervene in and regulate this 'sphere' of society as well. Yet, it is questionable to what extent governments should become involved in the so-called private sphere. We have finally been able to bring domestic violence to the forefront, at least in some areas of the world, and have it valued as a crime and injustice, not just as domestic quarrels. And, I believe this is a good thing. But, how much further do we want governments or states to intervene in the domestic lives of people? If every aspect of the private sphere became the political, state intervention into *legitimately* private matters could increase. I am not sure what the answer is, because maybe the price is worth paying if it means that women will no longer be victims of violence and robbed of freedom. This is another extremely difficult question and needs to be answered thoughtfully and democratically.

She also notes that her solutions are referring to both what theorists/social scientists and policy makers need to do.[27] Yet, she does not question the role of the social scientists and policy makers and the effects of their scholarship, i.e. the fact that there is no apolitical scholarship (Mohanty). In focusing on social scientists and scholarship, Okin's solutions, in effect, leave out the women whom she is trying to help or protect. As Aihwa Ong observes: "For the privilege of making cultural judgments which see their way into print, feminists often speak without reducing the silence of the cultural Other."[28] In my

---

[27] Susan Moller Okin, "Gender Inequality and Cultural Differences", op.cit., p. 17.
[28] Aihwa Ong, "Colonialism and Modernity: Feminist Re-presentations of Women in Non-Western Societies." *Inscriptions* 3:4 (1988): 79-93, here p. 3.

opinion, any real change cannot be spurred solely from social scientists, who tend to be Western Scholars, and policy makers. Real change must come from active participation of the people involved. Maybe Okin is correct to remind social scientists and policy makers that they must include women in their research and thinking about the world. Yet, I argue that this is not enough for women, especially women in poorer, less powerful regions of the world, to be included. For, as Claude Ake argues:

> Development [or improvement in the lives of communities] cannot be achieved by proxy. A people develops itself or not at all. And it can develop itself only through its commitment and its energy. That is where democracy comes in. Self-reliance is not possible unless the society is thoroughly democratic, unless the people are the end and not just the means of development. Development occurs, in so far as it amounts to the pursuit of objectives set by the people themselves in their own interest and pursued by means of their own resources.[29]

Okin seems to overlook difference in an attempt to arrive at a universal theory of justice based on a shared oppression of women. Yet, overlooking difference often means excluding those whose lives are different from the specific aspects from which a specific universal theory is based. Some argue that a dialogic feminism, similar to Jürgen Habermas' theory of discourse ethics, is what is necessary so that every women's voice is heard. Incorporating a dialogic feminism into democratic structures and interpersonal relationships, it is argued, will allow people from subordinated groups or parts of the world to be heard and to speak in their culturally specific ways. Thus, Ong puts forward:

> I can suggest a few tentative leads for recognizing a mutuality of discourse in our encounter with women in non-Western societies. We can resist the tendency to write our subjectively-defined world onto an Other that lies outside it (...) feminist scholarship tends to be riddled with natural, sexual, political and social categories when it comes to re-presenting the Other.

---

[29] Claude Ake, "The African Context of Human Rights," *Africa Today*, 34:1-2 (1987), p. 105.

> When we jetties on our conceptual baggage, we open up the possibilities for mutual but partial, and ambiguous exchange.[30]

These values, if practiced, will also allow others who are not in a particular culture to understand better the experiences of the members of that culture. In turn, this will allow for common bonds and awareness to be formed 'across difference and dominance'. And it will hopefully increase inclusiveness and equal status of individuals rather than exclude them.[31] Yet Okin disagrees objecting that listening and discussing are commendable and necessary for democracy, but, "If everyone were to speak only from his or her own point of view, it is unclear that we would come up with any principles at all."[32] Okin does not acknowledge that discussing, listening and debating over values and standards does not necessarily entail only thinking about oneself and one's own interests. Although we may never be able to escape our own standpoints and never actually be able to understand fully what it is like to be another person or what their exact needs and interest are (and individuals may not even be sure about their own needs), we may be able to respect others and take others' needs and voices into consideration as well as be able to change our own perspectives and views. Even though David Crocker, in his essay "Insiders and Outsiders in International Development Ethics", is primarily speaking of international development ethics, I think that what he says can be applied to approaches to developing just universal standards when he writes that:

> An approach to international development ethics is needed whereby an ethicist from a "developed" society can become convinced that a "developing" society offers some progressive ideas for the ethicist's *own* society; it could be something new and different that substantially alters the foreigner's ethical assumptions. Each ethicist starts from but need not end with the ethics inherited from his or her society. Genuine dialogue involves a "continual reweaving" of the web of the desires and beliefs of all those involved. North American and European development ethicists need to understand their activity in such a way that one upshot of international dialogue is that their own group's standards

---

[30] Aihwa Ong, "Colonialism and Modernity...", op.cit., p. 378.
[31] Alison M. Jaggar, "Multicultural Democracy" *The Journal of Political Philosophy* 7:3 (1999): 308-329, here p. 326.
[32] Susan Moller Okin, "Gender Inequality and Cultural Differences," op.cit, p. 18.

and practices might come to be seen as "bad" development or "anti-development."[33]

Dialogic feminism/ethics is not as unfruitful as Okin portrays it to be, even though it is not without its problems and difficulties. Instead, she recommends John Rawls theory of the veil of ignorance so that we might reach an 'objective standpoint'. This is important, according to her, because the veil of ignorance enables people (read Western academics and/or authorities), to take a critical distance as a committed outsider. This better prepares people to analyze and criticize social injustice from which "Third World" women need rescuing. This is the case because, "we are not always enlightened about what is just by asking persons who seem to be suffering injustices what they want. Oppressed people have often internalized their oppression so well that they *have* no sense of what they are justly entitled to as human beings."[34] One problem with this argument is that it is paternalistic and imperialist to the women and cultures to which she refers. Many of these cultures are deeply connected to religion and so the women in these groups often believe and accept that they are obligated to assume prescribed roles, even if it means restricting their freedom. And, these feelings and beliefs are extremely deep and powerful, so much so, that often they are willing to sacrifice a great deal in order to live in accordance with their religious beliefs even their own autonomy. To claim that these women all have been completely indoctrinated with false consciousness or brain washed is extremely condescending and disrespectful and may actually just be wrong.

Putting on a veil of ignorance may require us to consider many different sides of a situation as well as many differing traditions, customs and institutions so as to arrive at some type of so-called Archimedian point or objective standpoint which is fair and just. Yet, it is questionable that this is possible theoretically or practically. Practically, it is impossible to fully step out of one's own view point and understand fully positions and/or views of others, which was the same difficulty

---

[33] David A. Crocker, "Insiders and Outsiders in International Development" *Ethics & International Affairs* 5 (1991), p. 155.
[34] Susan Moller Okin, "Gender Inequality and Cultural Differences," op.cit, p. 19.

that Okin cited against dialogic feminism. And, theoretically, I doubt that it is possible for Okin to really be able consider all types of customs and traditions without previously ruling them out. Since she is committed, hitherto, to democratic and liberal values of equality and justice, she already eliminates many points of view which conflict with her and Rawls' views of justice. And, does Okin actually employ a veil of ignorance in her own work on women in "Third World" when she excludes so many of the women's voices?

Yes, it is questionable whether or not women in such cultures are truly autonomous and actually have the ability to choose to live within their cultures. No one really chooses their culture, but maybe after a certain age people can and do begin to question their cultural values and ways of life, even as insiders.[35] And, yet a certain element of unchoseness still remains in regard to being born into and raised within particular cultures and communities. But does this mean that all women within "Third World" cultures are duped with false consciousness and are merely rationalizing their oppression to make their lives bearable and thus need rescuing from Western liberal feminists? I am not convinced of this. Although this certainly may be the case at times, arguing that it is often the case deprives these women of any agency at all and may be worse. And doing so seems to be in direct contradiction with Okin's project of establishing autonomy for these women, with democratic principles and with ideas of justice. Not only does this deprive the women of agency, but Okin's assumes that autonomy is something that should always be preserved without question.

In speaking for others and "Third World" women, Western feminists position themselves as the autonomous individuals and the authorities. This renders the spoken for less than equal. This silences women from different backgrounds and from the "Third World" and gives the appearance that these women cannot speak for themselves. Okin must acknowledge and problematize these power relations that are present in her discursive acts especially since she is writing and speaking from a Western academic standpoint. Her standpoint is privileged and part of the Western/Northern hegemony. To ignore this di-

---

[35] See Uma Narayan, *Dislocating Cultures: Identities, Traditions, and Third World Feminism*, op.cit.

minishes the voices of "Third World" women because, in so doing, the privileged position is assumed as the norm and all others are marginalized as less than equal.[36]

Wielding sweeping judgments of these cultures and their practices without really attending to the cultural contexts and the viewpoints of individual and concrete women is as imperialistic and hegemonic as traditional liberalism. It represents the non-inclusive universalism that liberal feminists complained of in regards to traditional liberalism. This approach is imperialistic because in making such accusations about these cultures, 'Westerners' or 'Northerners' speak in the voice of the dominant "I" and ignore the own positionality as the supposed 'unmarked observer' who stands as the center or the norm to which all other cultures are to be judged.[37] Moreover, forming umbrella judgments based on a few practices, Okin in a sense demonizes the Other. Her judgments are insufficiently nuanced and portray these cultures as either all good or all bad.

Okin also seems to be assuming that humanity's just entitlements are better understood or more fully articulated by Western (liberal) feminists or academics. According to her, "Third World" women (again she uses the term so broadly, assuming that poorer countries and the "Third World" which includes a vast area of land and numerous different cultures and communities are all basically the same, less developed and less civilized), are often co-opted, duped or infused with false consciousness as a "survival strategy". Although false consciousness may certainly occur, this does mean that Westerns are the only qualified persons to speak for them on their so-called behalf. Doing so robs these women of any voice or agency and does not adhere to democratic values. She provides as proof that women in the "Third World" are often co-opted by presenting the fact that women perpetuate the process of foot binding, clitoredectomy, and purdah.

---

[36] See Chandra Talpade Mohanty, "Under Western Eyes: Feminist Scholarship and Colonial Discourses" op.cit., Linda Alcoff, "The Problem of Speaking for Others", op.cit, Jane Flax, "Race/Gender and The Ethics of Difference: A Reply to Okin's 'Gender Inequality and Cultural Differences' " op.cit., and Aihwa Ong, "Colonialism and Modernity...," op.cit.

[37] Chandra Talpade Mohanty, "Under Western Eyes: Feminist Scholarship and Colonial Discourses," op.cit.

She assumes without question that these practices are 'most cruel and oppressive'. She assumes without question that Western views of the good life are necessarily better and are universalizable, which is what she was trying to "prove" in the first place but is merely assuming. These practices may not be just or fair, but assuming so does not prove her point and using them to condemn an entire way of life and or to silence women within the relevant cultures flies in the face of her democratic and liberal values. Should we westerners go into such countries and fix things? Should we assume our culture is superior and silence the voices of the actual people and women?

Okin's comment, "What Moslem man is likely to take the chance of spending his life in seclusion and dependency, sweltering in head-to-toe solid black clothing?"[38], is a compelling and important question, but one that must be raised in dialogue with Moslem women and men. And, not a question to be cast out to castigate disparate communities and an entire religion with no regard to what the women and men in these communities might offer in response. Okin assumes forehand that her understanding of the religion or these various cultures is accurate, her judgments are more authentic or made with more authority, and her criterion of judgment (i.e. a theory of justice based on liberal and democratic values) transcend others'. These are all assumptions that she never questions even in light of much feminist scholarship and grassroots activism (from around the world) which advocate that she question these assumptions in order to question power and domination differentials.

Okin forgets to put her own culture and values to the same critical scrutiny. She assumes that liberal values are basically good at the expense of some alternate values. I think what is needed is a more careful and sufficiently nuanced method of criticizing cultures. Encouraging an open dialogue, discussion and argumentation, is a more appropriate avenue. In so doing, power differentials, domination, and hegemonic systems can be called into questioned and value systems can be constructed through process and change. We must listen to the voices of all women and hear their criticisms of their cultures as well as their criticism of Western views. Flax writes that, (…) such positioning

---

[38] Susan Moller Okin, "Gender Inequality and Cultural Differences," op.cit, p. 19.

denies the possibility that women in the First World have much to learn about themselves and others by seeing through their eyes. Taking the diversity of practices, locations, and meanings seriously entails placing Western, White women as the objects, not just subjects, of discourse. This approach is also more congruent with a commitment to justice; it treats others as persons deserving of respect and capable of exercising authority in their own lives and those of others. It does not presume in advance whose judgments ought to prevail when differences arise.[39]

We should be more concerned, together with the women of the Third World cultures, with creating a new range of options for women and "oppressed" people in general. It is difficult to know what a good or more positive range of options looks like, but it should be created in a fair and democratic process, through the voices of all.

Okin admits somewhat that cultural specificity is important to take into consideration at times, especially when one wants to help "Third World" women understand liberal democratic values and recognize their rights. She quotes Papanek to this effect; "And Papanek, too, shows how helping to *educate* women to awareness of their oppression requires quite deep and specific knowledge of the relevant culture" (italics added for emphasis).[40]

Again, she does not recommend truly focusing on the specificity of each woman or group of women and listening to their perspectives. Rather, we should learn about any given culture in order to understand how to relate to "Third World" women and to be able to *educate* them about their oppression. Okin believes that Western liberal feminists must teach "Third World" women of their rights because these other women do not seem to understand the injustices which they face. In Okin's view, the Westerners must help conceptualize these injustices for them. Although I agree that people can always learn from others and that Western liberals have something valid to share with "Third World" women, Okin does not realize the paternalistic (or maternalistic) and patronizing nature of her words. In effect, it seems that

---

[39] Jane Flax, "Race/Gender and The Ethics of Difference: A Reply to Okin's 'Gender Inequality and Cultural Differences'," op.cit., p. 904.
[40] Susan Moller Okin, "Gender Inequality and Cultural Differences," op.cit, p. 20.

Western feminists have already done the work, or constructed the issues and priorities on which all women should focus. And, now it is up to them teach these issues to other non-Western women.

In this way, the West has already articulated feminist's interests for all women.[41] And unfortunately, this has lead to a negative picture of "Third World" women as helpless and without agency. Chalpade Mohanty describes this negative picture when she writes that:

> This average Third World woman leads an essentially truncated life based on her feminine gender (read: sexually constrained) and her being "Third World" (read: ignorant, poor, uneducated, tradition-bound, domestic, family-oriented, victimized, etc). This, I suggest, is in contrast to the (implicit) self-representation of Western women as educated, as modern, as having control over their own bodies and sexualities, and the freedom to make their own choices.[42]

It may be the case that women qua their being female have all experienced some sort of domination or oppression from some men. Yet, this does not entail that women experience oppression in the same way and that differences of power, race, class, ethnicity, etc are not necessarily involved in women's experience of oppression. Many different influences factor in and have extreme effects on the lived experiences of women that their oppression is always experienced differently due to different localities and standpoints. Experiences of race, gender, class, and ethnicity interplay so much so that they may be inseparable. Since Okin refuses to concentrate on any socio-historical and cultural specificity, she is lead to inappropriate over-generalizations or vacuous truths. Women are constructed through cultural practices and institutions and are always part of the process of constructing these practices and institutions. Women are also constructed through class, culture, religion, belief systems and specific power relations.[43] Ignoring this denies the reality of the lives of women.

---

[41] Chandra Talpade Mohanty, "Under Western Eyes: Feminist Scholarship and Colonial Discourses," op.cit., pp. 256-257.
[42] Ibid., p. 258.
[43] Ibid., p. 262 (see also Ong's dicussion, op.cit p. 378 and Jane Flax, "Race/Gender and The Ethics of Difference...," op.cit.

In *Feminism, Women's Human Rights, and Cultural Differences*, Okin seems to agree with, though not admittingly and to a small degree, some of the feminist critics she previously argued against. She argues again that women suffer a similar oppression. Thus, women's human rights are universalizable and necessary to help end the subjugation of women. Although this is true, she admits that these rights should be established through dialogue, especially among women and including "Third World" women. Okin's writings yet remain problematic and paternalistic.

Okin argues that the difference between men and women's lives must be recognized so that women's formal human rights can take on more substantial meaning in their lives. She argues that what have been commonly known as human rights, have excluded concerns specific to the lives of women and so have hindered women's ability to enjoy such rights. Such issues as maternity leave, pregnancy and women's health care, gender based violence and affirmative action for women in education and employment are also necessary to focus on within human rights discussions and deliberation. And I do not doubt this is true.

She argues again that the accepted distinction between the public and the private in formulating human rights doctrines and taking the male head of the household as the referent, must be questioned because not doing so has contributed to the neglect of women in receiving human rights protections. For, private lives are protected by rights, but the lives within the private sphere are not. When only governments or nation-states are viewed as violating human rights, the fact that individual people violate others' human rights is gone unnoticed, especially men violating women's human rights. She writes, "Part of the reason for the "invisibility" of gender-based violations has been the neglect in human rights talk of the private or domestic sphere. For it is in this sphere that great numbers of the world's women live most (in some cases, virtually all) of their lives, and in which vast numbers of violations of women's human rights take place (Peters and Wolper 1995, 2)."[44]

---

[44] Susan Moller Okin, "Feminism, Women's Human Rights, and Cultural Differences" *Hypatia* 13:2 (Spring 1998): 32-52, here p. 36.

She goes on to argue that respecting cultural rights has been understood by many as allowing for the denial of human rights to many women. Issues of sexuality, marriage, reproduction, inheritance and power over children are cultural issues which, according Okin, directly affect the lives of women and have not been considered to be part of human rights. Women are also often considered to be the custodians of cultures and religions so that intervening in on issues which concern women ends up amounting to a violation of the entire culture and of cultural/religious rights. The precedence of cultural rights over women's human rights renders women's human rights as invisible, natural, or culturally justified. That is why paying attention to women's human rights as human rights necessarily involves not allowing for cultural exemptions.

Okin takes into consideration the objections of Mohanty and some other scholars who state that universalizing a shared oppression across race, class and cultures is ahistorical and impossible. They also argue that Okin's method denies women's agency, ignores contemporary imperialism and ignores power differentials among women. Okin asserts in consternation that such projects of anti-universalization inhibit the establishment of women's rights as human rights and so go against women's claim to equality and equal opportunity.[45]

Okin also argues that "Third World" feminist activists agree with her. She cites that many "Third World" feminist activists from many different regions of the world have been holding conferences, meetings and networking events with their own subgroups and with other such groups from around the world. She argues that in speaking with each other, "They found discrimination against women; patterns of gender-based violence; including domestic battery; and the sexual and economic exploitation of women and girls were virtually universal phenomena (Friedman 1995; Bunch 1994)."[46] Okin admits that these women have not claimed that all women's problems and oppression are exactly the same. But she argues that through these international conferences and women's NGO's, once silenced women now are being heard. I believe that these types of conferences are much needed in

---

[45] Ibid., pp. 43-44.
[46] Ibid., p. 44.

order for women to voice their sufferings of oppression and to problematize the different situations so that we can begin working to solve such injustices. Yet, Okin does not seem to realize that she is acknowledging that the women, in the "Third World" or anywhere women face oppression, do in fact need to be involved in the process, possibly with some help from "outsiders". And so she seems to almost be agreeing with her critics' arguments. For, here she admits that these "Third World" feminists need to get together, have a voice, problematize specific types of oppression, and work together (possibly with the help of outsiders) in order to battle such acts of oppression. And, she says that listening to once silenced voices is very important in ending oppression. Okin even admits that these women do not encounter the same experiences of oppression. Each community, and each individual for that matter, encounter any range of different experiences of oppression in which class, race, culture, gender, and etc. are all substantial factors. Thus, maybe Okin herself accepts that we must listen to everyone's voices in order to establish a more just standard of principles and values. This seems to stand in opposition to what Okin argued in her previous paper.[47]

Although I seemed to have been extremely critical of Okin's writings, I ultimately agree with her that liberal values can serve as an appropriate starting point or basis to supporting and developing a more just universal standard. What I have disagreed with was her method with which she tried to argue for the establishing of liberal values worldwide because it lacked the due care and specific attention to contexts that is required of such a grand project. So, I agree with Okin when she says, "If it was not clear earlier, surely it was clear now that bending over backward out of respect for cultural diversity could do a great disservice to women and girls."[48] Yet, making grand generalizations and demonizing numerous cultures is not the best way to "help" women and may, in fact, deny women the agency Okin is trying to preserve. I would advocate developing a more contextualized and nuanced approach in a revised method, however complicated this may

---

[47] See Susan Moller Okin, "Gender Inequality and Cultural Differences," op.cit, 14.
[48] Susan Moller Okin, "Feminism, Women's Human Rights, and Cultural Differences," op.cit., 46.

be. More generally, what I have intended to demonstrate was that arguing for seemingly good and just values systems has numerous difficulties that actually may lead to certain injustices. And this I think demonstrates the immensity of the problem of establishing a universal standard of justice. Although it is an extremely urgent issue, it cannot be "solved" without careful attention and primarily open dialogue.[49] The current structures of globalization and global injustice are issues that are pertinent to every person's life and so, I believe that it must be interrogated, questioned and analyzed by all. This must be done through real democratic means in order to level out unequal levels of powers and to give a voice to all rather than merely to the elite or oligarchies that have retained most of the power and decision making abilities.

---

[49] Some dialogue may need to be closed to certain groups especially oppressed groups so that they can find common bonds and strength from each other in order to develop a language that problematizes their oppression and establishes routes to overcoming it. Yet, eventually these groups will have to engage in open dialogue with others in order for their voice to be heard and to hear the voices of others. See Alison Jaggar's article "Globalizing Feminist Ethics" [*Hypatia* 13:2 (Spring 1998): 7-31].

Yvanka B. Raynova

CIVIL SOCIETY AND "WOMEN'S MOVEMENTS" IN POST-COMMUNIST EUROPE. AN APPRAISAL 25 YEARS AFTER THE FALL OF THE BERLIN WALL

Ten years ago, when I was invited to present a paper at a conference on women's movements in Eastern Europe, I at first decisively declined, because the notion of "women's movements" in a post-communist context appeared to me quite problematic. The organizers, however, felt that my position would incite a substantial discussion and therefore insisted on my participation. Thus, I explained my point of view at the conference, and argued it later in a larger study by presenting a thorough analysis.[1] I would like now to add some additional results, based on newer data, and to reflect on this subject in connection with the profound civil society transformations in the post-communist countries.

To begin with, what is a women's movement?

A number of scholars do not see any difference between a "women's" movement and a "feminist" movement. However, it is very important to distinguish women's movement, as a type of social movement, from the feminist movement, which often represents just a current of ideas, of theories or particular strategies, and which is therefore not necessarily connected to a women's movement. Women's movements are also not identical with women's organizations or political parties, which could become, under certain circumstances, its driving force or leader, but could also fail to organize women in a social movement.

Social movements have been commonly described as "collectivity acting with some continuity to promote or resist a change in the soci-

---

[1] See Yvanka B. Raynova, *Feministische Philosophie in europäischem Kontext*. Wien/Köln/Weimar: Böhlau 2010, pp. 93-144

ety or group of which it is a part."[2] One of the broadest definitions of a "women's movement" is given by Mary Katzenstein and Carol Mueller, who assert that it is characterized by a variety of issues and yet by a unity of purpose: that of the total transformation of societies' public and private gender institutions[3]. The fact that this definition is too broad becomes evident when we take into account that there are men's organizations and movements that also pursue the goal of a radical transformation of the gender institutions. A stricter definition of a "women's movement" can be found, for example, in the *Encyclopædia Britannica,* where it is defined as a "social movement (…) seeking equal rights and opportunities for women in their economic activities, their personal lives, and politics"[4]. But from this definition arises a serious question, namely, whether equality is or is not the sole and primary issue. If equality is the only issue, then, clearly, for those who think that gender equality has already been established, there is no further need for women's movements.

Most of the given definitions are problematic and not always helpful because they do not analyze the constituent elements of a women's movement or, if you prefer, its conditions. In my opinion those conditions are: (1.) women's oppression and discrimination as a prevalent situation, referred to by Simone de Beauvoir as "*la condition féminine*,"[5] which serves as a motive for a movement when this situation is deteriorating and turns out to be intolerable; (2.) ideas and concrete strategies on how to proceed in order to change this situation; (3.) some kind of organization and/or leading personalities, able to coordinate and unite women in a mass movement and to ensure continuity of action until the goals of the movement are

---

[2] Ralph H. Turner, Lewis M. Killian, *Collective Behavior.* Englewood Cliffs, N.J.: Prentice Hall, 1972, 1987, 223.

[3] Mary Fainsod Katzenstein, Carol McClurg Mueller (Eds.), *The Women's Movements of the United States and Western Europe: Consciousness, Political Opportunity, and Public Policy.* Philadelphia: Temple University Press, 1987, 5.

[4] *Encyclopædia Britannica*, Ultimate Edition DVD, 2014.

[5] Simone de Beauvoir. *Le deuxième sexe, II.* Paris: Gallimard, Folio, 1976, II, p. 328 (Engl. *The second sex.* Translated by H. M. Parshley. New York: Vintage Books, 1952/1980).

achieved; and (4.) large masses of women that are motivated and ready to fight resolutely for changing their situation.

From this point of view arises the question: are these essential components of, and conditions for, a women's movement to be found in post-communist Europe? This is a very complex issue as it is related to some country-specific particularities; therefore, the opinions about it are divided. The purpose of this article is twofold: first, I will indicate some fundamental tendencies in the post-communist social attitudes and civil society and scrutinize some empirical data in order to argue and to prove my thesis as to the lack of women's movements there; and second, I will analyze the reasons for the rejection of feminist ideas and the absence of women's movements in the post-communist countries, and try to clarify this situation from a new perspective.

1. Is the women's situation in Eastern Europe perceived by women as intolerable?

"You have been oppressed!" – this is the first thing that Western feminists said to "Eastern European" women at the beginning of the 1990s, when they started their mission of feminist "enlightenment" in the "other" Europe. This initiative was described by the Czech sociologist Hana Havelkovà as an ideological intrusion, through which the Western feminists stigmatized the post-communist societies as "sexist" or "patriarchal," and the "Eastern European" women as "second class citizens," who are "conservative, dependent, and discriminated."[6] This diagnosis has been largely rejected by Czech academics, and Havel-kovà has emphasized that she did not intend to persuade Czech women they were discriminated and oppressed if they did not feel so.

Although some "Eastern" European feminists also propagated and still propagate the idea of the patriarchal structures and the oppressed women in the ex-communist/post-communist countries, there are still many others who reject and resist this allegation. Thus, both sides

---

[6] Hana Havelkovà, "Real existierender Feminismus," in *Transit. Europäische Revue*, 1995, Heft 9, p. 146–158, here p. 147.

often accuse and reprove each other, mostly behind the curtain. One group believes that everyone who argues against the thesis of the women's oppression is seriously affected by the old "communist mentality," while the other group accuses the first one of being "servile," "ideologically assimilated," and even of being merely "paid servants" of the new *political correctness*.

The true reasons why most of the women are not convinced by such theses and do not conceive of their situation in the classical terms of "emancipation vs. oppression" are far different. On the one hand, many women in the academia tend to resist everything that seems to be just another type ideology or, even worse, a new "discursive colonization."[7] On the other hand, most women seem to be convinced that the emancipation and the equal status of women are already achieved, a thesis which was widely propagated during the communist era. Quite a few scholars and activists also believe that the women's condition in the post-communist countries depend on fundamental problems that are not only a "women's matter" – e.g., financial crisis, economic and political corruption, poverty, unemployment, organized crime, etc. – and therefore cannot be solved separately. Last but not least, an important tendency against women's emancipation is the *comeback* of traditional values and narrow views about the role of women in society. The reasons for such a backlash could be explained by the women's situation in the socialist past as well as by the new life circumstances arising from the post-communist transition to market economies. For many women, equality simply means a double burden, which they already had to carry under socialism as laborers, domestic workers and mothers. The nostalgia for being simply a housewife or the mistress of a wealthy man, who is able to offer her a "pleasant life," is becoming more and more a dream for many young women trying to escape the struggle for survival and the competition on the labor market. Finally, another particular reason for such a *comeback* in Poland is the

---

[7] Jiřina Šmejkalovà, "Gender as an analytical category of post-communist studies," in *Gender in Transition in Eastern and Central Europe. Proceedings*, Berlin: tra*f*o verlag, 2001, p. 52.

strong role of Catholicism there.[8] The problem which clearly appears in this context is, obviously, the conflict between two institutions, namely, the dogmas of the Catholic Church on the one hand and certain norms and regulations of the European Union (e.g., gender mainstreaming) on the other hand. However, this conflict is present in different shapes in other European countries as well.

2. Are there any feminist programs and ideas able to mobilize women?

Despite a number of very valuable studies and publications by Eastern European feminists in various fields of the social and human sciences,[9] "feminism" is still considered a dirty word not only in the public domain but also in the media and in academic debates. A deliberate misrepresentation, or even "a medialized 'horror' construction of 'feminism'," as it was described by Jiřina Šmejkalovà, has been propagated for years in the post-communist countries[10]. This is not the only reason, but is probably the main obstacle to serious reconsideration of, and a critical reflection on, the actual problems of women, as it is known that women's situation in the post-communist countries is deteriorating in many respects.[11]

---

[8] Maria Szyszkowska, Czeslaw Janik, "Zurück zu Kinder, Küche, Kirche – Die Lage der Frauen im 'demokratischen' Polen," *Die Linke*, 07-12-2006 (online: http://dielinke.at/ artikel/international/zuruck-zu-kinder-kuche-kirche-2013-die-lage-der-frauen-im-201edemokratischen201c-polen).

[9] Yvanka B. Raynova, op.cit., pp. 37-92; cf. Tatyana Batuleva, "Feminist Philosophy and Bulgarian Philosophical Culture: Readings and Emphases," in idem (ed.), *Philosophical Receptions: Transmissions, Affinities and Originality*, Sofia: "St. Ivan Rilski" Publishings, 2014, pp. 181-194; idem, "French Philosophy and Bulgarian philosophical culture," *Studies in East European Thought*, 53 (2001), pp. 21-36, idem. "Filosofska rezepzia I interkulturen dialog," in: idem (ed.). *Evropeijski vlijania v bulgarskata filosofska kultura*, Sofia: "St. Ivan Rilski" Publishings, 2013, pp. 11-20; idem, "Frenskata filosofia v Bulgaria," in: idem (ed.). *Evropeijski vlijania v bulgarskata filosofska kultura*, Sofia: "St. Ivan Rilski" Publishings, 2013, pp. 182-218.

[10] Jiřina Šmejkalovà, op.cit., p. 52.

[11] See Kirsten Ghodsee, *The left side of history: World War II and the unfulfilled promise of communism in Eastern Europe*, Durham and London: Duke University Press, 2015, p. XV.

Almost all experts dealing with Eastern Europe claim that feminism in this region is problematic. Their conclusions vary from total skepticism as to the possibility of deployment of some kind of "Eastern European feminism" to an organizational and communicative optimism based on the faith in common East-West projects. In an article on this topic, the sociologist Claire Wallace tells about her negative experience:

> When I arrived in Prague, I found out that the way of reception of feminist ideas in post-communist Europe was quite different: there is a lack of interest in it, and even a declared hostility. When I raised this issue, however, the students reacted in quite an inspired way: they were inspired to write essays about why feminism is irrelevant for Eastern Europe. I am not the only one who had such an experience.[12]

Nevertheless, Wallace tries to show that Eastern European women can make a valuable contribution to a common feminist self-criticism.[13]

Hana Havelkovà describes the failed exchange of ideas between Western feminists and Czech women scholars as follows:

> The final result of these difficult discussions was disappointment on both sides: on their part, because we did not allow them to lecture us, and on ours, because of their disrespect for our quite different experience and their inability to trust it and to take it seriously. For the sake of completeness, I will add that we do not hold joint meetings anymore: they hold theirs, and we hold ours. With this rather tragicomic story, I want to point out the general difficulty of Eastern-Western dialogue in the field of political philosophy. And this is not just my own unique experience.[14]

Her article ends with the conclusion that the post-communist experience led to extreme skepticism towards the great ideas of liberation, and also to an aversion for all "isms," so that feminism might be accepted by some individual women, but the overall incredulity to-

---

[12] Claire Wallace, "Eine Westfeministin geht in den Osten," *Transit*, 1995, Heft 9, pp. 128–145, here 128.
[13] Ibid., p. 134.
[14] Hana Havelkovà, op.cit., 1995, p. 147.

wards it will hardly disappear.[15] As additional reasons for the refusal of feminist ideas in Eastern Europe and the hostility against it, the authors usually refer to fundamental historical, cultural and political differences. According to Christiane Lemke, "the dominant political culture of the transformation societies includes strong patterns of political-cultural values and attitudes that stamp the perception of the gender problematic in a way that is in contrast to the feminist interpretations as well as to women's rights and interests."[16] Well, that may be true, but it is only one of the reasons for the resistance of the Eastern Europeans against feminism; for the "political-cultural values and attitudes" have changed since 1989, but the anti-feminist mindset remains mostly the same.

3. The role of feminist women's organizations

Let us take a closer look now at the more concrete question whether there have been and are some organizations in post-communist Europe that aspire to, and are capable of, organizing women in a social movement.

According to a study carried out at Queen's University of Belfast in the 1990s and funded by the EU 5th Framework Program, there are hundreds of women's organizations (NGOs) in post-communist Europe. The greatest number of such organizations was set up in Hungary – about 350; in Poland they were about 300, in Bulgaria, about 75-150, and in the other counties, between 50 and 70. But despite these impressive statistics, the author states that all these women's organizations cannot achieve a real women's movement:

> While individual NGOs are working on women's issues, there is not a uniform movement with common aims and platforms. Thus, members of most women's NGOs across Central and Eastern Europe deny

---

[15] Ibid., 157.
[16] Christiane Lemke, "*Frauen und Politik in den Transformationsprozessen Osteuropas*," in *Frauenbewegung und Frauenpolitik in Osteuropa*. Frankfurt/New York: Campus Verlag, 1996, p. 25.

the existence of a women's movement and fail to view many of their activities in this context.[17]

Unfortunately, in this study as well as in other research works, there is no analysis of the question *why* there was and still is a lack of women's movements in the post-communist European states. In my opinion, the primary reason lies in the fact that all organizations are fighting for subsidies, so they compete with one another. Every individual organization tries to show that its activities are more important for the women than those of all the other organizations and, consequently, that it is worthier of financial support. When there are dozens of organizations in a single country fighting for subventions, then the situation resembles a battlefield. As to the women themselves, they are so tired with all the struggles and crises after 1989, that they simply mistrust all politicians and organizations, including women's NGOs. But this alone could not explain the lack of women's movements in post-communist Europe. In my opinion, it is particularly important here to highlight the special case of Yugoslavia, which has usually been neglected.

At the beginning, I stated that women realize their gender-specific situation when it becomes intolerable. I want now to exemplify and argue this thesis in order to show that this is the fundamental reason why women unite and fight for the common objective of improving their and their children's situation. In the cases where this took place, as in former Yugoslavia, women's organizations were able to initiate, manage and guide a genuine women's movement. An emblematic example of such activist achievement was the women's organization *Women In Black*:

> It was a personal and political decision of feminists to oppose male violence against women, which included nationalist hatred, ethnic cleansing, mass rapes in war, prostitution for the soldiers, 4 million refugees, half a million dead and many injured. We decided to transform anger into action and in the last few years we organized initiatives for women. (…) After the start of the war, the political anti-war

---

[17] Amanda Sloat, "Fixing an Old Divide: The Political Participation of Women in an Enlarged Europe," 2003, p. 9, online: http://unpan1.un.org/intradoc/groups/public/documents/NISPAcee/UNPAN018544.pdf

group *Women In Black* formed in Belgrade. This group built itself as a model of the Israeli women pacifists who protested their government's actions against the Palestinians and the Italian and German women who protested their government's involvement in the Gulf War. Every Wednesday afternoon since 9 October 1991 *Women In Black* has stood in silence in the Republic Square in Belgrade to protest the war, militarism, nationalism and violence against women.[18]

The women's solidarity, which is often a missing link, was at work here in an exemplary manner: from Belgrade to Zagreb, women and women's organizations from mutually hostile, warring regions came together to protest against the war. There is no doubt that the women's organizations in this region of post-communist Europe played a positive role: with their remediating and peacemaking activities, they helped women to overcome the horror of the war and to rebuild their lives. It should also be remembered (sic!) that, even before the collapse of communism, Yugoslavia was a special case in regard to feminist theory and women's studies, as there was an important tradition of research in this field, such as was mostly absent in the other communist countries. This tradition of focusing on women and on gender problems has surely contributed to women's self-awareness and to the development of self-help strategies. However, from this and from some other Yugoslav examples, one cannot draw substantial conclusions about the rest of the women's organizations in the post-communist states. Due to the variety and the huge number of these organizations, it is not possible to give a general picture of them. But it is important to point out that opinions about the role and the efficacy of the women's NGOs are highly divided.

In regard to the *women's centers*, which carry out mostly academic activities and research, i.e., women's and gender studies, it could be indicated that some of them not only contributed to the import of Western feminist theories in post-communist Europe but also achieved substantive results of their own. Sharp criticisms appear when the issue is about "Western" money and "lucrative" projects

---

[18] Donna M. Hughes, Lepa Mladjenovic, "Feminist organizing in Belgrade, Serbia: 1990-1994," *Canadian Women's Studies/Les Cahiers de la Femme*, 1995, Vol. 16, No. 1, pp. 95-97.

that have been apparently distributed to women's organizations, mostly to NGOs.[19] This concern usually goes in two directions: first, how the subventions have been used, and, second, whether the results of the endowed activities are satisfactory. It is well known that a great part of the funds invested in the reconstruction of the "East" flowed into someone's "private pockets." So it is not to be excluded that this also happened to the subsidies granted to some women's organizations. However, there is another side to the coin: in some East-West feminist projects carried out in Central and Western Europe, women scholars from the post-communist countries did almost the whole work but got lower remuneration than their Western colleagues, who only supervised them. It is a fact that some people and even whole organizations, both from East and West, drew profits from this "collaboration." But it would be all too easy to take that fact as the sole explanation why the NGOs in post-communist Europe have been incapable of solving certain acute women's problems and/or organizinig women in a social movement, thereby contributing to the strengthening of civil society.

A detailed and empirically well-documented inquiry on this topic, which I want especially to outline, has been conducted by the American scholar Kristen Ghodsee. Her works[20] are of great importance because she spent many years in Bulgaria investigating the social changes, in particular, the role of women's organizations (she speaks Bulgarian herself), and also because she tries to throw light on the subject from different perspectives by providing a critical evaluation of both the Eastern European and the Western institutions. One of

---

[19] See Sarah Mendelson, John Glenn, *The Power and Limits of NGOs: A Critical Look at Building Democracy in Eastern Europe and Eurasia*, New York: Columbia University Press, 2002.

[20] Kirsten Ghodsee, "Feminism-by-Design: Emerging Capitalisms, Cultural Feminism and Women's Nongovernmental Organizations in Post-Socialist Eastern Europe," *Signs: Journal of Women in Culture and Society* 29, no. 3 (2004): 727–753; idem. *The Red Riviera: Gender, Tourism and Postsocialism on the Black Sea*, Durham and London: Duke University Press, 2005; idem. "*Nongovernmental Ogres*? How Feminist NGOs Undermine Women in Postsocialist Eastern Europe," *International Journal of Not-for-Profit Law*, vol. 8, no. 3 (May 2006): 44–59; idem. *The left side of history: World War II and the unfulfilled promise of communism in Eastern Europe*, Durham and London: Duke University Press, 2015.

her main theses is that the Western cultural feminism that was exported to Eastern Europe and was accepted by many women's organizations has been, maybe unwittingly, "complicit with the proponents of neoliberalism responsible for the very decline in general living standards that gave Western feminists their mandate to help Eastern European women in the first place."[21] Here, she uses David Stark's "capitalism-by-design" thesis,[22] which she exemplifies as follows:

> After the unexpected collapse of communism in Eastern Europe in 1989, billions of dollars in aid and assistance flowed from the United States and Western Europe into the former Eastern bloc. A virtual army of consultants and experts descended into capital cities to fashion the foundations of capitalism and liberal democracy from scratch (...) If the experts could create the proper institutions in a country, the rules of those new institutions would guide individual behavior, and one could create the conditions for the development of capitalism, literally by design. The capitalism-by-design paradigm still underlies the structural adjustment and stabilization practices of the World Bank and the International Monetary Fund in this region.[23]

According to Ghodsee, the cultural feminism exported to Eastern Europe plays a similar role and can be therefore described as "feminism-by-design." After the collapse of communism, Western feminists and women's organizations jumped on the "aid bandwagon," i.e., the World Bank, the International Monetary Fund, the American Agency for International Development, etc. They received abundant money for their activities in Eastern Europe, where they ordered studies that should prove the assumption that the economic transition from communism to capitalism would occur at the expense of the women, as the problems and the disadvantages of women in Western societies would be transplanted to the post-communist countries and would affect Eastern European women as well. Thus, many scholars failed to consider the possibilities of positive legacies of women's experience under socialism, and "the discourses produced by these

---

[21] Kirsten Ghodsee, "Feminism-by-Design," op.cit., p. 728.
[22] See David Stark,"Path Dependence and Privatization Strategies in East Central Europe," *East European Politics and Societies* 1992, 6 (1), pp. 17–54.
[23] Kirsten Ghodsee, "Feminism-by-Design," op.cit., p. 729.

scholars, activists, and international donors construct women as the natural and inevitable group of victims in the economic transformation period"; thus, they did them more harm than good.[24] She accuses the Western feminists of coming to Eastern Europe as "experts" without having a clue about the situation, but also blames Eastern European women of painting a very dark picture of women's position in the emerging post-communist societies in order to get financial support.[25] This is how a pile of studies and misleading reports was produced, which were based on the hegemonic Western culture-feminist concept of gender as an essentialist category of difference, and completely ignored the complex post-communist context.[26]

Ghodsee rightly poses the question: who profits from presenting the women in post-communist societies as oppressed and discriminated? The indirect answer she gives focuses on everyone who took part in the political legitimacy of neoliberalism. In the first place, these are institutions like the World Bank, the International Monetary Fund, the American Agency for International Development (USAID), etc.; in the second place, the Western feminists who fell into the trap of the "capitalism-by-design" paradigm; and in the third place, the Eastern European women's organizations acting out of self-interest and hence neglecting the women's interests in their countries.[27]

The main problem of most Bulgarians lies, according to Ghodsee, in unemployment and in the increasing gap between the incomes of the political mafia elite on one side and the rest of the citizens on the other. Despite this, a study by a well-known Bulgarian NGO claims that the highest priorities in the gender area are: 1) violence against women and sexual harassment; 2) discrimination of women at work and employment procedures; 3) limited access of women to decision making; 4) unequal distribution and different treatment with regard to paid jobs; 5) negative gender stereotypes in education and sexist

---

[24] Ibid., p. 734.
[25] Kirsten Ghodsee, "*Nongovernmental Ogres?*" op.cit., p. 50.
[26] Kirsten Ghodsee, "Feminism-by-Design," op.cit., p. 748.
[27] Ibid., p. 743.

publicity[28]. Using the data from the *National Human Development Report* of the United Nations, Ghodsee shows that the true situation of women in Bulgaria is quite different from the NGOs version: women outlive men, infant mortality for boys is higher than for girls, women have higher levels of education, women still enjoy longer paid maternity leaves than in most Western nations; in 2002 there were more female members of parliament than anywhere else in Central and Eastern Europe, and more than in many countries in Western Europe as well, Bulgaria has had a female foreign minister, a female deputy prime minister, and even, briefly, a female prime minister; and since 2001, men, not women, have made up the majority of the registered unemployed.[29]

Ghodsee emphasizes three points of critique regarding women's organizations in Bulgaria. First, she outlines that, by ignoring women's success before 1989, they put the whole blame for the deterioration of women's quality of life in the post-communist states on patriarchy, and thereby divert attention from those who are really responsonsible – the World Bank, the International Monetary Fund, and the Bulgarian government as their accomplice. Secondly, the Bulgarian NGOs misunderstood the fact that education and cultural capital are actually the key to women's success; consequently, they neglected the fact that there are not enough jobs in these sectors; instead, they focused on technical improvements relevant to social problems, avoided major controversial questions like economic injustice and social inequality, and simply followed the instructions of their Western donors. Thirdly, the women's rights problems tend to be used again as a means for supporting the dominant political and economic system.

The four solutions to these problems that Ghodsee proposes consist almost in one and the same thing, namely, in the advice to the Bulgarian women's NGOs to become more critical and independent of Western support.

---

[28] Kristen Ghodsee cites as a source of this study the research by Regina Indjeva and Stanimira Hadjimitova, "Mapping NGOs Dealing with Gender Issues," a report of the Women's Alliance for Development, 2002 (www.women-bg.org/index_en.html).

[29] Kirsten Ghodsee, "Feminism-by-Design," op.cit., p. 744.

First, she recommends to Bulgarian women's organizations to break away from the financial dependence of the Western governments and organizations so they can finally focus on the actual needs of women; this would also put an end to the distorted information received about the women's situation in Bulgaria. This is easier said than done, but according to Ghodsee, it is quite possible as the Western sponsors begin to withdraw from Eastern Europe.

Second, she suggests that the Bulgarian women's organizations should become independent of Western feminist expert advisers and the latter's gender projects. Women's projects developed in the USA or in Belgium are inappropriate for Bulgarian women, and that is why "NGOs leaders must be more creative in finding homegrown solutions to local problems."

Third, civil-society leaders and Western experts should recognize and accept the legacies of socialist feminism, and not continue to attempt to organize women as a biologically homogenous group in opposition to men. This means that, instead of reducing the Eastern European women to their sex and opposing them to men, they should take into account their group affiliation. The Bulgarian NGOs should treat women not only as women but try to organize them in professional associations according to their education, work, etc.

Fourth, the Bulgarian women's organizations and their leaders should reveal the negative influence of neoliberal capitalism:

> (…) nongovernmental organizations and their leaders need to publicly challenge the negative effects of neoliberalism and agitate for change. If the post-socialist state can no longer interfere in the market, then NGOs must step in to address the growing imbalances in society. Women's NGOs can play a very important role in the next generation, but only if they, too, are truly independent of the market. This means that NGO work cannot be a professional position, led by salaried employees of foreign governments. Their role, further, should not be to justify dismantling the welfare state, but to work against the most egregious excesses of free-market capitalism.[30]

---

[30] Kirsten Ghodsee, "*Nongovernmental Ogres*?" op.cit., p. 59.

Ghodsee's critical engagement with Bulgarian women's organizations definitely provides valuable food for thought. But I am, nevertheless, skeptical about the solutions she suggests.

First of all, I do not believe that the withdrawal of financial help from the Western donors would lead to a change in the attitude of the mentioned NGOs towards women's problems and needs. If there is no more funding, not even for gender mainstreaming, then the Bulgarian women's organizations and their gender projects will soon disappear and their leaders will turn towards other sources of subsidizing and other business opportunities.

Second, it is easier to follow the instructions of the Western "experts" and the gender policies of the EU rather than to think up new original solutions. Without a paid contract and without any prospect for implementation of the project results, nobody will rack their brains and search for "creative solutions" to women's needs or to any other social and economic problems. Supposing that a NGO or a research team finds such new and creative solutions, will anyone be interested in implementing these into practice? Everything that happens in the post-communist societies is a consequence of the will of the ruling powers; thus, a strategy can be implemented only if it is in accordance with the interests of the rulers, i.e., if it *serves* them. If the "creative solutions" do not match those interests or even oppose them, then they will just remain a dead letter. Ghodsee is right to accuse some Eastern European women scholars – the so called "educated middle-class women" – of writing artificial reports and of travelling all around the world to various women's conferences instead of concentrating on the real problems of women. But she disregards the overall picture of the deplorable situation of the human and social sciences in Europe. At a time when entire fields of knowledge throughout Europe, and not only in the post-communist states, are threatened with extinction, when highly-qualified scholars, both women and men, have to fight for survival or are forced to emigrate, it is not surprising that everyone is trying to save their own skins. Some Eastern European academics and pseudo-academics found their chance for a better life and good money in the subsidies for the implementation of the *feminism-by-design* ideology. The market needed them, and they needed the market. Personally, I doubt that the business was all that lucrative for all of them, but this is not the point. The point is that it is much easier to escape into activities fostered by the neoliberal market economy than to stand up for causes like women's life quality, social inequality, spiritual culture, fundamental research, etc. To take just one example from my own bitter experience: our long-standing struggle at the Bulgarian Academy of Sciences for the independence of scientific research from the political and market-based economy has failed. Fundamental research has become a *persona non grata* in Bulgarian academia, due to the fact that this is so throughout Europe. This does not mean that we should resign ourselves and accept it – on the contrary – but there is little prospect of change in this matter.

Third, it would be naive to assume that the Western experts would ever actively engage with women's problems in Eastern Europe and, even less, with their "socialist legacy." Such involvement would require a special commitment and a lot of time, which the experts and the fully-employed officials in Brussels do not have. The case of the Western feminists, who came as helpers to Eastern Europe, is a bit different. Some of them spent years in the post-communist countries, but finally they returned home with the same, or slightly revised, preconceived opinions they already had at the beginning.[31] Others, e.g., the American professor of law Frances Elisabeth Olsen, pointed out from the start the risks and the possibilities of the American engagement in Eastern Europe, showing the mistakes made by some American feminists.[32] Unfortunately, her brilliant critical analyses met with no response.

Fourth, Ghodsee is absolutely right when she suggests that Bulgarian women's organizations should begin to seriously face the authentic problems of women as connected with the consequences of the global market economy. But in my opinion, it is not necessary to

---

[31] Yvanka B. Raynova, *Feministische Philosophie in europäischem Kontext*, op.cit., pp. 154-161.
[32] Frances Elisabeth Olsen, "Feminism in Central and Eastern Europe: Risks and Possibilities of American Engagement," *The Yale Law Journal*, Vol. 106, No. 7 (May, 1997): 2215-2257.

carry out special research or to develop any "original" ideas; meanwhile, there is a large number of critical analyses of neoliberalism, including George Soros's debates on it.[33] The problem is that all these warnings and critical analyses have had no serious impact. The demands of some Bulgarian trade unions were also ignored. Years ago, an influential leader of one of the largest Bulgarian trade unions requested an increase in salaries and pensions and prompted resistance to the pressure of the International Monetary Fund. He argued that there is enough money, that the wage increase would promote sustainable consumption and would revive the economy. This man was more influential than any individual NGO but did not have enough power to break the dependence of the Bulgarian state and economy on the World Bank and the International Monetary Fund, nor to put into practice any project that would oppose their interests.

Last but not least, when Ghodsee requires from the Bulgarian women's organizations to engage with the main problem of unemployment, we should bear in mind that such engagement actually did take place in some post-communist countries soon after the fall of the Berlin wall. From 1991 to 1993 in Poland, for example, various women associations and foundations were launched, which provided valuable women's assistance via employment service, job application techniques and courses, labor market monitoring, expertise in discrimination issues, etc.[34] Such positive examples deserve greater

---

[33] See see George Soros, *The Crisis of Global Capitalism*. New York: Public Affairs, 1998, idem, *George Soros on Globalization*. New York & London: Public Affairs, 2002, idem. *The New Paradigm for Financial Markets: The Credit Crisis of 2008 and What it Means*. New York & London: Public Affairs, 2008, idem. *Financial Turmoil in Europe and the United States: Essays*. New York & London: Public Affairs, 2012, George Soros, Maria Bartiromo, "CNBC's Maria Bartiromo Speaks with George Soros, Chairman of Soros Fund Management, from the World Economic Forum in Davos," 2013 (see the Interview online: http://www.cnbc.com/id/100406050), George Soros, *The Tragedy of the European Union: Disintegration or Revival?* New York & London: Public Affairs, 2014. If I refer here especially to Soros, it is because his *Open Society Foundation* supported financially women's projects in Eastern Europe.

[34] See Gesine Fuchs. *Die Zivilgesellschaft mitgestalten. Frauenorganisationen im polnischen Demokratisierungsprozess*. Frankfurt, New York: Campus, 2003, pp. 118-119.

attention as they represent an important counterpoint to the negative image of women's organizations in post-communist Europe.

4. Women as "social actors"

Of course, unemployment and low salaries, which, according to Ghodsee, are the main problems of Bulgarian women, affect men as well. This is why many women in post-communist Europe do not consider their problems as *women-specific*; they feel neither disadvantaged, not suppressed; they reject feminism and the gender perspective as well, and do not see any need for a women's movement. In this context, some scholars from Eastern Europe emphasize that women's problems are interconnected with other basic problems and therefore cannot be solved *per se*.[35] This applies in particular to the specific issues of women in former Yugoslavia, stemming from politics, ethnic conflicts and war. As mentioned, the dependence between gender and politics was quickly recognized by Yugoslav women and led them to a collective political engagement. Similar tendencies could also be observed in Poland, e.g., on problems like abortion.[36] Nevertheless, women's political engagement in the post-communist countries is usually considered to be small. Vlasta Jalušič and Milica Antić describe the situation as follows:

> One problem we encounter when considering the relationship between civil society, or rather women's movements, and the formulation of equal opportunities politics arises in the first place from the fact that, in most CEE countries, feminist political activism is still quite unsystematic, or, in the words of P. Jedličkova, "Political activism in Czech women's NGOs is very rare and has an individualistic rather than a systematic character, while major achievements on the political scene (changes in legislation) have been achieved thanks to international support" (...) Feminist political activism within NGOs in CEE countries is rare. There is an aversion to collective action and institutional measures for increasing political participation. Some or-

---

[35] See Havelková, op.cit, p. 147; Šiklová, op. cit., p. 275.
[36] See Maria Kwiatkowska und Inga Pietrusiska, "Polen: Mein Bauch gehört mir!," *cafebabel*, 08.02.2007, online: http://www.cafebabel.com/eng/article/19941/polen-mein-bauch-gehort-mir.html

ganisations nevertheless support these measures while others provide training for the greater participation of women.[37]

This might be overall true, but such assertions tend to neglect the fact that the political engagement in some countries in Eastern Europe, which was relatively high after the collapse of communism, has sunk increasingly over the years, not only among women, but among the entire population. I still remember the first two years, right after 1989, when the Bulgarian people were obsessed with participation in political meetings and with political campaigning. The nation was literally split into two camps, and every single day one could observe how one group marched in the streets of the capital with blue flags, and the other, with red flags. That was the time of "political euphoria." What remained was just disappointment, annoyance, feelings of helplessness, apathy, and, consequently, decreasing electoral and political participation. Every once in a while, during the crises in 1997 and 2013, there have been moments of awakening and activation of civil society, but in general, the activeness of the citizens has dropped significantly in comparison with the period 1989-1991.

The thesis that women in the post-communist countries are less interested in politics than men is quite debatable. More important, in my view, is that, for women engaged in politics, their political convictions play a greater role than their gender. The interests that they defend are, consequently, not women-specific, but reflect their own interests and those of their party.

When Ghodsee interprets the fact that women are very well represented in government and in the parliament as being an achievement of the Bulgarian women, she is formally and statistically right. But the question is whether the women in parliament really contribute to women-friendly politics. In fact, the "beautiful" statistics and numbers that can be gathered from some studies and reports about the political participation of women in Central and Eastern Europe do not reveal anything about *women's policy* itself. Although the post-communist parliaments took some legal actions to implement the

---

[37] Vlasta Jalušič, Milica Antić, *Women – Politics – Equal Opportunities. Prospects for Gender Equality Politics in Central and Eastern Europe.* Ljubljana: Mirovni Inštitut, 2001, pp. 50, 68.

measures on gender equality demanded by the EU, we can hardly speak of a sustainable women's policy.

5. Conclusions

What conclusions can be drawn from this debate?

First, with the exception of former Yugoslavia, we cannot really speak of women's movements in post-communist Europe, but rather of active establishement of civil society organizations, including diverse women's associations and initiatives.

Second, the acute social and economic problems of women can be solved only through profound social changes; they are not just women's affairs and therefore should be achieved by means of political and civic activities in collaboration with men.

Third, specific women's problems like abortion, the double burden of professional and domestic work as well as parenting, different forms of discrimination and violence against women, etc., are still women's matters. Since in many cases the problem is not, or not *only*, about equal treatment, gender mainstreaming has proven insufficient, so there is a need for specific feminist strategies and for managing diversity.

Fourth, in regard to active citizenship and women's solidarity, it should be stressed that the cooperation between women's organizations from the warring regions in former Yugoslavia was really emblematic: it showed what a women's alliance can achieve, not only for the women themselves, but also at the social and political level. In other post-communist countries, however, where dozens of women's organizations have competed for funds, the urgent problems of women have often been neglected.

Fifth, the widely discussed number of women in the parliaments is specific to every country and reflects the complex power relations there, which are not always transparent. In 2013, Serbia was in the lead in this respect, with 33,2% of female members of parliament (more than in Germany – 32,9%, France – 26,9%, and England – 22,5%) [sic!], followed by Slovenia – 32,2%, Bulgaria – 24,6%, Croatia – 23,8%, Poland – 23,7%, the Czech Republic – 22%, Slovakia – 18%, Albania – 17, 9%, and Romania – 13,3%. A higher participation of women in the top ranks of politics is, no doubt, desirable for democracy, but it is no guarantee for a sustainable and proactive women's policy.

This general overview shows that women are, *nolens volens,* reliant on civil society precisely because they mistrust the politicians as well as the institutions, including the women's organizations. And vice versa, civil society needs women in order to disrupt some partial economic-political interests and monopolies, to revive diversity, and hence to be strengthened by the active involvement of various groups. But so long as women do not learn to use the public sphere more effectively in their own interest, their specific problems will not be seen and resolved. Or, as the saying goes, "No plaintiff, no judge."

PART II

COMMUNITY VALUES AND THE PRAXIS OF SOCIAL INTEGRATION AND EXCLUSION

9

Enrique Dussel

GLOBALIZATION AND THE VICTIMS OF EXCLUSION FROM A LIBERATION ETHICS PERSPECTIVE

To my friend the philosopher Prof. Dr. Odera Oruka from Nairobi University (Kenya) assassinated in December 1996

In this article I will merely refer to some fundamental theses.[1] The strategy of the argument will take the following path: I will begin with some older reflections by Paul Ricoeur about universal civilization and its particular cultures (part 1). I will summarize a non-eurocentric historical perspective that is pertinent to the Modern Globalizing System (part 2). I will describe the asymmetrical location of the "participants" that has resulted from the violent process of inclusion in the World System (part 3). I will point out to certain aspects through which one can see ethical and critical demands within the horizon of globalization (part 4). To conclude (part 5) I will suggest some relevant topics for future discussions.

1. Universal Civilization and particular cultures?

In 1961, as I arrived to Paris from a work-related stay of two years in Israel, I had the chance to attend some classes at the Sorbonne and to read an article by Paul Ricoeur published in *Esprit* and entitled "World Civilization and National Cultures."[2] According to Ricoeur, "World

---

[1] For more details see my book *Ethics of Liberation: In the Age of Globalization and Exclusion* (Durham: Duke University Press, 2013).
[2] See Paul Ricoeur, "Civilisation universelle et cultures nationales," in idem, *Histoire et Verité*, Paris: Seuil, 1964, pp. 274-288.

Civilization" — which already entails the entire problematic of "globalization" — is constituted on the basis of the scientific spirit,[3] the technical and instrumental structures, and a rationalized and universalized politics and economy which in turn generates a form of life that eventually becomes globalized ("the inevitable standardization of housing, clothing..." etc.)[4]. But when one asks with an optimism that is appropriate sometimes about the signification of such a civilization, Ricoeur points out that "this questioning amounts to come to terms with the only humanity,"[5] i.e. an entry of the masses to the elemental goods, a struggle against illiteracy, and an increment in the means of consumption and culture. Even though he already writes critically:

> En même temps qu'une promotion de l'humanité, le phénomène d'universalization constitue une sorte de subtile destruction ... (du) noyau créateur des grandes civilisations, des grandes cultures, ce noyau à partir duquel nous interprétons la vie (...) le noyau éthique et mythique de l'humanité.[6]

Indeed, world cultures have to reckon with the other cultures that belong to great civilization, regional cultures edified from an ethical and mythical nucleus,[7] cultures built by institutions that are not universal but rather particular:

> L'humanité ne s'est pas constituée dans un seul style culturel, mais a pris dans de figures historiques cohérantes, closes[8]: les cultures.[9]

---

[3] Science here is exclusively Greek and European, from Galilee to Descartes and Newton (Ricoeur op.cit., pp. 274-275). Thus, the scientific legacy of the Arabs and the Chinese is forgotten (See Joseph Needham, *Science and Civilisation in China*, Cambridge: Cambridge University Press, vol.1-5, 1985).

[4] Ibid., p. 277.

[5] Ibid., pp. 278-279.

[6] Ibid., p. 280. At its moment, I carried out a reflection that was applied to the Latin American reality [See Enrique Dussel, "Hipótesis para el estudio de Latinoamérica en la historia universal," Resistencia (Argentina): Universidad del Nordeste, 1966, and idem, *Nueve ensayos sobre la cultura*, trad.portug., São Paulo: Paulinas, 1996). It is important to note that over thirty years of the publication of Ricoeur's article, a work with almost the same title has just been released: *National Culture and the New Global System* (Frederick Buell, *National Culture and the new Global System*, Baltimore: The Johns Hopkins University Press, 1994.)

[7] Ibid., p. 282.

[8] A sort of non-communicable incommensurability is here suggested.

Cultures that cannot recreate are unable to develop, and thus they die.[10] Today those cultures that cannot adapt to "scientific rationalization" and to the secularization of nature will not be able to survive. It seems, then, as if Ricoeur believed that the westernization of the world is inexorable, since only a few cultures (the great cultures not withstanding) will be able to resist the affront of the Western and Christian culture that had produced a notion of westernization based on scientific rationalization and secularization:

> Il faut d'une part se réenraciner dans son passé, se refaire une âme nationale (...) Mais il faut en même temps, pour entre dans la civilisation moderne, entrer dans la rationalité scientifique, technique, politique qui exige bien souvent l'abandon pur et simple de tout un passé culturel.[11]

At any rate the question remains open for a move towards communication attempt that is similar to the Ethics of Discourse:

> Aux syncrétismes[12] il faut opposer la communication, c'est-à-dire une relation dramatique dans laquelle tour á tour je m'affirme dans mon origine et je me livre à l'imagination d'autrui selon son autre civilisation.[13]

However, the aporia remains unresolved: on the one hand, there is a civilization as a universal System – predicated upon instrumental reason, essentially at the level of scientific and technical abstract structure and also predicated upon the process of modern rationalization – and on the other hand, there are some other cultures (the great cultures) that are ultimately incommunicated, cultures that are particular rather than uni-

---

[9] Ibid., p. 284.
[10] "Telle est la loi tragique de la création d'une culture" (ibid., p. 285).
[11] Ibid., pp. 280-281.
[12] In syncretism lies the possibility of an intercultural dialogue from which a world culture that is the result of a syncretic unity of all cultures will be born. Ricoeur cannot accept a hybrid solution because of a Eurocentric a priori.
[13] Ibid., p. 288. Citing Heidegger ("It is necessary to lose ourselves in our own origins"), Ricoeur calls upon Europeans to return to their Greek, Hebrew and Christian origins: "pour avoir en face de soi un autre que soi, il faut avoir un soi" (ibid., p. 287). This is also the basic topic of Ricoeur's recent critics on Levinas in *Soi même come un autre* (Paris: Seuil, 1990).

versal, cultures that ought to mutually communicate but for which it remains to be seen how this communication is to be achieved.

One could conclude that there is universality at the instrumental level and particularity at the material level (in relation to the ethical and mythical nucleus) of each culture. In Latin America, Leopoldo Zea in 1957, in his book *America en la historia*[14] identified a similar problem to the one delineated above. On his part, the Caribbean Latin American Franz Fanon, confronted this very same problem in 1961 from the perspective of the oppressed colonials in *Les damnes de la terre*[15]; these questions were discussed at the time of my return to Latin America − after ten years in Europe.[16] In 1973, I would write in my work: *Para un etica de la liberacion latinoamericana*, a philosophical and critical statement expressed from the periphery of the World System:

> El europeo, y por ello su filosofía, ha universalizado su posición de dominador, conquistador, metropolí imperial, y ha logrado, por una pedagogía practicamente infalible, que las élites ilustradas sean, en las colonias, los subopresores que mantienen a los oprimidos en una cultura del silencio, cultura que no sabe decir su palabra, y que sólo escucha − por sus élites ilustradas, por sus filósofos europizados− una palabra que los aliena: los hace otros que sí mismos.[17]

Also, sometime after 1977, the same issue is being debated over in Africa through philosophical works of authors such as Eboussi Boulaga and Paulin Hontodji,[18] debates that fertilized the thought on particularism and universalism. This debates led to the multicultural trend of Postcoloniality, a trend that since 1986 has found a point of reference in

---

[14] See Leopoldo Zea, *América en la historia*, México: FCE, 1957.
[15] See Franz, Fanon, *Los condenados de la tierra*, México: FCE, 1963.
[16] See my works from that period: "Iberoamérica en la historia universal" [Enrique Dussel, "Hipótesis para el estudio de Latinoamérica en la historia universal," Resistencia (Argentina): Universidad del Nordeste, en rotaprint, 1966; idem, "Cultura, cultura popular latinoamericana y cultura nacional," *Cuyo* (Mendoza) 4, (1968), pp. 7-40].
[17] Enrique Dussel, *Para una ética de liberación latinoamericana*, Siglos XXI, Buenos Aires, vol.1, 1973, p.153; "Philosophy of Liberation" had already been born.
[18] See Fabien Eboussi Boulaga, *La crise du Muntu. Authenticité africaine et philosophie*, Paris: Présence Africaine, 1977 and Paulin Hountondji, *Sur la "Philosophie Africaine." Critique de l'ethnophilosophie*, Paris: Maspero, 1977.

Decolonizing the mind the politics language in African Literature[19] by Kenyan author NguNgu wa Thiong'o. In 1978, Edward Said published *Orientalism*,[20] a text which allowed for the discussion about anti-eurocentric theses.

The philosophical theme is always centered on the dialectics of universalism (of a modern civilization) and the notion of particularity (of the great traditional cultures of the colonial world). The question remains open to discussion; it is currently debated with fervor leading decidedly towards the problematic of "culture."[21] Charles Taylor writes advocating a multicultural yet non globalizing politics:

---

[19] Ngûgû wa Thiong'o, *Decolonising the Mind: The Politics of Language in African Literature*, Portsmouth: Heinemann, 1986.

[20] Edward Said, *Orientalism*, Random House, New York, 1978; See a revision of his thesis in idem, *Culture and Imperialism*, New York: Knopf, 1993.

[21] In effect, Featherstone [see Mike Featherstone (ed.), *Global Culture. Nationalism, globalization and modernity. A Theory, Culture and Society special issue*, London: Sage Publications, 1993], is coordinating a work on *Global Culture* that begins with the question: Is there a global culture? (p.1) a question that swiftly becomes: it might be possible to refer to the globalization of culture" (Ibid.). Robertson tells us that "during the second half of the 1980' s globalization (and its problematic variance, internationalization) became a commonly used term in intellectual, business, media and other circles – acquiring in the process a number of meaning, with varying degrees of precision" (Roland Robertson, *Globalization. Social Theory and Global Culture*, London: Sage Publications, 1994, p. 19.) Globalization, according him, is a recent phenomenon through which "all is structured as the whole." (Ibid., p. 20) This view implies that such a globalization begun to speed up since 1880 and that from 1960 it entered the "phase of uncertainty," especially in 1990. (Ibid., p.27) Robertson himself describes in his work *Globalization. Social Theory and Global Culture* (1994) the "global field" as a field with four poles:

   1 National Societies — 2 World System

   4 Self-identities — 3 Humankind.

This field determines sic different sets of relations: 1-2: Relativization of national society; 2-3: Real politic-humanity problematic; 3-4: Relativization of self-identities; 4-1: Individual-society problematic; 1-3: Relativization of citizenship; 4-2: Relativization of societal reference (p.27). This work is filled with suggestions to be taken into account. Frederick Buell (*National Culture and the New Global System*, 1994) makes an excellent description of debates in the USA about this problem, specially pertaining to the Post-colonial debate (pp. 217 ff) from within Marxist tradition (pp.265 SS), as well as within the debates on Postmodernity and Globalization. (pp. 325ff)

But merely, on the human level, one could argue that it is reasonable to suppose that a culture that have provided the horizon of meaning of large numbers of human beings, of diverse characters and temperaments, over a long period of time -that have, in other words, articulated their sense of the good, the holy, the admirable- are almost certain to have something that deserves our admiration and respect, even if it is accompanied by much that we have to abhor and reject.[22]

2. Towards a history of globalization

Immanuel Wallerstein, had already since 1974[23] advanced the notion of a "World System." Departing from this thesis Andre Gunder Frank asserts that the "World System"[24] does not originate in Capitalism but it has existed for at least 5000 years.[25] Similarly, Jim Blaut is of the opinion that Modernity does not exactly begin with Capitalism but rather with the European "invasion" of America in 1492.[26] I believe that this question is both complex and needs to be differentiated. Before entering this debate, and as a preamble, I would like to outline a certain historical

---

[22] Charles Taylor, *Multiculturalism and 'The Politics of Recognition'*, New Jersey: Princeton University Press, 1992, pp. 72-73.
[23] See Immanuel Wallerstein, *The Modern World-System*, New York: Academic Press, 1974; idem *The Politics for the World-Economy*, Cambridge: Cambridge University Press, 1984; idem, "The Insurmountable Contradictions of Liberalism: Human Rights and the Rights of Peoples in the Geoculture of the Modern World-System," *The South Atlantic Quarterly*, 94: 4 (1995), pp.1161-1178.
[24] See "The World System as Philosophical Problem," in Enrique Dussel, *The Underside of Modernity*, New Jersey: Humanities Press, 1966, pp. 214 ff.
[25] See André Gunder Frank, "The Shape of the World System in the Thirteenth Century," in Studies in Comparative International Development, XXII/4 (1987); idem, "A theoretical Introduction to 5000 years of World System history," in Review (Binghamton), 13/2 (1990), pp.155-248; idem, The centrality of Central Asia, Amsterdam: UV University Press, 1992; A. G. Frank, B.K. Gills (Eds.), The World System: From Five Hundred Years to Five Thousand, London/New York: Routledge, 1992.
[26] See Jim M. Blaut (Ed.), *1492. The debate on colonialism, eurocentrism and history*, Trenton (NJ): Africa World Press, 1992; idem, *The colonizer's model of the World*, New York: The Guilford Press, 1993.

perspective which will allow us to place the discussion within a different horizon (neither a Eurocentric, nor a Hegelian[27] one).

Many of the instances of the system that is nowadays globalized have an old history.[28] In our interpretation the "World System" has certain stages that we would like to briefly recall here.[29]

a. Stage I. Mesopotamia and Egypt. Of the six regions of what is considered the high Neolithic[30] culture (Egypt, Mesopotamia, India, pre Aryan China, Mesoamerica and the Inca region) only Egypt and Mesopotamia participate in an exchange of civilizing experiences that took place constantly since the IV. millennium B.C. At this juncture, a "system" that is now globalized begins to take shape historically, according to the plausible thesis of A.G. Frank.[31] In a non-eurocentric conception of history it is necessary to remember that Egypt has an originary Bantu component coming from the black African South.[32] Thus, in the Bantu

---

[27] For Hegel "world history travels from East to West; therefore, Europe is the end of universal history" (*"Die Weltgeschichte geht von Osten nach Westen; denn Europa ist schlechthin das Ende der Weltgeschichte,"* Gottfried Wilhelm Friedrich Hegel, *Die Vernunft in der Geschichte (1830)*, Hamburg: Meiner, 1955, p. 243). See also my lectures at Goethe Universität in Frankfurt (*The Invention of the Americas. Eclipse of the Other and the Myth of Modernity*, New York: Continuum, 1995, conf. 1).

[28] It might appear trivial to allude to the following ordinary examples; however, they reveal a deeper implication: the seven-day week originates in Mesopotamia; the scale that symbolizes justice is actually that of Osiris, with which she could weigh the good deeds performed in life by the dead ones of Egypt; our current dressing codes, for instance, the use of trousers, nowadays also widespread in women, was introduced in Mongolia by the horsemen of the Euro-Asian plains, approximately 8000 years ago; paper and the printing press was well known in China during the VI century BC.

[29] For a more detailed discussion see my *Ethics of Liberation* (Durham: Duke University Press, 2013), in the historical introduction section 1 and 2.

[30] The Neolithic revolution, contrary to Hegel's claims, travels from Mesopotamia and Egypt, right at the climax of the Paleolithic and without direct connections, towards the East: India, China and pre-Colombian cultures.

[31] I will not refer to it as "World System" because of the exclusion of "Amerindia" extended up to the European "invasion" at the end of the fifteenth century. Rather, I will refer to it as an Afro-Asian "Interregional System at the stage I."

[32] The Egyptian used to refer to himself as *kmt* which meant black, synonym of a civilized subject, while the white subject (in Egyptian language "red," a pejorative

culture the dead is buried with the instruments used while still alive (This can be observed both in a present day tomb in Ghana as well as in the pyramid of the Pharaoh Tutankamon whose hundreds of utensils can be seen at the Museum of Cairo). Similarly, the Osiris' myth of the resurrection of the dead (a myth which required a culture of Pyramids and mausoleums) arrives to Europe and America, via the Judeo Christian thought, where one can find cemeteries[33] like in the whole Muslim world, from Marroco to the Philippines. Normative enunciations such as "I fed bread to the hungry, gave water to thirsty, clothed the naked one"[34] or "that the powerful do not oppress the poor in order to do justice to the orphaned and the widow"[35] are today critical principles still in use in Western Culture and which come from the first stage of the "inter-regional system."

b. Stage II. The Culture of the Horse and Iron. Due to the use of the horse [36] and the use of iron,[37] especially in the manufacturing of weapons for the wars of the great invaders, the "inter-regional system" becomes connected. These peoples, inappropriately called "Indo-Europeans," have also been referred to as invaders even though their "invasions" cannot really be labeled as such. The "system" expands by becoming connected to China, and thus initiating what will be known as the "Route of Silk"; by reaching India and thus incorporating the "Aryans" of Rig Veda and by including the following civilizations: the Persians and Medes of Mesopotamia; the Hitites from Turkey, the Greek and Latins of the Mediterranean and the Germans in Northern Europe.

---

term) was the barbarian of the Mediterranean. It is, then, imperative to acknowledge a black- African component of Egyptian culture.

[33] The Greek, Indo-European tradition states the immortality of the soul; therefore, cremation of corpses is practiced since the body is the origin of all evil.

[34] Chapter 125, Egyptian *Book of the Dead.*

[35] From the Epilogue of the Babylonian Codex of Hammurabi.

[36] Horse as a means of transportation from Mongolia and China through the desserts of Euro-Asian plains to India, Persia and the Mediterranean (see Karl Narr, "Exkurs über die frühe Pferdehaltung," in *Saeculum Weltgeschichte*, Freiburg: Herder, Bd.1, 1965, pp. 578-581).

[37] A metal that produces a technological revolution: from the introduction of harnesses, nails, horseshoe, the ax, the shovel, pickax, to the improvement of agricultural plowing system, etc.

The "system" that becomes now globalized owes so much of the configuration of its "institutions" to the peoples from the Iron and Horse stage that it is frequently held that Modernity is the sole inheritor of the II stage of the Inter-Regional Asiatic-Afro-Mediterranean System; conversely, it is frequently forgotten that China, India and most of the Muslim world are just as authentic inheritors of this system as the previous ones. The unilinear syllogism Grece-Rome-Europe is false. Baghdad is an earlier and more relevant continuation of Athens than Paris or Köln – the first is more of an inheritor of Greek thought than the seconds. One should not forget either that Athens was a colony of the Egyptian Sais (its masters in economics, science and religion: the Neith, goddess of Sais is the Palas Atheneas, and Plato correctly asserted that the Egyptian Thoth had taught Greeks the numbers, calculus, geometry and astronomy)[38]. The armed riders of the Iron stage organized, then, the first political institutions and occupied vast territories, thus dominating many people that paid taxes and were frequently reduced to slavery. The Interregional system expanded from the Hitite Empire, whose capital was Hattusa, through the Persian Empire, the Indian kingdoms and the Chinese Empire, to the expansion of the Hellenistic world which founded Seleucia in the heart of Mesopotamia (capital of Seleucid Hellenes), city that was the "center" of the connections that sprang from China to Hispania. This primitive globalization was already intercontinental: from the Pacific to the Atlantic where an exchange of numerous techniques and findings related to astronomy, agriculture, economics and politics took place, an exchange that will persist in the present World System.

c. Stage III. From Byzantium to Bhagdad. It would seem that the domination of the Iron era produced endless oppression in the great empires. It would also seem, as Max Weber affirms, that, in the shacks of the slaves and the exploited ones, a critical ethics on the universalistic rebellion of the victims was propagated. The sage's critical formulations, exchanged with Egypt and Mesopotamia, were expressed in sacred books that, once re-read in situations of extreme material scarcity, produced as if by an explosion, the third stage of the "Inter-Regional System." This stage comprises the following cultures and territories: first of

---

[38] Phaedrus, 274d.

all, the Christian Byzantine culture; the Muslim culture (which will reach to Morocco in the Atlantic, to Poitiers in the north in 732 A.C., to the south of the Sahara, to the plateau via the golden Horde of the Mongols in what is now Russia, to Delhi, or Angra; and to the Mindanao in the Philippines in the fifteenth century through Malacca in the Pacific), and finally the Latin and Germanic cultures. The "System" will have as a central region from Samarkand and Bukhara (to the south of the present day Russia) up to Kabul around Bhagdad (founded in 762 and destroyed by the Mongols in 1258) which was the model of the "civilized" and "modern" for five hundred years.[39] The falasifa (philosophy in Arabic) acquires a classical splendor in the ninth century when Al Kindi (who dies in Kufic, Syria in 873 A.D.) initiates the first process of modern secularization in philosophy, thus making philosophy different from the Koran and using it as a rational hermeneutical method for its own commentary. Ibn Sina (Avicena, who dies in 1037 A.D.) who lived in Bukhara (now to the south of Russia), rediscovered and impeccably elaborated on Aristotle's logic. The Muslim Culture is the first great heir to Greek culture.[40] Europe, the Germanic Europe, was a peripheral region of the Mediterranean, a "remote" corner which was never central (not even during the Roman Empire) to the "Inter-Regional System" which encompassed China. The poorly labelled "Middle Ages"[41] were nothing but the European perception of its own darkness and its dependency on a "central" culture: the "Muslim culture." The first prominent European novel, though there are some others before, *Don Quixote*, "the

---

[39] In every culture from Egypt to China, from the Aztecs to the Incas, that which is modern signals to the center from which the best information of the "system" is managed; from which the best and newest instruments (material as well as symbolic) are used; from which political and religious power, and economic wealth is administered; in short, the modern signals to the most developed. The rest are "barbarians," non-humans, those who are outside, the "periphery." The modern in each culture is valuable because of its ethnocentricity. The "modernity" of the World System claims validity for all the other cultures; and this is a novelty in world history.

[40] Its octagonal mosques resemble Greek-Byzantine art, unlike later Gothic churches built with a different spirit.

[41] For world history, the label Middle-Ages is an invalid historical category; it does not make any sense for the Muslim world, India, China or Amerindia. It only works for Europe.

knight of the sad figure," (who fought against windmills)[42] is attributed according to his author to an Arab writer. Could a "barbarian" European write a "literary masterpiece" of such innovative style? It was more plausible to attribute it to those thought as "cultivated," undoubtedly the Arabs who were centenarian writers of subtle "stories" (protonovels), such as the *Arabian Nights*.

All of the elements, or at least most of them, that Weber identifies in the European Middle Ages and Renaissance as "internally" constitutive of Modernity, have been truly realized in the Muslim World centuries before [43].

d. Stage IV. The "World System": Europe as "center." Up until the "invasion" of the American Continent in 1492, the Baltic Sea (the industrial "Northern Europe" of Hegel) and the Sea of Japan, were the most remote regions from the "center" (at that moment Bhagdad and India).

The unexpected "invasion" of the Amerindian cultures (i.e: Mexico from 1519 and Perú from 1529) will give to peripheral Europe a "vantage point" when compared to China – more populated and at least at the same level of technological development as Renaissance Europe. The

---

[42] The windmill is a symbol of technological modernity. But one must not forget that windmills actually come from the Muslim world because, since 947 BC there were wind and water mills in Seistan, a town closed to Indo. Also in Basora, the Tigris' river flow was used to give motion to floating mill wheels. Modernity for Cervantes pays for the Armada with which Europeans, Spaniards, irrevocably defeat the Turks in the battle of Lepanto in 1571, a battle financed by the Latin-American silver extracted from the mines of Zacatecas and Potosí discovered in 1546.

[43] According to Braudel (1978) that because of a letter written by a merchant Jew from Cairo (1095-1099 A.C.) we know that Muslims knew all forms of credit and payment and all forms of commercial association; therefore, it was not in Italy that these commercial forms of transactions first emerged as it has been so readily accepted (p.65). There was an extensive commercial network with currency instruments that allowed for the management of money among the nations of the inter-regional system. Transactions of agricultural products developed the milling industry of cereals; for instance, 100 thousand camels were used exclusively for the commercialization of dates. Muslims caravans that connected India and China with the Mediterranean reached up to six thousand camels. This commercial network gave rise to multiple industries. Merchants began to make their calculations with Arabic numbers, which actually originated in India, and used the decimal system and the numeral zero, along with algebra, etc.

first Modernity,[44] in its humanistic and imperial sense will be advanced by Spain as a result of the unity of the Hispanic nation brought about by Castille and Aragon in 1476 through the Port of Seville; this unification (new center) will be the predecessor of what eventually will become the first (and only) "World System." The experience and wealth of Genoa and other Renaissance Italian cities was not pertinent to the lands where the Reformation occurred[45]. Such experience, along with that of the ancient Arab emirates (from the Caliphate of Cordoba...) was rather directed towards the Atlantic —an "ocean," up to that moment, devoid of culture—, a horizon that will extend to the Caribbean (the new Mediterranean) in the imminence of Capitalism.

Northern Europe, up to that moment always dependent and peripheral of the Latin Mediterranean world (with the relative exception of the Vikings and the Hansa Confederation, though these themselves were dependent on the Mediterranean) is now directly connected to the "center," as embodied by the Atlantic.[46] The emancipation of Holland from Spain (at the beginning of the seventeenth century) and its mighty fleet, transformed Amsterdam, since 1630, into the heir of Seville.[47] We

---

[44] See Wallerstein, op. cit., 1974, vol 1. Also see the eight volumes of Pierre Chaunu, *Séville et l'Atlantique (1504-1650)*, t.1-8, Paris: SEVPEN, 1955.

[45] For Hegel modernity covers a geography that, departing from the Renaissance (Italy) and passing through the Reformation (Alemania), the English parliament, and the French Revolution, reaches the Enlightenment (specifically in its German and French versions). As it can be gathered from this, there is nothing "modern" to Spain Portugal and Latin America. We have referred to this vision as provincial and Eurocentric, since it considers Modernity as developing from within, as a result of an intrinsic European development which began in the Middle-Ages. Such, however, is not the case. The fact is that Southern Europe (the "Latin" one), the center of the World System, makes of this region the departing point of Modernity. Latin America is the first periphery, a century before the Anglo-Saxon America (i.e. New Holland, colony of the Holland which at the time of settlement was a Spanish colony) became, in the seventeenth century, the New England of the thirteen original colonies.

[46] This explain that Luther's protest, which could have ended up as the rankings of one more heretic of Medieval Europe, could now "reach" the center of the System and thus could dispense away with the mediation of Mediterranean Rome, a Rome that along with the Mediterranean will become a peripheral culture of Atlantic Europe (thus inverting the ego-political situation). The Eurocentricity implicit in the so-called "discovery" of America thus explains the world scope of the Protestant Reformation.

[47] Immanuel Wallerstein, *The Modern World-System*, op.cit., vol. 2.

are now in the second Modernity, the properly bourgeois modernity of a mercantile "system" that will progressively replace the imperial Iberian superpowers. Since the "invasion" of Latin America in 1492, the "de-centralization" in the sixteenth century of the "ancient system" that gravitated around Baghdad, produces a shattering revolution of the scientific paradigm of the peripheral Medieval Europe. The sixteenth century is nothing but the period of this revolution – when in 1520 Magellan (El Cano) returns from "circling" the world, there begins, "empirically," a new phase of the world's astronomic cosmology. The new scientific paradigm is only "expressed" at the beginnings of the seventeenth century (as a result of the previous Hispanic revolution) with Galilee (condemned in 1616), Descartes (disciple of the Spanish Jesuits, devoted to the practice of the "examination of conscience," which in turn was the origin of the cogito and who writes in Amsterdam in 1636 *Le Discours de la méthode*), etc. The rest is already known. However, we would like to gather a few conclusions pertinent to our topic.

The "World System" that reaches a new stage of globalization at the end of the twentieth century is already five hundred years old – the Stage III, organized around Baghdad, was also five hundred years old. This System is that of Modernity, of mercantile Capitalism (first under Spanish and then under Dutch domination) of industrial capitalism (under British domination) and transnational Capitalism (under North American domination since 1945, end of the so-called Second World War). This "System" is not merely an instrumental one as Paul Ricoeur and others indicated; it also contains material cultural moments (symbols, myths, values and traditions). It is rather ambiguously a technological system (based on instrumental reason), but it displays also many material instances (such as the ones mentioned above) and discursive instances (i.e. political institutions), etc. Furthermore, for the first time a World System confronts all the other cultures which in the Asian and Mediterranean region (obviously from China to India up to the Middle East and Northern Africa) had been fertilized internally by ancient moments of the very same "system" (Stages II and III). China, for instance, is perfectly reticent to the modernity of the World System, because for thirty centuries it has lived with such system (from its Stages II and III); therefore, it has an internal capacity to assimilate and adapt. India, as a victim of colonialism is the exception. The Muslim reality, given its comprehension of the world, draws from internal resources, originating in its first philosophical and Aristotelian Enlightenment since the ninth century, in order to encompass the secularized world (fundamentalism notwithstanding, given that it is a nonessential epiphenomenon). Latin America was the first assimilated and co-opted modern periphery (Latin America is the originary "barbarian" required by Modernity for its own definition). With the exception of few ethnicities, still today resisting the invasion, destruction and assimilation, the destruction of the great majority of Amerindian cultures were the origin of "mestizaje." This is not the case with the Bantu world or any other "non-universal" indigenous culture, cultures whose process of "assimilation" is more complex.

At any rate, concomitantly with the globalization of modernity, the almost absolute exteriority of other sophisticated cultures has progressively diminished. But, suddenly, the capacity for expansion is halted and thus a process of exclusion begins, out of the internal crisis within this very World System. Let us consider, then, the processes of inclusion and exclusion that are both violent and mortal.

3. The asymmetrical inclusion of the victims of the World-System

From the fifteenth century onwards, Europe as a secondary and peripheral culture, dialectically expands its horizons and includes (subsumes) first and foremost Amerindia (from Mexico to Peru) the richest area in metal and whose urban centers were the most densely populated. For three centuries Europe will accumulate wealth and military technology, will monopolize power and will lead in the management of the World System's centrality (not anymore in the sense meant by Wallerstein, but incorporating many of the aspects of the autopoiesis of the "system" in the sense meant by Luhmann)[48] in order to territorially occupy certain regions of Asia and, since the Berlin Congress (in 1885, just a century ago), to prepare for the "invasion" of Africa. It was only since the fifteenth century that the purported "superiority" of Europe was exerted on the Amerindian cultures; these cultures did not know

---

[48] See Niklas Luhmann, *Das Soziale System. Grundriss einer allgemeinen Theorie*, Frankfurt m Main: Suhrkamp, 1984.

iron, gun powder and the horse. Such was not the case with Africa which resisted until the times of the Industrial Revolution, thus proving that until the fifteenth century the so called European superiority was ineffectual. The "colonial world" is the victim; it is a denied and divided world, an excluded world. In relation to this Franz Fanon wrote:

> Como es una negación sistemática del Otro, una decisión furiosa de privar al Otro de todo atributo de humanidad, el colonialismo empuja al pueblo dominado a plantearse constantemente la pregunta: ¿Quién soy en realidad[49]? (Fanon 1963, 228)

The point here is to locate historically, empirically and concretely this "negation of the Other."[50] The ethic of discourse indicates that if there is asymmetry among the participants concerned in the argumentative community, the justified decision is invalid. We will show how a radical invalidity blurs any present decision in the modern World System.

a. The Irrationality of Violence as Origin. From the fifteenth century onwards, the modern World System will always expand itself by means of an initial violence which constitutes the relation among systems, nations, cultures and people. Modern Europe, since the "invasion" of Amerindia in 1492, never initiated the process of "inclusion" of the other culture (The Caribbean Indians were exterminated in the course of one century; so, only the Mexican Conquest can be construed as the originary "inclusion" in reference to the whole process of inclusion car-

---

[49] This reality is found in exteriority – to express it in Levinas' words – it is and extra-ontological and extra-linguistic reality that pertains to the languages of the World-System; it is a prius that precedes the "being" of the "comprehension of being" of the modern World-System.

[50] In my work in progress *Liberation Ethics,* I devote the whole fourth chapter to analyze this "original negation," alienation as negation of alterity as I will architectonically refer to it in the future. This "originary negation" is the co-option of the other in the dominant system; it implies an alienation of the other's alterity, a negation of the other's possibility to live, a negation to participate in the center's discourse; in short, the inability of the other to accomplish his/her goals (including the cultural ones). See Dussel, 1973, 1985.

ried out by Europe).[51] The invasion of America originates the propagation of "modern subjectivity" in a practical sense: the *ego conquiro* (I conquer) precedes the *ego cogito*. Neither Europe (Spain, Portugal, England, France, etc.) nor the United States[52] ever initiated their relation with peripheral cultures (in Latin America since the sixteenth century and in Asia since the eighteenth century)[53] with a peaceful proposition based on rational arguments.[54] This relation was always and solely carried out by the violence of weaponry. Spanish, Portuguese, British, French and North American armies occupied strategic territories. These nations defeated their opponents on the basis of military technological superiority, unconditionally subjugating them to their domination. This is the "other face of Modernity," a face that has been ignored since Kant, a face which is constitutive of modernity's "being" and of the World System whose most recent globalization is herewith being considered (in the era of the transnationals and after the so-called[55] Second World

---

[51] See my book *The Invention of the Americas. Eclipse of the Other and the Myth of Modernity*, New York: Continuum, 1995 (conf. 3, pp. 37 ff).

[52] I am referring to the violent occupation of Puerto Rico, Cuba and the Philippines in 1988, approximately a century ago. The Philippines" courageous resistance against the North American "invasion" resulted in the loss of two hundred and fifty thousand lives.

[53] Before the Industrial revolution the "conquest in Africa and Asia was carried out solely in limited islands and territories (Because Portugal still had intentions of building a "World-Empire"--much in the manner of Charles V of Spain, who in the face of financial failure must abdicate in 1557 –, Angola and Mozambique were perhaps the exceptions to the pattern that characterized the conquest of Asia and Africa) Wallerstein makes it clear that the "World-System" does not have an imperial project (a project that would impose an official language, culture, religion; and political, military and economic organization). With a "Company of the West and East Indies," Amsterdam can commercially organize the system. There is, then, a simplification by negation of the quality in favor of quantity: only "black numbers" matter for book-keeping purposes.

[54] Bartolomé de las Casas in the midst of sixteenth century Latin America proposed in his work *De Unico Modo* that Europeans must rely on rational arguments and testimonies of morally virtuous life, rather than resorting to violence (see Dussel, 1995, confer. 5.3)

[55] I insist on the adjective "so-called," because it was not a "world" war, but actually an intra-capitalist war triggered by the hegemony of the World System. Germany and Japan attempted to participate in a market-economy monopolized by England, and to a lesser degree by France and other "traditional" Central European powers;

War). These are but a few instances of Modernity's violent irrationality: The colonial conquest in Latin America by Spaniards and Portuguese,[56] in North America by Anglo Saxons (who still celebrate at Thanksgiving the Native American offering so that the colonials would not starve, colonials who as a gesture of gratitude, initiated a fierce battle that did not spare a single Native American. This battle is still praised today in the American Western film where it meets with the universal complicity of audiences) in French Canada, in the enslaved Africa,[57] in the filibustering[58] of the Caribbean, in the opium war of China or in the violent occupation of India – murdering all those who would "compete" with the British textile industry, thus destroying the centenarian production of silk.

b. Economic exploitation as structure. The despotic dominance over the bodies of the new colonial servants was structured on the basis of an economic system which was founded not even on an unequal exchange, but on the simple extraction, pillaging or illegal appropriation of all resources that could be exploited through military dominance. Indians were sent by means of the system of *encomiendas* – a system characterized by gratuitous labor – to work in the fields; later to work in the haciendas, (farms) receiving fictitious salaries; they were sent to the mines

---

the United States defeat of Germany and Japan wrested the hegemony of the United Kingdom. We are specifically referring to the North American hegemony that since 1945 allowed for the colonial emancipation of Africa and Asia. From 1989 such hegemony for the first time in the history of humanity rests in the hands of *one military super Austin Power*.

[56] Some fifteen million Indians died as a result of violence carried out with sophisticated arms, with dogs trained to kill Indians; this violence was also evident in the slavery and devastation of Indians in plantations and mines and as a consequence of diseases foreign to the indigenous population of the Americas...the conquest was the first process of globalization.

[57] The Christian nations of England, Portugal, Holland and France, stained their white hands with the blood of over thirteen million African peasants, sold as beast of burdens in the south of the thirteen colonies, in Cuba, in Cartagena de Indias, in North -Eastern Brazil. In face of a sensitive and global ethical consciousness, the complicity of these nations still awaits for its own "Nuremberg Trial "

[58] Bandits who, in the name of England and France, looted Spanish ships filled with the silver extracted from the mines in Zacatecas, Durango Guancavélica and Potosí, at the cost of Indians who rested lifeless at the bottom of these mines.

where they labored their lives away in the mita; Africans were commoditized as slaves, used and slaughtered like animals (treated as pure merchandise deprived of fundamental rights such as marriage, paternity or any other right known to humans; their bodies could be used sexually or economically by the slave "masters" who had full rights over their lives, including their sadistic torture and their extermination). The mining wealth (gold and silver) was simply possessed by the colonials who had to pay taxes to the Crown; the rest of the colonials' revenues would then be funnelled into the European world market in Europe (the first true world market whose first currency was coined with the silver extracted by the indigenous contingent in Mexico and Peru, or by the African slaves later in Minas Gerais, Brazil) This is the "originary accumulation" of colonial extraction.[59]

When the mercantilism promoted by the extraction of metals and tropical products was transformed into Industrial Capitalism (circa 1750), the World System in its very center will start the accumulation of a surplus (*sensus strictus*). In Europe, such system would restructure the colonial contract under British economy, thus initiating an uneven exchange with the textile industry. Around 1870 the accumulation of wealth and technology allows for the expansion of imperialism, territorially opening railroad lines and crossing the oceans with steamships. Great areas (Argentina, Canada, Australia, etc.) are incorporated in the World System by means of the gigantic extraction of agricultural and mining products. The periphery will always remain in an asymmetric position.

The present stage of transnational capitalism now focuses on the periphery; its capital is now invested in industries of less relevance. By doing so, capitalism absorbs the low salary of miserable external proletariat (in Asia or Latin America). The Asymmetric relation is incontestable. The Great Seven (the group of the seven, G7) decide the destiny of the rest of humanity. The concentration of wealth in the hands of the United States, Japan and Europe (whose population does not reach 15% of the total world's population) controls, uses, consumes and destroys irresponsibly up to 80% of the non renewable resources of the world.

---

[59] See Enrique Dussel, *Hacia un Marx desconocido*, México: Siglo XXI, 1988.

c. The Metropolitan Political Domination: We are not addressing the structure of interstate politics. We are not addressing either the structure of national politics. Rather, we are referring to the political structure of the World System which has been around for five hundred years. The metropolitan system (in a *de jure* assumption) was organized on the basis of violence, a political system which was termed, for instance, in Latin America, the state of the Indies (Spanish America) or the state of Brazil: the state without rights. The colonies (or ultramarine provinces) were totally subaltern to the power of the European Kings (Spanish, English, French, etc.), to their courts, councils and other political organisms.

The political status of the inhabitants of the colonies was near to zero; these inhabitants had virtually no rights vis-a-vis the European power. In the World System the periphery was politically meaningless. The anti-colonial process of national emancipation (from the beginnings of the nineteenth century in Latin America and during the second half of the twentieth century in Africa and Asia) showed from its beginning the neo-colonial traces of the colonial period. The elites that led the emancipation process profited from the structural economic exploitation, from the military domination and especially from the cultural domestication. The neo-colonial situation is nothing but the continuation of the political and colonial dominance (included the military sense in which the Pentagon has replaced the military power of the old European metropolis, a power which is exerted via an incontestable computarized technology as it was witnessed in the Gulf War, where the dominance of the center gave a clear example to the peripheral nations as to their possible destiny were they to oppose the New World Order, an Order triumphantly proclaimed by President George Bush).[60]

d. Cultural Hegemony of the World System. In the fifteenth century begins the cultural penetration into territories that, up to that juncture remained peripheral. Europe as the center of the World System culturally penetrates these peripheries; this system is not merely an instrumental

---

[60] That so many European and North American philosophers based upon ad hoc arguments.

institution (as it could be suggested by Ricoeur), but also, and rather ambiguously, a value-ridden cultural development in the sense of the *Lebenswelt* of a particular culture with pretensions of universality[61] (European culture).[62] Over the centuries cultural transmission was implemented by an educational system that move from generation to generation (elementary and high school, higher and ecclesiastical, etc.; by means of books, newspapers etc.; by means of poetry, novels and theater, etc.). The metropolis was in charge of consolidating colonial elite that was loyal to the incumbent empire. Violent repression warned against the possibility of a much desired emancipation. In the neocolonial stage, on the most part, though with a few exceptions, the neocolonial elite was in many ways co-opted by the incumbent culture, a modern and hegemonic culture. Mimetism in the cultivated avant-gardes was a sad reality.

In the present times, the postmodern phenomenon,[63] has taken again this problem, since the cultural means of expansion have been revolutionized. The repercussion of this revolution, carried out by mass media industries such as the radio, the cinema and television, amounts to a

---

[61] The World-System is "global" but the fundamental European culture in the center of the system is "particular." The European is prone to assume that his/her culture even the post-conventional one is the universal culture of the future (indeed, many Marxist from the center fell into this fetishism). The World-System has certainly cultural elements but is not a culture in the truest sense of the word, since the world system culture has been instrumentally expanded in an external fashion upon other cultures, other cultures that, in keeping with their capacity of resistance or creativity, either accepted or rejected the cultural values of the "World-System" (from eating in Burger King through drinking Coke, to wearing blue jeans). In these examples "goods" are also cultural material objects which are consumed in different fashions: when eats them ones drinks them and wears them.

[62] Latin America constituted the periphery as a dependent, alienated and repetitive culture. Latin America, due to its constitutive "mestizaje," was the first to receive the "impact" of the process of acculturation: the christianization of the Amerindian cultures, and the forthcoming colonization (and here colonization is not used in the metaphorical sense implied by Habermas but in its original and real sense).

[63] Postmodernity viewed as the inherent culture of present "late capitalism." See Frederic Jameson's excellent work *Postmodernism, or, The Cultural Logic of Late Capitalism* (Durham: Duke University Press, 1991). Also consider Aijaz Ahmad "Jameson's Rhetoric of Otherness and the National Allegory" (Social Text 19, Fall, 1987, pp. 3-16); Ahmad will later criticize Said (*In Theory: Classes, Nations, Literature*, London: Verso, 1992).

radical change of the structure that underlies the constitution and consumption of cultural objects; therefore, the problem of exchange has been also altered as has been altered the cultural penetration of the peripheries carried out by the World System. These peripheries specifically referred to particular cultures affected by the process of globalization in the post colonial age.

e. The paradox of exclusion in globalization. But the mechanisms of inclusion in the World System, far from diminishing, have actually augmented peripheral heterogeneity, given that the aggressive actions of domination have not destroyed their exteriority but rather have pushed this exteriority to its limits via a non intentional politics of exclusion. Indeed, after five hundred years of the inauguration, development and global culmination of the World System, identified with transnational Capitalism at the economic level, two critical and absolute limits emerge to close upon the whole structure of the World System. The first, the ecological destruction, a non-intentional and irreversible process, the consequence of a devastating technology which springs from the following short-term selection criteria: the increment of the rate of profit[64] (the essence of capital as valorization of value). But, in relation to his previous idea, the second, embodied by the impoverishment of most of humanity located in the postcolonial peripheral horizon of late capitalism; this, in many cases, is the beginning of the end (hunger, AIDS, etc., like in Africa Bangladesh, Haiti, etc.); this is the possible extinction of the Homo species (more due to ecological effects than due to the nuclear holocaust). Therefore, the extinction of life on earth is the last limit of the World System. We are then addressing the plight of the victims of such System.

4. Ethical criticism of globalisation as exclusion

Ethics as practical philosophy, in order to be critical needs of a certain diagnoses; it requires the explanatory and interpretative mediation of the critical human and social sciences. We have seen the manner by

---

[64] Marx would have spoken of "surplus value." In real socialism the criterion, equally devastating, was that of the increase of the rate of production.

which the third criterion of demarcation allows for the discernment between the mere functional social sciences and the critical ones.[65] A moral that is purely procedural like the one characteristic of the ethics of Discourse, an ethics which presupposes the impossibility of an empirical perfect symmetry among the participants involved in the argumentative community, does not have the possibility to use this third criterion of demarcation because it has abandoned the material ethic. This abandonment is based on the opinion that such ethic is particular, linked to selfish impulses, to a "good life" or to cultural values exempted from universalist assumptions. Morality only offers the rules for the discussion on the fundamentation of practical norms, but it cannot offer material instructions to the very same discussion; rather, it leaves the discussion of topics under the responsibility of the "experts." But are these experts critical enough? Can discursive morality offer a criterion in order to discern which scientific experts are really functional and which are critical in relation to the system (a system that unintentionally excludes the ones who do not participate, despite their being affected by it)? None of this can be pondered by the ethics of Discourse. Let's then consider how can we approach the problem.

a. The Need of Criticism from the Symmetric and Anti-Hegemonic Community of Victims. The discursive reason whose intersubjective praxis reaches validity in a communication community could carry out its grounding and hegemonic praxis from the incumbent system[66] (in

---

[65] It would seems that there is an awareness of this issue in writing: " Something different happens with the political economy that in the eighteenth century competes with the rational natural law (...) As Political Economy, the sciences of economy still keeps , in terms of theory of the crisis, a relation with the global society (...). But, despite all this, it ends up destroying economy once it becomes a specialized science [read it as functional]. Today economic science treats economy as a sub-system of society and dispenses with questions of legitimacy" (Jürgen Habermas, *Theorie des kommunikativen Handelns*, Frankfurt am Main: Suhrkamp, 1981, Bd.1, p.17). Economy would not be in this predicament were it practiced as a critical social science (as it is practiced by those who exercise the discipline as a critical economy, just as it was practiced by Marx in his time).

[66] It is definitely "hegemonic" if the third criterion of demarcation is not explicitly put in the foreground. Yet it cannot carry it out because it is material (or the material has been abandoned at the beginning of its formal process.

keeping with our topic, from the center of the World-System which begins to be globalized since the Conquest of Mexico in 1519) or from a "community of victims." The latter could be exemplified by a group of women which become conscious of "machismo," a group of African Americans who struggle against racial discrimination, a group of marginalized subjects who struggle against urban exclusion...or the challenge of peripheral cultures and nations to a World System that becomes increasingly globalized. The ethic of Discourse has not yet imagined this perspective: the participants of an affected community of victims that in the hegemonic community are excluded or who are in an asymmetrical position can conversely acquire symmetrical participation when they are "among themselves." At the "bottom of history," as a person excluded from the process of globalization (as a woman, as a peasant, as an Indian and as a Guatemalan), a privileged victim reminds us:

> Me llamo Rigoberta Menchú. Tengo veintitrés años. Quisiera dar este testimonio vivo que no he aprendido en un libro y que tampoco he aprendido sola a que todo esto lo he aprendido con mi pueblo[67] y es algo que quiero enfocar (...)[68]

The discursive reason itself can be functional to the incumbent system or it can be intersubjectively critical. I think we have taken a step forward. We have departed from the strong and critical (negative and material) position of the first Frankfurt School; and, now, we also include, within the linguistic and discursive paradigm of the second Frankfurt School, such a "criticism." The criticism we are referring to has little to do with the theoretical "critical thinking" of someone like Stephen Toulmin and Hans Albert, neither does it have much to do with the Habermasian emancipation (Emancipation) as discursive Enlightenment (*Aufklärung*). The problem is really about an ethical criticism which departs from the notion of taking side, empirically and intersubjectively, with the victim, considering thus its material negativity (with "a" in German). When the supportive scientist (Gramsci's "organic intellectual") has adopted this intersubjective, practical and discursive perspective, and proceeds to project a program of scientific investi-

---

[67] The "community of victims."
[68] Rigoberta Menchú, *Me llamo Rigoberta Menchú y así me nació la conciencia*, México: Siglo XXI, 1985, p. 21.

gation which in turn seeks to explain –according to the best available scientific resources– the cause of the victims negativity, we come across with the position from which critical social sciences develop (and also Liberation Philosophy and its corresponding ethics which functions as its necessary introduction).[69] So, when Marx writes:

> Del hecho de que la ganancia pueda estar por debajo del plusvalor o sea de que el capital pueda intercambiarse por una ganancia pero sin valorarse en sentido estricto, se desprende que no sólo los capitalistas individuales, sino las naciones pueden intercambiar continuamente entre sí (...) sin que por ello hayan de obtener ganancias iguales. Uno puede apropiarse constantemente de una parte del plustrabajo de la otra, por el que nada da a cambio, sólo que en este caso, ello no ocurre en la misma medida que entre el capitalista y el obrero.[70]

Surely, Marx was not specially interested, mainly during his life time, in the competition of capital (and the national global capital) in the World Market. This, however, does interest me, since it has to do with the problem of the globalization of the productive capital and the globalization of the market. The surplus relation between the capitalist and the worker is intricately related to the "essence" of capital – which is what, historically, interested Marx and what was ethically presented to the English workers, in order to explain the cause of their material negativity: the misery of the working class. My interest in the problem of competition among national capital has to do with the misery of peripheral nations (with its peoples, ethnicities, groups, working class, etc.), as national capital is transferred as surplus from one nation to the other.

---

[69] The critical theory of Horkheimer formulated this question ambiguously, since it confused in a single program the critical social sciences and the ethical critical philosophy (a philosophy that I call "Liberation Ethics"). It is important to distinguish one form the other and to know how to articulate each one of them.

[70] Karl Marx, *Grundrisse der Kritik der politischen Ökonomie*, Berlin: Dietz, 1974, p. 755. See also Hinkelammert's lecture "Die Marxsche Wertlehre und die Philosophie der Befreiung" [in Raoul Fornet-Betancourt (ed.), *Für Enrique Dussel*, Aachen: Augustinus, 1995, pp.35-74]. In addition see my article "Marx's Economic Manuscripts of 1861-63 and the 'Concept' of Dependency" [in *Latin American Perspectives* (Los Angeles), 17, 1990/2, pp. 61-101].

Globalization has not yet advanced to the point of erasing national borders.[71]

The intersubjective consensus that claims validity and that is reached in the community of victims; a consensus that also integrates critical and scientific "explanations" is, however, inimical to the valid consensus of the "hegemonic community." For instance, the consensus of North American and European popular opinion about peripheral countries, an opinion which asserts that peoples from this countries do not work, that they are racially and rationally inferior, that they deserve their misery for their lack of a competitive edge, etc. All this accounts for a growing xenophobia as was ostensible in California during the debate around proposition 187, or in South Africa, or in the former socialist Eastern Europe. All this can be positively explained from the stand point of the social sciences used by the dominant system. It is not merely a coincidence that these sciences are formulated in Harvard, London or Frank-

---

[71] If this were to happen, the so-called transnational corporation would disappear, corporations that operate with the average difference *of national global capitals* in relation to their organic composition: they invest productive capital of high technological development in countries with low salaries; this, in turns, gives transnational corporation an advantage when competing with the capitals from the nation where the transnational headquarters are (absorbing high salaries); they also have an advantage over the capitals in the nations where the transnational operates (nations with a technological disadvantage.) This setting allows them to transfer value (surplus value) form the periphery to the center. The transfer of surplus value is achieved by means of diverse mechanism among which we will mention the following: the expiration of parts and whole products, collection of royalties, or simply profiting from high interests of phantom international credits. Only Marx has a theoretical categorical framework (of critical economy or of critique of the economy) that serves to "unveil" and "explain" these "facts," facts that are invisible to the "functional" economy (neo-classical, Keynesian, neo-liberal, etc.). the massive poverty of peripheral nations is a non-intentional effect of the globalization of the productive, commercial and financial capital, a fundamental material structure of the World-System. Since, as we have said, products (merchandise) are symbolic and cultural objects of consumption and thus such a system is also a cultural system: Coca-Cola is beheld "in its beauty," one can feel its "cool softness," one can taste its "bubbly flavor," it displaces traditional drinks (and really nourishing), it creates new needs and finally it must be purchased...thus transferring values to the "center" (vital human work that is objectivized). A country becomes richer while another becomes poorer; this is the contradiction that the Ricardian economist could not see in England and that we cannot see at the global level.

furt, or that the neo-classical economy, the economic neo-liberalism or the liberal "minimal" state came from Chicago. All these social scientific theories elaborated in the North, along with the recent geopolitical and military theories that buttress the fight against drugs, are nothing but an effective cover up for the actual occupation of the countries in the South.

Ethics has much to reflect and much to say in this sense. The little work by Kant *The Perpetual Peace* was an attempt during his time to propose a universal principle on international relations. This proposition is stated as follows:

> Las acciones referidas al derecho de otros seres humanos cuya máxima no admiten publicidad (Publizität) son injustas.[72]

That a maxim ought to be articulated publicly has to do with a formal and procedural principle. But once again we are riddled by uncertainties as we ponder our contemporary reality; so, can the international organisms begin to dialogue and discuss in a public manner, without taking into account a procedural requirement which amounts to a minimum of symmetry among the participants? Is there not power to veto in the United Nations? Is not there an asymmetrical dominance exerted by the "Group of Seven" (G7)[73] over decisions of economic and political world relevance? (a group which, as I write this lines today July 1, 1996, is

---

[72] Immanuel Kant, *Zum ewigen Frieden*, in idem, *Kant Werke*, Darmstadt: Wissenschaftliche Buchgesellschaft, 1968, vol. 9, B 99, A 93, p. 245. A maxim which cannot be published without provoking the failure of its very purposes, that must remain secret in order to achieve the desired success, that cannot be publicly proclaimed without causing the resentment in all towards my intentions [...] This maxim will never be based on nothing but injustice" (ibid., B 100, A 94) . It would be good to relay this to Admiral Canarys against Hitler, or to the heroes that died under Pinochet and Somoza's hands. Kant's law is applicable to a metropolitan "civil state" how would Kant have thought had he had been an Afro-Caribbean slave in Jamaica during the eighteenth century? Would he have made public his plan to flee the sugar plantation in order to reach the Central American Atlantic coast, thus reaching freedom?

[73] In the United Nations there are over one hundred and fifty nations represented, are these seven nations more human, and do they have more of a right and dignity than the rest? Would not the reason be simply based on the fact that these seven nations are more powerful and richer. We have schematically shown historical aspects of the accumulation of this wealth.

gathering in Lyon).[74] Furthermore, what is the criteria that guide this discussions? Is it not true that the valorization of value, of capital, the possibility to overcome the crisis and to increase the profits of transnational corporations, of banks constitute (International Monetary Fund, Inter American Bank of Development, etc.) the criteria that guide this conversations? What has ethics to say, apart from the establishment of certain rules, in order to determine the symmetrical participation of the affected ones, in order to reach a sense of fairness by establishing norms (...) whose possible conditions are, beforehand, known to be empirically inexistent? Apel in his talk on the dialogue East – West says with optimism in reference to "Towards a Macroethics of Humanity"[75]:

> Actualmente vivimos, por primera vez en la historia, en una civilización planetaria (...) la unidad de la historia humana se ha realizado hoy en un sentido (...) como una unidad éticamente deseable, y en parte existente, de cooperación respecto a la formación, preservación y reforma de las condiciones comunes de la civilización del mundo actual.[76]

After foregrounding the content of the universal ethical principle that makes itself present in those moral institutions, a principle that is advanced by the non-contingent propositions belonging to the institution (or philosophical meta-institutions – of argumentative discourse), he concludes again rather optimistically:

> Esta fundamentación aparentemente esotérica está, en cierto sentido, bien confirmada hoy (...) junto con aquellas declaraciones públicas que acompañan a los cientos de diálogos y reuniones sobre asuntos de importancia vital para la humanidad (...) pues estas reuniones y diálogos, en la mayoría de los casos, intentan al menos ser algo semejante a los discursos prácticos, luchando por soluciones aceptables para todos los seres humanos afectados.[77]

All impoverished peripheral countries, the oppressed classes of the center and the periphery, the Afro Americans and Hispanics in the USA,

---

[74] I read in *Cinco días* (Madrid), July 1, 1996: "The G-7 warns that globalization will increase employment and inequality" (p. 25)
[75] See Karl-Otto Apel, Hacia una macroética de la humanidad, trad.esp. México: UNAM, 1992.
[76] Ibid., p.21.
[77] Ibid., p. 30.

women all over the world, the homeless children from Bogota or Sao Paulo, the elderly in miserable retirement homes, the millions of marginalized people, and the millions of immigrant who flee their countries for economic, political and racial reasons; all these victims attest to the fact that Apel's optimism is misplaced due to the enormous asymmetry that characterizes all those meetings and dialogues where the affected ones are on the most part absent and the decisions taken are not "acceptable" by the great majority of humanity

b. From the Ethical Duties of the Production, Reproduction and Development of Life of Each One of the Community Human Beings. It seems apparent that the universal and discursive principle is by definition the last rational instance. However such is not the case. Wallerstein writes:

> We can assert, if we wish, that the principle of universalism both on a world-wide scale and within each of the sovereign states that constitute the interstate system is hypocritical. But it is precisely because there is in reality a hierarchy of states within the interstate system and a hierarchy of citizens within each sovereign state that the ideology of universalism matters.[78]

The domination among states, cultures and individuals can be measured by the quality of life, by the chance that life offers each of the affected parties to the full realization of his/her life. Nonetheless, for this realization to occur, human life must be one of the criterion also (not only as a discursive and public intersubjectivity); it must be a positive, universal criterion of practical truth (of the ethical and material reason), a criterion from which an ethical, material, universal and positive principle can be grounded, point of departure of the negative or critical principle (of the commitment to avoid the death of humanity).

As we have written, we propose the following initial description of the material universal principle of ethics, the principle of corporeality as sensibility, containing a pulsional order, a principle that functions as a cultural and valorative (hermeneutical and symbolic) point of reference for every norm, action, institution or ethical system, a principle whose

---

[78] "Culture as the Ideological Battleground" [see Mike Featherstone (ed.), *Global Culture. Nationalism, globalization and modernity. A Theory, Culture and Society special issue*, London: Sage Publications, 1993, p. 43].

point of departure is the universality of human life. He who acts ethically[79] ought to be (as an obligation or ethical inclination towards the good) reproducing and develop in a responsible manner the life of each and every other human being, having as a rule the normative enunciations with a truth claims in a life community. The point of departure, in cultural and historical terms,[80] ought to be a "worthy life" that is shared in solidarity with humanity and having humanity as an ultimate reference point, thus showing universalizing claims[81] (a "worthy life" with a manner to interpret happiness and with a sort of reference to the values implicit in the understanding of human beings).

This material principle of ethics includes the point of departure and contains the "matter" (*Inhalt*) of all the forthcoming moments (formal, procedural, factual, critical or of liberation). This moment constitutes the

---

[79] To make explicit the "ethical" action is redundant, since to be ethical is to be human. But in this case the redundancy is not gratuitous because it emphasizes the intention of the enunciation.

[80] Even in a nonconventional culture , where each individual must rationally justify his her decisions , and not only act by following the mores and conventions of tradition, the project of argumentative and intersubjective critique (by Apel or Habermas) are already a project of worthy and nonconventional life, a project that blooms in a historical culture and in a given moment, etc.

[81] The claim of universality in every culture (from the Eskimo or Bantú to the Aztec Nahuatl or Modern European nonconventional cultures) indicates the presence of the universal material principle within every culture; this opposes ethnocentrism. Ethnocentrism or cultural fundamentalism is the attempt to impose in other cultures the claim of universality inherent to my own (ours) culture, even before such claim was discursive or interculturally tested. Each culture serious claim to universality must be tested in a rational dialogue whenever there is a confrontation of cultures. And when cultures historically confront each other, the dialogue is only possible from the claim of universality that characterizes each one of these cultures; and materially, forms the principle of content that has to do with the reproduction and development that underpins each culture and all cultural subjects. This process allows for a material unveiling of real articulations, once the dialogue has been initiated on the manner in which a culture reproduces and develops, in a concrete fashion, human lives. The intersubjective and discursive moment is precisely the procedural moment which formally allows for such a dialogue without denying, however, the logic of the material content from which the participants must depart. All this was brought to failure by the Eurocentrism that Modernity implemented on peripheral cultures from the end of the fifteenth century until the present (See Dussel, *Etica de la Liberación en la edad de la globalización y de la exclusión*, Editorial Trotta, 3a. edición, 2000).

ethical content of all praxis and of all future projects of development: under any circumstances cannot be denied nor can it be overcome or ignored. . It is the room (place?) from which the facticity of the quotidian and ethical world as such is established. It is not merely a pathological or particular horizon that can be discarded in order to reach an a priori horizon of transcendental principles – as in the case of Kant or Apel. Neither does it consist exclusively of the cultural horizon – as in the case with the communitarians – or the incommensurable horizon – as in the case of the postmodern. But, furthermore, although such is the necessary departure point which is always presupposed in any moral system or ethics, it should not be forgotten that such is not a sufficient horizon, since in order for the validity, factibility or ethical critique, one must resort to other principles of co-determination.

But this very same positive principle is transformed in a negative critical principle. Ethical principles grounded from sets of criteria; now passing from "to be a life" to "ought to be" a life they must live. The following examples can clarify the question:

1. This is a hungry victim; therefore his/her life is in danger (it is a factual judgment or a descriptive enunciation).

2. I am responsible[82] for the hunger of this victim. Ergo (a normative enunciation is founded).

3. I ought (this is an ethical obligation) first of all, *to criticize* the norm, action, institution or ethical system partially or thoroughly, since those are the cause of this negativity of victim. Also and furthermore:

4. I ought *to transform* the norm, action, institution or structures that are responsible for such negation of the victim.

The point is then to negatively judge the system (norm, action, etc.) as the mediation that causes victims. This is the *Krisis* par excellence. This is the final judgment (in the manner of Benjamin's description of Paul Klee's work) carried out by the Court (from the standpoint of the victims) of History (*kriterion*) which measures all norms, actions, insti-

---

[82] In the irrevocable sense indicated by Levinas, but also if one considers all the necessary mediations, since any human, being a moment in the complex structure of human development cannot be declared as being absolutely innocent of anything, not even of non-intentional repercussions. There is always a sort of (direct, indirect, conscious or non-intentional) complicity in the victimization of the other, a complicity that binds us to all.

tution or ethical system in accordance to its goodness (or evil). The preamble to the judgement of the system with a negative "no" is the intention of "not" producing victims (if this victims did not exist, this critique would not be necessary). Therefore, the reason why the oldest and most venerable imperatives of humanity were always negative ones can be comprehended. Here one may place Wellmer's proposal[83] on the strength of the universal imperative as a prohibition of a non generalizable maxim.

The ethical and critical principle in its negative moments is, first and foremost, negative as a judgement related to the non-reproduction of the life of each human being; and, positive, as a demand for the development of the life of each human being. This principle can take approximately the following form: whoever acts ethically and critically has recognized that the victims of any norm, action, institution or ethical system etc. have been denied the possibility to live (in totality or in partial moments). Therefore, one is obliged, in the first place, to deny the "goodness" of the "cause" of such a victim; that is to say to criticize the "non-truth" (the *Unwahrheit* of Adorno) of the moment that causes the victim (which from this moment onwards appears as the dominant one). Secondly, to create in common solidarity the means, in order to transform this situation.

This material and critical universal principles make it possible to orientate abstractly and fundamentally the political organizations, conferences, forums and debates praised by the Ethics of Discourse, gatherings that take place in reference to the process of globalization. However, this material and universal principle (the asymmetry must always recall) and from such interpretation the victims ought to become aware of their situation; they should be moved to struggle for their recognition and for their rights, so that the impact of their acquired awareness move beyond the restricted space of these gatherings; and, thus, become useful in their daily lives. Liberation Ethics, then, quite beyond its formal principles will also articulate a material principle which can be exerted negatively as a critique of the World

---

[83] See Albrecht Wellmer, *Ethik und Dialog - Elemente des moralischen Urteils bei Kant und in der Diskursethik*, Frankfurt am Main: Suhrkamp, 1986, Kap. 1.

System that, due to its contents, becomes increasingly globalized at these levels: economic, ecological, pulsional etc.

c. The Philosophical Importance of North-South and South-South Discursive Dialogue. Philosophy, in its ethical dimension, has a responsibility, then, in this "orientation." It must promote a discussion between philosophers from the North and those from the South. In the promotion of this dialogue it is deserving of mention the asymmetry that characterizes these two regions: the philosophers from the North who enjoy an hegemony of material power in the form of universities and other educational structures, publishing houses, journals, research centers, funds, scholarships and grants, alliance with diverse areas: intelligence, the military and transnationals, etc. Conversely, philosophers in the South must develop a genuine discourse that springs from its underdeveloped situation, from its oppressive and marginalized reality, and even from its exclusion. This dialogue would endow philosophers form the South recognition amongst their peers and recognition within the civil society. From this recognition, philosophers in the South can then proceed to elaborate a critique of the peripheral systems that work in complicity with a globalization that excludes and destroys the cultural identities of the subjugated nations.

But, furthermore, it becomes necessary for the South to count with the aid of the North in order to initiate South to South philosophical dialogues; i.e. dialogues among Asia, Africa and Latin America. In this manner the acute problems, elicited non-intentionally from the process of globalization, could be dealt with solely from the demands characteristic of the South, thus dispensing with the tampering mediation (usually non-critical and influential) of structures from the North. Along with Prof. Odera Oduka,[84] I organized an international committee for the South-South philosophical dialogue in December 1994, in Cairo. He was scheduled to participate in a panel organized by the APA in April of 1995, in Seattle, Washington; but he was assassinated in 1995 by one of those dictatorial governments in the peripheral world that are fearful of critical philosophers. His death amounts to a testimony of loyalty to

---

[84] Professor of the University of Nirobi (Kenya), President of the African Philosophical Association, personal friend of the author of these notes.

criticism, to peripheral African philosophy, a truly "universal" and nascent philosophy.

5. Conclusion:
The principle of liberation in globalization's exclusions

These are nothing but a few words for a future discussion. Given that globalization produces non-intentional devastating effects in at least two thousand million humans and in countless cultures, cultures and peoples known as the victims of such process of globalization, Liberation Ethics must still forewarn that the function of ethics in relation to globalization does not end in the provision of discursive regulations needed to reach a consensus from which specific measures can be implemented. Its function does not end either in offering abstract guidelines (no matter how sufficient they might be) for the principle of reproducing and helping to develop the life of any human subject –a principle that is universal and from which the discursive principle functions as its moral mediation of application. Liberation Ethics, must still take into consideration the factibility of the decisions to which it arrives based upon the fulfillment of the two principles already discussed: the material and the formal principles.

Indeed, in the peripheral countries the factibility of the best decisions, the ones that are praiseworthy and meritorious, fix absolute limits: what is possible (from a technical, economic, political etc. point of view) determines a third area of the action and makes that a decision reached by consensus, a mediation of human life, become effective and actually possible. There is, then, an ethical principle of factibility that subsumes instrumental reason within the evaluation of the goals (from the material principle of life and the moral discursive principle: the principle of factibility should be nothing but mediation for life decided rationally and symmetrically by the affected ones). What is thus done is then "good." So, the process of globalization is "good" for the following instances: for certain countries, certain cultures, for corporations, political parties and some scientific and philosophical communities. But for the victims, as Adorno would say, the truthful becomes untruthful; and concerning the reproduction of life and their symmetric participation the "efficient" becomes inefficient. The ethical factibility for the reproduction and development of the life of the members of impoverished and peripheral countries and devastated cultures consists of halting such process of globalization, a globalization whose only criteria is the "efficient competition" in the market place (a principle of formal and instrumental factibility devoid of any ethical criterion or principle). This criteria solely tied to the "valorization of value" is responsible for the ecological destruction and ultimately for the destruction of life on earth and the concrete life of most of humanity. It is then at this juncture that an Ethics that founds the motivation of historical subjects (the victims in the process of concientization) becomes necessary, not only for the purpose of serving as a background to forums, conferences and debates, that seek to establish rational and ethical limitations to the "efficiency of the Total Market" in the midst of globalization, but also to materially found the norms, actions, institutions and ethical systems that the daily plight of the victims begins to organize in countless ways and as part of the so-called "new social movements" (feminist and ecological movements, poor nations, oppressed social classes, indigenous ethnicities, marginal urban populations, immigrants,, political refugees, anti-racial groups, homeless children, the unprotected elderly and so many other "liberation fronts"). The forging of a critical liberal Ethics, must occur in the interior of these new historical subjects to justify their goals, programs and decisions.[85]

---

[85] In Chapter six of the already mentioned *Liberation Ethics* I have discussed what I have now called the "Principle-Liberation," not included in this study.

Lester Embree

SCHUTZ'S THEORY OF THE HISTORICAL SCIENCES IN THE LIGHT OF THE WOMEN'S LIBERATION MOVEMENT[1]

According Alfred Schutz himself his highest contribution was in "the philosophy of law."[2] But when his colleague Leo Strauss praised him as a philosophically sophisticated sociologist for writing *Equality and the Meaning Structure of the Social World*, Schutz replied on October 20, 1955 that he preferred to be called a "sociologically sophisticated philosopher."[3] Then again, if his bibliography is considered, almost all of Schutz's writings are philosophical, some of them are interpretations of Husserl, James, Sartre, and Scheler, but most of them are phenomenological investigations. He did chiefly teach in a Department of Sociology and had several prominent sociological students, but he also taught had prominent students in philosophy. He appears, after all, to have been a philosopher and is no more a "phenomenological sociologist," as some say, than Merleau-Ponty is a child psychologist because he taught in that field for some years. But how was Schutz a philosopher and what did he in this field? The main thesis of this article is that Schutz's project offers a considerable beginning of a theory of the historical sciences; at the same time, he never abandoned his position that the social sciences in

---

[1] I thank Dr. Elisabeth Behnke for substantive suggestions as well as help with the expression on this essay. Professors Michael Barber, David Carr, Steven Crowell, Stanford Lyman, Nasu Hisashi, Thomas Seebohm, and Yu Chung-Chi are also thanked for their critique of the substance, but are nowise to blame for errors that remain. Dr. Martin Endress of the *Alfred Schütz Werkausgabe* is thanked for identifying two original German expressions in Schutz texts.
[2] Alfred Schutz, "Husserl and His Influence on Me," Ed. by Lester Embree in: *The Annals of Phenomenological Sociology*, 2 (1977), 48; idem, *The Theory of Social Action*. Edited by Richard Grathoff. Bloomington: Indiana University Press, 1978, 102.
[3] I thank Michael Barber for this information from the *Nachlass* on the exchange with Leo Strauss.

the strict signification are about the world of contemporaries and the historical sciences are about the world of predecessors, a position clearly incompatible with the position of some contemporary history understandings (f.ex. those of Susan Brownmiller and Kathleen Berkeley) dealing with the Women's liberation movement.

I. Schutz's theoretical project

A. The Theory of Science. One might call Schutz's project "philosophy of social science," although this expression does not occur in his oeuvre. But then both "philosophy" and "social sciences" need to be carefully comprehended. It is actually better to say that what he pursued was, to use his own words (although he did not use this exact phrase), the "theory of the cultural sciences." It is better to say "theory" than "philosophy," not only because "theory" includes more than a search for the rules of thinking or methodology in the narrow signification but also because it names a discipline that accommodates reflections on science by the scientists themselves as well as by philosophers: "It is a basic characteristic of the social sciences to ever and again pose the question of the meaning of their basic concepts and procedures. All attempts to solve this problem are not merely preparations for social-scientific thinking; they are an everlasting theme of this thinking itself."[4] "Theory" is not exclusionary, which "philosophy" can be.

Newly arrived in the United States, Schutz sought such reflections on methods and basic concepts by a scientist in Talcott Parsons unsuccessfully[5] and was earlier disappointed at what he found in Max Weber, "one of the greatest masters of the methodology of the social sciences":

> As he himself stated in various personal documents, he looked in vain for help in the epistemological writings of his contemporary philosophical colleagues, who belonged either to the neo-Kantian School or the so-called South-Western German School. These schools had influenced most of the writings of the historians and jurists studied by Max Weber at the beginning of his career, and he himself could not entirely escape

---

[4] Alfred Schutz, *Collected Papers, Vol. IV*, Ed. Helmut Wagner, George Psathas, and Fred Kersten, Dordrecht: Kluwer Academic Publishers, 1996, pp. 121, 203.

[5] Lester Embree, "Methodology is where Human Scientists and Philosophers can Meet: Reflections on the Schutz-Parsons Exchange," *Human Studies* 3 (1980), pp. 367-73.

their influence. But very soon he found that the conceptual frame of reference offered by these philosophers could not help him in building up a social theory applicable to the concrete sociological problems with which he was concerned. Therefore, he decided independently to investigate the methodological issues which he encountered, later professing his aversion to this job, which he compared with the sharpening of knives when there is nothing on the table to be carved. Guided by his intimate knowledge of the concrete problems of the social sciences and by an admirable feeling for relevant issues, he succeeded better than other social scientists in delimiting the realm of the social sciences and in describing the methods by which it can be explored.[6]

The meaning of basic concepts and procedures is clearly the aspect of science that deeply interested Schutz, but to what end? As he wrote to Adolph Lowe on October 17, 1955, "It is my conviction that methodologists have neither the job nor the authority to prescribe to social scientists what they have to do. Humbly he has to learn from social scientists and to interpret for them what they are doing."[7] He had earlier gone further in writing that "in this role, the methodologist has to ask intelligent questions about the technique of his teacher (i.e., the social scientist). And if these questions help others to think over what they really do, and perhaps eliminate certain intrinsic difficulties hidden in the foundation of the scientific edifice where the scientists never set foot, methodology has performed its task."[8]

Schutz is under no illusions that the science he reflects on took methodology to a philosophical level:

> On the one hand, methodology and studies in the logic of science have been concerned for more than two centuries primarily with the logic of the natural sciences and assume that their techniques of classification, measurement, theory-building, and empirical correlation are the only scientific ones. On the other hand, those social scientists did not have sufficient knowledge of the epistemological problems involved. They tried to overcome the difficulties they had encountered in elaborating the concrete problems of the social sciences with which they were con-

---

[6] Alfred Schutz, "Positivistic Philosophy and the Actual Approach of Interpretative Social Science: An Ineditum of Alfred Schutz from Spring 1953." Edited by Lester Embree, *Husserl Studies* 14 (1997), 123-149, here p. 126.
[7] Alfred Schutz, *Collected Papers, Vol. IV*, op. cit., p. 146.
[8] Alfred Schutz, *Collected Papers, Vol. II, Studies in Social Theory*, Ed. Arvid Brodersen, The Hague: Martinus Nijhoff, 1964, p. 88.

cerned by forging their own methodological tools without any attempt at clarifying the underlying philosophical position. They broke off their endeavors as soon as they felt themselves sufficiently equipped with the conceptual frame of reference needed for their concrete social studies.[9]

What Schutz urges might be called a gentle prescriptivism because not only are the sciences carefully studied to eliminate foundational difficulties and to foster clearer self-understanding in scientists, but also because Schutz seems to accept that it is for the scientists to decide whether or not to accept advice offered by philosophers.

If Schutz thus favors communication with scientists as well as close examination of what they do, what did he call the multidisciplinary endeavor he favored? One might call it "methodology" in the broad signification used above, but this word has a strict signification whereby "the description of ["definite operational rules"] is the business of a methodology of the social sciences"[10] and has come to designate merely formal techniques in many disciplines. What other titles occur in the oeuvre? Between 1940 and 1945 Schutz used the expression "methodology and epistemology" on six occasions,[11] nevertheless commenting to Parsons, "I fear that in this country the terms methodology and epistemology are used in a more restricted sense than their equivalents in German and I accepted these terms only because I could not find any better translation for "*Wissenschaftslehre*" which includes both logical problems of a scientific theory and methodology in the restricted sense."[12] This is the only time he uses "*Wissenschaftslehre*," but "*wissenschaftstheoretischen*" already occurs in the first sentence of *Der sinnhafte Aufbau der sozialen Welt* (1932),[13] mistakenly translated as "theoretical writings." Then

---

[9] Alfred Schutz, "Positivistic Philosophy...," pp. 125-126.

[10] Alfred Schutz, *Collected Papers, Vol. I, The Problem of Social Reality,* Ed. by Maurice Natanson, The Hague: Martinus Nijhoff, 1962, p. 255.

[11] Alfred Schutz, *The Theory of Social Action*, Ed. Richard Grathoff. Bloomington: Indiana University Press, 1978, pp. 9, 101; idem, *Collected Papers, Vol. II*, op.cit., p. 64, and *Collected Papers, Vol. IV*, p. 48, *Collected Papers, Vol. I*, p. 251.

[12] Alfred Schutz, *The Theory of Social Action*, op. cit., p. 101.

[13] Alfred Schutz, *Der Sinnhafte Aufbau der Sozialen Welt (1932)*, Frankfurt am Main: Suhrkamp, 1974, Engl. *Phenomenology of the Social World*. Transl. by George Walsh and Frederick Lehnert, Evanston, IL: Northwestern University Press, 1967; the English pagination will be offered after the German as *Der Sinnhafte Aufbau...*, p. 9/xxi, cf. ibid., p. 15/7.

again, "*wissenschaftstheoretischen Einstellung*" is used in 1936,[14] although oddly translated as "theoretical-scientific approach" when "science-theoretical attitude" would be more accurate. "*Theorie der Sozialwissenschaften*" is also used on the first page of the *Aufbau* and again in the German original of Schutz's last essay, "Some Structures of the Lifeworld" (1959), where Gurwitsch translated it as "theory of the social sciences"[15]; in letters to Schutz, Gurwitsch used "*Wissenschaftstheorie*" in 1941, 1945, and 1954,[16] which is correctly translated as "theory of science." Writing in English in 1945 and 1953, Schutz himself finally does use "theory of the social sciences."[17]

Incidentally, although its rigid translation is "science," "*Wissenschaft*" in German is best comprehended as designating a disciplined cognitive practice that can include deductive nomological theory and experimentation, but is in no way confined to them. Thus biography, for example, is a *Wissenschaft*, as is jurisprudence, the three *Wissenschaften* that especially concerned Schutz from the outset being economics, jurisprudence, and sociology, with political science coming soon after and ethnology and linguistics eventually added to the list.

In sum, there are at least three reasons why "theory of science" and its transform, "science theory" ("science-theoretical[ly]" is the modifier), appears to be the best expression for what Schutz was chiefly engaged in: (1) it can cover the clarification of basic concepts as well as the articulation of rules of procedure; (2) it can include both *scientific* science theory, i.e., theory of science done by scientists, as well as *philosophical* science theory done by philosophers; and (3) the theory of science is where scientists and philosophers can meet and learn from one another.

---

[14] Alfred Schutz, *Collected Papers, Vol. IV*, p. 121.
[15] Alfred Schutz, *Collected Papers, Vol. III*, p. 131.
[16] *Alfred Schütz Aron Gurwitsch Briefwechsel 1939-1959*. München: Wilhelm Fink Verlag, 1985. Engl. *Philosophers in Exile: The Correspondence of Alfred Schutz and Aron Gurwitsch, 1939-1959*. Transl. by Joseph Claude Evans, Bloomington: Indiana University Press, 1989, pp. 99/48,136/75, 273/172.
[17] Alfred Schutz, "Choice and the Social Sciences," in Lester E. Embree (ed.), *Life-World and Consciousness: Essays for Aron Gurwitsch*. Evanston, IL: Northwestern University Press, 1972, pp. 565-90, here 565, Alfred Schutz, "Positivistic Philosophy...," pp. 136.

One difference of philosophical science theory is the concern with founding all the other sciences in one discipline. For positivists, the founding discipline would be physics and for Husserl it would be transcendental phenomenology. What is the founding discipline for Schutz? Beginning in the *Aufbau*,[18] Schutz identifies his approach in the theory of science with what Husserl called "constitutive phenomenology of the natural attitude" or "phenomenological psychology." He writes that

> One can always reactivate the process which has built up the sediments of meaning, and one can explain the intentionalities of the perspectives of relevance and the horizons of interest. Then all these phenomena of meaning, which obtain quite simply for the naïve person, might be in principle exactly described and analyzed *even within the general thesis [of the natural attitude]*. To accomplish this on intersubjectivity is the task of the mundane cultural sciences, and to clarify their specific methods is precisely a part of that constitutive phenomenology of the natural attitude of which we have been speaking.[19]

One can still consider Schutz a philosopher even though he resorts to "phenomenological psychology" because that was not an independent positive science, but something distinguished *within* Husserl's philosophy. One should especially recognize "On Multiple Realities" (1945), which belongs "to the field of phenomenological psychology; that it is, it will be restricted to the constitutional analysis of the natural attitude" (IV 26), as well as Part II of the *Aufbau* as phenomenological psychology engaged in for science-theoretical purposes.

B. The Cultural Sciences. The probably unavoidable expression "philosophy of social science" is also problematical with respect to the genus and species of science that Schutz focused on. Regarding the formal sciences, he seems to have said nothing concerning the theory of grammar or the theory of mathematics, but he does agree with Husserl on the use of formal logic to unify all of science.[20] There are some remarks regard-

---

[18] Alfred Schutz, *Der Sinnhafte Aufbau...*, p. 55/43.
[19] Alfred Schutz, *Collected Papers, Vol. I,* pp. 136-137, 208, idem, *Collected Papers, Vol. IV,* p. 269). Cf. Edmund Husserl, *Ideas pertaining to a Pure Phenomenology and to a Phenomenological Philosophy, Second Book*. Transl. by R. Rojcewicz and A. Schuwer, Dordrecht: Kluwer Academic Publishers, 1989, pp. 412 ff.
[20] Alfred Schutz, *Collected Papers, Vol. I,* p. 49.

ing the naturalistic sciences that are interesting,[21] but they seem insufficient for inferring an outline of a theory of such sciences. The case is worse for psychology, where, although several Gestaltists are mentioned,[22] only William James is at all appreciated in anything like a science-theoretical perspective.[23]

What this leaves can be called "the social sciences in the broad signification." The general field of the social sciences in this signification is approached by adopting the theoretical attitude and by *not* performing the abstraction that thematizes nature for the naturalistic sciences.[24] Schutz's overlapping lists of particular disciplines in this genus are interesting. For example, in the *Aufbau* of 1932 Schutz writes that, "the social sciences [*Sozialwissenschaften*] include, according to our own concept, such widely separated disciplines as individual biography, jurisprudence, (...) pure economics, (...) history of law, history of art, and political science."[25] He also mentions history of politics,[26] economic history,[27] and the histories of music and philosophy.[28] In 1940, he lists "concrete sciences of cultural phenomena (law, the economic and social world, art, history, etc.)."[29] In 1953 he lists "sciences of human affairs – economics, sociology, the sciences of law, linguistics, cultural anthropology, etc."[30] In that same year and then later he mentions "a theoretical science of the mythological and religious experience of men."[31] Since he says "I can understand the acts and motives ... of the caveman who left no other testimony of his existence than the flint hatchet exhib-

---

[21] Alfred Schutz, *Collected Papers, Vol. I*, pp. 58, 129, 106; cf. *Collected Papers, Vol. IV*, p. 124; Alfred Schutz, "Positivistic Philosophy...," p. 135)
[22] Alfred Schutz, *Collected Papers, Vol. I*, p. 168; cf. idem, *Reflections on the Problem of Relevance*. Edited by Richard M. Zaner, New Haven: Yale University Press, 1970, pp. 93, 119.
[23] Alfred Schutz, *Collected Papers, Vol. III*, p. 1 ff.
[24] See Part III C below.
[25] Alfred Schutz, *Der Sinnhafte Aufbau...*, p. 341/242.
[26] Ibid., p. 191/136.
[27] Ibid., p. 192/137.
[28] Ibid., p. 297/211.
[29] Alfred Schutz, *Collected Papers, Vol. I*, p. 122.
[30] Ibid., p. 58.
[31] Alfred Schutz, "Positivistic Philosophy...," p. 131; cf. idem, *Collected Papers, Vol. I*, pp. 332, 337.

ited in the showcase of some museum,"[32] the genus may in addition be presumed implicitly to include archaeology.[33] Finally, Schutz's thought about literature might also belong here.[34]

It would be useful to find a better title than "social science in the broad signification" for this whole group of disciplines not usually taken together in the United States of late, particularly since Schutz also recognizes and chiefly refers to what can by contrast be called "the social sciences in a strict signification." He does use *Geisteswissenschaften* in the title of §28 of the *Aufbau*, where it is translated as "cultural science,"[35] and also in his 1932 review of Husserl's *Méditations Cartésiennes*, where it is translated as "human sciences."[36] "Human sciences" is a widely accepted translation of that expression today, but a German expression also actually accepted by Schutz himself is "*Kulturwissenschaft*," which is of course best translated as "cultural science." He repeatedly accepted this as well as "social science" as translation for *Geisteswissenschaft* in his "Phenomenology and the Social Sciences" of 1940, which originally had *Kulturwissenschaften* in its title, and the various sciences listed above can be thought of as thematizing different aspects of the sociocultural world. One can prefer "cultural sciences" for the broad signification sometimes expressed with "social sciences."

Whatever the genus of the cultural or human sciences be called, it has for Schutz two species. There are social sciences in the strict signification that thematize others who share time with a given self, i.e., those whom Schutz technically calls "contemporaries," and then there is history, which is concerned with "predecessors," i.e., those whose lives do not overlap those of the living. Among the former would fall cultural anthropology, economics, jurisprudence, linguistics, political science, social psychology, and sociology and among the latter would fall biography, history (including the histories of art, economy, law, literature,

---

[32] Alfred Schutz, *The Theory of Social Action*. Edited by Richard Grathoff, Bloomington: Indiana University Press, 1978, p. 53.
[33] See Alfred Schutz, *Der Sinnhafte Aufbau...*, p. 151/109, pp. 282/201, pp. 294/209, Alfred Schutz, *Collected Papers, Vol. I*, pp. 10, 17.
[34] Lester Embree, ed., *Alfred Schutz's "Sociological Aspect of Literature": Construction and Complementary Essays*, Dordrecht: Kluwer Academic Publishers, 1998.
[35] See Alfred Schutz, *Der Sinnhafte Aufbau...*, p. 9/xxxi, p. 22/14.
[36] Alfred Schutz, *Collected Papers, Vol. I*, pp. 164.

music, philosophy), and archaeology. It is not clear where the science of myth and religion would fall for Schutz. Interestingly, he actually mentions more historical sciences than social sciences in the strict signification. Then again, there are enough particular historical sciences corresponding to particular social sciences that one might wonder if such pairings are always possible for him.

Many seem to think that Schutz was a philosopher or theorist of the social sciences in the strict signification, but if most of his science theory relates to the social sciences in the broad signification, he is actually a philosophical theorist of the cultural sciences. The latter position would also be supported if a theory of the historical sort of cultural sciences can be discerned when his scattered remarks are collected and interpreted. This is the project of the present essay.

Schutz speaks in some places of the science of history (*Wissenschaft der Geschichte*[37]), mentions von Ranke and Burchardt in the *Aufbau*,[38] and in a late essay mentions historical writing by Marcel Granet, Arnold J. Toynbee, and Eric Voegelin.[39] Furthermore, in two letters to Voegelin in 1952 he also mentions the philosophy of history (*Philosophie der Geschichte*[40]), which would seem to include some efforts by Husserl.[41] And although they are scattered, there are far more remarks explicitly about the historical sciences than about the formal sciences and the naturalistic sciences put together, enough so that, except for one difficulty returned to in the last part of this essay, his theory of history can be fairly well delineated.

The present writer is not the first to consider a Schutzian theory of history possible. Schutz's friend Gurwitsch wrote that "the problem [of history and historical knowledge] does not play a role of primary importance for Schutz, who concerned himself rather with the relations between contemporaries living in the same world. (...) Clarification of the foundation of the social sciences (in the more restricted sense of the

---

[37] Alfred Schutz, *Der Sinnhafte Aufbau...*, p. 297/211; *Collected Works, Vol. IV*, p. 4.
[38] Alfred Schutz, *Der Sinnhafte Aufbau...*, p. 296/210.
[39] Alfred Schutz, *Collected Papers, Vol. I*, p. 333 n. 48.
[40] *Alfred Schütz Aron Gurwitsch Briefwechsel 1939-1959*, p. 296/188; cf. idem, *Collected Papers, Vol. IV*, p. 227.
[41] Alfred Schutz, *Collected Papers, Vol. I*, p. 139.

term) prepares for and contributes to the clarification of the foundation of the historical sciences."[42]

II. Some contemporary history: the Women's Liberation Movement

It will be convenient to interpret Schutz's statements relevant to his theory of the historical sciences in relation to an example of contemporary history. The following summary comes primarily from Susan Brownmiller, *In Our Time: Memoir of a Revolution*,[43] and secondarily from Kathleen Berkeley, *The Women's Liberation Movement in America*.[44] Brownmiller is a journalist who relies on what she explicitly calls participant observation. She herself led some of the movement's actions, participated in more, interviewed over 200 participants, and gained access to documents not yet archived. She appears the most insider of insiders for Women's Liberation. Kathleen Berkeley, by contrast, also draws on a wide array of sources, but they are chiefly books by fellow historians; she writes as a historian, and there is no sign that she was ever a participant in the movement, which would be all the more significant if she had been.

Berkeley and Brownmiller agree that the Women's Liberation Movement strictly so-called began in the mid-1960s and ended in the mid-1980s. Berkeley explains how it is part of the larger Women's Movement that goes back to the middle of the 19th century and continues today. Both agree that there were two wings to the recent movement, a liberal wing and a radical wing. Berkeley covers both, with more emphasis on the liberal wing, and Brownmiller strongly emphasizes the radical wing. The radical wing is what the expression "Women's Liberation Movement" strictly denominates, but this title is often extended to refer to the whole movement in that time, because, as both again agree, innovation regularly spread from the radical to the liberal wing during the twenty years of Women's Liberation.

---

[42] Alfred Schutz, *Collected Papers, Vol. III*, p. xxxi.
[43] Susan Brownmiller, *In Our Time: Memoir of a Revolution*, New York: Dell Publishing, 1999.
[44] Kathleen Berkeley, *The Women's Liberation Movement in America*, Westport, CT: Greenwood Press, 1999.

The questions that a historian ought to ask about such a movement for social change must include: (a) Who conducted it, which includes the question of what sort of groups was in it? (b) How was it motivated and how did it begin? (c) What were its actions? And (d) how did it end? Some of Schutz's thought can be connected with these questions in the following exposition under these headings, while other thought will be related in subsequent parts.

A. *What Type of Group Led Women's Liberation?* Schutz always recognized that there are social groups, and this is especially evident in "Equality and the Meaning Structure of the Social World" of 1955. For him, a group is a set of interacting individuals; as he once wrote, "The attempts of Simmel, Max Weber, [and] Scheler to reduce social collectivities to the social interaction of individuals is, so it seems, much closer to the spirit of phenomenology than the pertinent statements of its founder."[45] In addition, it bears remembering that Schutz asserts in no fewer than sixteen places that the individual is an abstraction from social life,[46] which is to say from the groups to which she belongs, something well reflected if we follow Schutz and some sociologists, e.g., George Psathas, in speaking of "members" rather than "individuals."

Schutz divides groups in two ways. One distinction is between voluntary groups and involuntary or existential groups. The latter are based on such things as sex, national origin, mother tongue, and race, and the former include marriage, friendship, and partnership.[47] Although concerned with differences in sex, the groups making up the Women's Movement were voluntary, some of them including men. The other distinction – one Schutz accepted from William Graham Sumner – is that between in-groups and out-groups. Little needs to be said here about how groups understand themselves and one another, but clearly it is an important issue for history. Indeed, one could interpret "Equality and the Meaning Structure of the Social World" with gender substituted for race as the topic of prejudice, particularly with regard to the question of

---

[45] Alfred Schutz, *Collected Papers, Vol. III*, p. 39.
[46] Alfred Schutz, *Collected Works, Vol. I*, pp. 10, 11, 13, 53, 124, 167, 208, 218, 278, 306, 318, 347; idem, *Collected Works, Vol. II*, p. 167; idem, Alfred Schutz, *Reflections on the Problem of Relevance*, pp. 73, 134, 173.
[47] Alfred Schutz, *Collected Papers, Vol. II*, p. 250.

groups striving for equality without assimilation to the dominant group – i.e., something concerning gender that is analogous to multiculturalism. Also on the basis of that essay, it can be presumed that while certain sexual differences would have been recognized on the biological level, the Women's Movement emphasizes cultural differences akin to those Schutz alluded to when he asked, "Could Marian Anderson sing Negro Spirituals in her unsurpassed way if she did not share with her fellow Negroes this specific cultural heritage, this specific conception of the world of which the Spirituals are a partial expression?"[48]

Even though her memoir does chiefly refer to individual members, Brownmiller is emphatic about there being two types of voluntary groups within the movement:

> NOW [the National Organization of Women] was a dues-paying membership organization that welcomed the participation of men; its organizational structure, with an elected national board and state divisions, was determinedly hierarchical. Women's Liberation, in name and spirit, sprang from the radical ferment of the civil rights, antiwar, and counter culture movements. Decentralized and antihierarchical, it functioned and flourished within an amorphous framework of small, ostensibly leaderless, usually short-lived groups (...) in which a male presence was unthinkable. NOW's commitment to equality of opportunity in employment was its strong suit. The fast-beating heart of Women's Liberation was analysis and theory. As a general rule, NOW preferred to rely on traditional forms of protest: committees and picket lines, lawsuits and lobbying, while Women's Liberation broke new ground through theoretical papers, imaginative confrontations, and inventive direct action. The explosive creation of the antiviolence issues – rape, battery, incest and child molestation, sexual harassment – and later on, the controversial development of antipornography theory, belonged to the domain of Women's Liberation, as did the early surge of lesbian feminism and the rise of a vital, alternative feminist press.[49]

B. How Did Women's Liberation Begin? Alfred Schutz does not explicitly address how a movement for social change begins, but he does offer an account derived from W. I. Thomas about how crises occur in

---

[48] Ibid., p. 259; cf. *Collected Papers, Vol. I*, pp. 350, 248/155.
[49] Susan Brownmiller, *In Our Time: Memoir of a Revolution*, p. 7.

society.⁵⁰ Before a crisis there is "thinking as usual" relying on "cookbook" knowledge:

> Any member born or reared within the group accepts the ready-made standardized scheme of the cultural pattern handed down to him by ancestors, teachers, and authorities as an unquestioned and unquestionable guide in all the situations which normally occur within the social world. The knowledge correlated to the cultural pattern carries its evidence in itself – or, rather, it is taken for granted in the absence of evidence to the contrary. It is a knowledge of trustworthy *recipes* for interpreting the social world and for handling things and men in order to obtain the best results in every situation with a minimum of effort by avoiding undesirable consequences.⁵¹

This "thinking as usual" would seem to characterize American culture before the 1960s. Of course it was recognized that women were somehow different from men, and there were no doubt pockets of recognition of injustice to women, but the notion of women as having shared concerns of their own – much less organizations and intentions to change society – was not at all widely recognized. Both Berkeley and Brownmiller venture into how that "consensus" itself arose, but it is sufficient here to say that there was then a pre-crisis state of "thinking as usual" about women.

Schutz goes on to state four related assumptions that must hold for thinking as usual to continue: (1) that social life will continue such that the old solutions will still work; (2) that knowledge handed down by "parents, teachers, governments, traditions, habits, etc." can be relied on; (3) that knowledge about the general type or style of events suffices; and (4) that the systems of "recipes as schemes of interpretation and expression" are not our private affair, but are likewise accepted and applied by our contemporaries (II 96). It would seem, then, that a movement for social change can begin when one or more of these assumptions fails. In that case, Schutz, following Thomas, says, "a 'crisis' arises which (…) 'interrupts the flow of habit and gives rise to changed conditions of consciousness and practice'."⁵²

---

[50] I am grateful to my colleague Stanford Lyman for reminding me of this part of Schutz's position.
[51] Alfred Schutz, *Collected Papers, Vol. II*, p. 95.
[52] Ibid.

Did a crisis arise for American women in the mid-1960s? Within what became the liberal wing of the Women's Movement, President Kennedy's Commission on the Status of Women in 1961 offered some help; he himself, however, was indifferent about feminism, and sex-discrimination was left out of his civil-rights legislation. President Johnson was no better, hesitating to link the advancement of African Americans with women's rights. What became Title VII of the Civil Rights Act was added by a Southern conservative in an attempt to derail the entire bill, and then the Equal Employment Opportunity Commission established by that law began by practically ignoring sex-discrimination. According to the historian Berkeley, this became "a critical factor in the 1966 resurgence of a mass feminist movement similar to that which existed at the height of the Progressive Era (1900 – 1920)."[53]

The origin of the radical wing is different. In 1964 a kind of memo was written for a retreat of the Student Nonviolent Coordinating Committee by women volunteers tired of being confined to clerical and domestic tasks during the Mississippi Freedom Summer. It included this comparison: "The average white person doesn't realize that he assumes he is superior. So too the average SNCC worker finds it difficult to discuss the woman problem because of the assumption of male superiority. Assumptions of male superiority are as widespread and deep-rooted and as crippling to woman as the assumptions of white supremacy are to the Negro."[54] Later during that retreat Stokeley Carmichael infamously joked: "What is the position of women in SNCC? The position of women in SNCC is prone."[55] Similar events occurred in other radical organizations. In one a woman was told, "Cool down, little girl, we have more important things to talk about than women's problems."[56]

The first radical women's group was soon formed in Chicago. Brownmiller quotes a member:

> We talked incessantly. We talked about our pain, we discovered our righteous anger. We talked about our orgasms, and then we felt guilty for talking about our orgasms. Shouldn't we be doing actions? After all, the New Left was about action. We talked about the contempt and hos-

---

[53] Kathleen Berkeley, *The Women's Liberation Movement in America*, p. 20.
[54] Quoted at Susan Brownmiller, *In Our Time: Memoir of a Revolution*, p. 13.
[55] Ibid.
[56] Ibid., p. 18.

tility that we felt from the males on the New Left and we talked about our inability to speak in public. What had happened? All of us had once been such feisty little suckers. But mostly we were exhilarated. We were ecstatic. We were ready to turn the world upside down.[57]

That group published a mimeographed newsletter until 1969. Overall, it would not seem difficult to identify the recipes within New Left thinking-as-usual that had failed for these women.

That is what happened within the Women's Movement. What of American society in general? In that context, the initiating event was Betty Friedan's *The Feminine Mystique* of 1966. It was based on some 200 questionnaires sent to her class of 1947 at Smith College in preparation for their fifteenth class reunion. Berkeley reports that "the book identified and popularized 'the problem that has no name' that afflicted not only Friedan's Smith classmates but also hundreds of thousands of educated, white, middle-class suburban women who had exchanged their diplomas for a marriage license."[58] "The problem," she continues, "was one that each suburban housewife struggled with alone, until Friedan named it, collectivized it, and popularized it. 'As she made the beds, shopped for groceries, matched slipcover materials, ate peanut butter sandwiches with her children, chauffeured Cub Scouts and Brownies, [and] lay beside her husband at night, she was afraid to ask the silent question – Is this all? What kind of woman was she if she did not feel this mysterious fulfillment waxing the kitchen floor?'"[59] Brownmiller says: "I'd read it in paperback a year later, around the time I went to Mississippi, and although Friedan had defined the problem largely in terms of bored, depressed, middle-class suburban housewives, who downed too many pills and weren't making use of their excellent educations, I'd seen myself on every page. *The Feminine Mystique* changed my life."[60] In short, the recipe whereby marriage, children, and a house in suburbia will bring happiness was widely recognized to have failed, especially for white, middle-class, and college-educated women.

---

[57] Ibid.
[58] Kathleen Berkeley, *The Women's Liberation Movement in America*, p. 27.
[59] Ibid., quoting Friedan.
[60] Susan Brownmiller, *In Our Time: Memoir of a Revolution*, p. 3.

C. What Were the Actions of the Movement? In twenty years there were over a dozen issues that engaged the radical groups. The most important were childcare, sexual satisfaction, standards of beauty, abortion, rape, sexual abuse of children, battery, sexual harassment, women's health, lesbianism, and pornography. The exclusion of unescorted women from restaurants was easily eliminated, but a campaign against prostitution was abandoned when call girls protested the threat to their incomes. What constantly went on, however, were meetings of groups and a type of communication within them called "consciousness raising." This appears to be the fundamental action, no matter what particular issue was at stake or what further kind of action emerged from it. For Schutz, action includes social action, which is action that "involves the attitudes and actions of others and is oriented to them in its course."[61] Thus a style of group communication that is not only motivated by prevailing conditions in society, but is also designed to alter the attitudes of each new member as she enters the group, as well as strengthening the new attitudes emerging among all the participants, is already an example of social action before another specific action is chosen and carried out.[62]

At least as something deliberately engaged in on a regular basis, *consciousness raising* is something original to Women's Liberation, where it was also named. Brownmiller calls it "a group exercise designed to unlock the door to collective truths unmediated by the opinions of men."[63] She went to her first meeting two weeks after the Miss America protest. There were thirty women in blue jeans, long hair, and no makeup. Soon they were talking about the abortions they had had or had not been able to get. Brownmiller seems to have trumped everybody when she reported having not one but three.

> Saying "I've had three illegal abortions" aloud was my feminist baptism, my swift immersion in the power of sisterhood. A medical procedure I'd been forced to secure alone, shrouded in silence, was not "a personal problem" any more than the matter of my gender in the newsroom was "a personal problem." My solitary efforts to forge my own destiny were fragments of women's shared, hidden history, links to the past and future

---

[61] Alfred Schutz, *Collected Papers, Vol. II*, p. 13.
[62] Alfred Schutz, *Collected Papers, Vol. I*, p. 67.
[63] Susan Brownmiller, *In Our Time: Memoir of a Revolution*, p. 5.

generations, and pieces of a puzzle called sexual oppression. The simple technique of consciousness-raising had brought my submerged truths to the surface, where I learned that I was not alone.[64]

Brownmiller emphasizes that such realizations led to recognizing the political dimensions of the personal:

> Small-group consciousness-raising took hold ... suddenly and spontaneously among American women in the suburbs and the cities ... Not everyone was temperamentally suited to the c.r. process, which required a high degree of honesty about intimate matters in front of relative strangers. Many of the "naturals" had been in group therapy or just adored talking about themselves. Others (I include myself in this category) had to overcome an inbred reluctance to speak confessionally, thinking it somewhat narcissistic. But we all believed in the political importance of our task. We expected that the pooled information would clear our heads and lead to analysis and theory, and it did.[65]

For example where theory is concerned, Artist Pat Mainardi's paper is called "The Politics of Housework." In it she examines every weaseling excuse that men put forward to avoid sharing the household duties, culminating, of course, with "Housework is too trivial to even talk about." Mainardi's paper is a knockout. It gives political importance to a formerly private and personal female complaint. In a household where both partners work, why are *we* the sex that does the unpaid, repetitive, boring, time-and-energy-consuming tasks? Where is it written in the book of law that we're supposed to do the laundry, dust the table, and wash the dishes? After I read Pat Mainardi's paper, I no longer thought of housework as my private battle with the man in my life. It's part of the universal male-female problem. – New thinking that flows from a reexamination of women's daily lives is what this new movement is all about. As Pat Mainardi insists, "Participatory democracy begins at home." As Carol Hanish writes in her paper on consciousness-raising and action, "The personal is political." – *The personal is political?* Housework is political. Abortion is political. Standards of feminine beauty are political. Women's oppression is political. Sexual satisfaction is political. A reevaluation of male-female relations is political. What else were we on the verge of discovering? What other so-called trivial

---

[64] Ibid., p. 7.
[65] Ibid., p. 79.

issues and private battles consigned to the "personal" will we bring to light and redefine as political?[66]

Many insights were gained in such meetings, and some gained outside them were brought to them for refinement.[67] This eventually led to challenges about members claiming individual authorship and royalties for books. In fact, there was actually quite a bit of conflict within and between groups.[68] But there was still a series of impressive direct actions that impacted on the wider American society. In 1968 there was actually no bra burning in Atlantic City, but there was a Freedom Trash Can into which girdles, high heels, falsies, eyelash curlers, fake lashes, tweezers, and tubes of mascara were thrown.[69] Also, the policy of speaking only to women journalists began then, as did national media coverage.

Then again, the technique of the *sit-in* was borrowed from the civil-rights movement. Over one hundred women staged one at the editorial office of the *Ladies Home Journal*:

> The decision to target the *Journal,* the quintessential magazine of the 'American Housewife" with a readership of 14 million, was a political statement in and of itself. As the demonstrators anticipated, their action netted media attention; once reporters and camera crews were in place, a statement was handed out that indicted the *Journal* for "dealing superficially, unrealistically, or not at all with the real problems of today's women: job opportunity, day care, abortion (…)' After a protracted standoff, a settlement was reached in which the women were given the opportunity to produce an eight-page supplement to be included in a future issue. When the supplement appeared in the August 1970 issue, it contained information on women and work, how to start consciousness-raising groups, a contact list of women's liberation groups, a proposal for a housewife's bill of rights (…)[70]

Another technique was the *speak-out*. Brownmiller writes: "Speak-outs based on the New York women's model were organized in other cities within the year, and subsequent campaigns to change public opinion in the following decade would utilize first-person testimony in a full

---

[66] Ibid., p. 45.
[67] Ibid., p. 96.
[68] See ibid., pp. 53 ff.
[69] Ibid., p. 39.
[70] Kathleen Berkeley, *The Women's Liberation Movement in America*, p. 47.

range of issues from rape and battery to child abuse and sexual harassment. The importance of personal testimony in a public setting, which overthrew the received wisdom of 'the experts,' cannot be overestimated. It was an original technique and a powerful ideological tool."[71] On Berkeley's account, one action began from a conference.

> The 1970 publication of *Women and Their Bodies* (soon to be retitled *Our Bodies, Ourselves*) gave the women's health movement its proverbial shot in the arm. This project, conceived and written by a small, radical feminist collective from Boston, grew out of a workshop held during the spring of 1969. Following the success of the conference, a dozen women conducted a free course on women's health issues for individuals and community groups; so popular was this course that the women, who eventually incorporated themselves as the Boston *Women's Health Book* Collective, decided to publish their research on women's health issues. The book became a runaway best-seller with over 200,000 copies sold by 1973 and over 2 million by the end of the decade. Much of the book's focus, like the women's health movement in general, centered on such topics as heterosexuality and homosexuality, reproduction (from menstruation to menopause), abortion, violence against women, and lessons in self-defense. The authors' growing awareness of the politics of health care also led them to include a critique of the American health-care system.[72]

Brownmiller's account of the workshop on women's health is slightly different. When the chair of the overflowing workshop expressed outrage at her obstetrician, it "unleashed a freewheeling exchange on patronizing male doctors, childbirth, orgasm, contraception, and abortion that was so voluble and intense that nobody wanted to go home. – 'Everybody had a doctor story ... We put aside our prepared papers and did consciousness raising'."[73]

Brownmiller wrote a book on rape, and considers the theorizing on this issue to be the radical movement's "most successful contribution to world thought."[74] This is not the place to present that theory, but her remark to *Good Housekeeping* can be quoted: "Rape is to women as

---

[71] Susan Brownmiller, *In Our Time: Memoir of a Revolution*, p. 109.
[72] Kathleen Berkeley, *The Women's Liberation Movement in America*, p. 63.
[73] Susan Brownmiller, *In Our Time: Memoir of a Revolution*, p. 181.
[74] Ibid., p. 194.

lynching was to blacks. It's a conscious process of intimidation that keeps all women in a state of fear."[75] There was the action of *monitoring* of rape cases that came to trial.[76] Hotlines were established; by 1976, there were over 400 Rape Crisis Centers across the country and every state in the union had revised its laws on rape.

Pornography was and is the most divisive issue for the movement. This is also not the place to analyze the antiporn and anti-antiporn theories, but the direct action of *browsing* deserves mention: "While pretending to peruse the porno racks in convenience stores, they'd drip glue on the magazine pages and insert messages such as 'Pornography Hurts Women'" (SB 301). On a larger scale there was a campaign of tours of the sex industry in New York's Times Square, which the media especially loved (SB 305). Brownmiller remarks in 1999 that the "anti-porn initiative constituted the last gasp of radical feminism. No issue of comparable passion has arisen [since 1985] to take its place."[77]

D. How Did Women's Liberation End? Why the Women's Liberation phase of the Women's Movement ended is not clear. How such a phase ends is as much a historical question as how it started. There was the usual burning-out in the radical groups, but for some reason, a new generation of volunteers did not arise.[78] Could it be said that a new pattern of "thinking as usual" was established? It is said that the *Zeitgeist* changed with the election of President Reagan and the rise of the New Right, but this is not clearly an explanation. The movement lost the public's attention by the mid-1980s. Pornography was the last and most divisive issue for Women's Liberation. The liberal wing has of course continued. Comparison with other radical movements for social change in that and other eras would no doubt shed some light.

Finally, that much was accomplished in the two decades of Women's Liberation might be recognized in retrospect:

> Imagine a time – or summon it back into memory – when a husband was required to countersign a wife's application for a credit card, a bank loan, or automobile insurance, when psychiatrists routinely located the cause of an unsatisfactory sex life in the frigid, castrating, ball-breaking female

---

[75] Ibid., p. 204.
[76] Ibid., p. 218.
[77] Ibid., p. 324.
[78] Ibid., p. 329.

partner, when abortion was an illegal, back-alley procedure, when rape was the woman's fault, when nobody dared talk about the battery that went on behind closed doors, or could file a complaint about sexual harassment. And remember the hostile humor that reinforced the times: the endless supply of mother-in-law jokes, the farmer's daughter, the little old lady in tennis shoes, the bored receptionist filing her nails, the dumb blonde stenographer perched on her boss's lap, the lecherous tycoon chasing his buxom secretary around the desk.[79]

Alfred Schutz died in 1959, which is before the radical social movements against racism, the Vietnam War, sexism, homophobia, etc., of the 1960s began, but he had become sympathetic with the efforts of oppressed groups to attain equality, and included age- as well as sex- and race-based inequalities in his concern.[80] Against the revolutionary position, he was a reformer who advocated a "strategy by which the evil of social tensions can at least be diminished. This educational goal can in my opinion be reached," he wrote, "only by a slow and patient modification of the system of relevances which those in power impose on their fellow-men."[81] The efforts of Women's Liberation were hardly slow and patient, but one might wonder if their wider impact on American society was not through the persuading of those in power, e.g., magazine editors, to impose a different relevance system. This would seem decidable through historical research.

III. The historical sciences in Schutz's theory of the cultural sciences

Does Schutz's theory of the cultural sciences, which is usually comprehended as specified for the social sciences in the strict signification, include the historical sciences? The more the inclusion of the historical

---

[79] Ibid., p. 3.
[80] Lester Embree, "The Ethical-Political Side of Schutz: His Contributions at the 1956 Institute on Ethics concerned with Barriers to Equality of Opportunity," in Lester Embree (ed.), *Schutzian Social Science*, Dordrecht: Kluwer Academic Publishers, 1999, p. 254.
[81] Alfred Schutz, *Collected Papers, Vol. II*, p. 262. Cf. Lester Embree, "Schutz on Reducing Social Tensions," in Kevin Thompson and Lester Embree (eds.), *Phenomenology of the Political*, Dordrecht: Kluwer Academic Publishers, 2000, pp. 81-102.

sciences becomes clear, the more urgent becomes the question of whether the historical sciences are a different species, and this question becomes critical if the difference urged by Schutz proves, on Schutzian grounds, no longer to be valid. The question of the difference of the historical sciences will be addressed after a brief discussion of (a) the theoretical attitude, (b) basic concepts, and (c) some methodological postulates specifiable for the historical sciences. Attempts to particularize historical science into history of art, history of law, archaeology, etc., are plainly possible, but will not be ventured here. The reader will be further referred on various occasions to the case sketched above in Part II in order to be the more persuaded of the plausibility of some interpretive assertions.

A. The Historian's Attitude. The outlines of a cultural-scientific account of science can be discerned in general statements referring to all science as well as history-specific statements in Schutz's oeuvre. Thus, "scientific activity itself occurs within the tradition of socially derived knowledge, is based upon co-operation with other scientists, requires mutual corroboration and criticism, and can only be communicated by social interaction."[82] There can be "we-groups and they-groups of scientists."[83] And, "considered purely as a human activity, scientific work is distinguished from other human activities merely by the fact that it is constitutes the archetype for rational interpretation and rational action."[84] Schutz's emphasis, however, is on a contemplative attitude:

> The attitude of the social scientist is that of a mere disinterested observer of the social world. He is not involved in the observed situation, which is to him not of practical but merely of cognitive interest. It is not the theater of his activities but merely the object of his contemplation. He does not act within it, vitally interested in the outcome of his actions, hoping or fearing what their consequences might be, but looks at it with the same detached equanimity with which the natural scientist looks at the occurrences in his laboratory.[85]

---

[82] Alfred Schutz, *Collected Papers, Vol. I*, p. 37; cf. idem, *Reflections on the Problem of Relevance*, p. 154.
[83] *Alfred Schütz Aron Gurwitsch Briefwechsel 1939-1959*, p. 142/79.
[84] Alfred Schutz, *Collected Papers, Vol. II*, p. 69.
[85] Alfred Schutz, *Collected Papers, Vol. I*, p. 36.

Recognition of this attitude is essential to Schutz's theory of science. If the above passage is comprehended as referring to social science in the broad signification, i.e., the cultural sciences, then this description would subsume the attitude of the historical scientist. The work of Brownmiller illustrated above is then not strictly scientific. Although they may be less involved in the situation than most expressions in non-scientific life, memoirs and writings by journalists are hardly disinterested. For the historian, they are source materials. Schutz recognizes everyday life as the opposite of scientific thinking, and within it recognizes the roles of the "eye witness," "insider," "analyst," and "commentator,"[86] "reporter," which must include the journalist Brownmiller, being added to the list later.[87] The historical work of Berkeley would, however, appear scientific because it is produced in a theoretical attitude.

But is it the case that the historian is a scientific observer? When a historian observes predecessors, they are observed in the same way in which absent contemporaries are observed in the social sciences in the strict signification. It is clear in §41 of the *Aufbau* that historical observation of predecessors includes the direct form whereby one remembers others who are now dead. Then again, predecessors can be known through intermediaries who are alive now but knew those now dead. Thus the line between predecessors and contemporaries is constantly changing. Beyond that, however, there are only signs, i.e., records and monuments, through which one can observe for the purposes of history (SASW 294/209).

B. Clarification of Basic Concepts for the Historical Sciences. The fact that Schutz's concern with basic concepts is as much a part of his theory of science as his methodology strictly so-called is a fact that may not yet be widely recognized. If so, this may be because the expression "basic concepts" does not occur frequently in the American writings. It and a synonym do occur in the opening sentences of an essay written in 1945: "Choice and decision are fundamental categories of the theory of human action and therewith of the theory of the social sciences. Yet

---

[86] Alfred Schutz, *Collected Papers, Vol. II*, p. 132.
[87] Alfred Schutz, "Memorandum to Harold Lasswell of June 7, 1956," in Lester Embree (ed.), *Schutzian Social Science*, Dordrecht: Kluwer Academic Publishers, 1999, p. 293.

with very few exceptions social scientists have so far failed to clarify these basic concepts of their sciences."[88] The first page of the *Aufbau*, however, contains this list of "*geisteswissenschaftlichen Grundbegriffe*": "the interpretation of one's own and others' experiences, meaning-establishment and meaning-interpretation, symbol and symptom, motive and project, meaning-adequacy and causal adequacy, and, above all, the nature of ideal-typical concept formation, upon which is based the very attitude of the social sciences."[89] And then the penultimate section of Schutz's book begins, "having completed our analysis of the most important basic concepts [*Grundbegriffe*] of interpretive sociology..."[90] This list can be expanded. The very first sentence of the *Aufbau* reports that Schutz was long concerned with the science-theoretical (*wissenschaftstheoretischen*) writings of Max Weber (it will be recalled that cultural scientists as well as philosophers can participate in the theory of science for Schutz). The logical structure of Weber's sociology includes the concepts of social action, social relationship, communal relationship, associative relationship, etc.[91] Schutz's objection to Weber, however, is that although he saw the need for secure foundations for the social sciences, he was interested in science-theoretical problems only insofar as they bore directly on his specialized research and thus, for example, his concept of the meaningful act of the individual does not define a primitive, as he thinks it does.[92] Schutz's project in the *Aufbau* thus includes going deeper than Weber did in clarifying basic concepts.

Clarification of basic concepts can have negative outcomes, but nevertheless disclose fundamental insights:

> In his specialized studies [Georg] Simmel made lasting and valuable contributions, although very few of his basic concepts [*Grundbegriffe*] have survived critical scrutiny, not even his key concept of reciprocal effect (*Wechselwirkung*) (...) However, Simmel's underlying idea has proven fruitful and is still utilized. This is the notion that all concrete social phenomena should be traced back to modes of individual behavior

---

[88] Alfred Schutz, "Choice and the Social Sciences," in Lester E. Embree (ed.), *Life-World and Consciousness: Essays for Aron Gurwitsch*. Ed. Evanston, IL: Northwestern University Press, 1972, p. 565.
[89] Alfred Schutz, *Der Sinnhafte Aufbau...*, p. 9/xxxi.
[90] Ibid., p. 340/241; cf. *Collected Papers, Vol. IV*, pp. 121 ff.
[91] Alfred Schutz, *Der Sinnhafte Aufbau...*, p. 13/5.
[92] Ibid., p. 15/7.

and that the particular social form of such modes should be understood through detailed description.[93]

Finally, while there may be additional basic concepts for the specifically historical sciences, those mentioned above are clearly of use in the investigations done in the historical as well as the social sciences in the strict signification and are, as Schutz was aware, cultural-scientific basic concepts. Sixteen basic concepts are expressed in the passages quoted in this subsection. It does not seem worth the space to show that each and every one of these basic concepts is relevant for the understanding the Women's Liberation Movement sketched above.

C. Some Methodological Postulates for the Historical Sciences. Mere consultation of the indices of volumes I and II of the *Collected Papers* shows that Schutz discusses at least six methodological postulates (there are at least that many more). Three will be presented here to show that they hold for the historical as well as other cultural sciences. The inclusion of history is clear: "the researcher who occupies himself scientifically with the objects of the world of nature is in no way in the same relationship to the objects of his interest as the sociologist, the economist, the theorist of law, or the historian. Any well-founded consideration of the methodological problems of the social sciences needs to begin with the clarification of this difference."[94] Briefly, in order to have the observable nature their theories refer to, the naturalistic sciences require an abstraction from how the world in everyday life is originally sociocultural, while the cultural sciences do not perform that abstraction but rather retain the concrete sociocultural world as their subject matter.[95] Positively put, "the constructs used by the social scientist are, so to speak, constructs of the second degree, namely constructs of the constructs made by the actors on the social scene, whose behavior the scientist observes and tries to explain in accordance with the procedural (...) rules of his science."[96] Naturalistic science abstracts from primary constructs.

---

[93] Ibid., p. 12/4.
[94] Alfred Schutz, *Collected Papers, Vol. IV*, p. 121.
[95] Alfred Schutz, *Collected Papers, Vol. I*, p. 58; Alfred Schutz, "Positivistic Philosophy...," p. 133.
[96] Alfred Schutz, *Collected Papers, Vol. I*, p. 6.

Schutz uses the word "postulate" most of the time, but he also uses "rules," which seems short for "the rules of procedure" or "the procedural rules" as used by his friend Felix Kaufmann, "a body of accepted rules of procedure of thinking [being] called the method of science."[97] It will be remembered that it is the task of philosophical but also scientific science theorists to make such rules explicit for the consideration ultimately by scientists.

1. The postulate of subjective interpretation. The principle whereby "any phenomenon of the social world (...) has a different aspect for the sociologist and for the man who acts and thinks within it" is "the most important contribution of Max Weber's methodological writings to the problems of social science."[98] Here Schutz uses "aspect" to translate Weber's *subjektiver Sinn*, which he usually renders literally as "subjective meaning" but also increasingly in the later writings renders as "subjective interpretation" even though he considered it an "unfortunate term."[99] He was especially hesitant about "objective meaning (*objektiver Sinn*)":

> It was Max Weber who made this distinction the cornerstone of his methodology. Subjective meaning, in this sense, is the meaning which an action has for the actor or which a relation or situation has for the person or persons involved therein; objective meaning is the meaning the same action, relation, or situation has for anybody else, be it a partner or observer in everyday life, the social scientist, or the philosopher. The terminology is unfortunate because the term "objective meaning" is obviously a misnomer, in so far as the so-called "objective" interpretations are, in turn, relative to the particular attitudes of the interpreters and, therefore, in a certain sense, "subjective."[100]

One might go beyond Schutz's letter and experiment with the expressions "insider interpretation" and "outsider interpretation." Thus, one can say that the insider interpretation is that of the actor of her own action, relation, or situation and that in contrast there are the common-sense outsider interpretations produced by her partners and observers in everyday life. (Insider interpretations are what Brownmiller's book chiefly

---

[97] Ibid., p. 5.
[98] Alfred Schutz, *Collected Papers, Vol. II*, p. 92.
[99] Alfred Schutz, *Collected Papers, Vol. I*, p. 24.
[100] Alfred Schutz, *Collected Papers, Vol. II*, p. 275.

contains.) In further contrast, there are then the outsider interpretations of the scientist and the philosopher. These are not in the practical but in the theoretical attitude and would be (a) scientific theory of sociocultural things, e.g., Berkeley's book, or (b) scientific theory of science, as found in to some extent in Weber but not in Parsons, while (c) the science theory of Schutz is a matter of philosophical outsider interpretations. And as seen above in Part I, it is through reflecting on the practices of scientists that the science theorist is able to conceive rules that the scientists may or may not accept and attempt consciously to follow in order to do their science better.

The rule or postulate of subjective interpretation is formulated repeatedly by Schutz; perhaps the following two formulations together show, among other things, how gentle is his prescriptivism:

> The social scientist must ... ask, or he must, at least, always be in a position to ask, what happens in the mind of an individual actor whose act has led to the phenomenon in question. We can formulate this *postulate of the subjective interpretation* more correctly as follows: The scientist has to ask what type of individual mind can be constructed and what typical thoughts must be attributed to it to explain the fact in question as the result of its activity within an understandable relation.[101]

> What is really meant by the postulate of subjective interpretation is that the actor understands what he is doing and that, in daily life as well as in science, the observer who wants to grasp the meaning of an action observed has to investigate the subjective self-understanding of the actor. Strictly speaking, it is only the actor who knows where his action starts and where it ends. The observer sees merely the segments of the ongoing course of action which becomes manifest to him (...).[102]

If one thinks about what a historian does and considers, e.g., how Berkeley could use work like that of Brownmiller, it is plausible that the historian's work includes asking about the insider interpretations of the actions of historical actors, which may or may be expressed by those actors. But does Schutz's account explicitly extend that far or, in other words, is he using "social scientist" in the above passages to express the broad signification best expressed as "cultural scientist" that subsumes

---

[101] Alfred Schutz, *Collected Papers, Vol. II*, p. 85.
[102] Alfred Schutz, "Positivistic Philosophy...," p. 138.

the historical scientist? Although he does not mention "subjective interpretation" in the following passage, there is clearly a place for it:

> Now historical research does not take as its primary object the subjective experiences of the authors of source materials. Yet these sources refer throughout to the direct and indirect social experience of their authors. As a result, the objective content communicated by the sign has a greater or lesser concreteness. The procedure of historical research is at this point the same as that used in interpreting the words of someone who is speaking to me. In the latter case I gain through communication an indirect experience of what the speaker has experienced directly. In the same way, when I am reading a historical document, I can imagine myself face to face with its author and learning from him about his contemporaries; one by one his contemporaries take their places within my world of predecessors.[103]

2. *The postulate of adequacy*. The following passage expresses not only what this postulate consists in, but also its significance, although it also deserves to be noted that what is called "scientific system" in this passage is called "scientific model" in a later statement:

> Each term used in a scientific system referring to human action must be so constructed that a human act performed within the life-world by an individual actor in the way indicated by the typical construction would be reasonable and understandable for the actor himself, as well as for his fellow men. This postulate is of extreme importance for the methodology of social science. What makes it possible for a social science to refer at all to events in the life-world is the fact that the interpretation of any human act by the social scientist might be the same as that by the actor or by his partner.[104]

For example, this would signify that Brownmiller, like any other contemporary participant, could find Berkeley's account intelligible and reasonable, which does not imply that it is found to be in all respects true. When it is a question of predecessors, the historian asks whether, if the actor were alive, she would or would not find the historian's account understandable and reasonable.

3. *The postulate of logical consistency*. The system of typical constructs designed by the scientist has to be established with the highest degree of clarity and distinctness of the conceptual framework implied and must

---

[103] Alfred Schutz, *Der Sinnhafte Aufbau...*, p. 294/209.
[104] Alfred Schutz, *Collected Papers, Vol. II*, pp. 85-86.

be fully compatible with the principles of formal logic. Fulfillment of this postulate warrants the objective validity of the thought objects constructed by the social scientist, and their strictly logical character is one of the most important features by which scientific thought objects are distinguished from the thought objects constructed by common-sense thinking in daily life which they have to supersede.[105]

Since Brownmiller's memoir is well written and has no obvious obscurities and confusions, a contrast with Berkeley's also lucid history is not conspicuous. But if one thinks about the information that Brownmiller gathered from others through interviewing and reading as well as from her own memory, then the contrast between their accounts might become greater.

There are more postulates to Schutz's theory of science, but enough has been done to show that some of his postulates for the social sciences in the strict signification hold also for the historical sciences and hence are postulates of method for the social sciences in the broad signification, i.e., for the cultural sciences. It has also been shown above that the basic concepts as well as the attitude of the social scientist in the strict signification are shared by historical sciences.

IV. How are the historical sciences different?

From his scattered remarks, it is clear that the Schutz offered a considerable beginning of a theory of the historical sciences. At the same time, he never abandoned his position that the social sciences in the strict signification are about the world of contemporaries and the historical sciences are about the world of predecessors, a position first expressed in the *Aufbau* of 1932[106] and also expressed in his last essay, "Some Structures of the Life-World."[107] Yet the example presented in Part II is clearly incompatible with that position. Those whom Berkeley writes about were mostly alive when she wrote about them. Either Schutz has no place for contemporary history or contemporary history is a social science in the strict signification. Few would doubt that Berke-

---

[105] Alfred Schutz, *Collected Papers, Vol. I*, p. 43.
[106] Alfred Schutz, *Der Sinnhafte Aufbau...*, p. 23/14.
[107] Alfred Schutz, *Collected Papers, Vol. III*, p. 119.

ley's book is a work in history. Accordingly, there is need for a new *differentia specifica* for Schutz's theory of the historical sciences.

Schutz became implicitly prepared for this situation. Originally he seems unprepared to recognize how historians can redefine their scientific field.[108] Later on, however, he said: "Of course, the theoretical thinker may choose at his discretion – a choosing solely determined by inclinations rooted in his intimate personality – the science in which he wants to carry out his investigations. But as soon as he has made up his mind in this respect, the scientist enters a pre-constituted world of scientific contemplation handed down to him by the historical tradition of his science."[109] "There are," in other words, "the historical boundaries of the realm of his science which each scientist has inherited from his ancestors as a stock of approved propositions."[110] The interesting question of how the structure of a preconstituted world of scientific contemplation can change can be set aside. But if the science of history came to have a species called "contemporary history" in which living others are thematized, which Berkeley's work shows that it does, then Schutz would have accepted it. How he would then have differentiated the historical from the other cultural sciences is not so clear.

Are there any other clues about differences of the historical sciences in Schutz's oeuvre? Three have been noticed. Given the then recent *Methodenstreit* in German speaking philosophy, it is curious that Schutz has so little to say about the ideographic/nomothetic contrast:[111]

> The dogmatization of the purported contrast between the two types of sciences has frequently originated from an unjustified identification of the problems and methods common to all the social sciences with those of one particular social science. Because history has to deal with unique and non-recurrent events, it was contended that all social sciences are ideographic and thus seek singular assertory propositions, whereas natural sciences are looking for laws.[112]

---

[108] Alfred Schutz, *Der Sinnhafte Aufbau...*, p. 41.
[109] Alfred Schutz, *Collected Papers, Vol. IV*, p. 47.
[110] Alfred Schutz, *Collected Papers, Vol. II*, p. 87-88.
[111] I thank David Carr for reminding me of the *Methodenstreit* in Schutz's recent past.
[112] Alfred Schutz, "Positivistic Philosophy...," p. 127.

Schutz does not accept the ideographic/nomothetic difference as holding between the naturalistic and cultural sciences, but does he consider the historical species of cultural science ideographic?

It does appear that he recognized unique and non-recurrent events:

> In order to grasp the subjective meaning an action has for an actor, the social scientist has, however, only rarely if at all to turn to a concrete individual actor and his acts. To be sure, to any individual actor the meaning of his action has to be necessarily unique and individual because it originates in the unique and individual biographical situation of the actor. We have learned from Whitehead that all sciences have to construct thought objects of their own which supersede the thought objects of common-sense thinking. The thought objects constructed by the social sciences do not refer to unique acts of unique individuals, occurring within a unique situation. By his particular methodological devices, the social scientist replaces the thought object of common-sense thought relating to unique events and occurrences by constructing a model of a sector of the social world within which merely those typified events occur that are relevant to the scientist's particular problem under scrutiny.[113]

By this passage it would seem that the social sciences in at least the strict signification can indirectly refer to unique and presumably non-recurrent events at least insofar as they are referred to in the common-sense interpretations or constructs that scientific constructs are about. But would the situation not be the same for the historical sort of cultural sciences?

Considering the example given above in Part II, it seems difficult and perhaps impossible for the historian not to think in terms of types where phenomena such as Women's Liberation are concerned. The recourse to consciousness-raising meetings, for example, was not a unique but a recurrent event. Was there not a type of activist, a type of problem, and a type of direct action? Then, while the movement as a whole is a unique episode, is it not compared by the historian with the Civil Rights Movement and the Environmental Movement, on which there are books in the same series with Berkeley's book, and which can also be called typical social movements in the United States of the 1960s? Indeed, can one even use language in everyday life or in science without using

---

[113] Alfred Schutz, "Positivistic Philosophy...," p. 145.

types? Then again, are there not unique phenomena that social scientists in the strict signification seek to understand, e.g., a particular election investigated by a political scientist? In sum, both species of cultural science have ultimate reference to unique and non-recurrent events but both also resort to types in attempting to establish knowledge about them.

Secondly, the following passage may seem to differentiate the two species of cultural science (It can also be taken to confirm that the methodological postulates hold for the historical sciences).

> The principle of relevance, the postulate of the subjective interpretation, and that of adequacy, are applicable at each level of social study. For instance, all the historical sciences are governed by them. The next step would be to circumscribe within the social sciences the category of those we call the theoretical ones. The outstanding feature of these theoretical sciences is the interpretation of the social world in terms of a system of determinate logical structure (…)[114]

If "social study" here is synonymous with "cultural science," this passage might be taken to signify that the specifically social sciences are theoretical while the historical sciences are not. This is not "theoretical" in the signification of the theoretical attitude, which all sciences share. It would also seem not to refer to the contrast of theory and fact.[115] In one place, Schutz does list "all the theoretical sciences of human affairs – economics, sociology, the sciences of law, linguistics, cultural anthropology, etc.,"[116] which are social sciences in the strict signification. But if a difference of the historical and the social species within "social study" is alluded to, it is difficulty comprehend on the basis of Schutz's oeuvre what it might be. Historical accounts certainly have at least implicit logical structure, so that the postulate of logical consistency applies to them, and what "determinate" might signify in this connection is also not clear.

Thirdly and finally, Schutz once interestingly characterizes the seer by saying that "he would proceed like a historiographer, except that the

---

[114] Alfred Schutz, *Collected Papers, Vol. II*, p. 86; cf. *Collected Works, vol. IV*, p. 23. I am grateful to Nasu Hisashi for reminding me of this distinction mentioned by Schutz.
[115] Alfred Schutz, *Collected Papers, Vol. IV*, p. 150.
[116] Alfred Schutz, *Collected Papers, Vol. I*, p. 58.

latter explains the present situation by events looked at in terms of the past tense or the present perfect tense, or a past situation by events looked at in terms of the pluperfect tense" (II 279; cf. IV 65). One problem with this position is that that the events by which something is explained are always in the past of the explanandum, and thus historical explanation is not, or at least not yet, distinct from explanation used in the social sciences in the strict signification. Perhaps, however, it is a matter of how far one goes back in searching for an explanation.

Schutz's does recognize not only teleological explanation in terms of in-order-to motives, but also aitiological explanation, as it may be called, in terms of what he calls "because motives." This model can be extended from individual members to groups such as Women's Liberation. Yet aitiological explanations in contemporary history and sociology, for example, are not different if they explain events by earlier events in the region of contemporaries. But contemporary history is different from the social sciences in the strict signification if its explanations reach back into the realm of predecessors. Schutz does not say or imply this, but is a difference in essence rather than merely in emphasis. Differently put, contemporary history follows the influence of predecessors into the realm of contemporaries, which the social sciences in the narrow signification do not need to do. In addition, this is something that is done, for example, in Berkeley's history of women's liberation, i.e., in the concrete practice of science that Schutz's science theory fundamentally respects. Other types of historical science would begin as well as end their explanations in the realm of predecessors. This solution to the problem of the difference of the historical sciences is not Schutz's, but it does seem Schutzian.

11

Dimitrios E. Akrivoulis

THE EFFICACITY OF HISTORY AND THE LIMITS OF EMANCIPATION: REINHART KOSELLECK AND PAUL RICOEUR

What is the content we could meaningfully ascribe to emancipation today? What is the deep reason for the internal contradictions of emancipation? What is the situation we find ourselves in, when claiming for an emancipated future? These are the core questions that the paper will attempt to tackle by drawing on Paul Ricoeur's hermeneutics of historical consciousness. Our "drawing on" Ricoeur will pass by way through Reinhart Koselleck's work, to which Ricoeur's own discussion on the efficacity of history is much indebted. Although discussed in two separate sections, the works of the French philosopher and hermeneutic thinker and of the German theorist of history and historiography will be examined in unity. Yet, rather than focusing merely on Ricoeur's own usage of Koselleck's earlier work, *Futures Past*,[1] the paper will attempt to keep their dialogue alive and open by reading Ricoeur's hermeneutics of historical consciousness, as elaborated in the third volume of his *Time and Narrative*, in conjunction with Koselleck's latest work on the limits of emancipation. Thus reconciled their investigations of the receptivity and efficacity of the past, as well as their accounts of two core *meta*-historical categories that condition history, namely the "space of experience" and "the horizon of expectation," will guide our own explorations in the initial disproportionality marking the concept of emancipation.

---

[1] Reinhart Koselleck, *Futures Past: The Semantics of Historical Time*, transl. by Keith Tribe, Cambridge: MIT Press, 1985.

Following Koselleck's historical semantics of emancipation, the first section will examine the noematic metamorphoses of the concept and will ponder on the limits, backlashes, and retardations relating to its legalization process. It will be suggested that these situative aporias could be read as fundamental expressions of a certain paradox relating to the inability of any emancipatory struggle to fully escape its internal contradictions reflecting, in turn, the tension between lived experience and future anticipation intrinsic in any emancipatory demand. Drawing on Ricoeur's hermeneutics, the paper will argue in its second section that emancipation is not only a critical interrogation of our lived experiences from the "vantage" point of an aspired future; it is always already a projection towards our political future *from* our historical present, and hence should respond to both the lived experience of the past and the necessities and callings *of* the present. As time becomes thematized into historical past, present and future, there comes forth the issue of legitimacy of both our lived experiences and our aspired futures. There emerges, that is, the need for an ahistorical transcendental that would not return to a principle of radically monological truth. It is here that the significance of reading Ricoeur and Koselleck in unity becomes apparent. We have to ensure, the essay will conclude, that both our horizon of expectations opened up by our emancipatory demands *and* their validation are articulated on the basis of thinking about history in terms of the "future-being-affected-by-the-past."

1. Rescuing the concept

In the early Roman Republic, as Koselleck reminds us, *emancipatio* described the legal act by which a *paterfamilias* exercised his exclusive right of releasing his son from paternal power. The son was not legally entitled to claim for his own emancipation, since it was simply unthinkable in Roman legal tradition that one could emancipate oneself. During the Middle- Ages, *emancipatio* also appeared in the German common law. As a legal concept it was now related to civil independence attained not through a unilateral act, as in the Roman Law, but rather automatically when certain socio-economic criteria were met or the age of maturity was naturally reached. It was not until the eighteenth century that the actual differences in terms of rank and legal status were affected by emancipation. It was not until the Enlightenment that emancipation, whether naturally or unilaterally attained, presupposed *domination*. It then came to signify the general release from domination and finally acquired its revolutionary potential.

This decisive transformation of meaning, first evident in the verb and adverbial usage of emancipation was brought about not by the language of law but rather by its sociopolitical and philosophical usage. Hence, whereas the reflexive verb "to emancipate oneself" was initially employed by the poets, the philosophers, the cognoscenti who sought to liberate themselves from the pregivens, it was soon broadly used to refer to institutions, peoples or groups. Connoting self-liberation from God and reason (Rabelais) or the rules of nature (Montaigne), this noematic metamorphosis was directed against the church, tradition and political authority. To emancipate oneself did not only or merely connote to challenge and subvert the given. To declare oneself free always entailed a self-authorization drawn from a number of sources of modern legitimation, such as nature, reason or free will. It was in the triangle "between natural pregivens, subjective or collective self-authorization, and the establishment of legal norms, [that] "emancipation" gained its new historical quality," which it maintained through the present years without significant alterations.[2]

By the beginning of the nineteenth century, emancipation has turned into a concept of social change and historical movement. It has become a new criterion of justice that aimed at radically subverting domination of humans by humans and inequality in society, politics, economy and the law. As Koselleck again notes, "it was both liberal, in favor of the rule by law, as well as democratic, in favor of the sovereignty of the people; it was interpretable in a socialist fashion, in favor of a community of property, as well as being the sup-

---

[2] Reinhart Koselleck, "The Limits of Emancipation: A Conceptual-Historical Sketch," in idem, *The Practice of Conceptual History: Timing History, Spacing Concepts*, transl. by Todd Samuel Presner, Stanford: Stanford University Press, 2002, p. 254.

posed means for abolishing economic domination."[3] At the same time, though it became a sort of a catchword. Gradually added in the political rhetoric as a maxim or slogan, it was employed to register various political meanings expanding both its polysemy and its social efficacy. It was employed to connote political struggle at all levels: to procure equality of individual rights under pregiven civil and legal predicaments; to contest for equal rights for subjugated social groupings or entire peoples; to strive for freedom from domination and for universal equal rights.

Drawing from a number of historical findings, Koselleck ponders on certain limits relating to the legalization of emancipation. His first assertion concerns the fact that the various political, social, economic and religious claims of emancipation expressed in the legal acts of a historical and culturally specific society usually buttress one another resulting not only to certain retardations to emancipation but also to irresolvable contradictions. Since legal acts of equalization can equally uphold or impede the effectuation of civil rights, legal emancipation has proven to be a necessary but rather insufficient condition for effective equal rights. Second, given that emancipatory struggles may result in long and vengeful conflicts or civil war posing a serious threat to human existence, this danger can only be averted "if the legal principle of equal rights for all human beings around the world is proclaimed not only as a legal norm but *practiced* as a politically necessary and conscientiously enforced principle of justice"[4] (emphasis added).

A third obstacle is posed by the insufficiency of legally relating the equal rights of the social groupings struggling for emancipation directly to the very individuals that form these groupings. Although such an individualizing perspective, based on a liberal understanding of both subjectivity and rights, could render possible a general act legally granting equal rights to all human beings, it has historically led to a political impasse, namely the danger of those belonging to a group, a nation or a race being disappeared not as individuals granted equal rights, but exactly *as* a group, a nation or a race. Fourth, and as

---

[3] Ibid.
[4] Ibid., p. 257.

a corollary, it is only when our deliberations on the historical development and the possible future of emancipation include the vast array of concrete units of action, that we could meaningfully talk of the equality of all human beings as the theoretical premise of their equal rights. It is only when we acknowledge, Koselleck concludes[5] certain relative guarantees of existence to concrete historical communities in their diversity that the universal premise of justice could be realized as a minimal imperative.

As we have seen, in his investigation of the historical semantics of emancipation, Koselleck provides us with four situative aporias in which legal emancipation has found itself. The result of these aporias has been that a legalisation of emancipatory demands has deterred their full realization, creating new problems that could be hardly solved solely through legal means. In an attempt to move beyond the level of law, Koselleck further evaluates the concept of emancipation with respect to both its legitimacy and use. First he refers to the basic meaning of the concept, the "*natural substratum*" of emancipation, that every subsequent generation finally reaches the age of maturity[6]. As the members of newer generations succeed the older ones, there arise the incessant need and possibility to liberate themselves from the pregiven bonds. To this extent, "while preserving a common legal heritage, emancipation is a fundamental category of all conceivable histories."[7]

Second, Koselleck refers to the paradoxical situation resulting, on the one hand, from the diversity of both the heterogeneous units of emancipatory action and the pregivens they struggle to overcome and, on the other, from the emergency of contemporary global problems and threats (i.e. ecology, the atomic threat) that call for an immediate recognition of the general right of all human beings to this earth. The paradox puts forth the necessity of bringing about a minimal consensus of possibility for life. This minimum would be feasible, according to Koselleck, only through a re-explication of the utopian demand of the Enlightenment for complete freedom of rule and

---

[5] Ibid., p. 259.
[6] Ibid., p. 261.
[7] Ibid.

its reduction "to its actual core, namely to achieve the distant goal of equal rights today. (...) That politics is only possible and can only be mediated via particular and small-scale aggregated units of action, without, however, losing from sight the universal claim of an empirically present humanity, is today's challenge."[8]

Finally, Koselleck points out the "*temporal ambiguity*" of the traditional concept of emancipation. On the one hand, the concept connoted the singular legal act by which the state granted equal rights, the effectuation of which legally presupposed certain means of enforcement. On the other hand, the concept also meant the longitudinal social process of bringing about equal rights through gradual reconciliation, habituation or self-emancipation. It is essential, for Koselleck, to clearly distinguish between these two meanings so that the concept would be saved from ending up into a multivalent catchword. As he interestingly notes (emphasis added): "If we apply the patent ambiguity of our modern concept of emancipation to our situation, then the following conclusion can be drawn: the temporal dimension of gradual change and the temporal dimension of unique action evidently *move together*. Not just the spans of action but also the spans of expectation become shorter."[9]

At least in our reading of Koselleck, the general aim of his detour through the historical semantics of emancipation is two-fold: on the one hand, to explore the deeper reasons of the phenomenal limits of emancipation evident at the level of its legalization and, on the other, to investigate the ways in which contemporary emancipatory demands could still efficiently respond to current challenges at the global scale. In other words, this means to rescue the concept without necessarily passing through its legalizing process which has brought us in a state of aporia. But is not this aporia, we would ask, but the fundamental expression of a certain paradox relating to the inability of the very emancipatory struggles to fully escape their internal contradictions? Is it not the case that the inescapability of this paradox is only made apparent or further empowered by the inability of any

---

[8] Ibid., p. 262.
[9] Ibid., p. 263.

attempted legalisation of emancipation to resolve its inherent problems?

What is involved here, we think, pertains less to the insufficiency of law, as the product of social emancipatory struggles, to resolve these situative aporias than to the very paradoxical tension between lived experience and future anticipation inherent in almost any demand for equality. Hence the crucial question is not whether or how the law could temporally resolve and adequately contain the inherent contradictions of emancipatory claims. We prefer to ask instead: What is the situation we find ourselves in when bearing such claims? In what sense, if any, have the inherent contradictions of our emancipatory demands conditioned and continue to underpin our temporal existence? Indeed, these questions could be hardly answered if our explorations of the past and future of emancipation remain merely at the level of its legalization. But equally they could not be adequately met if our investigations of its possibilities abstain from exploring our historical present as the temporal space that brings such emancipatory demands to life, imperfectly mediating the relationship between our given experiences and our future anticipations. It is this subtle relationship that we will now attempt to investigate by drawing on Paul Ricoeur's hermeneutics of historical consciousness.

2. The tension within

In the third volume of his *Time and Narrative* Ricoeur calls for a practical yet imperfect mediation between past and future in a sort of a "pluralistic unity," so that our mere receptivity of history would be extended to our being-affected-by-the-past. The historical present is hence appreciated as the temporal cross-point between past and future, when the weight of the already made history is laid down or deferred by the past, and when the fantasy of the what-is-yet-to-come is surrogated into a responsible decision. Interestingly enough, Ricoeur builds here upon two regulative concepts developed in Koselleck's earlier authoritative work, *Futures Past*: "space of experience" and "horizon of expectation." Following Koselleck, Ricoeur interprets the dialectic between "space of experience" and "horizon of expectation" under the light of three related topoi in which these categories were instantiated by the philosophy of the Enlightenment: first, the belief that the present age has an unprecedented perspective on the future; second, the belief that these new times are also accelerating times, and that changes for the better are rapidly progressing faster; and third, the belief that human beings are increasingly more capable of making their own history.

Citing Adorno and Horkheimer's critique of enlightenment, Ricoeur suggests that the first of these topoi (new times) appears suspect since hardly could anyone claim for a progressive distinctiveness of the modern age. The second topos (acceleration of history) is equally challenged, as the belief in the accelerated pace of progress is put in serious doubt. Koselleck himself admits that the modern age is characterized by an increasing distance between our space of experience and our horizon of expectation. But does not this entail, asks Ricoeur, that our emancipatory dream of a reconciled humanity becomes more and more uncertain and suspended *sine die*? As to the third topos (mastering history) Ricoeur notes that its vulnerability is divulged not only by the unintended results of human actions and the contingency of historical change at the levels of both emancipation and need, but also and most crucially by a cardinal misapprehension of history itself: our disregarding that we are always already thrown into a history, which conditions both our existence and our anticipations. This is something against which even Marx[10], one of the preponderant exponents of this topos, has cautioned by suggesting that "men make their own history, but not as they please. They do not choose for themselves, but have to work upon circumstances as they find them, have to fashion the material handed down by the past." What is downplayed through this topos of modernity is the fact that in "making" history we always already find ourselves affected by what has been given to us as history and by the history we ourselves make.

The internal contradiction of emancipation to which we referred above lies exactly on this subtle paradoxical relationship between our

---

[10] Karl Marx, *The Eighteenth Brumaire of Louis Napoleon*, transl. by Eden and Cedar Paul, London: Allen and Unwin, 1926, p. 23.

historical action and a received past which was only given to us. In that sense, any emancipatory struggle involves not only a claim directed towards a new political future, but also the necessity of critically re-examining our relation with tradition. It involves both a certain future-oriented project of *making* history and our being always already *affected by* history. If we are to follow Ricoeur's thesis and take Koselleck's categories of "space of experience" and "horizon of expectation" as genuine transcendentals in our thinking of historical action, then we imply that the tension between them "has to be preserved if there is to be any history at all."[11] Furthermore, and as a corollary, we imply that only if this tension is preserved could the realization of our emancipatory demands be feasible and our path towards it be delineated.

Warning against the aphoristic assertion that the future is always open and contingent, whereas the past is always closed, rigid and finite, Ricoeur counsels that we have to re-open the past so that its undisclosed possibilities would be revivified. We have to undertake a double critical meditation directed towards the past *and* the future. Then the past would be disclosed as a "living tradition" rather than as a *fait accompli*. Since our emancipatory struggles are the bearers of this unrealized future, the significance of this assertion is hard to be overemphasized. Rather than slipping their anchorage in past and present experience, our emancipatory projects should fall instead *within* the scope of social action. It is our open-ended task of formulating a path towards the realization of our claims, under the penalty of these claims being cancelled as soon as they lose their foothold in experience.

It is our imperative task not only to preserve the tension between experience and expectation within our emancipatory demands, but also to make sure that this tension is not turned into a schism. This entails that our emancipatory dream is not only an immanent critique

---

[11] Paul Ricoeur, "Ideology and Utopia as Cultural Imagination," in Donald M. Bochert and David Stewart (eds.), *Being Human in a Technological Age*, Athens, OH: Ohio University Press, 1982, p. 215; cf. idem, *Lectures on Ideology and Utopia*, ed. G.H. Taylor, New York: Columbia University Press, 1986; idem, "Ideology and Utopia," in *From Text to Action: Essays in Hermeneutics II*, transl. by Kathleen Blamey and John B. Thompson, Evanston: Northwestern University Press, 1991.

of the present, a critical gaze towards our historical present from an anticipated future "elsewhere." It is always already a projection towards this "elsewhere" *from* our historical present. It is a projection that by being always already inscribed *in* the present should respond to the necessities, callings and commitments of present political experience. In that sense, there has to be sustained a tensional relevance between our present political experiences and future expectations within our demands.

Even when our emancipatory claims project a radically different future, we still are the heirs of past discourses and practices, for the temporal distance that would separate us from this past "is not a dead interval but a transmission that is generative of meaning." No matter how distant our future anticipations might seem, we would never be in the position of being "absolute innovators," but rather we would be "always first of all in the situation of being heirs."[12] Hence the paradox: We cannot struggle for a different kind of politics and anticipate an alternative political future altogether without breaking with the inequalities of the present. But equally we cannot suppose that our hopes about this future become more meaningful in deficit of any historical household. There must be a double inscription of our emancipatory demands in both the present and the past. In that sense, we could say that what we have been so keen on overcoming, rejecting and substituting, is finally what has constituted and continues to underpin what we allow ourselves to hope for through our emancipatory dreams.

It should be emphasized here however that neither this implies that we should render tradition the criterion of truth for our future claims, nor, conversely, that our theme "the-future-being-affected-by-the-past" could be read as an apology for tradition. This is an immanent danger which we will unavoidable face if we "easily succumb to the sterile antithesis between a reactionary apology of the

---

[12] Paul Ricoeur, *Time and Narrative*, vol. 3, transl. by Kathleen McLaughlin and David Pellauer, Chicago: University of Chicago Press, 1998, p. 221.

past and a naïve affirmation of progress."[13] Rendering our-being-affected-by-the-past more intelligible involves a passage by way through a clarification of the very notion of tradition. Here Ricoeur distinguishes between three different problems discussed under the headings of "traditionality," "traditions," and finally "tradition."

First, traditionality refers to the transmission of past heritages to future generations. It is the temporalization of history through certain dialectic between our being *passively* affected by history and our *active* response to history. On the one hand, traditionality resists both the total abolishment of the past and the Nitzschean idea of a hiatus between changing horizons that would dissolve history into a multiplicity of incommensurable individual perspectives. On the other hand, it also resists an idealist synchronization of past and future that would reduce the diversity of history to the absolute identity of contemporaneous understanding. Drawing on Gadamer, Ricoeur suggests that traditionality proposes instead a *fusion of horizons*, where the past is disclosed as a temporal horizon that is both distinguished and included in the horizon of the present.

The second category examined by Ricoeur is that of "traditions." Whereas "traditionality" is a formal concept referring to the historical transmission of meaning, "traditions" refer to the concrete material contents of tradition. It is exactly at this level that when struggling for emancipation we find ourselves to be the heirs of the past rather than the *ex nihilo* creators of something altogether new. Here the consciousness of being exposed to the past becomes supplemented by our interpretative response to the texts that communicate the past to us. A material dialectic of contents is hence added to the temporal distance that separates us from the past. Our being-affected-by-the-past takes here the form of a Gadamerean answer/response model: "As soon as, by traditions, we mean the things said in the past and transmitted to us by a chain of interpretations and reinterpretations, we have to add a material dialectic of the contents to the formal dia-

---

[13] Richard Kearney, "Between Tradition and Utopia: The hermeneutical problem of myth," in David Wood (ed.), *On Paul Ricoeur: Narrative and Interpretation*, New York / London: Routledge, 1991.

lectic of temporal distance. The past questions us and calls us into question before we question it or call it into question."[14]

Whereas, according to Ricoeur, the imperfect classification between consciousness exposed to the efficacy of history and the receptivity of past texts allowed Gadamer to move from the Heideggerean theme of understanding historicality to the opposite problem of a historicality of understanding, we would say that it is the process of constant (re-)interpretation involved in this transmission that supplements Heideggerean historicality for Ricoeur. It is through such (re-)interpretations that what has been independent from the temporality of *Dasein* is now appropriated into human existence. Even more crucially, it is through the transmission of historical meanings that a certain aura of sociality is added to historicality, surpassing the rather monadic ontology of Heidegger's *Dasein*. Experiencing time as past, present and future through the transmission of historical meaning, rather than as a series of equally weighted instants, is to experience historicality by way through "traditionality" and "traditions." Thinking of history as historicality, thus understood and supplemented, is what conditions the efficacy of the past in our emancipatory claims.[15]

The third and final category of the historical past questioned by Ricoeur is Tradition with a capital T. It is here that the above mentioned danger of understanding the efficacy of the past as an apology for tradition is more immanent. At this point Ricoeur rejoins the famous polemic between Gadamer's hermeneutics of tradition and Habermas' critique of ideologies, a polemic which Ricoeur finds not to be insurmountable. As he notes, a hermeneutics of tradition already involves a critique of ideologies insofar as we accept that tradition is not a mere dogmatic fixation, but an ongoing dialectic full of historical continuities as well as ruptures, internal crises, rivalries and revisions,

---

[14] Paul Ricoeur, *Time and Narrative*, vol. 3, transl. by K. McLaughlin and D. Pellauer, Chicago, IL: University of Chicago Press, 1998, p. 222.
[15] See also Patrick L. Bourgeois, Frank Schalow, *Traces of Understanding: A Profile of Heidegger's and Ricoeur's Hermeneutics*, Würzburg /Amsterdam /Atlanta: Königshausen /Neumann /Rodopi, 1990, p. 138.

which themselves open up a critical space for interpretation. But this interpretation raises, in turn, the question of legitimacy.

On the one hand, Ricoeur is suspect of Habermas' appeal to an ahistorical ideal of undistorted communication rather than to the ideologically distorted historical language of tradition as a criterion of legitimacy and truth. The possible danger here lies, for Ricoeur, in our finding refuge in a utopian future that is not anchored in our space of experience. On the other hand, our resorting to a transcendental reflection in order to provide universal norms of validation runs the risk of our being encircled by a Kantian monological transcendental of truth. Hence, no ideal of undistorted communication could be possible without a dialogical dimension rooted in the dialectics between our horizon of expectation and our space of experience. It is only upon such a ground that our emancipatory demands could be validated, without leading us either to a schismatic negation of the given or to an unconditional acceptance of past and present inequalities.

To summarize Ricoeur's discussion of these three categories of the historical past and relate them more closely to the issue of emancipation, we would say that, first, traditionality indicates the necessary interconnectedness between what has been already given to us and what we allow ourselves to hope and anticipate through our emancipatory dreams. In that sense, it designates the interplay between effective-history and our being-affected-by-the-past which underpins the very historical semantics of emancipation. Second, traditions refer to the actual transmission of past meanings and their reception within a certain symbolic order. They are the material contents of tradition, the baggage of past meanings passed to us through texts and narratives. Tradition, third, brings us in front of the crucial question of legitimacy; it involves a certain claim to the truth and validity of what we have already received from the past and what we could anticipate from our futures in our emancipatory struggles. If we fail to acknowledge that our historical past is also designated by the two first categories, traditionality and traditions, it is highly probable either that emancipation would be deficit of any meaning at all, or that its historical household would be completely lost: We would have to either uncritically vindicate the given or find total refuge in an unrealizable utopia that fails to respond to our current necessities, commitments and callings.

3. Conclusion

The observations made above lead us to the following conclusions. Our being-affected-by-the-past is always already caught in a subtle relationship with the anticipations disclosed by our horizons of expectation. The situative aporias discussed by Koselleck on the limits of emancipation hence reflect less the inability of its legalization to overcome them, than to the internal contradictions underpinning our emancipatory dreams, demands and struggles. These contradictions are but the manifestation of the dialectic between the space of experience, from which these dreams, demands and struggles are born and strive to depart, and the horizon of expectation disclosed by our dreaming, claiming and fighting for an emancipated future. A hermeneutic exploration of the efficacity of history involves exactly an investigation of the dialectic between past and future internal to our space of experience. Such an exploration proves helpful in two respects: On the one hand, it renders possible the reanimation of our supposedly closed past, opening up its forgotten possibilities and lost meanings, as well as its aborted or repressed endeavors. On the other hand, it alerts us against letting the tension between past and future degenerate into an absolute schism.

It is our task to situate our future anticipations in parallel with our past and present experiences within our emancipatory demands. This in-parallel-situating of tradition and innovation could then demonstrate better that our demands always already bear an unsurpassable internal contradiction; that they are always already conditioned by this contradiction. Investigating what variations or hybrids the dialectics between past and future might bear in our emancipatory struggles appears to be a task both timely and demanding. But even our mere posing the question is already pregnant of more, newer difficulties. It presupposes a certain act of instantiation that leads us to a state of aporia. As time becomes thematized into historical past, present and future, and as new meanings are given to the past there comes forth the issue of legitimacy of both our lived experiences and our aspired futures. And with the question of legitimation there emerges the need for a meta-historical transcendental, a new ethical standard. What is going to validate our future aspirations? How could we avert the danger of returning to a principle of radically monological truth?

This is a political moment, a moment of risk and fragility. Our criteria of truth and legitimacy need a dialogical dimension rooted in history. We have to ensure that both our horizon of expectation opened up by our emancipatory claims and the validation of these claims are articulated on the basis of thinking about history as historicality (understood as the future-being-affected-by-the-past). In that sense, our anticipations would be conditioned by a fusion of horizons rather than a multitude of distinct, incommensurable ones. In this fusion of horizons the historical past, present and future are bound together in a form of dialectics. It is our task to keep this dialectics alive. Perhaps then we could come closer to the realization that the utmost significance of our emancipatory struggles as well as the paradox born from their internal contradictions are of an intrinsically political essence. Perhaps then we could speak of politics as always open and unfinished; perhaps then we could speak of politics a polemical concept provided by the dialectics between the space of experience and the horizon of expectation.

Tatyana Batuleva

RESPONSIBILITY BETWEEN ONTOLOGY AND ETHICS: HANS JONAS AND EMMANUEL LEVINAS

What does "being responsible" mean? When it has passed into the public space, does responsibility remain genuine or does it imperceptibly degenerate into irresponsibility, travestied behind the mask of good intentions? Is responsibility born in the field of the intimate or, to the contrary, do its modern dimensions necessarily include some collective subject and object? What are the demands of responsibility in a world where, the more precise the steps of reason become, the more difficult it is to take those steps legitimately and safely? Responsibility becomes increasingly needed in a world, where humankind has pushed aside religion and the sacred and must put limits to its project for total domination.

According to the Polish anthropologist József Tischner, responsibility derives from the consciousness of meaningful action in the present. When responsibility is real, something actually depends on you, your standpoint may bring about changes, hence, it represents a hope that springs from the present moment. To the contrary, when responsibility is fictitious, you simply conduct yourself as if something depends on you. Tischner views authentic responsibility as something that "has to be discovered, described and measured," and in this sense, it cannot be a "free creation of the imagination."[1] This is in contradiction with the views of other thinkers as well. Likewise in contrast with Tischner, Derrida links real responsibility not to the possible but to the impossible.[2]

---

[1] József Stanisław Tischner, *Myślenie według wartości*. Kraków: Znak, 1982, pp. 433-434.
[2] Jacques Derrida, *L'Autre cap* suivi de *La Démocratie ajournée*. Paris: Minuit, 1991 (Engl.: *The Other Heading: Reflections on Today's Europe*. Bloomington: Indiana University Press, 1992).

Bulgarian public thought is also sensitive to the topic of responsibility. But it seems that in present-day Bulgarian discourse on responsibility, this concept is usually used as synonymous with guilt – which testifies to its actual absence in real life. We remember to think about responsibility when something shocking and unacceptable has already happened – then we resort to phrases like, "who will bear the responsibility?," or "dilution of responsibility"; the causes and culprits are looked for, but the circle is never actually closed. The responsibility that should accompany every choice, i.e., in a certain sense, that should be an initial element, in such cases has the features of something secondary, and is deprived of its own justifications, turning into an addition to and function of a certain context, thus becoming the contrary of responsibility.

If, in an accusatory aspect, responsibility is used as synonymous with guilt, in a justificatory aspect it can be reduced to a synonym of reaction. François Furet warns of the possibility of confusing the study of the origin of a certain phenomenon with the reduction of responsibility. Accepting the hypothesis of Ernst Nolte that Nazism originated as a reaction to the Communist threat, it should be said he nevertheless points out that such an interpretation can lead "if not to a justification, at least to a partial disinculpation of Nazism."[3] Jean Starobinski points attention to this fact. Under certain circumstances, the reaction represents a result. Then, says Starobinski, "the whole share of responsibility ascribed to the antecedent can be deduced from the testimony of an accused."[4] The question he raises is the following: it is true that understanding a given event requires taking the context into account, but still, "does understanding mean forgiving everything?" Starobinski concludes that ascertaining a causal dependence should not decide beforehand the ethical grounding, of which responsibility is an element.

However, Tischner is right when he stresses the dynamism of responsibility, the fact that its qualitative contents change over time, "with the progress of consciousness, technology, with the development

---

[3] François Furet, *Penser le XX-e siecle, Robert Laffont,* 2007, p. 380.
[4] Jean Starobinski, *Action et réaction. Vie et aventures d'un couple*, Paris: Seuil, 1999, p. 302.

of the public conscience."[5] Indeed, it becomes increasingly difficult to talk about the subject and about responsibility in the present-day globalized world, in a society interwoven with networks, when the illusion of inviolable privacy increasingly gives way before the dissolving boundaries that separate the inner from the outer – under conditions of growing anonymity and the intervention of chains of intermediaries. The question arises, whether the break-down of the subject makes responsibility impossible or, conversely, the assumption of responsibility leads to the construction of a new type of subject. We should, in any case, note that postmodernity, for all the reproaches that have been leveled at it regarding the lack of a common horizon and perspective, focuses attention on otherness by attempting to build a new type of relation between the Self and the Other, a relation in which otherness is not repressed, not made negative or assimilated, a relation that generates a new dynamic whole beyond the "reconciling" synthesis of two elements. "Being-for-the-other" and "hospitality" – these terms, favoured by postmodern thinkers –, may be viewed as an attempt at and guarantee of building a new type of responsibility.

Reflections on guilt and responsibility have been an inseparable part of the life of mankind. In this field of thought, the work of Hans Jonas holds a special place as his conception of responsibility. As a disciple of Husserl and Heidegger, he strove to link ethics to the new principles that take into account the vulnerability of nature and the moral dimensions of technology, and argued the need for a new categorical imperative. Jonas created an ethics oriented to the future. But he specified that this ethics has nothing to do with the Utopian projects of Marxism, nor with Messianic religious ideas. Orientation to the future, in this case, refers to the need for farseeing prognosis and assumption of responsibility in order to overcome the unprecedented impending dangers for humanity and the planet. While this conception, which is based on metaphysics, seems to be at the opposite pole of Levinas's one, which is based on ethics, the aim of this essay is to make a comparison between the two thinkers in order to show that finally they both arrive to very similar conclusions.

---

[5] Józef Stanisław Tischner, op.cit., p. 433.

1. Knowledge and moral verification

Is knowledge the key to everything, or would it be truer to say that it has imperceptibly displaced religion and has turned into an "opium for society"?[6] Is it a value in itself, or does some ethics always have to be added to it in order to make it a value? What is the relation between knowledge and responsibility? Do scientific discoveries always deserve our applause, or is knowledge inevitably accompanied by acquaintance with sin? The work of Hans Jonas presents an attempt to answer these questions; it is a reflection oriented to safeguarding "our descendants from the consequences of our present deeds."[7] Jonas expands the dimensions of responsibility, including within them not only mankind but humanness and life in general, not only our neighbour or the Other, but also the unforeseeable otherness of a future mankind. He goes beyond the concrete and invites us to discern not only the threat of physical annihilation but also that of the concealed manipulations that automatize our life and efface responsibility per se.

Jonas constantly argues the need for ethically-based interpretation, for moral verification of everything related to science and technology as typical human activities, because every activity has both its constructive and destructive sides. But the need for ethical norms here has a more concrete motivation insofar as modern science is a very particular case. Jonas pointed out several factors that might turn the growing power of science into an uncontrollable disaster. First of all, he pointed out the "ambivalence of consequences." He had in mind not the misuse of various capabilities, the possession of which is, in itself, always a good thing. The point is not to possess a certain power but not to permit abuse of that power – an issue that acquires meaning if we assume that ethics can be the judge of what is good and what is bad. It is far more difficult, says Jonas, when we are faced with an action where every usage, regardless of the good intentions underlying

---

[6] Roger-Paul Droit, Dan Sperber, *Des idées qui viennent*. Paris: Odile Jacob, 1999, pp. 55-57.
[7] Hans Jonas, *The Imperative of Responsibility: In Search of Ethics for the Technological Age*. Translated by Hans Joas with the collaboration of David Herr, Chicago, IL: University of Chicago Press, 1984, p. 31.

it, carries "increasing bad consequences"; when these "bad consequences" are inseparable from the desired and fathomable "good consequences," so that ultimately they begin to predominate over them. Because not only the misuse of scientific achievements, but also the best intentions and the most legitimate goals might represent a threat in the long term. There are situations in which evil grows through the good and useful; when success, not failure, holds dangers. That is why Jonas appealed for an ethics that takes into account the polyvalent nature of technological action.[8]

Another particularity is related to the fact that, in general, any knowledge can postpone its application. The possession of a capability does not yet imply the use of that capability. For instance, a person who is a gifter orator does not talk constantly. But this is not true of the technical potential of a society: as soon as a potential capability has been discovered (especially by science), society has what is required to apply it and to turn this application into a constant necessity of life. In this permanent process, human power is no longer ethically neutral; moreover, it lacks the ability to separate the possession from the exercise of power.[9]

A particularly important aspect, according to Jonas, is the fact that the scale and consequences of modern technological practices are such that they introduce previously new and unknown dimensions of ethical values. Modern technology is meant for large-scale use; its achievements extend to the entire planet. This is also true for its consequences, which extend to countless future generations. What is done today mortgages future life. The entry of far-reaching, future and global dimensions into our daily practical decisions is something ethically new with which technology has burdened us; and the ethical category that enters the scene in this new context is called *responsibility*. This opens a new chapter in the history of ethics, where responsibility grows in proportion to the manifestations of power.

Having long since overcome the horizon of spatial-temporal proximity, human power has already succeeded in breaking the anthropo-

---

[8] Hans Jonas, "Technology as a Subject for Ethics." *Social Research* 49 (1982/4): 891-898, here p. 892.
[9] Ibid., p. 894.

centric monopoly of traditional ethical systems. In those systems, the ethical scope is not very broad, the human always dominates in it, and the object of human duty is only people. But now, the whole biosphere of the planet proves to be vulnerable. And since man is the only living being capable of assuming responsibility, he must expand his ethical horizon. Responsibility towards other people remains, but it also takes it upon itself to strengthen interpersonal solidarity. However, the correctly understood human responsibility transcends the immediate pragmatic viewpoint. In this perspective, what is good for humans is connected with life as a whole, and the preservation of the gene fund of all living things, accumulated over the centuries, becomes the transcendent duty of man. Responsibility attains cosmic dimensions. Man here and now, and the projected future man are in need of protection; life itself is in need of protection.

Thus, Jonas argues why technology becomes the starting point of a new type of ethical reasoning that delineates the complex dilemmas confronting modern technology. It is customary to believe that while the atomic bomb is something bad, the use of nuclear energy for peaceful purposes is good. But in the long-term perspective, it too may prove to be an uncontrollable evil: and the "long-term perspective" of growing consequences is internally linked to the use of modern technology. The treacherous element is that, while as concerns an eventual atomic war there is always a safeguarding difference between the potential and the actual danger, between the actual possession of means and their potential use, in the case of peaceful use of nuclear power, the negative consequences (Jonas refers to the "apocalyptic threat") may remain unnoticed for a long time. The bomb might go unused, but the "peaceful" atomic reactor accumulates, undisturbed, its poisons for the coming thousands of years.[10]

Owing to its inherent tendency towards excess, many well-intentioned ventures of high technology become a source of very dangerous risks. It is precisely the advantages of technology that make people increasingly dependent, and that may turn the blessing into a curse. That is why regulatory morality is the only supporting point of an ethics of technology. In response to the long-term threat held by

---

[10] Ibid., p. 898.

technology, Jonas proposes the notion of long-term responsibility and formulates the idea of the technological syndrome and "the quasi-coercive element that characterizes progress." This element transforms technological power into an independently acting force to which people, though they are its possessors, become subjected. Freedom becomes the hostage of its own objectified manifestations. This tyrannical element of modern technology turns inventions into our masters; it imposes the inexorable logic that forces people to constantly multiply inventions – something that also demands an ethical response. Jonas's conclusion: only control external to technology can provide an adequate response to the galloping growth of technology. Such is the demand of human autonomy and dignity.

2. Responsibility as ethical mediation between two ontological poles: The categorical imperative

The role that was traditionally assigned to religion and that which, according to Levinas, is assumed by the "first philosophy"[11], for Jonas finds its justification in metaphysics. It is to metaphysics that Jonas links the destructive potential of technology and its threat to the existence of the human race and even to the conditions for a higher life on earth – metaphysics, the guardian of justifications, which answers the question why there should be a humankind; why the genetic heritage of humankind should be preserved; why there should be life; which risks are admissible and what is the new categorical imperative of humankind. This link to metaphysics also passes through the transformation of being, which is value-laden, and "affected," by man, into a sort of instance, into an actual object of human responsibility. It is precisely the valorization of being, perceived as significant in terms of value, as not indifferent, and as including "not only that for which I am responsible at the moment but also that before which I shall always be

---

[11]Emmanuel Levinas, *Totality and Infinity: An Essay on Exteriority*. Transl. by Alphonso Lingis, Pittsburgh, PA: Duquesne University Press, 1969, p. 304; idem, *Alterity and Transcendence*. New York: Columbia University Press, 2000, pp. 97-98; idem, "Ethics as First Philosophy," in Séan Hand (ed.), *The Levinas Reader*, Oxford, Cambridge: Blackwell, 1989, pp. 76-87..

responsible," it is this valorization that imposes requirements on the subject. Thus, the command of responsibility does not stem from a humanness that is linked with God, but from the voice of being itself. It does not come prior to, and does not lead beyond, being, but, on the contrary, is indissolubly tied to being – *firstly*, as a gesture that springs from freedom, whereby a person becomes guarantor of some being, of somebody's being; *secondly*, as a gesture of which the silent judge is not someone else but precisely that previously valorized being. That is why responsibility does not come before ontology, does not simply imply being, but is an "ethical mediation between two ontological poles: human freedom and the integrity of being.[12] In this case, being's primordial right is linked to a transposition: Nature is not the embodiment of the forces that dominate man, which he gradually masters; the vulnerable one is not man but the being of all living things that are exposed to the consequences of human action. Such an inversion of the relation is typical for Levinas as well, for whom the other is not the absurd, is not hell, is not he who negates me by his presence, but is vulnerability itself.

For Jonas, metaphysics is the guardian of the justification that humanness (in terms of both spirituality and physical body) must not disappear. This is so because the imperative of metaphysics goes far beyond the biological imperative of continuation of the species. Unlike postmodern thinkers, who see in metaphysics the basic cause of man's distancing from the human in terms of the senses and the body, see it as a constraining grip, a one-way groove that has left the stream of thought without an alternative, Jonas believes that the positivistic attitude of humankind has long since cut man away from metaphysics. In this sense, the sought foundation of the ethics of the future lies not in surmounting metaphysics but in a return to it, in the "ontological specificity of man, in his quality of being the only creature that can bear responsibility."[13] "The increased freedom has as its correlate increased responsibility. We have no right to mortgage the existence of future generations out of carelessness. Now we are responsible not

---

[12] Hans Jonas, *The Imperative of Responsibility*, op.cit., pp. 35-36.
[13] Hans Jonas, *Mortality and Morality: A Search for Good After Auschwitz*, Evanston, IL: Northwestern University Press, 1996, p. 40.

only for our neighbour and for our immediate proximity but for the distant as well."[14] According to Jonas, "this dimension of the distant appeared only after the Second World War, when man himself became a paramount natural force capable of putting in question the existence of future generations (the atomic bomb at Hiroshima) or the dignity of man (Auschwitz)."[15] Thus, Jonas makes of responsibility an *ontological object*: it is not only responsibility for something concrete but is an immanent command to preserve responsibility as such, and its future carriers.

Jonas's theory rests on the following premises: man has the gift of cognition on one hand and of freedom on the other; i.e., people can act in various ways. Man is the only creature on earth capable of assuming responsibility; and he cannot escape responsibility. The growth of human power is due to the growing potential of knowledge. But this does not mean that man's deeds have become wiser. The misuse of nature is deeply rooted in the Western world. But knowledge has another side as well: it shows us the possible consequences of our actions. Through it, freedom becomes aware of the need to impose inner limitations of its own. Just as society is based upon voluntary self-restrictions, so too are restrictions needed with regard to humankind's relation to nature. The diversity of life is a value in itself. Jonas appeals to the imagination for the assumption of responsibility, because the imagination is what shows us what can be done but also what would happen if something is not done. "It is much more likely for fear to obtain that which reason failed to obtain, and to reach where reason failed to reach. It is paradoxical, but I believe hope lies in education through the mediation of disasters. Only they will impose on us to change our habits of life, will make us abandon unbridled consumption in favour of a high ideal, because he who does not feel immediately threatened does not resolve to radically change his way of life."[16]

For Jonas, knowledge has a prognostic and preventive role: it must warn us of the possible future consequences of present-day human activity. There can be no progressive development without preventive

---

[14] Ibid.
[15] Ibid., p. 41.
[16] Hans Jonas, *The Imperative of Responsibility*, op.cit., 57.

thinking. In the present age, however, the balance has been upset and the impacts of human activity exceed the scope of possibilities for regulating them. A new "categorical imperative" is necessary. That is why Jonas paraphrases Kant's categorical imperative and formulates the following maxim: "Act in such a way that the consequences of your action would be compatible with preservation of real life on Earth." Also, "Act in such a way, that your actions will not be destructive of future possibilities for life."[17] This new imperative must be taken into consideration when pursuing any scientific activity, or any political action, in order to avoid the dangers arising from uncontrolled development of new technologies that put at risk the survival of humankind and humanness. Human power has already grown to a point where it is in need of a new ethical system that might go beyond the boundaries of the anthropocentric model. Human rights and the call to "love the neighbour" remain in force. But they are not enough, for they are strictly focused only on the human, in the aspect of human vulnerability. Now, not only man is vulnerable, but life itself, the variety of life. That is why man's duty is to think about life, to preserve it not only here and now but for the future generations as well, for those whose chances of life lie in the hands of the people of today and who have not yet received the possibility of having their word be heard. This life must not be a hostage to the headlong pursuit of short-term benefits and artificially created needs. Jonas gives a strikingly precise formulation of the present-day situation: the dimensions of the future and of the global are invading our everyday practical decisions; likewise accurate is Jonas' formulation that "the requirements for responsibility grow in direct proportion to the manifestations of power."[18]

The link of responsibility to knowledge on one hand, and to values on the other, inevitably raises questions concerning the balance between science and ethics. Some reproaches addressed to Jonas include qualifications that he is anti-democratic, tying action to fear, and sacrificing freedom in the name of freedom (in his view, insofar as the ontological capacity for freedom is inseparable from man's essential nature, it is invulnerable – it "may temporarily be excluded from pub-

---

[17] Ibid., p. 58.
[18] Hans Jonas, *Mortality and Morality*, op.cit., p. 42.

lic space but it cannot be destroyed"), the presence of goal-setting in being, Jonas' valorization of nature and effacing of responsibility (Bernard Sève, for instance, reproaches Jonas for his lack of concreteness – both the subject of responsibility and the negation of responsibility are anonymous and collective, they are everywhere and nowhere[19], and his anti-scientific pathos.

Marie-Angèle Hermitte views Jonas' standpoint as favouring values at the expense of distancing himself from science. She accepts the need for a "culture of anticipation," but, according to her, the emphasis should be placed not on the political decision but on the debates that have led to that decision. Nevertheless, Hermitte concedes that Jonas' views lead to several important conclusions: he grounds the expansion of the boundaries of responsibility; he underlines the need for mastering the mastery (of nature); he introduces, as a fundamental element, the inner duty of knowledge itself to anticipate what may be foreseen.[20]

Unlike her, Jean-Pierre Dupuy accepts that we should talk not about risks but about evils that derive both from nature and from people. In the September 11 attacks and in global warming, a combination of both kinds of factors is present. In the case of global warming, evil comes from nature itself, but is also a consequence of the development of technology, while in the 9/11 attacks, violence is in fact the result of a reversal of the power of technology, which was initially aimed at mastering nature. Dupuy sees the cause of all this as lying in the incapacity of humankind – which has suppressed religion and the sacred – to impose limits to its project for total technological domination. This lack of limitation turns power into a threat and even into a fatal predetermination.[21]

---

[19] Bernard Sève, "Hans Jonas et l'éthique de responsabilité," *Esprit*, Octobre 1990, p. 31.
[20] Marie-Angèle Hermitte, Dominique Dormont, "Propositions pour le principe de précaution à la limite de l'affaire de la vache folle," in Ph. Kourlisky. G. Viney, *Le principe de Précaution*, Paris: Odile Jacob, 2000, p. 361.
[21] See Jean-Pierre Dupuy, *Pour un catastrophisme éclairé. Quand l'impossible est certain*. Paris: Seuil, 2004; François Furet, *Penser le XX-e siecle*, Paris: Robert Laffont, 2007, p. 24.

Accepted or criticized, Jonas' theory is a possible answer to the complex and ambiguous connections between responsibility, knowledge and metaphysics in our contemporary global, "post-modern" or "post-metaphysical" world – a world that strives to combine the vision of a united humanity with the diversity of choices and possibilities, of voices and perspectives; a world in which every rational action is already marked by the shadow of irrationality, in which the dividing line between instrumental rationality and the extremes of irrationality becomes ever thinner; a world in which the more precise the moves of reason are, the more difficult becomes the legitimate and safe application of those moves.

3. Jonas and Levinas:
The paradoxical dimensions of responsibility

Similar in this to Levinas, Jonas links responsibility to humanness. Unlike Levinas, however, who refers to the violence of ontology and declares ethics to be the first philosophy, here responsibility is not pre-ontological; on the contrary, for Jonas, *ontology* serves as the source and inspiration of responsibility. He situates his reflection not beyond metaphysics, but in the seemingly abandoned fields of metaphysics, which had been declared fruitless, and proposes the justification of an "ethics of the future."

While in Levinas, responsibility is primordial[22], coming before awareness and arising independently of human will, goals and mutuality, in Jonas it is connected precisely to awareness, and its orders spring from ontology. In Levinas, the motivation of responsibility arises in the encounter with the face of the other in front of me[23], while in Jonas the stake of responsibility is mankind as a whole and its future on earth. Levinas situates his reflections in the space of intimacy, in the between-two (l'entre-deux) of the encounter, while in Jonas it is inscribed in the global fate of mankind. In fact, their different paths

---

[22] See Emmanuel Levinas, *Ethics and Infinity: Conversations with Philippe Nemo*. Transl. by Richard A. Cohen, Pittsburgh: Duquesne University Press, 1985, pp. 85-86.
[23] See Emmanuel Levinas, *Totality and Infinity: An Essay on Exteriority*, op.cit., 1969, pp. 293 ff.

lead both of them to the same view: responsibility springs from an elevating and obligating image of human being.

Unlike Levinas, for whom responsibility comes before all knowledge inasmuch as knowledge is viewed as grasping, appropriating, turning the Other into an object – in other words, as an operation that effaces the otherness of the Other[24], Jonas considers knowledge to be a necessary condition for the possibility of assuming real responsibility. This difference in views is determined primarily by the different fields in which the two authors are situated. While for the former, responsibility arises in immediate proximity, in the between-two of encounter, the latter outlines the field of an unpredictable in scope meeting with the otherness of the future, with the coming generations. That is why to assume responsibility for this otherness would be impossible without a degree of predictability that only knowledge can provide. Jonas explains the paradoxical role of contemporary knowledge, of the growing power of mankind, which, on one hand, is the cause of imminent danger and, on the other, is a means for overcoming evil. The ethics of the future is tied to knowledge because, due to modern technology, the present-day situation entails a high degree of unpredictability. Even the most that mankind could hitherto do to nature and to itself pales by comparison with what it has the capacity to do now. Jonas ties responsibility to knowledge in several aspects.

Firstly, responsibility entails the command to increase knowledge about the consequences of our acts and about how they determine and endanger the future of mankind. Secondly, it requires that we distinguish what is permissible and what must be avoided. But there is one other particularity here. Knowledge is one of the conditions for assuming responsibility, but not the only condition. Jonas again turns to metaphysics. Knowledge must not be all-powerful but should go hand in hand with the interpretation of values. Responsibility always includes a perspective on the good, on what man ought to be. Responsibility takes into consideration not only knowledge about the factual condition of things but about values as well; it considers not only what might be but also what ought not to be. Here we should note one other

---

[24] See Emmanuel Levinas, *Otherwise Than Being or Beyond Essence*. Dordrecht / Boston / London: Kluwer Academic Publishers, 1991, p. 10

difference between Levinas and Jonas. While Levinas proceeds from the individual Self, from the individual subject of action[25], Jonas chooses a different perspective, that of the collective subject and the long-term consequences that his actions entail; this is a subject that carries the burden of responsibility for the collective other – moreover, this is a collective other that cannot be fitted into the concrete here and now but is characterized by the indeterminacy of that which will come, which has not yet been, which has not yet been born. This characteristic situates that other beyond visibility. This is true for Levinas as well, but while for him the characteristic of being beyond visibility is related to the fact that the face is always more than ordinary morphology and hints of the Divine presence, for Jonas this beyond-visibility gives us an intimation of the commands of being itself. That is why, despite the differences between the two thinkers, we may ask ourselves: is this responsibility for being and in being, this care for future life, is it not a supreme form of Levinas' asymmetry? That is, a responsibility that awaits no answer regarding a future which, in its unpredictability, is completely vulnerable to the present day, a future the voiceless answer of which can only be detected in the silence of being. This is a meeting between the present and the future that should take place beyond total predetermination and, thus, should remain a kind of separation. A look beyond visibility, beyond the immediate results of our actions, beyond the consequences that, at first glance, are harmless, such a look involves the imagination in the field of responsibility. That is why "anticipation" is the term that best describes this responsibility which springs from metaphysics – not from the negation of metaphysics – a responsibility committed to preserving future life in general, and whose dimensions refer not only to the existential but to the ethical as well. This directedness at knowledge and at the imagination on the Other requires an interdisciplinary "futurology of warning," i.e., a scientifically guided distant projection of what our current action might lead to. In addition to this combination of knowledge and imagination, futurology has the advantage of providing emotional motivation as well, for it awakes in us the horror of what might be and

---

[25] Ibid., pp. 55-57, 118ff.

mobilizes us to prevent it, makes us be on the alert with regard to the good.

For Jonas, responsibility derives from the very being of man, because the very fact that man *can* carry responsibility means he already *does* carry it, he is placed "under its command."[26] While for Levinas the responsibility for the Other, which is there before all choice, leads to freedom, for Jonas it becomes possible precisely through the primordial human freedom, the burden of which the acting subject is called upon to carry. That is why, for him, responsibility comes not before all choice but is derived from the possibility of choice. It is true, though, that for both thinkers the command of responsibility is unconditional. But while for Levinas, this unconditionality derives from the fact that God Himself speaks to me through the immediate proximity of the face of the Other, for Jonas it does not depend on whether anyone (God or judge) can hold me responsible – its judicial instance is internalized, is human conscience, and its roots lie in "the ontological capacity of man to choose with knowledge and by his will between alternative action."[27]

Whereas for Levinas, God Himself speaks through the face of the Other, for Jonas, God continues to speak through the voice of man, who is the guarantor of the preservation of what God has begun. For Levinas, by means of the encounter between two persons, the Self attains an expanded identity entering into spaces in which death may be avoided; for Jonas, man bears the burden of his freedom, his responsibility, and hence of a divinity that is set in him. For Levinas, the presence of the Other is ensured, at least until the encounter of the Other with the Self; while for Jonas, the eyes of the other in front of me are absent: even the very birth of the other depends on the subject, on the collective Self.

In the case of Levinas, the responsibility that does not await a response and the hypostasis of the Self in the Other is tied to a subject that has lost his/her individual centre and who, emancipated from the narrative that is imposed on him/her, is the independent writer of

---

[26] Hans Jonas, *The Imperative of Responsibility*, op.cit., p. 34.
[27] Ibid., pp. 35, 38, 40; cf. Hans Jonas, "The Concept of God after Auschwitz: A Jewish Voice." *Journal of Religion* 67, no. 1 (1987): 1–13.

his/her own life. For Jonas, responsibility is aimed not only at the other facing me, but also at the yet unborn, at all living things and at the capacity to assume responsibility in general. To use Levinas' terms, this highest level of cosmic responsibility also carries responsibility towards the social subject that has become my neighbour, and carries the appeal for justice – an appeal provoked by the advent of the third, whose horizon is the asymmetry of responsibility in the meeting-parting. At that level is situated the flexible subject, whose boundaries are mobile; his/her responsibility serves as a path towards the discovery of his/her own uniqueness, towards the transcendent, towards a space where the "project without a future" may be avoided. This responsibility expands the horizon of the subject – not only because he/she has been able to forgive and turn caring for the Other into a reciprocal relation (Ricoeur)[28], not only because the weakness of the other has unlocked the subject's own capacity to act, but also because the resolution of his "narrative," current or postponed, now lies in his/her own hands.

This responsibility makes of the subject a continuer of God's work. Here the vulnerable one is not only the unborn Other, who, in his total predetermination, is entirely dependent on the subject. God Himself, Who has "become silent" and withdrawn, is vulnerable. Will the fact of being a "collective subject" help the subject to assume this unbearable responsibility bequeathed to him/her by metaphysics – the guardian? Or will he/she renounce responsibility, effacing thereby not only the other and him/herself, not only life, but the very possibility of openness, which is inseparable from humanness?

This subject views the tension that exists between the same and the other as a source of strength and as a future full of inexhaustible possibilities. While allowing for the possibility of absolute hospitality that is open to being-for-the-other and reciprocal asymmetry, Levinas nevertheless underscores the need for preserving a separating distance.

---

[28] See Paul Ricoeur, *La mémoire, l'histoire, l'oubli*, Paris: Seuil, 2000, pp. 594-595 (Engl. *Memory, history, forgetting*. Transl. by Kathleen Blamey and David Pellauer, Chicago, London: University of Chicago Press, 2004).

Regardless of whether ethics is a first philosophy (Levinas)[29] or whether its roots reach ontology (Jonas), regardless of whether it is linked to God's presence or God's absence, responsibility is in all cases paradoxical. It invites us to gaze beyond the visibility of the face, of the images created by media noise, and turns for help to the imagination – in order for us to be able to see the faces of those who already belong to the past or to those whose birth depends on us. Responsibility stakes on humanness, on something that is before duty, before rational action, before the conventions of communication. It exists in the connection to the Other, but through it, the subject overcomes his own boundaries, in it the Self is substituted by the Other – not in order to be overwhelmed by the Other but in order to assume the status of something unique.

Responsibility is paradoxical also because it manages to transform a past that is heavy with suffering, and with the will to revenge, into an always open possibility and promise for a future full of hope and lightness (Ricoeur). It is paradoxical in its striving to preserve the double imperative, to open possibilities in the impossible (Derrida). In a certain sense, is the silent God of Jonas not also the Other, the vulnerable? Is He not someone Whom I can nihilistically deny, but for Whom I decide to assume responsibility instead? Responsibility is a liberating, magic gesture that is inscribed in the very status of the subject. It leads to deconstruction of the closed subject, but in this deconstruction lies its awakening. Through it, the subject discovers his/her identity, because movement and change is inherent to the identity of the subject.

---

[29] See Emmanuel Levinas, "Ethics as First Philosophy," in Séan Hand (ed.), *The Levinas Reader*, Oxford, Cambridge: Blackwell, 1989, pp. 76-87.

Mark Zlomislic

DERRIDA AND THE ETHICS OF COMMUNITY

Postmodernism and deconstruction are usually associated with a destruction of ethical values. Richard Rorty argues that while deconstruction is important on a private level it is "pretty much useless when it comes to politics" and is "largely irrelevant to public life and political questions."[1] In a recent interview Ronald Dworkin expresses the view that postmodernism "is silly, indeed incoherent."[2] I believe that Derrida's answer to his critics can be found in the afterward to Limited Inc., entitled, "Toward an Ethic of Discussion", where he writes:

> For of course there is a right track, a better way, and let it be said in passing how surprised I have been...by the use or abuse of the following argument: Since the deconstructionist (which is to say, isn't it, the skeptic-relativist-nihilist!) is supposed not to believe in truth, stability...how can he demand of us that we read him with pertinence, precision, rigor?.... The answer is simple enough: this definition of the deconstructionist is false...it supposes a bad...and feeble reading of numerous texts, first of all mine, which therefore must finally be read or reread. Then perhaps it will be understood that the value of truth (and all those values associated with it) is never contested or destroyed in my writings, but only reinscribed in more powerful, larger, more stratified contexts...from the point of view of ethics, "deconstruction" should never lead either to relativism or to any sort of determinism.[3]

---

[1] Richard Rorty, *Contingency, Irony and Solidarity*, Cambridge: Cambridge University Press, 1989, p.83

[2] Ronald Dworkin, "Tyranny at the Two Edges of Life: A Liberal View," *New Perspectives Quarterly*, Winter 1994, p.17

[3] Jacques Derrida, *Limited Inc.*, transl. by Samuel Weber, Evanston: Northwestern University Press, 1988, pp. 148-149. In "Passions: An Oblique Offering," Derrida contends that "Some minds believing themselves to have found in Deconstruction... as if there were only one, a modern form of immorality, of amorality or of irresponsibility

Leslie Armour argues that the "application of metaphysics to social and political philosophy theory is a necessity and not simply an option".[4] Derrida, however seems to be arguing the opposite, namely, that the overcoming of a certain type of metaphysics is a necessary if there is to be genuine community.

The present essay has three parts and will proceed in several interrelated transactions. In Section one, Derrida's critique of metaphysics as restricted economy will be examined. In Section two, the postmodern approach to the question of community will be explored in light of the debate between Gadamerian Hermeneutics and Derridean Deconstruction. Section three, will examine what type of community could emerge from the results of deconstruction. Contrary to those critics who have equated postmodernism with a destruction of ethical values[5], I will argue that Derrida has opened a space in which the question of ethics and community, can be pursued in a productive manner.

1. Deconstruction and the Critique of Metaphysics

I have used Bataille's distinction between restricted and general economy as a starting point from which to think about postmodern ethics and community. In The Accursed Share, Bataille argues that: "Changing from the perspectives of restrictive to those of general economy actually accomplishes a Copernican transformation: a reversal of thinking-and of ethics."[6] Construed in the light of its etymology,

---

(etc.: a discourse too well know, I do not need to continue), while others, more serious, in less of a hurry, better disposed towards so called Deconstruction today claim the opposite; they discern... increasingly intense attention, to those things which one could identity under the fine names of "ethics", "morality", "responsibility", "subject", etc" (see David Wood [ed.], *Derrida: a critical reader*, Oxford: Blackwell Publishers, 1992, pp.13-14). Whether or not we should accept Derrida's interpretation of his own work is an issue that needs to be explored. In other words, can Derrida's work be subjected to the same critique which he reserves for other authors?

[4] Leslie Armour, "The Metaphysics of Community", unpublished manuscript.
[5] For example, see John H. Elllis, *Against Deconstruction*, Princeton: Princeton University Press, 1989, and Gillian Rose, *Dialectics and Nihilism: poststructuralism and law*, Oxford: Oxford University Press, 1984.
[6] Georges Bataille, *The Accursed Share, Volume 1*, transl. by Robert Hurley, New York: Zone Books, 1988, p.25.

the word economy means "law of the house". Derrida argues that "economy is in a way an idea based on sameness, the *oikos*, that which remains within the 'home' of the same."[7] An economy which is based on sameness is restricted. Derrida argues that a general economy would "stress another dimension of differance, which is, by contrast, that of absolute heterogeneity, and therefore of otherness, of radical otherness."[8]

Derrida defines metaphysics as a system that depends on a first principle upon which a hierarchy of meaning can be constructed. Metaphysical theories have created a chain of source words that have acted either as a foundation or model. Some of these source words include arché, form, soul, God, Truth. While these metaphysical source words have thrived, the question of ethics has been forgotten. As Bill Martin argues: Derrida wants to dispel the notion that it is imperative that we figure out "what came first", this identity-logic in the theoretical sense (and as especially perfected by Kant and Hegel) or the practice of sequestering persons and social groups deemed "impure." This search for "first philosophy" regardless of whether it arrives at a materialist or an idealist starting point, is itself part of the problem.[9]

Metaphysics, in Derrida's view is logocentric because it based upon an Ultimate Authority or source. Logocentrism posits a Transcendental Signified that gives all other signs their meaning. The metaphysical tradition, according to Derrida can be read as a history of binary oppositions. Derrida's deconstructive strategy is to disrupt binary oppositions such as truth/falsity, master/slave, presence/absence, etc. Deconstruction aims to undo the history of binary oppositions in order to show that rigid and restricted boundaries cannot be drawn. To cite Derrida:

> In a classical philosophical opposition we are not dealing with the peaceful co-existence of a vis-a-vis, but a violent hierarchy. One of the

---

[7] Raoul Mortley, *French Philosophers in Conversation*, London: Routledge, 1991, p. 99 (my emphasis).
[8] Ibid., p. 99.
[9] Bill Martin, *Matrix and Line: Derrida and the possibilities of postmodern social theory*, Albany: SUNY Press, 1992, p.175.

two terms governs the other, or has the upper hand. To deconstruct the opposition first of all is to overturn the hierarchy at a given moment.[10]

The first movement of deconstruction consists in overturning the hierarchy. Many critics of Derrida's work, have only focused on this first movement of deconstruction. Thus, Derrida's authorship has been read as a privileging of absence over presence, madness over reason, immorality over ethics. Of course, Derrida realizes that simply overturning a hierarchy is not an overcoming. Overturning the hierarchy still results in the continuation of metaphysics.

The second movement of deconstruction consists of "the irruptive emergence" of a new "concept", a concept that can no longer be, and never could be, included in the previous regime."[11] Derrida offers the word differance as an example of a non- metaphysical concept. Derrida argues:

> Not only is there no kingdom of differance, but differance instigates the subversion of every kingdom, which makes it obviously threatening and infallibly dreaded by everything within us that desires a kingdom, the past or future presence of a kingdom.[12]

A metaphysical ethic that has emerged from a restricted economy, has sought to justify itself from an Archimedean point. Throughout the history of philosophy, the Archimedean point has received various names, i.e. The Forms, The Good (Plato) Arete (Aristotle), the Categorical Imperative (Kant). These Archimedean theories have sketched a restricted metaphysical picture of what it means to be human, and ethical, while outlining what kind of existence is essentially good or virtuous for the human individual. The Archimedean ethic rests on a conception of the human individual as a rational agent who must act within the limits of reason alone. Anything outside of these restricted limits, is immediately labeled as amoral or unethical.

Restricted economies reduce everything to one fixed center, or to what Derrida calls a fixed point of presence. Derrida argues:

---

[10] Jacques Derrida, *Positions*, transl. by Alan Bass, Chicago: University of Chicago Press, 1984, p. 41.
[11] Ibid., p. 42.
[12] Jacques Derrida. *Margins*, transl. by Alan Bass, Chicago: University of Chicago Press, 1982, p. 22.

> The function of this center was not only to orientate, balance and organize the structure – but above all to make sure that the organizing principle of the structure would limit what we might call the play of the structure.[13]

The center provided stability and unity at the expense of arresting the proliferation of differences. Derrida argues that the history of philosophy may be read as the domination of stabilizing centers such as Truth, Being.. A restricted metaphysical economy prevents the proliferation of differences in order to insure itself against loss or instability.

Derrida makes it clear that the deconstruction of a restricted metaphysical economy does not lead to nihilism:

> What survives deconstruction should have new forms. It couldn't be a new system for instance, because the idea of system is one of the targets of deconstruction... But the fact that this form, this structure, has been deconstructed doesn't mean that after deconstruction (if there is such a thing as 'after deconstruction') we will have nothing or chaos. We are in the process of deconstruction and there are new things and things which fall apart... it is not a new order but it is a permanent process of disordering order.[14]

The deconstruction of Metaphysics, is an ethical task which facilitates "the necessity for a change of terrain."[15] By focusing on the debate between Gadamerian Hermeneutics and Derridean Deconstruction, we will be in a position to explore the landscape of this new terrain.

2. Postmodern Charity and The Undecidable: Gadamer and Derrida

In the analytic and hermeneutic traditions, the concept of charity refers to the stance adopted by the interpreter or critic. Charity as a basis for interpretation would ask the question "How does a critic comprehend, interpret or welcome a text"? Within a postmodern

---

[13] Jacques Derrida, *Writing and Difference*, transl. by Alan Bass, Chicago: University of Chicago Press, 1978, p. 99.
[14] Lisa Appignanesi (ed.), *Postmodernism ICA Documents*, London: Free Association Books 1989, p. 223.
[15] Jacques Derrida, *Margins*, op.cit., p.135.

framework, charity forces use to ask, "How do we welcome a friend or stranger into our economy.[16] Derrida would argue that the analytic and hermeneutic traditions operate according to a restricted economy; that is to say, they have called for a denial of Otherness. A restricted economy in Derrida's words, "intends to know and to master its margins".[17] A restricted economy "watches over its margins as virgin, homogeneous, and negative space, leaving its outside, outside".[18]

For proponents of the analytic and hermeneutic traditions, charity, in principle, represents the quest for legitimacy and validity. But the word charity, betrays the hermeneutic / analytic quest. Charity is a cognate of the Latin caritas, suggesting dearness, costliness, high price (the cost of a gift), and carus, dear, valued, esteemed, beloved. The concept of charity is also affiliated with the Sanskrit word kama (love), the Slavic kamata, suggesting a place of exchange, or being indebted to the Other. Ironically, charity construed in the light of its etymology, resonates with significations of illegitimacy instead of the legitimacy and security of a fused hermeneutic horizon. Charity reflects both a giving and taking; an open-heartedness and cold-heartedness. In Derridean terminology, the word charity is an undecidable.[19] In other words, it cannot be comprehended solely on the basis of its oppositions.

---

[16] The postmodern charity being articulated here shares an affinity with the concept of potlach. Leslie Armour points out that the Haida and Kwakiutl Indians in British Columbia "centered their concept of property around the concept of the potlach. If one wanted to hold a public office or take on a new name, one had to organize a potlach at which one gave away property.... property was thus something whose power centered on its being given away." ("The Metaphysics of Community", unpublished manuscript). The concept of potlach embraces another logic, whereby one gains by losing. I would argue that economically the concept of potlach can be interpreted as the giving away of property, ethically, potlach exhibits generosity toward the other. For a detailed analysis see Georges Bataille, *The Accursed Share,* New York: Zone Books, 1988, pp. 63-77.

[17] Jacques Derrida, *Margins*, op.cit., p. XXIV.

[18] Jacques Derrida, *Margins*, op.cit., p. XXVII.

[19] Other undecidables would include, *differance*, which means both to differ and to defer; *pharmakon*, which means both poison and remedy, and *supplement*, which means both addition and substitute. For a detailed exposition see Jacques Derrida, "Differance", in *Margins, op.cit.*, idem, "Plato's Pharmacy" in *Dissemination* and idem, "Nature, Culture, Writing", in *Of Grammatology*, op.cit.

A postmodern charity, does not give the Other gifts from a restricted reserve, from which there will be "some return, redemption or gain".20 A postmodern charity is not calculated in advance, like a modern business plan or forecast. A postmodern charity forsakes profit and is "owed to the Other before any contract".[21] The Derridean understanding of charity implements a shift to undecidability. It accepts the imperative of decision-making, but immediately submits every decision to the risk of deborderment.

Derrida, in developing a postmodern approach to charity, asserts a minimum of three distinct meanings for undecidablity. In Dissemination, Derrida notes that initially he used the term undecidability as "that which resist binarity or even triplicity. For the later Derrida, this determination of undecidability was "too anti-dialectical, hence too dialectical". Undecidability is used, in his subsequent work to mark "within the order of the calculable, the limits of decidability, of calculability or of formalizable completeness". Derrida also uses undecidablity in a sense that remains heterogeneous both to the dialectic and to the calculable; a sense that expresses a more lively interplay of the rival perspectives of Heraclitus' flux and Parmenides' unity. This sense of undecidability is crucial for decision making:

It opens the field of decision or of decideability. It calls for decision in the order of ethical-political responsibility. It is even its necessary condition... There can be no more or political responsibility without this trial and this passage way of the undecidable.[22]

Hermeneutic strategies for containing undecidability, in Derrida's view, shelter us from options that might otherwise appear. Hermeneuts, marked by an excessive fear of incomprehensibility, choose to take a protected passage through the undecidable. This guardedness invoked by hermeneutic questioning is not, in Derrida's view, a prerequisite for making choices. There is no requirement to guarantee truth. Decisions, at least by those with a higher tolerance for uncertainty, can be made in the face of a set of equally compelling al-

---

[20] Jacques Derrida, *Spurs: Nietzsche's Styles*, transl. by Barbara Harlow, Chicago: University of Chicago Press, 1979, p.111.

[21] Jacques Derrida, "Force of Law," *Cardozo Law Review*, Volume II, 1990, p. 965.

[22] Ibid., p. 961.

ternatives. Crossing interpretative horizons, and introducing new perspectives, increase both the difficulty and freedom involved in decision making. In giving decision makers more options and no independent basis for ultimately selecting from these options, the Derridean decision calls for "an increase in responsibility".[23]

An ethics of community recognizes a necessary level of calculability or programmability in generating options but places greater responsibility on the individual decision maker in choosing. To cite Derrida:

> In short, for a decision to be just and responsible it must... be both regulated and without regulation... Each case is other, each decision is different and requires an absolute unique interpretation, which no existing, coded rule can or ought to guarantee absolutely.[24]

A hermeneutic text can only be analyzed alongside a limited set of alternatives. Positions which depart too far from the story that the tradition tells or positions which simply fail to cohere with the hermeneutic horizon are excluded from consideration. The hermeneutic and analytical thinker can always seek refuge in the posited unity and certainty of the tradition or system.

Derrida's notion of dissemination, in contrast, invokes a shifting or crossing of interpretative spaces or contexts (as opposed to no contexts). In Derrida's words: The undecidable is not merely the oscillation or tension between two decisions, it is the experience of that which, through heterogeneous, foreign to the order of the calculable and the rule, is still obliged- it is of this obligation that we must speak- to give itself up to the impossible decision, while taking accounts of laws and rules. A decision that did not go through the ordeal of the undecidable would not be a free decision, it would only be the programmable application or unfolding of a calculable process.[25]

The result of udecideability, is a shifting interpretative topology where political, philosophical or ethical positions can no longer be protected by the exclusionary policy of a restricted economy.

Gadamers' allegations that Derrida's work is marred by wrongful confusion or incomprehensibility is, from Derrida's perspective, a

---

[23] Ibid., p. 955.
[24] Ibid., p. 961.
[25] Ibid., p. 963.

product of a lower tolerance for uncertainty and shifting boundaries. Derrida argues that the hermeneutics restricts the play of the understanding to the more familiar. Gadamerian hermeneutics is flexible enough to view its interpretative processes as a conversation in which we are played and under which "no one knows what will come out".[26] But its play is curtailed by its commitment to a constrained or internal horizon of interpretation. Hermeneutic philosophers acknowledge the value of a skeptical mind, but declare that the only worthwhile skepticism is of the engaged, internal kind. The internal skeptic accepts the demands of coherency which requires that we all work with the same pre-interpretative data, the same language or the same tradition (i.e. the same community of meaning). We cannot, in Gadamer's view disagree on the basic order or horizon in which all interpretation is conducted and from which all understanding is produced. To proclaim that we can exceed the limits of the interpretative horizon is to step out of our tradition, (i.e. into nihilism).

Derrida concurs with Gadamer that "no completeness is possible for undecideability."[27] The necessity and value of operating within a situation or context is never denied. In fact, Derrida accepts the proposition that hermeneutic decision making processes have value. Hermeneutic processes claim the importance of maintaining the openness of the question. Derrida purports, however, to mark out the limitations of the hermeneutic techniques. In the appropriate contexts, these philosophical techniques continue to play a role in a variety of decision-making structures. By claiming, however, to extend these processes to all levels of decision making, hermeneutics arrests the necessary recoiling[28] movement of the undecidable.

For Gadamer, a hermeneutic "discipline of questioning and research... guarantees truth."[29] For the analytic thinker, the regulative principle of a restricted charity ensures understanding. Derrida however offers no reassurance. For the postmodern economist, understand-

---

[26] Hans-Georg Gadamer, *Truth and Method*, transl. by G. Barden and J. Cumming New York: Seabury, 1975, p.345.
[27] Ibid., p.115.
[28] See Charles E. Scott, *The Question of Ethics, Nietzsche, Foucault, Heidegger*, Indianapolis: Indiana University Press, 1990.
[29] Hans-Georg Gadamer, op.cit., p. 447.

ing, like the currency of a vibrant political community, is produced by a variety of competing internal and external economic activities, rather than backed by a reductive internal gold standard. Within a postmodern economy, one is indebted to the institution of the Other. As the narrator of the Postcard tells us:

> I am founding an entire institution on counterfeit money by demonstrating that there is no other kind. There is only one good institution, my love, it is us.[30]

Merely adhering to the insular limits, of the techniques of hermeneutic and analytic thinkers, arrests the undecidable. Each of these schools of thought places greater emphasis upon obtaining the best fit with the tradition or the prevailing paradigm, rather than cultivating vital questioning. The deference to the demands of compatibility, violently excludes other world views and reduces the "liberty of the question."[31] The liberty of the question, involves an interplay between self and Other.[32] How we question and how we respond reflects the tolerance we show toward the Other. Our response towards any question can take the form of "yes" or "no". As Derrida points out:

> One always has, one always must have, the right not to respond, and this liberty belongs to responsibility itself, that is, to the liberty that one believes must be associated with it. One must always be free not to respond to an appeal or to an invitation- and it is worth remembering this, to remind oneself of the essence of this liberty.[33]

---

[30] Jacques Derrida, *The Postcard,* transl. by Alan Bass, Chicago: University of Chicago Press, 1987, p.178
[31] Jacques Derrida, *Writing and Difference*, op. cit., p. 80.
[32] Leslie Armour asks "For how does one reach into the possibilities of individuality and come out with a particular life ? One chooses. But how? By seizing the opportunities which one conceptualizes. But that in turn is done through language, and language again requires a community to nurture and shape it... I speak and you respond." The Metaphysics of Community", unpublished manuscript. (my emphasis). In "Derrida and the Ethics of Dialogue" (*Philosophy and Social Criticism*, 19:1, p.4), Richard Kearney develops a similar argument, he writes, "For an ethical subject to respond, an ethical other must first have addressed the subject in a language the subject can hear and (at least minimally) understand".
[33] Jacques Derrida, "Passions: An Oblique Offering" in David Wood (ed.), *Derrida: a critical reader*, Oxford: Blackwell Publishers, 1992, p. 15.

Derrida argues that choices and decisions must be made, but they cannot be defended by recourse to hermeneutic and analytic conceptions of truth and charity. The postmodern economist is prepared to work with rival interpretative frames, without the assistance of a comprehensive coordinate system. The instability of undecideability produced by the crossing of contexts is valuable. This destablizing approach, according to Derrida, "should never lead either to relativism or any sort of indeterminism."[34] As Derrida argues in Limited Inc.:

> To be sure, in order for structures of undecidability to be possible (and hence structures of decision and of responsibilities as well) there must be a certain play, difference... Difference is not indeterminacy. It renders determinacy both possible and necessary.[35]

Deconstruction deploys the classical exegetical methods in order to open a reading, rather than shield that same reading from further development.

Derrida contends that indecision is a product of rival semantic, ethical and political paradigms or determined poles which are "on occasion terribly necessary" and "always irreplaceably singular".[36] Far from being nihilistic, "undecideability is always a determinate oscillation between possibilities" which are "themselves highly determined in strictly defined situations (for example... political, ethical, etc). They are pragmatically determined."[37]

The cultivation of the undecidable is not for everyone in a community to practice. Personal tolerance for uncertainty varies considerably within any political structure. For those with a limited tolerance for shifting boundaries, the protection afforded by secure objective rule structures is beneficial. Those who emerge as leaders in a community are those who have a higher tolerance for uncertainty, they must have the freedom and ability to resist the leveling forces of dominant conceptual schemes. These individuals, in Derrida's view, must be able to work the limits of divergent conceptual schemes, to integrate rival conceptual schemes with existing political structures, to regulate re-

---

[34] Jacques Derrida, *Limited Inc.*, p. 148.
[35] Ibid., p.149.
[36] Ibid., p.148.
[37] Ibid., p.149.

sulting non-coherencies, and in the process, to maintain a tension between the competing demands of comprehensibility and undecidability. There is no easy way of expressing this postmodern posture towards an ethics of community. It calls for a much more rigorous and multi-faceted charity. That there is no thematic unity to resolve rival interpretations, places greater responsibility on the decision-maker. In the next section, I want to examine what type of community could emerge from the results of our investigation.

3. Postmodern Justice and the Prayer of the Other

The injustice of a restricted economy is both passive and active. It is passive, insofar as it oppresses the Other with certain codes and imperatives. It is active to the extent that it uses force to enforce any violation of the code. In The Use of Pleasure, Foucault writes that with code orientated moralities:"the important thing is to focus on the instance of authority that enforce the code, that require it to be learned and observed, that penalize infractions."[38] An ethics that takes its position from the codes of metaphysics has placed its trust in the principle of reason. This blind trust is connected to the violence and repression that metaphysical authority exerts and exhibits. An ethics which is reduced to the observance of codes cannot respond responsibly to the call of the Other.

Justice within a restricted economy is reduced to the violence of the law which is imposed as a safeguard against the Other. As Derrida argues, "justice as law is not justice".[39] Justice is to be found in a general economy which is beyond mere calculation. As Derrida argues: "Law is not justice. Law is the element of calculation... but justice is incalculable, it requires us to calculate with the incalculable."[40] Within a restricted economy, justice "will have been buried and repressed.[41] The

---

[38] Michel Foucault, *The Use of Pleasure*, transl. by Robert Hurley, New York: Vintage Books, 1985, p. 29.
[39] Jacques Derrida, "Force of Law," op. cit., p. 939.
[40] Ibid., p. 947.
[41] Ibid., p. 963.

deconstruction of a restricted economy provides a "maximum intensification of a transformation in progress."[42]

In "Force of Law", Derrida maintains that deconstruction corresponds "to a double-movement".[43] In very Kierkegaardian language, Derrida describes how deconstruction "operates on the basis of an infinite idea of justice,"[44] which is beyond calculation. This deconstructive justice is "owed to the Other before any contract."[45] Deconstructive justice annuls the restricted phenomena of injustice that has oppressed, marginalized and excluded the Other.

A deconstructive justice exposes the violence inherent in all restricted economies. Within a restricted economy, a metaphysical blanket protected dominant forces, while systematically smothering and threatening Otherness. To borrow Lyotard's insights, a restricted economy has embraced a metaphysical meta-narrative and has formulated laws in order to suppress Otherness46. In short, a restricted economy employs a resistance to Otherness, whose final aim is the total elimination of Otherness.

Deconstructive justice consists of a double-movement. The first movement consists of "responsibility before the very concept of responsibility."[47] In this movement, deconstructive justice calls for an increase in responsibility. In Kierkegaardian terminology, this first movement suspends the merely ethical sphere. This first movement goes beyond all calculable systems of restricted and coded prescriptions. The second movement of deconstructive justice embraces "a sense of responsibility without limit."[48] This second movement is attuned to the call of the Other. Situated in between these two movements is an ever present anxiety. Derrida argues:

---

[42] Ibid., p. 935.
[43] Ibid., p. 953.
[44] Ibid., p.965.
[45] Ibid., p. 965.
[46] See Jean-François Lyotard, *The Differend*, transl. by George Van Den Abbede, Minneapolis: Univeristy of Minnesota Press, 1988, and idem, *The Postmodern Condition*, transl. by Geoff Bennington, Minneapolis: University of Minnesota Press, 1983.
[47] Jacques Derrida, "Force of Law," p. 955.
[48] Ibid., p. 953.

This moment of suspense, this period of epoché, without which, in fact, deconstruction is not possible is always full of anxiety... (But) ... this anxiety ridden moment of suspense is also the interval or space in which transformations take place.[49]

Following Kierkegaard, Derrida argues that deconstructive justice addresses itself with responsibility to the single individual. Deconstructive justice "always addresses itself to singularity, to the singularity of the Other."[50] Deconstructive justice is an affirmation of the value of the Other.

Derrida's meditation on the call of the Other intersects with Heidegger's thinking concerning the call of Being and Levinas' reflections on the face of the Other.[51] Throughout his dialogue with Heidegger, Derrida asks, if Being gives or sends itself, what mechanisms or routing systems are in place, so that Dasein can hear the call? Derrida argues that there cannot be a direct line to Being. It would be impossible to calculate the trajectory of such a call. In describing the call of Being, Heidegger writes:

The call does not require us to search gropingly for him to whom it appeals... the call undoubtedly does not come from someone else who is with me in the world.[52]

Heidegger's emphasis on the call of Being short circuits the call of the Other, and thus closes off the possibility for ethics. In *Of Grammatology*, Derrida makes it clear that "there is no ethics without the presence of the Other."[53]

In Derrida's postmodern general economy, "one answers (responds) first to the Other: to the request, the prayer...the appeal."[54] The appeal

---

[49] Ibid., pp. 955, 957.
[50] Ibid., p. 955.
[51] See, Emmanuel Levinas, *Totality and Infinity*, transl. by Alphonso Lingis, Pittsburgh: Duquesne University Press, 1983.
[52] Martin Heidegger, *Being and Time*, transl. by John Macquarrie and Edward Robinson, New York: Harper and Row 1962, pp. 318, 319, 320. See also Avital Ronnell, *The Telephone Book*, Lincoln: University of Nebraska Press,1989.
[53] Jacques Derrida, *Of Grammatology*, transl. by Gayatri C. Spivak, Baltimore: John Hopkins Press, 1976, pp. 140-141.
[54] Jacques Derrida "The Politics of Friendship" *The Journal of Philosophy*, Volume 85, Number 11, p. 639.

comes from the Other, and is "assigned to us by the Other."[55] What is at stake here, is not responding to the Other because of the duty imposed by a metaphysical theory. We should respond to the Other, because we recognize our own vulnerability through the Other.

Through its restrictions and prescriptions, a metaphysical ethic, helped to perpetuate the exclusion of the Other. The Other to borrow Levinasian insights is the widow, the stranger and the orphan, the marginalized and the excluded.

The call of the Other is a prayer which is addressed to me. The prayer of the Other draws me out of my own selfish concerns. A prayer may also be called a petition. To pray is also to invite. The prayer of the Other is an invitation which calls one to make an expenditure without fear of loss.[56]

If there is to be a metaphysics within a postmodern community, then ethics must be the basis of metaphysics. In other words, we should not ask "what the final form of community is." The question to ask is "what institutional structures will allow people to both reinvent community and to continually postpone the question of the community's 'final form'."[57]

An ethics of community begins with what has been excluded. It moves beyond the barriers of a restricted economy in order to recover community from the crisis of its enclosure.

---

[55] Ibid., p. 634.

[56] The invitation of the other which calls one to make an expenditure without fear of loss shares an affinity with the concept of potlach. Leslie Armour writes: "But to a Kwakiutl or a Haida, property was not just a collection of blankets, fish oil and coppers. It was essentially a social bond, and in giving it away one showed exactly how one was bound to the recipients. In showing that one could give it away, one validated one's social position by showing that one could care well for the community. The Haida could certainly see the bundles of blankets and the buckets of oil. But to him the community was as real as its members and to give was not to part with the goods but to bring the community to tangible life. The community was seen through its members" ("The Metaphysics of Community", Notes for March 14/1994, p. 16).

[57] Bill Martin, *Matrix and Line*, op.cit., p.180.

14

Susanne Moser

THE IMPORTANCE OF VALUES FOR SOCIAL AND POLITICAL INTEGRATION OF EUROPE

Social cohesion is vital to every society, yet our era is increasingly challenged by growing inequalities and social fragmentation. This holds true for Europe as well as for the United States. As the gap between rich and poor widens, so does the gap between cultures. In the United States, Christians have launched a renewed attack against abortion, homosexuality and the separation of church and state. In Europe generous social welfare systems and labor standards, already under strain from an aging population, may wilt further from exposure to the winds of globalization. And, as the European Union continues to admit new member states, it must now contend with greater wealth disparities, more baffling cultural differences and more varied types of taxation and welfare.

In this paper I will focus on the recent debate that has been taking place within the Frankfurt School, and its shift away from a value-neutral position to a position focusing on values and recognition. Axel Honneth, who can be seen as the third representative of the Frankfurt School after Adorno, Horkheimer, and Habermas, points out that it would be wrong to speak, as Habermas or Luhmann does, of capitalism as a system of economic procedures free from inherent norms and values. Not only capitalism, but our modern democratic system itself is based on fundamental values that have led historically to a long and profound transformation of society. In *The Struggle for Recognition* Honneth shows that a long struggle for recognition was necessary to realize the fundamental values of modern democracies.[1] But what are these fundamental values? In the eighteenth cen-

---

[1] Axel Honneth, *The Struggle for Recognition: The Moral Grammar of Social Conflicts*, Cambridge: Polity Press, 1995.

tury, the fundamental value of personal freedom was approved, at least in some countries such as England, and realized in the form of the liberal rights of freedom (also called negative rights) protecting everyone's freedom, life and property from the infringements of the rulers; in the nineteenth century the value that everyone should participate in political decisions was introduced as the positive right to voting and assemble; and, in the twentieth century the idea that everyone should have enough to eat and to live on, in order to be able to take part in political decisions, was established together with the social right of fair distribution. This fundamental change of values went hand in hand with a great shift taking place within society itself, a shift from a traditional system of rights to a post-traditional one. In a traditional society the dignity of a person derives from that person's position in society, his or her social recognition. The social role endows certain rights and duties. In post-traditional societies the dignity of a person is connected to his or her autonomy. Autonomy means following only those norms and rights that we have all agreed upon together. In post-traditional societies the system of rights must be seen as the expression of the generalized interests of all members of society, in such a way that exceptions and privileges are no longer accepted. The idea that members of society have to follow only those norms and rights they have agreed to as free and equal persons means also that they have to recognize each other as persons who are able to decide autonomously on moral and legal norms. That means that subjects in modern systems of rights recognize each other as being able to make rational decisions; in other words, they reciprocally recognize their imputability. But how to judge the imputability of a person? If we say, with Kant, that every person is an end, this does not yet say how this universal claim can be applied concretely.

In *The Struggle for Recognition* Honneth points out that it is exactly in this area of concrete applications that struggles for recognition take place. The emergence of new ideas and values does not yet mean that they are realized in general, because certain groups claim them only for themselves, excluding all others. A long historical process was necessary, in which there occurred a broadening of what could be seen as a legitimate individual legal and moral claim. To demonstrate this process Honneth refers to T. H. Marshall. Marshall points out that the big difference between traditional rights and modern rights lies in the uncoupling of individual rights form social status and social recognition. The principle of legal equality means that no exceptions and privileges are allowed any more. To be equal means to be a fully adequate member of the political community. If we look at the historical situation in the nineteenth century we find that the right to participate in political decisions was confined to a man with a certain income and property. Marshall argues that rights to political participation as well as social rights were brought into being and broadened by forces fighting for the idea that all people should be full members of a political community. What stands behind all this is the idea that everyone should be able to participate in political decisions. Therefore, every kind of exclusion should be eliminated. Poverty, not having enough material resources to be able to participate in political decisions, has to be overcome too. Thus, social rights are necessary to guarantee that everyone can be an adequate person in the community. Marshall summarizes his historical overview with the following thesis: "The urge forward along the path thus plotted is an urge towards a fuller measure of equality, an enrichment of the stuff of which the status is made and an increase in the number of those on whom the status is bestowed."[2]

Honneth argues that people suffer from the experience of misrecognition and disregard if they are excluded from certain rights. It is his conviction that a struggle for recognition is possible within the legal sphere. Social conflicts and struggles intend to widen the material content as well as the social reach of the status of a legal person.[3] It is not possible to develop self-esteem if one lives without individual rights. "Having rights enables us to 'stand up like men,' to look others in the eye, and to feel in some fundamental way the equal of anyone. To think of oneself as the holder of rights is not to be unduly but properly proud, to have that minimal self-respect that is necessary to be worthy of the love and esteem of others. Indeed, respect for persons may simply be respect for their rights, so that there can-

---

[2] Ibid., p. 118.
[3] Ibid.

not be the one without the other; and what is called 'human dignity' may simply be the recognizable capacity to assert claims."[4] Honneth uses the example of the black civil rights movement in the United States, which argued that legal recognition is a necessary prerequisite for self-respect. The same is true of the women's liberation movement and its claim for equal rights and the gay rights movement fighting for the right to free sexual orientation and for equal rights concerning same-sex partnership.

When we look at a statement of the European Commission, that "through modernisation, we will preserve our values," we can understand this statement as an invitation to think over and work over our fundamental values in order to maintain them. As the example of the fundamental value of legal equality has shown us, it was a historical process of modernization that led to the transformation of large parts of society. Women and black people are no longer excluded from political participation and many countries of the European Union have accepted same-sex partnerships.

At the very moment that the fundamental value of equality seems to be realized in the legal sphere, inequality rises in the socio-economic sphere. In *Redistribution or Recognition?*, his discussion with Nancy Fraser, Honneth points out that it is not enough to call for redistribution, but to look for the reasons that make redistribution necessary. It is due to certain values that material distribution functions. Capitalist society, according to Honneth, was organized from its beginning in a very hierarchical way, one with an undoubtedly ideological character: what was valorized as personal achievement, as work, was valorized according to a system of values focused on the male citizen. What was called "work" was in fact the consequence of a group-specific value setting, excluding all those activities that were necessary to reproduce society such as housework, child-rearing, taking care of old people and so on. For Honneth, the social order of contemporary capitalist societies contains material repressions in the way that its ideological structure valorizes types of activity and work and determines the resources people gain for their individual lives–and this of course not only in the case of gender but

---

[4] Joel Feinberg, "The Nature and Value of Rights," cited in Honneth, op. cit., p. 120.

also in the case of race, ethnicity, class and so on. The institutional framework that valorizes activities and work is not value-neutral, but the consequence of a process in which certain groups have asserted their interests. To understand this better, Honneth contrasts the modern capitalist system and social order with traditional social orders such as feudalism or other premodern societies in which rights were directly derived from the honor or status a person had in this society. Legal respect and social recognition were directly linked. The social hierarchy determined not only social recognition, but also the subjective legal rights of a person. In post-traditional societies, such as modern democracies, legal recognition "splits off from the hierarchical value order insofar as the individual was in principle to enjoy legal equality vis-à-vis all others."[5] This, according to Honneth, led to a revolution in the moral order of society: every single individual should now be respected by all other members of society as having equal rights. At the same time a new hierarchical order of social values was established: social recognition was no longer bound to descent but to personal achievement. For Honneth this new social order contained from the beginning elements of material violence. What is judged and valorized as achievement decides what resources people get to live on. Thus, a new status hierarchy comes into being containing all those capitalist values that determine the hierarchy of social recognition and the distribution of resources. For Honneth this all shows that it is important to take into account the cultural values that flow through the principle of achievement and competition into the institutional constitution of the economic sphere.[6] He points out the suffering people are drawn into by referring to Pierre Bourdieu's study *The Weight of the World*: "the 'feminizing' of poverty, which primarily affects single mothers with limited job qualifications; long-term unemployment, which goes along with social isolation and private disintegration; the depressing experience of the rapid disqualification of job skills that had enjoyed high esteem at the start of a ca-

---

[5] Nancy Fraser and Axel Honneth, *Redistribution or Recognition? A Political-Philosophical Exchange*, trans. Joel Golb and Christiane Wilke, London: Verso, 2003, p. 140.
[6] Ibid..

reer ...; the immiseration of the rural economy ...; and finally, the everyday privations of large families."[7] Besides this, Bourdieu regrets that the category of the social now has the image of being antiquated and thus nobody wants to speak about it.

Neither Bourdieu nor Honneth mentions the situation in Easten Europe. Thus, it would be interesting to apply their studies to the transformation process that has been taking place for the past fifteen years in Eastern Europe. I think that here we will find the same phenomenon Honneth and Bourdieu are talking about: if social problems reach a level where they attain public attention, they become part of those social movements that deal with conflicts arising around claims for cultural recognition. These so-called "identity politics" follow the interests of groups seeking recognition for their claims, mostly ethnic groups, women or homosexuals. "The 'new social movements' idea is, however, problematic and obscures the greater significance of identity politics. Without much theoretical rationale, it groups together what seem to the researchers relatively 'attractive' movements, vaguely on the left, but leaves out such other contemporary movements as the new religious right and fundamentalism, the resistance of white ethnic communities against people of color, various versions of nationalism, and so forth. Yet these are equally manifestations of 'identity politics' and there is no principle that clearly explains their exclusion from the lists drawn up by NSM theorists."[8] Honneth rejects the assumption that a critical theory should be orientated normatively by social movements. This would mean narrowing the whole spectrum of social unease and suffering to those social movements that have succeeded in obtaining attention. Social unease and suffering have for Honneth a normative core: they contain the experience that something unjust has been done by society. The procedural model that Jürgen Habermas presents is not sufficient for Honneth: it would require new categories in order to adopt the normative point of view from which subjects judge and valorize their social order. Basic notions and values should be orientated on a theo-

---

[7] Ibid., pp. 118-119.
[8] Craig Calhoun, *Social Theory and the Politics of Identity*, Oxford: Blackwell, 1994, cited in Fraser and Honneth, op. cit., p. 121.

ry of recognition, where the denial of social recognition, the phenomenon of humiliation and disregard form the core of all experiences of injustice.

This is not the place to discuss the difficulties in which Honneth gets involved by trying to find new categories for measuring the unease and suffering of people and the strategies it would need to reverse the increasing deterioration taking place across the whole of Europe, but I think that he poses questions that are of immense importance to the future of the European Union–above all, the question of which values we want to realize in the future. In an article titled "The Revolt of the Superfluous," Ulrich Beck recently posed the question: What happens to all those who are excluded from the brave new world of globalization? The new globalized rich don't need the poor any more, in order to get rich. They are simply superfluous, useless and this is something that happens not only in Africa but in the heart of Europe.

Jürgen Habermas sees a way out of this threatening scenario in a strong European Union with its own constitution. In his June 2001 article in *Die Zeit* he makes it clear that the Maastricht intergovernmental agreement is not strong enough to create the power for a consolidation that only "a political act of foundation" can bring. A strong Europe is needed to defend its culture and way of life, threatened more and more by a neoliberal paradigm that does not fit into the normative self-understanding of the European people. For Habermas the neoliberal paradigm is characterized, first, by the anthropological idea of man as a rational entrepreneur, who deploys his own capacity for work; second, by the social and moral idea of a postegalitarian society that accepts marginalization and exclusions; third, by the economic idea of a democracy that reduces citizens to members of a market society and the state to a public services enterprise for clients and customers; and fourth, by the strategic belief that the best politics are those that are carried out by themselves, automatically. In his article "Remarks on Dieter Grimm's 'Does Europe Need a Constitution?'" he sees the greatest danger as coming from global networks and markets contributing more and more to the fragmentation of public consciousness.⁹ If these systemic networks don't get strong political institutions on their side, it could lead to a paralyzing fatalism and to mistrust of political consciousness and action. The postindustrial misery of those who are superfluous–the Third World in the First World–would lead to the moral erosion of the whole community. Only a strong Europe can handle this threat and is powerful enough to develop new visions. Economic reasons are not sufficient to motivate people; this needs, as Habermas says, orientation on common values. The disapproving attitude of the population toward the European Union can only be surmounted, if the European project is no longer a project only for experts, but a project discussed in a broad political arena. For this it would be necessary to create a European civil society, to construct a European public sphere and to create a political culture that all Europeans share.

But what are these common values that could motivate people to engage in a strong Europe? How should the social integration of Europe take place? What are those common values Habermas speaks of? These questions are not so easy to answer, because Habermas modifies his position concerning values over the course of his work. In *Between Facts and Norms* he defines values as intersubjectively shared subjective preferences, but in his later work he distinguishes values from preferences: What is valuable and authentic for us is imposed on us and must be distinguished from bare preferences by a binding quality that transcends the subjectivity of needs and preferences. It is the feeling of being moved by and attracted to something that characterizes the experience of values.¹⁰ But what are we moved by? In *The Theory of Communicative Action* he argues that social integration that is no longer guaranteed by a sacral ritual praxis can be achieved by communicative action. The authority of the sacral is replaced by rational consensus. The banishing power of the sacral is transformed into the binding power of norms that can be criticized. This almost utopian and optimistic position is retracted by him in his later works. The assumption that religious world-views can be re-

---

[9] Jürgen Habermas, "Remarks on Dieter Grimm's 'Does Europe Need a Constitution?'" *European Law Journal*, 1, Nov. 1995, pp. 303-307.
[10] Jürgen Habermas, *Between Facts and Norms*, Oxford: Blackwell, 1997.

placed by an universalist ethics of responsibility subsides into the realization that argumentative consensus contains only a weak power of rational motivation. Because of its weak motivation this morality needs to be supplemented by law, which has the power to compel. Law is obligatory, universal and intersubjective.[11]

From 1988 on, Habermas distinguishes between the pragmatic, the ethical and the moral use of practical reason. Pragmatic questions arise from the point of view of someone who looks for the best means to reach certain ends and preferences. The actor acts rationally, if he acts in accordance with certain reasons and knows about this. Ethical questions arise from the perspective of members of a certain community, who want to make clear which way of life they want to share and which ideals and values they want to guide their lives. Ethical questions are placed around a common ethos: it is important to know how we should understand each other, how we shall live our lives, how to orientate in the community, and how to know what is the best for our lives with respect to the intersubjectively shared tradition we inhabit. The attractiveness of values is not something we can choose easily, as we can do with preferences and ends. Habermas warns us not to mix up values and interests. Conflicts arising from different interests can be solved through compromise. Ethical conflicts arising around different values cannot be solved in the same way. This would hurt the identities of those expressing their way of life and self-understanding through these values. Relations of values can be changed only by discourses about the self-understanding of people, not on the way of finding a compromise. Fundamental values, which are constitutive for the identity and thus for the self-understanding of the members, are not negotiable. The mixing up of fundamental values and interests is a grave mistake, Habermas points out. What enters into the definition of identity is not subject to compromise. Infringements of this kind would be an attack against human dignity and thus would be not permissible for legal reasons.

In moral questions it is the normative perspective from which we examine how our living together is regulated in the common interest

---

[11] Jürgen Habermas, *The Theory of Communicative Action*, Oxford: Blackwell, 1989.

of all. A person assumes a moral perspective when he or she acts like a democratic legislator and checks if the praxis that would follow from a hypothetic norm could be accepted by all other co-legislators. From the moral point of view all the ends, preferences and values are brought under examination. Thus, Habermas distinguishes between moral questions, dealing with problems of justice, and ethical questions concerning self-understanding. Questions of justice look for norms that are good *for all* in the same way, whereas questions of self-understanding deal with who we are: with our identity. The latter contains values in which we express what would be a good life *for us*. In both cases, we maintain a distance from current praxis, but from the ethical standpoint the distance we maintain need not be as great as it has to be when we assume the moral standpoint. Dealing with ethical questions we remain within our cultural horizon. When we answer moral questions we have to decide in a broader horizon, one including those who do not belong to our social and cultural environment, to consider those who are foreigners separated by geographical, historical, cultural or social distances. Habermas assumes that it is possible to come to a decision that is good for all. Discourse opens up a wider horizon in which it should be possible to find a solution that is accepted by all, without being forced to solve the conflicts of values on the ethical level.

Habermas is deeply skeptical about the contribution of values to the social integration of modern societies. Universalist morality and, where this is too weak, modern law, is for Habermas the best way of integrating modern societies. He thinks that law is very well suited for the social integration of economic societies, because it refers to the actions of individuals pursuing their special interests. But law also has to consider the needs for a social integration that is realized best by a communicative process guaranteed by the liberal and political rights of citizens. In *The Genealogy of Values*, Hans Joas criticizes Habermas for arguing that a moral community is constituted *only* by the negative idea of doing away with discrimination and suffering and by inclusion of the marginalized into a reciprocal consideration.[12] Habermas, however, would still have another approach

---

[12] Hans Joas, *The Genealogy of Values*, Chicago IL: Chicago University Press, 2001.

to morality and law. In *Between Facts and Norms* he speaks about morality and law as guarantees in case of the failure of the socially integrative efforts of all other institutions. This lets us know that morality and law should not stand in the foreground of social action. Of course, Joas admits it would not be possible to rely only on integration by common values, and of course these bonds always have to be corrected due to the universal claim of the normative, but it is important to see that we need the reproduction of values as much as we need the procedural rationality of rights. The reproduction of values is not automatically guaranteed by relying on the weak motivation of rational consensus and the legitimating effect of civic freedom. Social solidarity can be regenerated in the forms of communicative practices, but not only in them.

Thus far in the discussion we have seen that Honneth and Habermas take quite different positions concerning the importance of values for the social and political integration of Europe. Habermas sees the importance of values for the self-understanding and identity of people but is skeptical about their contribution to social and political integration. Honneth, on the other hand, points out that we have to do with values on all levels: even the modern democratic system itself is based on fundamental values that have historically been modified and modernized in the way we have already seen. And the capitalist system itself is not as value-neutral as people want to make us believe.

After all, what can we say about the importance of values for the social and political integration of Europe? Why should people feel motivated to vote for a European constitution? If we look at the great majority of the European population we find most people occupied with questions concerning their way of living, how can they lead a good life? Will Europe bring them a better life? Most are fearful about their future standard of living, most feel that things are getting worse. We can classify all of these under what Habermas calls "ethical questions," because ethical questions deal with the identity and self-understanding of people and, as we have learned, this category of the ethical, dealing with values, must not be mixed up with the category of the pragmatic, dealing with interests. While people in the economic field are mostly motivated by their interests, social and political integration needs more than a compromise on interests. Social and political integration touches the level of identity and values. As Habermas says, love or recognition cannot be exchanged for money, one's mother tongue or religious confession cannot be exchanged for job positions. It needs a common self-understanding, a self-understanding that can be found only in "discourses of self-understanding," as Habermas calls them. Is it enough to create a European civil society, to construct a public sphere and to create a political culture, as Habermas instructed us, to overcome the disapproving attitude of the population towards the European Union? What does Europe stand for? Is it the neoliberal paradigm that will get the upper hand, as many people fear, or is it on the contrary the European Union that can save us from this threatening scenario, as Habermas believes? It is up to the European people to make up their minds which values they want to guide their lives. The great majority of the European population does not even know on which fundamental values the European Union is based or should be based in the new constitution. Until now, the European Union has failed to open a discussion about values. People in France and the Netherlands have rejected the European Constitution, afraid that the European Union would realize the neoliberal paradigm. If we look at the latest European Social Survey we learn that only two out five people in Austria, that is, less than half, are content with how democracy functions in Austria, and in the Czech Republic, Italy and Poland the number is even lower. Far from being proud of what has been attained, far from being aware of the fact that modern democracies are based on the participation of all of us, people feel more and more powerless and helpless. And as concerns the belief in the democratic structures of the European Union, the situation is even worse than on the national level. What is needed now is a Europe-wide discussion on what we want the European Union to be for all of us and of what visions we have about the future of the European Union. Values play a crucial role in this process as they influence our identity and self-understanding and, thus, are essential for the social and political integration of Europe.

15

Yvanka B. Raynova

THE EUROPEAN VALUES – A "DICTATORSHIP" OR A CHANCE FOR UNION?

"Today, no one who is anybody speaks of 'good' and 'bad.' Instead, everyone speaks of values. Political parties debate values; constitutions are regarded as 'systems of values.' We supposedly live in a time of decaying values, or perhaps of changing values. Even NATO, says British Prime Minister Tony Blair, should no longer be viewed as an alliance for the common defense of territories, but as an instrument for the defense – and expansion – of common values."[1] This observation by the German philosopher Robert Spaemann is a well-formulated expression of the fact that in the recent past the discourse on values began to play a central role in the social and political life of the West and, more especially, in the European process of enlargement. It is particularly the question of whether Europe should constitute a community of values or a community of rights that then came to occupy the center of the debates. Therefore, the main proposition of my paper is to analyze these debates, to discuss their problematic points and to indicate some new possible issues.

1. The Danger of the European Discourse on Values

I wish to begin with the main arguments of the opponents to the Idea that Europe should constitute a community of values. Therefore I will present briefly the critical objections made by Robert Spaemann

---

[1] Robert Spaemann, "The Dictatorship of Values," online: http://www.iwm.at/index.php?option=com_content&task=view&id=213&Itemid=27

and Krysztof Michalski, who discussed this question already in 2001 in Transit,2 the Journal of the Institute for Human Sciences in Vienna.

In his article "Europe – A Community of Values or A Legal Order?" – abridged and translated into English as "The Dictatorship of Values" – Spaemann emphasizes that the discourse on values is *trivial and at the same time dangerous*. It is dangerous because of its ambiguity and it is trivial because we know very well that every society is based on certain common values. It is true that the common supply of all that we esteem and all that we detest shrank Western societies because of the increase in the variety of life styles and convictions or in the rise of so-called pluralism. However, according to Spaemann, even pluralist societies require some common values and value judgments, which lie at the basis of fundamental rights. This is not just a fact, but a necessity, because a radically pluralist society could never survive; there must be a legal framework in order to preserve the domestic peace of the state and the freedom of its citizens.[3]

But the danger of the discourse on Europe as a community of values emerges for Spaemann from the fact that "there is a tendency to substitute the speech of fundamental rights with the speech of fundamental values."[4] This danger is shown more concretely by the fact that a state begins to legitimize the use of violence by referring to certain "higher values" in order to proscribe something that the law on its own would not permit it to forbid. In such a case values are used as a legitimization for the transgression of the norms of law.[5] This was, e.g., the case of the Third Reich, which was a sort of value order called the *Volksgemeinschaft* (national community), wherein the state was merely the agent of different "higher values" such as Nation, Race, Health, etc., and the National Socialist Party, which was directly committed to these values, in certain circumstances gained much more power than the state and could dominate it. According Spaemann, there is actually a similar danger within the European community and, in order to illus-

---

[2] See *Transit. Europäische Revue,* 21, Sommer 2001.
[3] Robert Spaemann, "The Dictatorship of Values," op.cit.
[4] Ibid., p. 175.
[5] Ibid., p. 176.

trate this, he gives five examples from the praxis of the internal and external politics of the European Union.

A first indicator of the danger of a liberal totalitarianism is, according Spaemann, the persecution of sects. The term "sect" is usually utilized as a negative expression, designating smaller religious communities, which split off from the traditional church, especially the Christian church. But in a political sense, a sect designates a community defined by common beliefs, a strong hierarchical structure, and often having a charismatic leader at its head. Religious and political sects are characterized by strong internal bonds and discipline, as well by the "missionary" propagation of their activity. Spaemann observes that the inclusion of a community in the list of sects is at the discretion of the owners of the interpretation monopoly, that is, of the representatives of the state since all of these characteristics are very vague and, in liberal states there is no prohibition against belonging to such groups. Sects are therefore persecuted informally by discrimination against their members and leaders. "Why do many states object to sects?" Spaemann asks. And he answers: "Only when the state defines itself as a 'community of values,' comparable to an established church that excludes non-believers, do hostile official attitudes toward 'sects' become comprehensible."[6] In this way the difficult achievement of the liberal state's rule of law is abandoned because the state is conceived as a liberal community of values, which no longer represents a legal order, but a worldview (*Weltanschauung*).

A second indicator of the danger of a liberal totalitarianism for Spaemann is the deployment of state institutions in order to ostracize certain political ideas, even if they conform to the constitution. This is actually the case in Germany, where attempts have been made to prevent a public discussion of the question of immigrants; restrictive positions or an ethnic-cultural self-understanding of the nation are a taboo subject because they are associated with acts of violence against foreigners. There is no danger, according to Spaemann, when people protest against the extreme right, but there is a danger to democracy when the state itself organizes these demonstrations with the help of the President. The state as an "alliance against the Right" – that is in

---

[6] Ibid.

fact a community of values which takes the place of the state based on law, and here the alarm bells must ring.[7]

The third example given by Speamann is closely connected to the second. He emphasizes that the state can neglect its obligation to remain neutral by privatizing national institutions, in which it retains the majority share and therefore the say-so, and it can then use this position in order to discriminate against some inconvenient organs. This was the case in Germany when the German Postal Bank blocked the accounts of the weekly paper *Junge Freiheit* – a right-conservative intellectual newspaper with neither extremist leanings nor National Socialist tendencies. The attempt to strangle the newspaper, which the regime deemed politically incorrect, failed because of massive public protests. The boycott against the newspaper was in the end cancelled, but such an attempt gives enough reason to be watchful.

As a fourth example Spaemann brings to attention the sanctions imposed on Austria in the beginning of the year 2000. Refugee centers were burned in Germany, immigrants were harassed in Spain, Neo-Nazis demonstrated in Sweden, etc. Nothing of this kind happened in Austria. However, the EU decided to blacklist this country because of a lack of political correctness in the face of the so-called "European values." Fortunately in this case justice triumphed over the community of values after a re-appraisal by the "three wise men," but, as Spaemann remarks, this did not prevent the German government from continuing the proscription of its neighbor for a while.

As a fifth and final example he gives the Kosovo war. This war was led in the name of "our values." The main presupposition was that military intervention to prevent a people being expelled from their homeland is without doubt a "just war." However, the management of such a war was incompatible with existing international law – a fact which Henry Kissinger and Helmut Schmidt referred to, among other things. International law recognizes only defensive war against attacks on one's own territory or on the territory of allied states. What therefore gives cause for worry is that the new circumstances did not lead to a revision of international law to allow for the persecution of a war of aggression; the legitimizing discourse on values simply authorized

---

[7] Ibid., p. 179.

those who acted in their name to ignore the valid legal rules. Here again, one who acts in the name of the community of values stands above the law, a state of affairs that in the past was called totalitarianism.

In other words, against the Idea of Europe as a community of values, Spaemann argues that values are used in the European Union in order to legitimize different kinds of discrimination and to hoodwink existing laws. Spaemann reinforces his arguments by referring to Nietzsche's critical discourse on values. According to Nietzsche, behind all moral norms there stand some elementary valuations. But what is most important for the value-endowing subject it is finally power. Power is the highest value and people extol as values those characteristics and activities which promise to help them to gain power. Spaemann emphasizes that this is exactly what is happening now in Europe in the form of a strange dialectic between the dominating subjectivist relativism of values and the absolutist pretensions of the valuations made. On the one hand, the term "community of values" is a relativistic and voluntaristic one. It is based on the fact that the Good is something relative, e.g., on the belief that we are the community of the good ones. On the other hand, this community of values reclaims an absolute validity, but this validity is a voluntaristic one. In fact, the values of each community are set. But if values are set, then those who have power are those who set the values, and their fight for values is nothing other than a masked fight for power. Therefore, in a community of values, one must ask about the hidden interests: who benefits from a certain value order? Who is the interpreter and the trustee of the highest values? The legal order of modern states is based on value insight, e.g., on the insight of the constitutive value of internal peace and tolerance. These values were derived from the nature of the person and lie at the basis of fundamental rights. These rights, human rights, cannot have had everywhere the same development as in Europe. The right to participation in any community does not automatically include the right to participation in every community, and it cannot also have everywhere in the world the form of parliamentary elections. The Aristotelian natural right, on which Spaemann depends, is based on the insight that human nature permits very different cultural and historical developments which, however, are not arbitrary. There exist, measured by the yardstick of human self-implementation, better and worse law orders, and there is a lower limit defining what a legal order has to be. The value basis of a modern legal order, however, requires that the rights of citizens and of civil society do not depend on the value approbation of citizens, it being presupposed that they obey the laws. One must obey the legal order not because one belongs to this community of values, but because one values domestic peace, *pax illis et nobis*, as Augustine wrote. In this sense Spaemann concludes that: "The future Europe should be a legal community that accepts and protects smaller communities with their own values, but refrains from being itself a community of values."[8]

A similar position, but elaborated with the help of other arguments, has been presented by Krzystztof Michalski in his article "Politics and Values."[9]

Michalski claims that nothing which we do is morally neutral, but the moral meaning of our acts is ambiguous and there are no a clear indications of how to attain the good in this world. Politics and values are always closely connected because politics has to do with moral values, which cannot simply be reduced to material interests. Politics operates in a space of moral customs and expectations, of concepts of good and bad, of values. "Because society is defined by historically developed values, no community, no society – and this applies also to 'Europe' and to 'Austria' – can renounce the exclusion of other societies with other 'values'; only by this exclusion ... does each human community become what it is and get its specific character. Only when we are able to defend a certain way of life and its rules (our 'values') against this of others (...) do we become who we are. This is the reason for the existence of the explosive tension in the culture in which we live: modern European culture."[10]

Michalski underlines that values have a meaning only in regard to someone – they are values only for a subject. Values are set by someone, whether they are understood as "relative" or "absolute." The idea of harmony is utopian because, in a world of values which are set by

---

[8] Ibid., p. 185.
[9] Krzystztof Michalski, "Politik und Werte," *Transit. Europäische Revue*, 21, Sommer 2001, pp. 208-217.
[10] Ibid., p. 211.

someone, there can never be an identity of all subjective desires and representations, but rather a conflict between the subjects of different value systems. The task of politics today is thus "the solution of conflicts in an incurably heterogeneous human world."[11] This means, according to Michalski, that our pluralistic world needs "something other than a morality, understood as valuation; it needs a politics in the sense of the art to resolve conflicts or at least to limit them. We do not decrease the conflict and the danger of a heterogeneous world by referring to values: values do not connect, values separate."[12] This belief leads Michalski to the following conclusion: in order to solve conflicts, one must try to contemplate all values (which Michalski identifies with preferences, representations and desires) from a certain distance, instead takeoff taking a moral point of view: "Our common life must be regulated not by values, but by norms, which (...) are recognized as objective. If we grasp conflicts in moral categories, thus as value conflicts, we grasp them from the perspective of those involved (...) The value perspective on conflicts makes them still more dangerous."[13] In order to underpin this opinion, Michalski quotes Carl Schmitt's statement that the imposition of one's own values devalues the values of the opponent as non-values and operates without any respect. Michalski concludes: "Values can become regulators of social life and its conflicts only if they are changed into objective norms. Legal norms allow us to view social conflicts (...) from a distance."[14] Michalski admits that politics and legal norms need values and "live" on them, so that it would be an illusion that "we could eliminate the possibility of a dangerous conflict in this world," but he does not explain what this means exactly.

2. European Values: Between Politics, Culture and Identity

In 2004, on behalf of the Dutch Presidency, the Nexus Institute at Tilburg University in the Netherlands organized a series of interna-

---

[11] Ibid., 215.
[12] Ibid., 216.
[13] Ibid., 217.
[14] Ibid.

tional conferences on European values and their significance for our future. A few hundred prominent thinkers and decision makers participated in debates on this subject in The Hague, Warsaw, Berlin, Washington and Rotterdam. In these debates special attention was paid to building bridges between values and politics. In this second part of my paper I will present briefly some of the results and some of the arguments, expressed by the defenders of the idea that Europe should constitute a community of values and not just a political and economic alliance.

The main results or statements of the opening conference, whose theme was "The Politics of European Values," can be summed up as follows:

- Most universal values originated in Europe. European values are the product of a process spanning many centuries, in which crowning artistic and cultural achievements have alternated with extremes of injustice and violence. Bitter experience has taught Europe just how fundamental its values are. It has taken two world wars for Europe to realize that its values must indeed be shared.

- However, Europeans have not yet made up their minds about whether they are Europeans because of the past or because of the future. The EU seems less like a community sharing the same fate and more and more like a club. And the question of whether to join is no longer "why?" but "why not?."

- Values have an important part to play in the quest for a European identity, especially since many people now perceive their existence to be increasingly uncertain as a result of globalization, technological change, immigration and a changing "social contract."

- In themselves, values are pale, abstract concepts, yet they do guide our actions. Even the most technical European legislation is based on clear-cut values. These must be protected and upheld in the face of indifference, scepticism and selfishness, by making them explicit and discussing them. Such discussion need not necessarily lead to consensus: values can be disputed, as long as there is willingness to compromise and, at the very least, to agree to disagree.

- The question of what European values actually are, and how they are interrelated, can be answered in different ways, but the common thread is respect for human rights, freedom, equality and solidarity. Some speakers stated that it is not the rule of law and solidarity that make the European Union unique – these can just as well be found in Norway, Canada or Australia – but the way in which the Union has shaped transnational relations.

- The EU is the only federal structure that seeks to be a community of diversity rather than a nation – which is why the Union's neighbors do not see it as a threat. Nevertheless, the post-war principle "thou shalt compromise" has given Europe influence and moral authority. Europe does not seem sufficiently aware of its power, or at least does not do enough to wield it, despite the fact that many non-Europeans expect so much of it.
- In fact, it is this unique attribute – Europe's "soft power" – that makes it so hard for citizens of the Member States to identify with the EU. This lack of loyalty within its ranks – this reluctance on the part of citizens to "join the club" – is a serious failing.[15]

The Introductory Address was given by the Dutch Prime Minister Jan Peter Balkenende, who linked the importance of reflecting on values to the vitality and energy of the EU. Values are not possessions – they are a task, a motivation, an incentive to take action, he said. The EU is the product of Christianity, Judaism, classical antiquity, humanism and the Enlightenment, as well as of dialogue with Islamic and Arabic culture. Europe is a community of values that has been built up over many centuries – the Europe of Michelangelo and Montesquieu, but also the Europe of the guillotine and the gas chamber.

Respect for human rights and human dignity, freedom, equality and solidarity are moral, universal values that united Europeans and were anchored in their treaties. Continuing integration now offered the prospect of a Constitutional Treaty. The Constitution for Europe should be seen as an important step forward because shared constitutional values are the glue that binds the expanding Union together, for governments as well as citizens. Freedom, solidarity and respect for

---

[15] See: "Europe: A Beautiful Idea? The Debate on the Idea of Europe by the Dutch EU Presidency 2004. A Series of Conferences organised by the Nexus Institute." Revised edition, Tilburg: Nexus Institute, 2005, pp. 17-18.

one another are the values that did, and should, guide us in our actions and in our efforts to achieve:
- Sustainable economic growth and social justice.
- A society in which people can realise their full potential.
- Freedom, peace and prosperity for as many people as possible.

Balkenende emphasized also that we must use values to achieve what could not be achieved by purely economic means: European citizens must "accede to Europe." They must prevent Europe from becoming a spiritless machine and grinding to a halt.

In his keynote address at the first session Valéry Giscard d'Estaing accentuated the importance of the series of conferences. European values had always played a part during the Convention, if only in the background, but Giscard believed that not enough use had been made of them. Values should not be confused with rights, and there should be more emphasis on duties. He stated that many values had originated in Europe, but were now universal. Respect for human dignity, tolerance and the social dimension are typically European values. More generally, Europe has an unmistakable culture of its own, but this has not been explicitly elaborated. Europeans are the vehicles of a culture that has become universal: the Hellenic philosophical tradition, the Roman legal tradition, the Judeo-Christian tradition, democratic freedom (the Enlightenment), science in the nineteenth century and research in the twentieth century. The EU can therefore be seen as a "pioneer of values." It is up to us to re-examine these values critically and cast them in a new mold. How are newcomers to adapt to our societies and function within them? How shall we deal with clashes between freedom, equality and emancipation? It is our task to be the vehicles of European culture and continue to give it shape in a transnational context.

Joseph Weiler considered the debate on values essential to the emergence of a European political identity. Values are not something isolated – they are present in everything we do. Every rule laid down by the Union – from the Common Agricultural Policy to security – is based on a particular value. These values will always have to be made explicit in order to clarify the choices and make clear what Europe stands for.

Weiler noticed that Europeans had not yet made up their minds about whether they were Europeans because of the past or because of the future. Meanwhile, values have effectively taken the place of such traditional unifying elements as race and religion. However, this does not mean that they will always be the same: values can be disputed, as long as there is willingness to compromise and, at the very least, to "agree to disagree." Europe appears to have succeeded in this, and in that sense it has an exemplary role, and indeed power. It is not the rule of law and solidarity that makes the European Union unique – these can just as well be found in Norway, Canada or Australia – but the way in which the Union has shaped transnational relations. The EU is the only federal structure that seeks to be a community of diversity rather than a nation or state.

In the discussion treating the question of whether present-day Europe is a community of values it was underlined that only philosophers can come to grips with global values not bound to time or place; politicians, however, know that they must apply values to specific national situations. In this connection, some speakers asserted that when national politicians make those values a central issue in their discussions with their constituents, the debate will be about national issues, national tensions and national minorities.

The question of whether Europe could limit itself to being a legal community came up several times because values – whether or not they conflict – are reconciled in law in the form of clear, recognizable norms such as "the EU is a legal community, an abstract system of norms not related to specific groups." For many speakers, this relative "freedom of values" in law was precisely the reason to argue for a community of values to supplement a legal community. In addition, it was pointed out that a legal community with a separation of powers always needs a political counterweight. The history of Belgium, for example, shows that a legal community without political accountability is doomed to fail. It was posited that, in its most extreme form, the "rule of law" equates to the "rule of judges." The case of Iran shows where that can lead. It was suggested that, in many ways, the Council of Europe, the European Convention on Human Rights, the International Criminal Court and the Yugoslavia Tribunal personify European values better than the institutions in Brussels.

The closing conference, "Europe: A Beautiful Idea?," was held on 4 December 2004 in Rotterdam. It focused on the major topics of the conference series: European citizenship, European culture and education, and European values. The lectures gave rise to the following observations. On the one hand, Europe is unique in its diversity. The question which arises is how – despite the differences – to find and sustain the common ground on which the European project relies. To some degree, that common ground can be found in the values and related fundamental rights now enshrined in the Constitutional Treaty. Those values are fundamental and unite Europeans in their diversity. However, the Constitutional Treaty does not answer all the questions about Europe's essence, and the answers it provides are not definitive. Spiritual and moral values remain vulnerable, opinions on the definition of a good society are always divided, and times change. On the other hand, values are under attack, not on account of differences between cultures or beliefs, but from small groups of radicals in Europe and elsewhere. A free, democratic Europe depends on responsible citizens. Freedom and responsibility go hand in hand. Education, culture and the arts play a vital role, and openness is a characteristic of European civilization. Europe is a project of inclusion. Europe must not define itself as the opposite of something or someone else but must fight the ghosts of its own past.

At the end of the lectures, the Dutch Prime Minister Jan Peter Balkenende identified the following five points for action and strengthening of fundamental values within Europe:

- Europe's fundamental values are inviolable. The EU must act with this in mind. The legal order and basic rights must be defended inside and outside the EU because they are the cornerstones of the rule of law.

- Education is vital in transferring values which contribute to active citizenship in Europe. Cooperation and exchange of experiences in the area of citizenship education should be promoted as much as possible. The values enshrined in the Constitutional Treaty should be made part of the education system of member states.

- Mobility in Europe is a prerequisite for European citizenship and must increase.
- European politicians must break "the conspiracy of silence." "Communicating Europe" is still urgently needed.
- Europe needs to be united in its diversity. Newcomers should have the opportunity to become fully-fledged members of European society and assume their responsibilities as fellow citizens.

3. European Values: Paradoxes, Dangers and Issues

Although today "everyone speaks of values," as Spaemann underlines, most citizens of Europe do not understand what the expression "European values" means or what values are at all. That is why I would like to indicate in this last part of my paper some major paradoxes and dangers in the actual discourse about the so-called European values, as well as possible new issues regarding this subject.

The main question that emerges when we speak about "European values" is doubtlessly: What are values at all?

Allusion has often been made to the fact that values and also fundamental values are "idealistic and abstract terms," which form the basis for fundamental rights and human rights. In the above-mentioned conference series, "Europe: A Beautiful Idea?," it was also claimed that "values are pale, abstract concepts."[16] But are values really only that?

In general terms a value is something that is regarded as valuable. Besides that, values play the role of a world-view orientation and function as regulative ideas for personal and social action. Values are not only set, they are also discovered, recognized and invented. This does not mean that a value is something purely subjective or that it is a purely voluntaristic creation or invention. In any case, values should not be confused with valuation, as Spaemann and Michalski do. A value always represents a certain object, a phenomenon. Valuation, on the other hand,r is a subjective judgment, that is, a relation to this object or phenomenon. The valuable object or phenomenon can have an objective, material nature (e.g., a sculpture, a picture, Wittgenstein's

---

[16] "Europe. A Beautiful Idea?" p. 17.

house in Vienna, etc.) or an ideal character (the idea of the Good, the True, the Beautiful, etc.); it can be present or absent, real or unreal, something which has to be realized; a value can be purely subjective and personal (what we love, esteem, aspire to), but it could also be recognized by a certain community of specialists or a society as something objectively valuable (e.g., Leonardo's Mona Lisa, Shakespeare's plays etc.).

Both the opponents and the defenders of the idea of Europe as a community of values speak either about values in general, or they differentiate values as moral phenomena from norms as legal phenomena, or completely confuse values from different registers, that is, moral, political, legal and cultural values. But there are no "values in general," except at the definition level of the theory of values, where more precise definitions of values and their functions have to be given. This last is certainly a *conditio sine qua non* for the understanding of the meaning of values, but it is not sufficient. If one speaks of values, then he/she must state clearly whether it is about ethical, aesthetic, cultural, social, political, legal or personal values. Furthermore, it should be explained how these different kinds of values stand in relation to each other, whether they function in parallel spaces, or whether they overlap or even clash with each other, etc. The use of the expression "European values" raises in particular the question as to which register of values we have to do here. Balkenende claims that the values of Respect for Human Rights and Human Dignity, Liberty, Equality, Solidarity are "universal moral values which bind us and are enshrined in our treaties."[17] In a similar way the manifesto "Realising the Idea of Europe – Ten Conclusions for the Political Leaders of the European Union" defines "European values": "Europe is united in its diversity. Unity in diversity is a historical and a moral principle. It refers to the universal values which have come to constitute the foundation of European civilisation over more than two thousand years: respect for human dignity, freedom, democracy, equality, the rule of

---

[17] See "Speech to be given by Prime Minister Jan Peter Balkenende at the conference 'The politics of European values', The Hague, 7 September 2004," online: http://docenti.unimc.it/sharifah.alatas/teaching/2014/2000004080/files/lm38-i-anno-reading-for-oral/at_download/file

law and respect for human rights. These are the fundamental values that protect a pluralistic, tolerant society from absolutism, relativism and nihilism. These fundamental values are inviolable."[18]

But are "European values" only moral values? And is value just a moral category?

Is the respect for human dignity and for human rights not also a social and political value? Are human rights fundamental values or fundamental rights? Or are they both? Is liberty a value *per se*? Could liberty be also a condition or a real situation, or, on the contrary, an ideal, that could never be fulfilled completely? Aren't there differences between a moral, a social, a political, a legal and a personal liberty? What does the assertion that all these "European values" are universal mean? How can it be stated on the one hand that 'European values" are historical products which are constantly changing, and, at the other hand, that they are at the same time abstract and universal?

To all these questions and paradoxes one finds no answer in the current value debates. There is also a missing link between values and norms. It is tacitly accepted that values have a moral character and that norms, on the contrary, have a legal one, without taking into consideration that there exist not only legal, but also moral, political, and cultural norms. Regarding the debate about whether Europe should be a community of values or a legal order, it is important to emphasize that values, in contrast to legal norms, are a "softer" notion with an informal, non-constraining character: values are something that "ought," that "should be" (*ein Sollen*), but they are not something that "must be" (*ein Müssen*), that is, something obligatory. Like norms, values have a regulative function but this does not represent an obligation. Values could became norms and then and only then would they assume this character. The opponents of the idea of Europe as a community of values are completely right when they point out that values today degenerate into a totalitarian style of action when they are used for to legitimize illegal discrimination against people, groups and states, and when they are placed over the legal order. A difference must, however, be drawn between what values are – that is, the fact that they do not implicitly contain an authoritarian character – and the

---

[18] See "Europe: A Beautiful Idea?" op.cit. p. 11.

ends for which values are used – that is, the fact that they could serve authoritarianism and the will to power. But values do not have to be automatically a masked form of the will for power, as Spaemann, following Nietzsche, maintains. In the Christian and also in many far-eastern traditions we encounter some higher spiritual values that have nothing to do with power, such as compassion, unselfishness, helpfulness, devotion, generosity, etc., and we sometimes meet human beings and groups who personify these values.

We cannot also say that values initiate only conflicts, as Michalski claims, nor that they are merely binding and identity-building, as some politicians claim. The question here is to find out under which conditions and circumstances values lead to conflicts and under which they could function as bridges between humans, groups and nations.

A serious danger is represented, in my opinion, by the statement of some politicians that we have to defend "our values" against the "enemies of European values," e.g., some groups of radicals, because it is unclear what this concretely means and we get the impression that this is just a new form of the old cold war discourse on "our enemies" that should be cause for fear.

Another danger is represented by the fact that the values in the European Constitution are indeed "pale and abstract," without any concrete content, and therefore I doubt that they are really binding. The European Union sees itself as a fighter for liberty, but the Americans did the same when they marched into Afghanistan and into Iraq, and so do the followers of the Jihad, who pretend to deliver the Arab world from the Americans.

A further danger lies in the treatment of the above-mentioned "European values" as exclusive products of European civilization and culture (Balkenende, Giscard d'Esteing, et. al.). This form of Eurocentrism leaves out of consideration the fact that respect for human being and human dignity, liberty, tolerance and solidarity were already leading values in some communities of the oldest civilizations and cultures, e.g., in India or China. We should rather ask: How can the European Union pretend to be "the pioneer of the values" if it cannot even explain to its own citizens what values are?

Finally, I would like to amplify the question whether Europe should be a community of values or a legal order? It is not clear at all why the question has been posed in these terms, the terms of "EITHER/OR." Why has it not be posed in the terms of "BOTH? AND"? Is this question not similar to the question about which came first, the chicken or the egg?

The opponents of the community of values assume that a state constituted as community of values is already totalitarian, because it is just an "agent of higher values," of a world view based on a relativistic and voluntaristic set of values instead of being a legal order. But, as already said, values are not just set voluntaristically and they are not only a masked striving for power and influence. Conversely, a legal state is not automatically somehow better than a value community. The former Tibetan state, which was also a community of values, based on the Buddhist world view, can be given as an example of liberty and tolerance, excluding any violence and authoritarianism. The real danger consists, as Spaemann observes, in the replacement of the legal order by an order of values. But, conversely, a legal order can also take the form of a dictatorship and a police state, where fundamental values and also fundamental rights (!) are constantly hurt. What is lacking in the current debates is a clear understanding of the fact that *there is a non-suspensive circularity between values and rights*. Social, political, moral, cultural, and personal values need the cover of legal norms in order to obtain a strong legal status. But legal norms also need political and parliamentary consent as well as legitimization from commonly accepted values. Not least, both values and rights need a sort of recognition by the majority of the public, if the state or the community is to avoid protests and internal social tensions. Therefore it is clear that, first, a community of values and a legal order do not exclude each other; second, that they should not be played against each other but reconsidered as closely interconnected; and, third, that the public should be more actively included in the debates on values and rights. In this connection I would like to point out some conditions for a positive reconsideration of the problem of "European values" in order to avoid the above-mentioned paradoxes and dangers. These conditions consist in the necessity:

- To reconsider the expression "European values," which is misleading, because it suggests an essence or a quality of the values that does not exist; there are no "*European* values" in the way that there are "*red* apples"; it should rather be "values of the European Union";
- To clarify the question of why human dignity and human rights, liberty, equality and solidarity are considered the fundamental values of the European Union and if they are the only one which are of fundamental significance;
- To interpret and define more concretely the fundamental values of the European Union, instead of giving only abstract and contentless formulations under which could be subsumed completely opposed meanings;
- To elucidate the relation between values as historically and permanently changing phenomena or notions and values as general concepts in law and the constitution;
- To articulate clearly the difference and the connection between fundamental values and fundamental rights;
- To explicate the difference and the correlation between "national," "Europe-wide" and "universal" values.

Values are at the core of world views, of conceptions of human being, of beliefs, of social and political projects as well as of legal orders. Because it is impossible to implement values by force, every attempt to utilize them as a new ideology and to impose them from above on the citizens, the politicians, the educators and the cultural milieus in Europe, and then to try to oppose this ideology to other value orders, would doubtless cause more harm than good. If the European Union wants to make its leading values the lynchpin for "unity in diversity," it must be added that its old values should incessantly acquire new contents in order to stay alive and contemporary, and that at the same time *new common values*, which correspond better to our current situation, should be created and tested through the common practice of community building.

CONTRIBUTORS

Dimitrios E. Akrivoulis is an Associate Professor of International Political Relations in the Balkans at the Department of Balkan, Slavic and Oriental Studies, University of Macedonia, Thessaloniki, Greece. He holds a PhD in International Relations from the University of Kent, UK. He is author of numerous books, some still in progress, including *Eleftherios Venizelos, the Great Powers and the Balkans, 1928-1932* (Thessaloniki: Epikentro, 2009), *Introduction to the European Post-Socratic Political Philosophy* (Athens: Kritiki, 2007), *The Foreign Relations of Greece during the Eleftherios Venizelos's Administration, 1928-1932* (Athens: Greek Parliament, 1995).

Tatyana Batuleva is an Associated Professor of Philosophy at the Institute for the Study of the Societies and Knowledge at the Bulgarian Academy of Sciences. Her research interests are in the fileds of French philosophy, Bulgarian philosophical thought, and feminist theory. She is the author of *French Philosophy between Modern and Postmodern Rationality* (Sofia: Petrov Publishings, 1994), *Subject and Responsibility* (Sofia: St. Iv. Rilski Publishings, 2010), as well as editor of the collections *The Europen influences in Bulgarian Philosophical Culture* (Sofia: St. Iv. Rilski Publishings, 2013) and *Philosophical Receptions: Transmissions, Affinities and Originality* (Sofia: St. Iv. Rilski Publishings, 2013).

Enrique Dussel is a professor in the Department of Philosophy in the Metropolitan Autonomous University (UAM), in Mexico City and has also taught at the National Autonomous University of Mexico (UNAM). He has acquired a doctorate in philosophy in the Complutense University of Madrid, a doctorate in history from the Sorbonne of Paris, and has also a license in theology from Paris and Münster. He is the founder with others of the Philosophy of Liberation. Author of more than 50 books in different languages, including English: *A History of the Church in Latin America. Colonialism to Liberation (1492-1979)* (Grand Rapids: Willian B. Eerdmans, 1981), *Philosophy of liberation* (NY: Orbis Books, 1985), *Ethics and*

Community (NY: Orbis Books, 1988), *The Invention of the Americas* (NY: Continuum Publishing Group, 1995), *The Underside of Modernity: Apel, Ricoeur, Taylor and Rorty* (NY: Humanities Press, 1996), *Towards an Unknown Marx. A commentary on the Manuscripts of 1861-63* (London: Routledge, 2001), *Beyond Philosophy* (Maryland: Rowman and Littlefield, 2002) *Twenty Theses on Politics* (Durham: Duke University Press, 2008), *Ethics of Liberation: In the Age of Globalization and Exclusion* (Durham: Duke University Press, 2013).

Lester Embree is a William Dietrich Scholar and Professor of Philosophy at Florida Atlantic University at Boca Raton. He was till 2005 Director of the Center for Advanced Research in Phenomenology and initiator of the Organisation of Phenomenological Organisations. He is author of the books *Reflective Analysis. A First Introduction to Phenomenology*, dual language text, trans. into Castelian by Luis Román Rabanaque (Morelia: Editorial Jitanjáfora, 2003), *Environment, Technology, Justification* (Bucharest: Zeta Books, 2008), and of over 200 other publications. He has also edited several dozen volumes, including *Phenomenology of the Cultural Disciplines* (Dordrecht, Kluwer, 1994), *Encyclopedia of phenomenology* (Dordrecht, Kluwer 1997), *Problems of the value of nature in phenomenological perspectives or what to do about the snakes in the grass* (Dordrecht: Kluwer 1997), *Schutzian social science* (Kluwer 1999), and *Handbook of Phenomenological Aesthetics* (Dordrecht: Springer, 2010).

Maria Luisa Feminias is a professor of Philosophical Anthropology and Director of the Interdisciplinary Center for Gender Studies at the La Plata University in Buenos Aires. She is author of numerous books in Spanish: *Inferioridad y exclusión: un modelo para desarmar* (Buenos Aires: Grupo Editor Latinoamericano, 1996), *Aristoteles filosofo del lenguaje?* (Buenos Aires: Universidad Nacional de La Plata, 1997), *Sobre sujeto y género: lecturas feministas de Beauvoir a Butler* (Rosario: Prohistoria Ediciones, 2001/2012), *Judith Butler, introducción a su lectura* (Madrid: Siglo XXI Ediciones, 2003), Judith Butler [1956] (Madrid: Ediciones del Orto, 2003), *Feminismos de París a La Plata* (Buenos Aires: Catalogos, 2006), *Perfiles del feminismo ibero-*

americano (Buenos Aires: Catalogos, 3 vol., 2002, 2005, 2007), *El Genero del Multiculturalism* (Bueanos Aires: Universidad Nacional de Quilmes Editorial, 2007), *Violencias cotidianas en la vida de las mujeres* (Rosario: Prohistoria Ediciones, 2013), *Multiculturalismo identidad y violencia* (Rosario: Prohistoria Ediciones, 2013), *Aspectos del discurso jurídico* (Rosario: Prohistoria Ediciones, 2014). She is co-editor of *Mora*, the Interdisciplinary Journal for Gender Studies of the Philosophy Faculty of the Buenos Aires University.

Alison Jaggar is a College Professor of Distinction at the University of Colorado at Boulder in the departments of Philosophy and Women and Gender Studies, and also a Research Co-ordinator at the University of Oslo's Center for the Study of Mind in Nature. She is author of *Feminist Politics and Human Nature* (Harvester Press, 1983) and *Living with Contradictions: Controversies in Feminist Social Ethics* (Boulder: Westview Press, 1994). She also edited and co-edited several books, including *Gender/Body/Knowledge: Feminist Reconstructions of Being and Knowing* (New Jersey: Rutgers University Press, 1989), Morality and Social Justice: Point Counterpoint (Lanham: Rowman and Littlefield, 1995), *The Blackwell Companion to Feminist Philosophy* (Oxford: Blackwell, 1998), *Just Methods: An Interdisciplinary Feminist Reader* (Boulder: Paradigm Press, 2008), *Abortion: Three Perspectives* (Oxford University Press, 2009), *Pogge and his Critics* (Cambridge: Polity 2010), *Gender and Global Justice* (Cambridge: Polity, 2013) and was co-editor of the book series "Feminist Theory and Politics" at Westview Press as well as Associate editor of *Hypatia: A Journal of Feminist Philosophy*.

Sonia Kruks is is the Robert S. Danforth Professor of Oberlin College. She is the author of several books on existential thought and feminist theory, including *The Political Philosophy of Merleau-Ponty* (Humanities Press, 1981/1994), *Situation and Human Existence: Freedom, Subjectivity, and Society. Problems of Modern European Thought* (London, Boston, Sidney, Wellington: Unwin Hyman, 1990), *Retrieving Experience: Subjectivity and Recognition in Feminist Politics* (Ithaca: Cornell University Press, 2001), *Simone de Beauvoir and the Politics of Ambiguity* (Oxford University Press, 2012). She is also co-editor of *Promissory Notes: Women in the*

Transition to Socialism (New York: Monthly Review Press, 1989), and serves on the Editorial Board of *PS: Political Science and Politics, an official journal of the American Political Science Association*, as well as on the editorial boards of *Hypatia: A Journal of Feminist Philosophy* and *Sartre Studies International: Journal of Existentialism and Culture*.

Susanne Moser received two master degrees, one in economics at the University of Economics in Vienna, and one in philosophy at University of Vienna, where she also earned her PhD in 2001 and teaches courses on Philosophy and Business Ethics. She is also lecturer at the Karl-Franzens University in Graz and other High Schools in Austria. She is author of *Freiheit und Anerkennung bei Simone de Beauvoir* (Edition Diskord, 2002), published in English as *Freedom and Recognition in the Work of Simone de Beauvoir* (Frankfurt a. M.: Peter Lang, 2008), and co-editor of *Die Feministische Philosophie: Perspektiven und Debatten* (Sofia: Nauka i izkustvo Publishings, 2000), *Simone De Beauvoir: 50 Jahre nach dem* Anderen Geschlecht (Frankfurt a.M.: PeterLang 2003), *Das Integrale und das gebrochene Ganze: Zum 100. Geburtstag Von Leo Gabriel* (Frankfurt a.M.: PeterLang, 2005). She is managing editor of *Labyrinth: An International Journal for Philosophy, Value Theory and Sociocultural Hermeneutics*.

Yvanka B. Raynova is a Professor of Philosophy at the Institute for the Study of the Societies and Knowledge at the Bulgarian Academy of Sciences and Director of the Institute for Axiological Research Vienna. She is author of numerous books, including *Between the Said and the Unsaid. In Conversation with Paul Ricoeur* (Frankfurt a.M.: Peter Lang, 2009), *Etre et être libre: Deux passions des philosophies phénoménologiques* (Frankfurt a. M.: Peter Lang, 2010), *Feministische Philosophie im europäischen Kontext. Genderdebatten zwischen "Ost" und "West"* (Wien, Köln, Weimar: Boehlau 2010), *Lebenswelt, Sprache und Werte* (Frankfurt a. M.: Peter Lang, in print), and of over 200 articles. She translated a number of books and studies from French into Bulgarian, among other Sartre's *L'être et le néant* and Paul Ricoeur's *Le conflit des interprétations*. She is Editor of *Labyrinth: An international Journal for Philosophy, Value Theory and Sociocultural Hermeneutics*, as well as of several books and book series, inter alia of "Philosophy, Phenomenology and Hermeneutic of Values" at Peter Lang.

Mary-Kate G. Smith received her M.A. in philosophy from the University of Colorado at Boulder (2001), and earned a law degree from the University of Connecticut School of Law (J.D., with honors, 2004), where she was recognized for her service in the Asylum and Human Rights Clinic representing international refugees and received two CALI Excellence for the Future awards. She serves as the interim-president and secretary of the board of directors for the Women's Mentoring Network, a Stamford-based educational, career and personal resource program that promotes economic empowerment for low-income women. She has been selected to the "Rising Star" list in New England Super Lawyers Magazine (November, 2013) and Connecticut Magazine (February 2014) in the practice areas of general litigation, employment & labor, and land use/zoning.

Mark Zlomislic is a Professor of Philosophy at Conestoga College, in Kitchener, Ontario where he teaches courses in ethics, aesthetics, postmodernism, critical theory and social/political philosophy. He is the author of *Zizek: Paper Revolutionary. A Franciscan Response* (Eugene, OR: Wipf and Stock, 2015), *Jacques Derrida's Aporetic Ethics* (Lanham: Lexington Books, 2007), and of *The Sorrowful Mysteries: a postmodern poetics* (with David Goicoechea, Zagreb: Sipar, 1998), *Joyful wisdom: Zarathustra's joyful annunciations* (Thought House Publishing Group, 1995) and has published numerous articles on Derrida, Nietzsche, Scheler, Foucault, Genet, and Kristeva. He is also the Editor of *Joyful Wisdom: a journal for postmodern ethics* and of the "Postmodern Ethics Series" at Wipf and Stock where he co-edited *Cross and Khôra: Deconstruction and Christianity in the World of John D. Caputo* (2010) and *The Poverty of Radical Orthodoxy* (2012).

www.ingramcontent.com/pod-product-compliance
Lightning Source LLC
Chambersburg PA
CBHW070807300426
44111CB00014B/2445